Educational Research in Britain

Educational Research in Britain

edited by H. J. Butcher
with the assistance of H. B. Pont

AMERICAN ELSEVIER PUBLISHING COMPANY INC.
NEW YORK 1968

AMERICAN ELSEVIER PUBLISHING COMPANY, INC.
52 Vanderbilt Avenue,
New York, N.Y. 10017

Library of Congress Catalog Card No 68–8974

Printed and bound in Great Britain

Contents

CONTENTS

The Contributors

H. J. Butcher
Professor of Higher Education, University of Manchester

Brian Cane
Senior Research Officer, National Foundation for Educational
Research in England and Wales

Maurice Chazan
Senior Lecturer in Education, University College of Swansea

T. Christie
Lecturer in Education, University of Manchester

R. R. Dale
Senior Lecturer in Education, University College of Swansea

D. Graham
Senior Lecturer in Psychology, University of Durham

J. Heywood
Senior Research Fellow in Higher Education, University of Lancaster

Harry Kay
Professor and Head of the Department of Psychology,
University of Sheffield

Kenneth Lovell
Reader in Education, University of Leeds

E. A. Lunzer
Senior Lecturer in Child Psychology, Department of Education,
University of Manchester

T. Gordon Monks
Senior Research Officer, National Foundation for Educational
Research in England and Wales

A. E. G. Pilliner
Senior Lecturer in Education, University of Edinburgh; Director of the Godfrey Thomson Unit for Educational Research

Jessie F. Reid
Lecturer in Education, University of Edinburgh

D. F. Swift
Tutor in Sociology, Department of Education, University of Oxford

D. A. Walker
Director of the Scottish Council for Research in Education

W. D. Wall
Formerly Director of the National Foundation for Educational Research in England and Wales. Now Dean of University of London Institute of Education

John Williams
Research Officer in charge of the Section for Mathematical and Conceptual Studies, National Foundation for Educational Research in England and Wales

Stephen Wiseman
Formerly Professor of Education and Director of the School of Education, University of Manchester. Now Director of the National Foundation for Educational Research in England and Wales

Acknowledgments

The editor, authors and publishers would like to thank the Department of Education and Science and H. M. Stationery Office for permission to reprint table 1, page 275, from *Higher Education*, Report of the Committee on Higher Education (The Robbins Report); Manchester University Press for permission to reprint figures 1 and 2, pages 268 and 269, from Wiseman's *Education and Environment*; the National Foundation for Educational Research in England and Wales, the Department of Education and Science, and H. M. Stationery Office for permission to reprint table 1, page 220, from Report on Education no. 36 (May 1967); and Messrs Oliver & Boyd for permission to reprint figure 3, page 273, from Wiseman's 'Environmental and innate factors and educational attainment' in Meade and Parkes' *Genetic and Environmental Factors in Human Ability*.

Introduction

During the last five years or so the amount of educational research carried out in this country has increased almost explosively, to such an extent that lecturers in universities and colleges of education have often had difficulty in keeping up to date with important findings. They may have a particular field of interest and be familiar with the literature in that field, but it is common experience accidentally to come across some finding in quite a different area that is of great interest and relevance.

If lecturers are in this position—and there is little doubt that they often are—the plight of students attempting a first piece of research is more acute. Before deciding upon a topic, they need to have a general idea of what work has been done; and it is by no means easy to obtain access to the breadth of information required. Our experience in supervising a large number of research students in education suggests that this is by far the most difficult stage. Once the topic is firmly and sensibly fixed, its scope limited and an experimental design decided upon, the battle is half won.

Before this can be done, the student must make himself familiar with a considerable literature. The difficulty of this task, even to an intelligent and highly motivated person with access to well-stocked libraries, is usually underrated. To search through the possibly relevant journals and other publications has become a much more difficult undertaking. The *British Journal of Educational Psychology* has recently doubled in bulk, papers on research in education are to be found in a wide range of sociological journals, and new publications appear practically every year. *Educational Research*, published by the National Foundation for Educational Research in England and Wales, although quite a new periodical, has had to be supplemented by *New Research in Education*. The increase in educational research in Scotland has led to the appearance of *Scottish Educational Studies*. Nor does this boom in publications exaggerate the amount of valuable work being done. On the whole, the space available barely keeps up with the volume of research, and the standard of published work has certainly not fallen.

There is therefore a clear need for up-to-date and authoritative surveys to provide guidance about where to find the most important articles. Our aim is to satisfy this need—not to save the student the trouble of reading the original papers, but to help, guide and evaluate, and especially to cover a wide variety of topics within one volume. It is intended to fill the gap between narrow, specific research papers and elementary, often outdated, introductory textbooks.

Introductions are to skim through, not to taste word by word; if they become prolix, they waste the reader's time and, like a too substantial *hors d'oeuvre*, spoil appetite for the main meal. In the present case, the meal is a solid one, and we shall be correspondingly brief. Only two points require to be made—first, the need for a book of this kind, and secondly, an explanation of the principles on which contributors and topics have been selected.

The main reasons for producing this book have already been outlined; they are the rapid expansion of educational research in Britain, the consequent spate of publication, and the resulting difficulty, or even impossibility, for anyone other than the full-time professional, to keep abreast of current knowledge. The developments that have led to this healthy state of affairs are documented by Dr Wall in the first paper, which describes the expansion of the National Foundation for Educational Research and some of its recent projects. A similar abundance of solid work north of the border is described by Dr Walker. These two papers cover many of the large-scale inquiries conducted by teams of research workers investigating problems beyond the capacity of individuals.

Apart from these accounts of the work of the national research institutions, our selection of topics and contributors requires some explanation, particularly about the intended coverage, the level of writing and the readers for whom the book is designed.

Topics have been chosen so as to provide a representative selection of current research in Britain. Within the scope of a single volume, it is necessarily a *selection*, and one that has no doubt been influenced by the experience and interests of the editor. But the range is wide, and the overall picture of recent work almost certainly more comprehensive than in any other book. Authors have been chosen as being actively engaged in empirical research in the fields they review, and as acknowledged experts in their subjects. They have been encouraged not only to survey the British literature in these fields, but also to describe their own projects, often still in progress. In many cases they have been unduly modest in this respect.

'Educational research' covers a multitude of activities. It is interpreted here as empirical research, based on experiment, on social surveys and on the clinical study of individuals. We have not been able to include historical or philosophical studies or accounts of the organization and economics of education. This has been a general policy, not a rigid prescription. In some papers, such as those of Mr Dale on co-education and of Mr Monks on comprehensive education, some discussion of the organization and administration of education has been essential. Even the restriction implied in the title of this book—that it should be confined to research in Britain—has been interpreted quite freely. In his paper on children's thinking Dr Lunzer has had the arduous assignment of compressing the virtually incompressible literature on cognitive development. A large proportion of the seminal work in this field can hardly be evaluated without reference to related work in other countries. In that paper and to a lesser extent in several others, the intention has been to provide a comprehensive and unified account, even if this has involved occasional wandering across national boundaries. In general, however, foreign research is described only where it has provided important theories and experiments that research workers in this country have been concerned to test or replicate.

Wherever possible, the authors have avoided jargon, educational, psychological or sociological, and have written their reviews plainly and directly. We must say 'wherever possible', because one man's jargon is another man's technical precision, and distinctions of this kind are relative. We have tried to err in the direction of plain words, and to avoid pretentious or unnecessary technical terms. Although some of the research described depends upon statistical techniques, none of the reviews assume more than a very elementary knowledge of statistical procedures. Few papers require any preliminary specialized knowledge, and it is hoped that many will be intelligible and interesting to the general reader. But the main readers for whom the book is meant will have some professional connection with education, whether as teachers, student teachers, lecturers, educational psychologists or research workers. We also thought it likely that readers abroad would find this book useful as a reasonably concise summary of research in

Britain; and contributors were therefore asked not to take for granted a detailed knowledge of the organization of education in this country.

The eighteen papers provide a good sample of British empirical research, but obviously nothing like a comprehensive collection; other editors with different interests and preconceptions might have produced another volume with the same title but with hardly any overlap in content. We should have produced a broader collection if all the authors approached, often at unduly short notice, had been able to contribute. We had hoped to include papers on individual differences in ability, personality and creativity, on medical education, on the Nuffield projects, and also to devote additional papers to sociological studies and to research in higher education. These latter topics, although dealt with, clearly merit fuller treatment.

We hope that these omissions and many others will be repaired, by the time the present words are in print, in the preparation of a second volume. Despite our efforts to produce the present book promptly and rapidly, small cumulative delays inevitably occurred, some, it must be admitted due to one or two authors not keeping to the agreed time-schedule. If a paper appears less up to date than some others, this will be a sign of the author's efficiency in delivering his manuscript on time. Conversely, the more up-to-date papers covering articles well into 1967 (such as that by Butcher) will be by contributors whose punctuality was less evident!

H. J. Butcher and H. B. Pont
January 1968

W. D. Wall

The Work of the National Foundation for Educational Research in England and Wales

1. *The early years*

For more than twenty years, the National Foundation for Educational Research in England and Wales has existed as both a formal and a working partnership of all those professionally concerned with the public educational system. It was set up following the Education Act of 1944 by the professional associations of teachers, the local education authorities, the universities, and the then Ministry of Education. For the first years of its existence it was fostered by the University of London Institute of Education, and particularly by Sir Philip Hartog, Sir Fred Clarke and Sir Cyril Burt. Sir Fred Clarke and later, Dr C. B. Jeffrey were the first Chairmen of the Executive Committee. The Armed Services and the whole spectrum of educational associations also joined from the outset, and as the educational system has changed and developed, new categories of membership have arisen, which include specific representation for such fields as technical education, teacher education, and the like.

For the first twelve years, the Foundation's resources were so severely limited that its programme was forcibly restricted to a few projects which by modern standards were small. It did, however, undertake a variety of studies connected with the measurement of attainment and ability, ways of solving some of the social, educational, administrative and psychological problems of allocation to secondary education, the educability of cerebrally palsied children, the teaching of reading and mathematics in the primary school, rewards and punishments, pupil record cards, and similar topics. It has contributed substantially to the change in our views about ability and its measurement; it has pin-pointed the precise practical problems which surround the learning of reading and mathematics in the early school years, and has provided through its Test Services and Test Agency, an array of professional instruments for the use of teachers and psychologists in the understanding and guidance of pupils.

All this was during a period when there was little general interest in educational research. At this time, too, educational research in the universities was even more restricted by lack of finance and of trained staff, and was to all intents and purposes confined to the type of study appropriate to postgraduate degree work.

2.   *A changed climate*

The last six or seven years have been marked—in part because of the Foundation's own efforts at presenting the case (Wall 1959)*— by an almost explosive increase in interest in educational research and in the finance available to support it. In 1958, it was possible to demonstrate that expenditure of all kinds on research relating to education represented no more than 0·01 per cent of all expenditure on education; in 1967, the proportion may well be thirty times as much, and will probably grow over the next decade.

This rapid infusion into educational research of interest and money directly and indirectly from the Government, as well as the development of an initiatory and directive role by private foundations, has led to a somewhat chaotic and uncoordinated growth, and particular themes of inquiry have leaped almost overnight to the forefront in ways which make it difficult to distinguish the merely modish from the permanently useful.

It has come to be recognized, too, that objective inquiry, a readiness to listen to its outcomes, and the general prestige of research can be a threat to the cosy amateurism which by and large still characterizes much educational decision-making. Teachers, administrators, and the public are uneasily aware of this; and not unnaturally there has been a growing tendency to seek to control both the directions of research and the manner in which its findings impinge upon policy. Equally naturally, there have not been wanting pressure groups who carry out quick 'cream-skimming' surveys and publish the results in support of their particular viewpoints. Finally, we should draw attention to the

----

* All the references are given on p. 355 ff.

role played by such committees as Crowther, Robbins, Newsom, and Plowden, in recognizing that a background of verifiable facts is essential, even if policy-making recommendations have still for practical (or social) reasons to go far beyond any supporting evidence which can be obtained.

3. *Problems of expansion*

We now seem to be in a phase where the several dangers of rapid growth are apparent. There is an acute shortage of the sophisticated man-power which adequate research in so complex and difficult a field as education demands. It is not enough to have a grounding in the research methods of one or other of the basic sciences. Living experience of the schools, high-level administrative skills and the ability to bring a variety of disciplines to bear in concert are all equally necessary. And since education is a long-term process, the research worker or, more usually, the research team has to plan at least for a five-year period of follow-through. This is a long way from the concept of academic research for an M.A. or Ph.D. completed in two or three years.

Other limitations may in the long run prove more serious still. Even ten years ago, teacher training contained relatively little to suggest to the neophyte that his art had a growing technological basis and that the ability to understand and apply the results of research was an essential part of the teacher's equipment. Still less was the profession generally armed to play a leading role in the scientific professional study of education. Paradoxically, however, the bulk of the research so far done—and almost all that can claim to be seminal—has been the work of men and women with considerable practical experience of teaching who have trained themselves through higher degrees in education and psychology and have become members of university education departments, of colleges of education or of the Inspectorate. For example, teachers and inspectors—notably Sophie Bryant, Kimmins and others —formed the backbone of the Child Study Association founded by Sully in 1898; furthermore, research in education from 1920 to 1950 was dominated by such men as Hamley, Valentine, Godfrey Thomson, C. A. Richardson, Sir Cyril Burt, all of whom had been teachers or inspectors and were engaged not only in university teaching but in many cases in applied educational psychology. The fact remains that much of the delay in the application of results and almost all the indifference, if not latent hostility, to research is a result of a communication barrier which only improved teacher education—initial, in-service and further—will remove (see Van der Eyken 1965).

A more serious problem is that of reconciling the demands for co-operation made on schools and other institutions with the efficient conduct of their main educational task. In any one year as many as 25,000 teachers and their pupils may be involved in N.F.E.R. programmes alone. If to this we add the questionnaires and forms emanating from universities, colleges of education, and the Department of Education and Science, and the even heavier contribution which an increasing activity in curriculum development seems to involve, it is not difficult to foresee a time when schools and teachers are so overloaded that their ordinary work is interfered with.

4. *Change in the N.F.E.R.*

Even so sketchy and summary an allusion to the changes which began to make their evident impact in 1961* underlines the idea that at present (and it seems likely to continue for a decade) we are in a highly dynamic but confused situation where tensions and profound and sincere oppositions of opinion cut across professional affiliations and interests, and from which research in education seems likely to emerge very different in conception, in resources, in prestige and in the roles ascribed to it from anything in the past or that we can readily conceive at the moment.

The last years have seen a profound change in the N.F.E.R. From an organization with a total staff of thirty-nine and a budget of £37,000 in 1960, it has grown in 1967 to an institution spending over £260,000 annually and with a staff of 120. This rapid growth has been accompanied by adaptation both in its scientific policy and in its relations with other bodies. From being virtually alone in its concern with such problems as the impact of various forms of educational organization on children's learning and general development, or the ways in which particular aspects of curriculum fit into the general pattern of schooling, the Foundation is now one of many often overlapping instances. The process of change is likely to continue—particularly as the new bodies

* The Research and Intelligence Branch of the Department of Education and Science was set up in 1961, and substantial funds were put at its disposal to encourage the development of educational research.

like the Educational Research Board of the Social Science Research Council, the Schools Council for Curriculum and Examinations, and the Planning Branch of the Department of Education and Science begin to find roles and fields of interest specific to themselves, and as the quickened interest in education shown by academic departments of psychology, economics, sociology and statistics in universities begins to make an impact. Hence what follows is in a very real sense an interim description of a situation in rapid evolution.

5. *Field research*

It should be made clear that the N.F.E.R. has always been concerned mainly, but not exclusively, with applied research and principally, though again not exclusively, with field studies. Here we may make a distinction, admittedly only partly sustainable, between work in the basic sciences of psychology, sociology, economics and the like which may incidentally contribute to education because it contributes to general theory building; and work in such sciences which begins with a direct educational interest and relevance—e.g. child development, educational sociology, educational psychology, learning theory, psychometrics— and which contributes directly to the construction of specifically educational theory. The insights and theories from basic research on, for example, learning can rarely be applied naively to the day-to-day working of an educational system: experimental applications of insights derived from the learning of rats and monkeys are at best only partially and fitfully transferable to the problems of Jane grappling with fractions in a crowded classroom. Even concepts from other applied fields such as industrial cost-benefit analysis cannot be applied directly to school systems. Basic theory is immensely valuable; but fundamental research in real or closely simulated educational systems is an essential further step before we can begin to draw specifically educational insights; and even this takes us only so far. So many factors of all kinds enter into real educational situations, even the simplest, and they enter in ways which are qualitatively different from the simply cumulative that, even more than in agriculture, the relatively untidy field study is an essential ultimate phase in the assimilation of theory into practice, as well as being immensely important in its own right.

Such field studies form the staple of the Foundation's programme and are, as it were, the outward presentation of its work. The programme is, however, more than an *ad hoc* collection of large projects—in spite of the somewhat *ad hoc* sources of finance which come in part from subscription income and in an increasing degree from outside sources, governmental and private. Each research project is conceived in such a way that it fits with others to deal with some major practical or theoretical problems. For example, a great deal of attention has been and is being given to teacher attitudes and their effects on children's learning, in the work on the teaching of reading, on streaming and other forms of grouping in the primary school, and in the studies of comprehensiveness in education at the secondary level. Another major theme, running through the studies of primary, secondary and technical education, is that of guidance, which in its turn is connected with the work of Test Services. A number of overlapping projects are being devoted to immigrants and overseas students, leading up to a major study, in nursery, infant and junior schools, of the ways in which different forms of cultural deprivation of native-born and immigrant children may be met. In its turn, this is connected with the work concerned with the ways of positively influencing school climates which is the basis of the 'Constructive education' project. There are others.

Inevitably, in an area of study where the theoretical sub-structures are not yet very strong, problems arise in field studies which demand basic research. Hence a good deal of time and attention is devoted to small theoretical studies, mainly but not exclusively of a psychometric kind. The Foundation has been incidentally concerned in this way with work on concept formation, on attitude change, on differential growth in ability, and on motivation.

6. *Policy orientation and independence*

The fact remains, however, that all the Foundation's research projects are policy oriented and concerned with the solving of practical administrative and teaching problems in the day-to-day setting of the schools and institutions of further and higher education. It is here that its peculiar constitution and its governing philosophy are of importance. Any kind of educational policy decision—from the choice of methods by which to teach mathematics to the choice among ways of organizing secondary education—implies an attempt to answer a number of questions, only some of which imply scientific research. All those questions which involve moral or value judgments are obviously matters of opinion and philosophy. 'Is it a *good* thing to educate children of different social and intellectual groups together?' is such a question. By research we may perhaps answer a number of questions, on the responses to which the value decision will rest in practice: such, for example, as 'Is it *possible* to educate such children together and under what conditions?' or 'if you have educated such children together, how far have you attained the "good" that you sought?' and—a question often forgotten in the heat of reforming zeal—'what, in terms of other "goods", have you lost?'

Being what it is, surrounded by emotion and increasingly becoming the centre of political and social pressures, education is difficult to view without prejudice, open or concealed, in any of its aspects. Hence institutions which have no axe to grind, which are manifestly independent of government and of pressure groups, and which studiously avoid any kind of political, social, religious or philosophic commitment are essential for the conduct of certain kinds of research. In the case of the N.F.E.R. this non-commitment is ensured by its fully representative constitution and by the consequent make-up of its Executive Board, which is the overall governing body so far as policy is concerned. The Board is appointed by the local authorities, teacher organizations, universities, and has observers from the Department of Education and Science, the Armed Services and the Schools Council; its Chairman is independent and elected. In terms of the conduct of research this freedom is further guaranteed by the relations between the staff and the Board: the staff being responsible for the scientific execution of research; and the Board for policy decisions such as the acceptance of a commission from outside, the choice of areas for investigation, and the authorization of publication of any reports on completed studies or studies in progress.

Complete independence and non-partisanship in research are becoming of crucial importance in view of other developments. Departments of state are increasingly conducting research on their own behalf in support of policy, as well as commissioning it from universities. Quasi-governmental organizations like the Schools Council, the Modern Languages Committee, and the Council for Educational Technology have sprung up to provide services of development and advice to education, and private foundations are intervening to back particular views of what children shall be taught and how. Disinterested and non-partisan examination of enthusiatic claims of all kinds, wide evaluation of the educational effectiveness of new curricula, of organizational change and of the impact on children and society of innovation should form a part of the essential checks and balances of our system. Some of this work is done by the Foundation, and an increasing amount by universities; but it is true to say that much currently fashionable change escapes real evaluation. The great problem for the future is that of achieving a reasonable balance between the enthusiastic force of innovation and the colder, more objective and less spectacular task of scientific investigation of its effects upon children.

7. *Method*

The peculiar position and methods of the N.F.E.R. may be illustrated by two pieces of field research in progress, each of which has grown out of an acute contemporary controversy. Both are financed by grants from the Department of Education and Science in such a way as to leave the Foundation free to conduct the work according to its own principles and to publish the results. These are the inquiries into streaming and other forms of grouping of pupils in primary schools, and the study of comprehensiveness in secondary education.

When these inquiries began, it was clear from published material that no one knew in detail what kinds of practices existed in the schools, nor indeed what were the basic questions to which answers should be sought. Accordingly, in each it was necessary to undertake a preliminary survey on a national scale. In the case of streaming, approaches were made to nearly 2,000 primary schools in 1963. These revealed that so far from 'unstreaming' being a common and increasing practice, it was, in its genuine form, a relatively rare arrangement. Moreover, schools which described themselves as streamed in fact employed a considerable variety of arrangements including age-groupings, setting, within-class grouping, vertical streaming. Many schools were too small to stream in any real sense of the word, but nonetheless went to considerable lengths to put children of similar levels of ability together for the purpose of instruction. Similarly, the attitudes of teachers to the issues involved were far from homogeneous and often not in accord with the expressed philosophy of the school in which they served (Lunn 1967).

A similarly complex picture emerges from the preliminary study of comprehensiveness. The fact-finding survey concerned itself at first with a description of things as they now are and revealed how far from the truth were such statements as that comprehensive secondary schools tend to be very large—few, indeed, were over 1,000 pupils—or that, in their present stage, they cater for a real cross-section of the age-group (Department of Education and Science 1967b).

Such fact-finding studies are the preliminary to research proper. They serve to define and refine questions and hypotheses and to delimit the kind of sampling necessary. From them follows the main study which, methodologically, is a combination of cross-sectional and longitudinal approaches and is in fact characteristic of most work of this kind. Details of the 'Comprehensive education' project are given elsewhere in this book (see the paper by Monks). Hence we shall concentrate on an outline of the further stages of the 'Streaming' inquiry.

One of the ways of comparing the outcomes of two different systems is to take representative matched samples of each and apply measures of attainment or of any other criteria to pupils in their final year. This is a cross-sectional approach, and it may be given increased richness by measuring various kinds of educational outputs at points between the first and the last year. The weakness of such a method lies in the assumption that different pupils at different stages of their growth and development are in fact similar basically—that second- and fourth-year pupils tested now give the same picture as would have been obtained if we had tested them in their second year and then compared them with themselves two years later. In other fields of child development, this has been shown not to be entirely tenable as an assumption. Moreover, it is difficult, if not impossible, to tease out cause and effect without following individuals through and at the same time observing changes in the institutions which influence them.

The cross-sectional type of study which was undertaken in the 'Streaming' inquiry in 1964 was useful in getting some rapid results to show the different nature of the outcomes of the two kinds of organization, and particularly in throwing up hypotheses, in testing measures, and in directing attention to the problem of defining criteria. But the critical work lies in the longitudinal follow-through of the progress of whole classes of children in a large sample of primary schools carefully matched for such basic variables as size and catchment area, and contrasted in their practices. This longitudinal study was begun in 1964 and the field work will be complete in 1968, though it is hoped that funds will be found for further follow-up at the secondary stage.

8. *Definition of objectives*

This kind of inquiry throws into relief what is the core problem of educational research of this kind—that of defining the objectives to be served by education, and of seeing to it that the inevitable selection of what to assess and measure is fairly representative of all sides in any controversy there may be. It is easy to measure some, particularly the more conventional, kinds of attainment. Often such measures are emotionally rejected by the innovators who insist upon other 'goods'. Increasingly, therefore, a major function of any research team is becoming that of working with groups of educators with opposing views in an attempt to get agreed operational statements of the outcomes they hope for; and then of embodying these in acceptably accurate and valid measures. When this is done effectively, the upshot of most well-conducted research is not in fact to settle the controversy once and for all, but to sharpen up the real issues for decision. Not infrequently we find that all the methods or organizations suggested produce very similar results over a wide area, that sometimes ends are achieved that the innovator did not set out to attain, and sometimes the traditionalist, unknown to himself and without intention, arrives at the innovator's goal. The choice is, in fact, revealed not in black and white, but in terms of how much of this you may get in exchange for less of that. Even more important is the way that such research may highlight the practical problems of innovation: the fact that, for example, a head may destream his school and yet have colleagues of undoubted loyalty whose attitudes to children are 'streamed'. We can see something of the way in which this conflict in the teacher's mind affects not merely the attainments of his pupils but their personality (Lunn 1967).

9. *Action research and curriculum evaluation*

Another research study which has been in progress for three years illustrates how action research and the evaluation of curriculum innovation may go hand in hand. It will be recalled that the Nuffield Foundation set on foot a project to introduce the teaching of French to children from the second year of their junior school. The Department of Education and Science arranged for special training courses for the teachers involved, and the experiment began in 1964. In collaboration with a team of H.M. Inspectors, the Foundation's staff has been engaged in a thorough follow-through of the children. This study, as well as involving the preparation of a variety of measures of attainment in French of a new type to conform to the mainly oral approach, has also concerned itself with the problems posed by particular groups of children—the less able, for example—and with the effects on the rest of children's learning, particularly in the mother tongue, of the introduction of a new subject. The more elusive effects of the work on pupils, its general bearing upon the life of the schools, and the practical organizational problems it raises have been studied by H.M.I.s in collaboration with the N.F.E.R. team.

Earlier work of the N.F.E.R. on the evaluation of curriculum and educational method is illustrated by the long series of researches on *reading* and primary school *mathematics* which are reaching their culmination in a number of publications. They have been of the nature of operational research; an ongoing study of things as they are without any experimental attempt to alter them. Each of them had an extensive sampling framework involving sixty or more schools and several thousand children over a period of years; and each had within it sub-samples of schools and children increasingly intensively studied. In all cases the novel dimension has been the attempt simultaneously to study the sociological variables which do much to determine the background against which the teacher does his work, the school variables of size, organization, location and so on, which condition what he can do, and the characteristics of individual pupils learning more or less effectively according to the methods adopted by their teachers.

10. *School climates*

Much current work of the Foundation suggests that curriculum content and even teaching method are less important than they may seem, and that the central problems for research lie in the climate and atmosphere of the schools regarded as transitional, artificial and therefore manipulable communities. Features of organization and of method are important much more for the way in which children interpret them than for themselves. Being in a D stream, for example, may well have different meanings and therefore profoundly different effects on a pupil, according to whether he perceives it as a rejection or as a remedial device aimed to see that he gets what he needs. So, too, the kind and quality of a pupil's learning is very much a function of what his teacher says and does, of the teacher's skills, insight and attitudes.

One attempt to study this series of problems is the 'Constructive education' project, financed jointly by the Home Office and the Department of Education and Science. This is an action research in which the innovations and changes spring in part from the attempt to generalize practices which have been found to be effective, and in part from an attempt to draw out from the teachers themselves suggestions as to how school climates might be changed. It has begun with a study of secondary schools in districts where the incidence of adverse social factors is high and where some of the schools are strikingly more successful in the prevention of delinquency, maladjustment and backwardness than others; and it will proceed with what may broadly be described as a school-centred approach—modifications of curricula, internal organization, and the like—and a contrasting, community-centred approach—an attempt to improve and make more fruitful the relations between the school and the life around it and among services ancillary to education, such as the school psychological, medical and social services.

11.   *Teachers and teaching*

Many of the Foundation's inquiries have incidentally studied aspects of the teacher's function, attitudes and training. During the past year this set of topics has become of increasing importance. Staff have just completed a major review of research on teaching and teacher education and the N.F.E.R. has sponsored two working conferences of research workers and others particularly interested in the matter. In 1966 two preliminary studies were initiated, designed to explore areas to which, hitherto, little attention has been directed in this country.

The first is a pilot project on the in-service training of teachers. It has been planned and conducted in collaboration with the Surrey Educational Research Association, a group consisting largely of heads, teachers, teacher trainers and the local authority inspectorate. This group has piloted a questionnaire and other methods of study which have been widely used in the county and will be used for the intensive study of teacher needs and views and of the resources of training available in three other counties.

The second is in an even earlier pilot stage. It is concerned with the feasibility of studying what it is that teachers are called upon to do professionally, both inside and outside the classroom—a kind of job analysis without which, incidentally, the training and education of teachers must be something of a hit-or-miss business and research on children's classroom learning lacking in a major dimension. The immediate first step is that of investigating the effectiveness of various kinds of recording device and technique, including such things as self-observation, participant observation, tape recording and closed-circuit television. The work illustrates an important aspect of the Foundation's approach to educational research. The feasibility exercise arose out of discussions with a group of Slough head-teachers. They have set up a working party which, with the assistance of the N.F.E.R., is devising the whole range of instruments, conducting the preliminary trials, and will continue to act as a professional steering committee for the research which will follow.

12. Technical education

Technical education has since the war and particularly in the last ten years seen more change and given rise to more public anxiety than any other sector of the public system (see also the paper by Heywood). It is a peculiarly difficult field for research because of the nature of its population, the immense variety of arrangements, and the fact that many of its teaching staff have part-time appointments. Not surprisingly research activity is scattered and in relation to other areas, somewhat thin.

Recognizing this, the N.F.E.R. set up a small informal liaison group of research workers interested in the field, and under the aegis of this, *Technical Education Abstracts* was set on foot, and two conferences devoted to a synthesis of research in technical education have been held. The liaison group has also prepared a handbook on research methods, which will shortly be published.

Two major research programmes on aspects of technical education are nearing completion. One has been concerned with educational and vocational guidance at the *transition from school to further education,* and the other, financed by a grant from the Department of Education and Science, with the relative advantages of *Block and Day release.* Both have

shown the extraordinary difficulty inherent in a field subject to so rapid
a series of changes and in a population which fluctuates; both suggest
that the key problem for inquiry is that of the kind of learning and
motivations to learn involved in technical education and vocational
training, and have highlighted the need for much more adequate
techniques and systems of guidance. It is on these problems that future
work will be concentrated.

13. *International work: research in comparative education*

A word should be said about the very considerable international
activity in which the Foundation plays its part (see also the paper by
Walker). There are many problems in education which cannot
adequately be studied within the context of one school system. Some
years ago the Foundation organized a meeting of the staff of educational
research centres in Europe and across the world, with the specific
object of strengthening working relationships. At this meeting and at
another, in which the Foundation played a leading part, organized by
the Unesco Institute for Education, Hamburg, the idea arose that
collaborative research was feasible and likely to be a most powerful
instrument for the advancement of knowledge. A pilot study of
thirteen-year-olds in twelve countries showed the problems of such
work and demonstrated its feasibility (Unesco Institute for Education
1962). From this the *International Evaluation of Educational Attainment
project* was born. For more than five years now, some dozen or more
research institutions in countries as far apart as Sweden and Japan,
America and Israel, the United Kingdom and Australia have collaborated
on comparative studies of educational outputs from their systems. The
first piece of work, concerned with the learning of mathematics at the
age of thirteen, school leaving and the threshold of higher education, has
been completed and published (Husén 1967, Pidgeon 1967). The group
is now going on to the systematic study of further subjects of the
secondary curriculum—science, the mother tongue, social studies
(civics), and a foreign language. It is only in this world framework
that the spectrum of possible decisions on such things as the degree of
educational investment, the gradations of selectiveness/comprehensive-
ness in school systems, and the effects of parental, cultural and class
attitudes can adequately be studied. The I.E.A. has given a new
dimension to comparative education.

14. *Services to the education system*

A) TEST SERVICES

The major research programmes of the Foundation are only one—though a very important—part of its whole activity. In addition, a considerable range of services is provided which can only be effective on a national scale. The longest established of these are the Test Services. Over nearly twenty years, the Test Services have been devising psychometric tests of ability and attainment. Some of these have been specifically for use by local authorities in their allocation procedures, and some are designed for the use of teachers in the diagnosis of educational difficulties, in the day-to-day evaluation of their pupils' work, and in educational guidance. Nearly a hundred different tests covering the whole age-range of the junior and secondary school and the subjects of the basic curriculum are now available to teachers. All of them have comparable norms, have been widely standardized and conform to high standards of construction. What is perhaps even more important is that, although the Foundation is responsible for the technical tasks of a psychometric and statistical kind, the content of the tests and the items of which they are composed are the work of practising teachers. Similarly, many of the guidance procedures which are still in use in many authorities at the transition from primary to secondary school are based in part on specially devised instruments, the specification and contents of which are the work of teacher committees, with the N.F.E.R. providing the strictly technical services necessary.

B) E.T.R.U.

Of a similar nature is the *Examinations and Tests Research Unit*, which was established in 1965 with funds from the Schools Council and the D.E.S. Its main purpose is to study means of ensuring comparability of standards among the fourteen C.S.E. examining boards. The current procedure for this is the use of a scholastic aptitude test as a common yardstick for making broad inter-board and inter-subject comparisons. Experiments are, however, going on which include the use of mathematics and English achievement tests, an essay test as well as the comparative judgments of chief examiners from different boards. A novel procedure under investigation involves the development and use of an 'item bank'—a collection of standardized examination questions, the validity, reliability and difficulty of which will be known, as will their applicability to any given educational objective. From such a bank it will be possible to draw a selection of questions—all of them originally devised by teachers—to assess reliably any selection of educational objectives. In this way it is hoped to reconcile the liberty of the teacher both in the choice of objectives and in the way in which they are measured with minimum national standards of comparability.

The Unit is also concerned currently with a follow-up of secondary school pupils who, having taken the c.s.e., either stay at school or leave to enter work. A study, too, is being made of attitudes to science as a school subject and as a career choice.

c) TEST AGENCY

Still in the field of guidance and measurement is the N.F.E.R. Test Agency. This agency exists to provide, either by producing and publishing the work of British test constructors or by import from outside the country (mainly the United States), tests and other psychological materials required by psychologists working in school psychological services, child guidance and psychiatric clinics and in industry. Increasingly, too, it provides the instruments asked for by educational guidance officers and school counsellors. It also operates an advisory service on tests. Most of the instruments concerned are prepared for those specially trained to use them. In consequence the Foundation, in collaboration with the British Psychological Society, operates a scheme of control and accreditation.

d) INFORMATION

Another series of services provided by the Foundation is concerned with the dissemination of information on research, the maintenance of a clearing house, and the publication of a considerable variety of journals, pamphlets, bibliographies and books. Such services are expensive to operate and difficult to build, and we are very conscious of the gaps which exist—only some of which are beginning to be of interest to other agencies. The Information and Documentation Centre answers a thousand or more major inquiries a year. It maintains a register of research in education still in progress as well as publishing lists of completed research. There are three periodical publications, *Educational Research, New Research in Education,* and *Technical Education*

Abstracts. The Foundation's own research is published in a series of book-length research reports of which some fifteen have been issued to date. An *Occasional Publication* series also exists to provide an outlet for valuable research work done by others which is too lengthy for publication in a journal and unlikely to find a commercial market. A series of pamphlets explaining the bearing of the Foundation's own research work on the teacher's problems is in preparation, as is a series of paperbacks presenting the results of research in particular areas. As and when a matter of educational relevance becomes the centre of public controversy—as did the 11-plus some time ago—the Foundation may prepare an *ad hoc* pamphlet to set out such evidence as exists, or it may—as in the case of the i.t.a. research—organize and publish a critical symposium (Downing 1967b; see also the paper by Reid).

15. *Conclusion*

In a brief space, it is difficult to bring out more than a few of the main aspects of the work of an organization like the N.F.E.R., which has no precise parallel either in the United Kingdom or abroad. It is an independent research institute with a broad brief, as wide in theory as the educational system itself. On the other hand, it is as much concerned with the dissemination of information arising from research as it is with the conduct of research, and to do this as completely and as impartially as possible. Members of staff are constantly called upon, by local authorities, by the Department of Education and Science, by individual teachers, university and college of education staff, by industry and by organizations the world over, for advice and information. At any one time, three or four advanced students, administrators or inspectors from England or abroad will be found receiving informal in-service training in one or other of the Foundation's programmes. It provides a research base for senior workers from overseas who wish to conduct comparative inquiries in English schools; and staff co-operate in a great many inquiries and studies—such, for instance, as the Population Investigation Committee follow-through study of children born in 1946 (Douglas 1964) or the National Child Development Study, 1958 Cohort (Pringle *et al.* 1967)—conducted by others.

On the other hand, all its work is conceived and conducted in the closest collaboration with the teaching profession and educational administration. Apart from the formal representation of the professional associations of teachers, of the universities and colleges of education and of the local education authorities at all points in its government, direct links with the field are very close indeed. Research projects arise from discussions with teachers, local authority staff, the Inspectorate and the departments of state; the planning is done in continuous consultation with groups of advisors drawn from the field to be studied; even the instruments of measurement are devised and refined, piloted and amended with the help of working groups of consultants drawn from schools. Finally, all the field work is conducted by teachers, local authority staff and working psychologists.

This close informal collaboration with the public educational system is probably more effective than would be a formal structure of committees. It is certainly educative both ways: it enables research staff to be aware of what is going on in the schools and, by involving the practitioner from the outset, provides him with a kind of in-service training which has done much to prepare the way for current developments* and which will help to ensure that research and practice become more fully integrated in the future.

*The willingness of teachers to take part in research has grown considerably over the past decade, and in a recent direct inquiry 80 per cent of teachers expressed willingness to take part in research conducted by the N.F.E.R.

D. A. Walker

The Work of the Scottish Council for Research in Education

The Scottish Council is probably best known for its mental surveys, which were conducted in 1932 and 1947. In each of these, group tests were administered to a complete age-group of eleven-year-olds, numbering 70,000 in 1932 and 87,000 in 1947. The 1932 survey was probably the first occasion on which the same test had been given to a complete age-group in any country. But the Council does more than conduct mental surveys; it has published more than fifty volumes in the field of educational research, and the following account gives some idea of the projects with which it is now concerned or which have been recently completed.

The Scottish Council for Research in Education was established in 1928, following discussions between the Association of Directors of Education in Scotland, who are the administrators of the thirty-five counties and cities into which Scotland is divided, and the Educational Institute of Scotland, which represents most of the teachers. Its purpose is to encourage and organize educational research in Scotland. The Council has in its membership representatives from the local education authorities, the Educational Institute of Scotland, the Association of Directors of Education, colleges of education, universities, and other interested bodies. The Scottish Education Department, which is the national body administering education, is represented by assessors.

The work of the Council can be summarized under the following seven main heads as:

1. Conducting research through committees set up by the Council.
2. Sponsoring research to be conducted by persons or groups on the Council's behalf.

3. Co-ordinating the research efforts of others, and arranging for facilities to be provided for projects approved by the Council but executed by others.
4. Publishing the results of educational research conducted in Scotland.
5. Maintaining registers of current and completed research in Scotland and a library of research journals.
6. Advising bodies or persons engaged in research.
7. Making grants to persons requiring financial assistance to undertake research projects.

Investigations undertaken directly by the Council

If the Council decides to undertake a research project under its own auspices, it usually entrusts the work to a committee whose members are appointed for their knowledge of the particular field and their skill in research. These members receive their expenses for attending meetings, but no fee for their services. The normal practice in recent years has been for the Council to have eight or nine projects under way at the same time. This has the advantage that the Council has operated on a wide front, sometimes extending from the nursery school to the university; but it has the disadvantage that too much has been attempted, with the result that the completion of projects has been delayed and reports have been published a long time after the inquiries were made in the schools. The temptation to start a new project on an interesting topic is a very real one for those engaged in research in education, where there is so much innovation, and where some measure of evaluation is required before important decisions on organization, curricula and teaching methods are made.

The following sections contain a brief description of each of the major projects that are now being undertaken or have recently been completed by the Council.

A) THE MENTAL SURVEYS

These are included, although fieldwork is completed and the final report will be published shortly. The first survey (Scottish Council for Research in Education 1933) had as its aim the application of a group test of intelligence to the age-group of eleven-year-olds in 1932, numbering about 87,000 children, and of an individual test to a sample of 1,000 children from that year-group. In both of these the Council was very successful, thanks to the co-operation of the administrators and teachers in Scotland. The results gave more reliable estimates than had hitherto been available of the great range of individual differences in measured intelligence, and showed that the difference between boys and girls in average score was negligible, but that the scatter of the boys' scores was greater than that of the girls. This second result recurs in other investigations, and must be borne in mind whenever comparisons are made between the sexes on measures at the extremes of distributions; e.g. the proportion of boys who score very highly tends to be greater than that of girls who score very highly; and so also does the proportion of very low-scoring boys contrasted with that of girls.

In the years following the first survey, the attention of those working with intelligence tests was drawn to the fact that children from large families tended to have lower scores than those from smaller families. The fear was expressed that this might lead to a steady fall in the national level of intelligence. A second survey (Scottish Council for Research in Education 1949), on the same scale as the first, was therefore carried out, the 1932 test being again used.

The results confirmed the finding that average score was negatively associated with size of family, but they showed that the average score made by the eleven-year-olds in the test had increased rather than decreased over the fifteen-year interval between the surveys.

The debate on the possible causes for the increase still continues, but it seems likely that environmental changes are part of the explanation. Perhaps it was with this in mind that the planners of the second survey included a sociological schedule which was completed by the teacher and a random sample sociological schedule, on a more extensive scale, which was completed for a random sample of about one-tenth of the age-group. The findings obtained from the analysis of these schedules and the test scores have been described in two further reports (Scottish Council for Research in Education 1953, 1958).

Another selection from the random sample produced a group of 1,208 children, known as the 'Six-day sample' because of the method of selecting them. (They were the children born on the first day of the second, fourth, sixth, eighth, tenth and twelfth months of the year 1936.) This method of selection ensured that they were scattered over the length and breadth of Scotland. The Council decided to keep in touch with these pupils and to record their progress and subsequent careers; it succeeded in carrying out this follow-up over a period of sixteen years, i.e. until the young people had reached the age of twenty-seven years. In the early stages they were still at school, and reports could be obtained from the school authorities. When they left school, a system of home visitors was organized, many of these being teachers. When the follow-up was completed, some visitors had an unbroken record of keeping in touch with the sample member throughout the whole period. The work was voluntary, only travelling expenses being paid, and it says much for the willingness and enthusiasm of these home visitors that at the end of the follow-up the Council was still in touch with 1,084 of the original 1,208. A pleasing feature was that in the final years of the follow-up about one-third of the sample members were returning their own questionnaires, and many of them have asked that they should be told when the final report is published. The early years of the follow-up were reported by Macpherson (Scottish Council for Research in Education 1958).

A further extension of the survey involved the testing of the younger brothers and sisters of the sample members as they reached the age of eleven. This provides additional information on the relation between intelligence and size of family. For this the Council was indebted to psychologists in the employment of education authorities or on the staffs of universities and colleges of education. The final report of the survey is nearing completion, and will be published at an early date.

b) THE SCHOLASTIC SURVEYS

The mental surveys just described provided little evidence on the scholastic attainments of the pupils, and the Council decided to conduct a scholastic survey in 1953 on the same lines (Scottish Council for Research in Education 1963). Once again the co-operation of all schools in Scotland was obtained. On this occasion the group chosen was the ten-year-olds—to avoid any conflict with the arrangements for allocating children to secondary courses—and the subjects tested were arithmetic and English.

The tests were designed and tried out by committees of teachers. One great difficulty experienced by the committee arose from the variations between areas in the curricula, especially in arithmetic. Four tests were constructed, two in each subject, and these were given to the whole age-group in May 1953. Additional information about the pupils and the schools from which they were drawn was supplied by the schools.

The analysis of the data from over 72,000 pupils taking four tests was a time-consuming task, and it was not until the data had been entered on punched cards that swift and accurate progress was possible. The detailed results included comparisons between urban and rural areas, between sexes, and between schools of different sizes. It was noteworthy that the one-teacher school produced on average as high a level of attainment as the larger school with seven or more teachers.

In addition to this type of analysis, the committee which had designed the tests closely examined samples of scripts, and two chapters of the report were devoted to their findings on the reactions of pupils to particular items and to recommendations to teachers on teaching methods.

Since the tests had not been published in the interval between their use in 1953 and the publication of the report in 1963, it was possible to use them again for a survey in 1963. This was done on a sample basis, with the school as the sampling unit, and about 7 per cent of the schools in Scotland were selected. The analysis was on this occasion effected much more speedily and the report (Scottish Council for Research in Education 1968) is now available. The smaller numbers made the data easier to handle, but the method of sampling introduced complications of a different kind. The calculations have underlined the need for care in handling the statistical analysis where the sampling is of 'cluster' type, in this case with the school as the primary unit. These calculations indicate that the sample size of just over 5,000 has yielded the same precision as a simple random sample of about 700.

The findings of the second survey are encouraging. They show that the ten-year-olds of 1963 are more proficient in the basic skills than were their predecessors of 1953.

c) THE STANDARDIZATION OF THE WECHSLER INTELLIGENCE SCALE FOR CHILDREN

Lest it be thought that the Council is interested only in surveys, the third example chosen is of another type. The Wechsler Intelligence Scale for Children, commonly known as the w.i.s.c., has been employed by psychologists in Scotland for some years as an individual test. The norms, however, are based on children in the United States of America, and a request was made to the Council that an effort should be made to provide Scottish norms.

In accordance with its usual procedure, the Council formed a committee, in this case composed mainly of practising psychologists. Their first task was to examine the Scale for possible amendments, replacing American usages by the equivalent Scottish terms. These amendments were kept to a minimum. Arrangements were then made to have the amended test given to a random sample of children, numbering about 200 in each year-group, for the age-groups 5 to 15. The testing was conducted by qualified psychologists, who had not only to record responses in a more detailed way than is usual in the testing situation but also to carry out extra procedures.

The responses were then analysed, partly by the members of the committee and partly by clerical staff adequately briefed. New norms were constructed on the lines indicated by Wechsler.

At the end it was found that the Scottish norms differed only in minor respects from those in the w.i.s.c. handbook, although there were variations in the sub-tests (Scottish Council for Research in Education 1967). The amendments and Scottish norms have been made available to those who use the w.i.s.c. test.

Once again the Council has been indebted to the group of people, in this case psychologists, who made their knowledge and time available for the task.

D) ASSESSMENT FOR HIGHER EDUCATION

The Council embarked on this inquiry in 1962, with the aid of a grant from the Carnegie Trust for the Universities of Scotland, and with the collaboration of the Department of Psychology of the University of Edinburgh. The project is described in the paper by Butcher.

E) BIBLIOGRAPHY OF EDUCATION

Research in education embraces not only the experimental and the survey approaches, but also the work done by the historian of the subject. For the benefit of those doing research in this field, a committee has been engaged for some years in recording references to Scottish education. The material examined has included books, periodical literature and pamphlets but not manuscripts, and many libraries have been visited. The mass of data is so great that it has been decided that the bibliography will run to at least two volumes, the first of which, covering the period to 1872, is nearing completion.

F) ORGANIZATION OF SECONDARY COURSES

The course of research in education does not always run as smoothly as some of these accounts might appear to show. In 1965 the Council launched an inquiry into the effects of changes in the organization of secondary courses which had followed changes in the Scottish system of school examinations. Questionnaires for a pilot inquiry were constructed, but it was then found that the changes were taking place with such speed and to so great an extent that an inquiry on the usual time-scale would be of little value. Even if it had been possible to obtain the data, the analysis and conclusions would have had purely historical interest. The research in this field, which is also concerned with the problems arising from the transfer to comprehensive education, will therefore have to be operational.

G) MATHEMATICS IN THE PRIMARY SCHOOL

In this case, too, difficulties have been experienced in designing the project. The committee began by considering three lines of inquiry. The first was to design a test which would enable pupils in the primary school with high mathematical aptitude to be detected and given appropriate courses. The attempt failed, partly because of the lack of agreement on what mathematics is, and partly because it was impossible to separate aptitude from the knowledge acquired in the various school curricula.

The second and third lines were concerned with the arithmetical attainments of average and below-average pupils in the upper part of the primary school. This would, it was hoped, indicate the level of competence to be expected of the average pupil and the amount and nature of the failure of others. It was found that there was so great a variation in content, order of presentation and level expected in the various schools that this approach had to be abandoned.

Until the objectives of teaching arithmetic and mathematics in the primary school have been agreed and defined, research on the extent to which different methods of teaching or learning succeed in attaining their objectives cannot be carried on with any degree of assurance.

Sponsored research

It is not possible nor it is desirable that the Council's staff should be responsible for administering research on all the topics which the Council wishes to investigate. There are some topics, such as national surveys, which are obviously best conducted from a central point. There are others in which a local approach is more desirable, and still others where a single investigator with a special knowledge of the topic may do the best work. The support of the Council, which may be financial or clerical or merely consultative, can make possible research which might otherwise not be carried out.

The Council uses the term 'sponsored' to denote research which it wishes to have carried out; it effects this by requesting an institution, a group of investigators or a single investigator to undertake the necessary work with the support of the Council. Three examples may be quoted.

A) AGE OF TRANSFER

The question of the optimum age for transferring a child from primary to secondary education is continually under discussion. One has only to mention the fact that the present age for transfer is eleven in England and Wales and twelve in Scotland to show that there is no agreement on the question. The earlier physical maturation of young people with its effects on the educational system has reinforced the need for research.

Being aware of the great volume of work that had already been carried out in Aberdeen City, the Council asked Professor J. D. Nisbet of the Department of Education in the University of Aberdeen to undertake an inquiry into the age of transfer, and offered substantial financial aid. The team which Professor Nisbet leads embarked in 1963 on a five-year project, in which an age-group has been followed from the second highest class in the primary school to the third year of the secondary school. A first report (Nisbet and Entwistle 1966) has shown that the evidence is in favour of a gradual transition from primary to secondary education, based on the steady progressive nature of children's development. The research continues, and further reports are awaited with interest.

B) HANDWRITING

In Britain in recent years there has been a spate of new methods of handwriting, each with its enthusiastic advocates. Few, if any, however, are based on thorough research into the subject, and the claims of their advocates cannot always be substantiated. Education authorities and groups of teachers have also been grappling with the problem, and some have devised new schemes of teaching writing in the primary school; but these schemes, too, have had to be based on slender evidence. The Council therefore asked Dr G. G. Neill Wright and his wife Dr Helen Wright, who had been engaged on research on this topic for some years, to extend their work and prepare a report for publication.

This report will be in two volumes. The first is devoted mainly to the history of handwriting in the Western world, with its implications for the present controversies on teaching method. The second volume is planned to include descriptions and discussions of experiments which have been carried out in Scottish schools, both primary and secondary, and with adults.

C) HISTORY OF THE TRAINING OF TEACHERS

As there is no up-to-date history of the training of teachers in Scotland, the Council requested Dr M. A. Cruickshank, at that time a member of the staff of Jordanhill College of Education, to undertake the task of writing one. Its preparation involves a search of the printed records and an analysis of a great deal of manuscript material in the individual colleges. The report will include a description of the present-day expansion, the administrative reorganization which has accompanied it, and the innovations in the curricula of the colleges which reflect the new trends in education.

D) HISTORY OF THE SCOTTISH DEGREE OF BACHELOR OF EDUCATION

This degree was instituted in Scottish universities just after the First World War. Those who gained the degree have filled important posts in the academic world, in the administration of education, and in other fields. It was a second degree, denoted by the letters B.Ed. or Ed.B., and the advent of the B.Ed. as a first degree has brought to an end this era. Courses of the same type will continue to be provided, but will lead to the degree of M.Ed.

The Council has asked Mr R. E. Bell of the Department of Education in the University of Edinburgh to write a history of the original Scottish degree; work on this is now nearing completion.

Grants in aid of research

A third way in which the Council has been able to aid research in Scotland has been in making grants to applicants. In these cases the project is suggested by the applicant, and the Council has to decide whether the project comes within its field, whether the proposed research is soundly based, and finally whether it is of sufficient importance to warrant a grant from the Council's funds. Until recently the funds were so limited that only a few grants could be made, but financial support from the Scottish Education Department has increased in recent years and the Council has been able to make more grants.

Topics which are being covered in this way include children's thinking, methods of teaching chemistry at university level, subject choice in secondary school with special reference to the shortage of university-trained scientists, slow speech development, the social and emotional adjustment of the deaf, computer procedures for school timetables, and the recruitment of teachers.

Publication of educational research

The publication of reports of educational research is not usually an attractive commercial proposition. The Council has helped to make available in printed form reports which might otherwise not have been published. The research thus published has not necessarily been carried out on behalf of the Council or with its aid. A notable early example of this is the work of McClelland on educational selection (1942), carried out in Dundee Training College for the International Examination Inquiry Committee. The findings of this report no longer hold, since school conditions have altered so greatly since 1942, but the experimental method and statistical analysis are still valid. A later example is Fraser's research on education and home background (1959), which is now recognized on both sides of the Atlantic as a notable contribution in this field.

It is the Council's policy to make available to scholars, teachers and the public a series of histories of education in the different regions of Scotland. Only when the series nears completion will it be possible to write a balanced account of the history of education in the whole country. The Council therefore welcomes offers of suitable manuscripts, and has been able to publish histories of education in Aberdeenshire, Angus, Ayrshire, Stirlingshire and Edinburgh. Other volumes include a history of the Inspectorate in Scotland and a collection of shorter studies.

International research

In recent years there have been great developments in the field of international co-operation between research centres, and in this the Scottish Council has played an active part. In its simplest form this may mean only providing information about the Scottish system and linking the investigator from overseas with the institutions or schools in which research is to be carried out. An inquiry of this kind, conducted in 1962 by a group from the University of Michigan, compared the achievements in reading and spelling and quality of handwriting of English, Scottish and American children.

More direct participation has occurred in the International Project for the Evaluation of Educational Achievement. This arose from meetings of heads of research centres in 1959 and later years, the first result being a pilot project (Unesco Institute for Education 1962) in which thirteen-year-old pupils from twelve countries were given tests of reading comprehension, mathematics, geography and science. In this project the research centres co-operated with the Unesco Institute for Education in Hamburg, and the co-operation was continued in a full-scale investigation into the teaching of mathematics in secondary schools (Husén 1967).

This involved the construction, with the help of practising teachers, of tests of mathematics appropriate to thirteen-year-olds and to pupils in the final year of the secondary school in the twelve countries taking part. Some countries, including Scotland, also administered tests to pupils at the 'O' grade stage, corresponding roughly to English 'O' level. Questionnaires recording the pupils' opinions and attitudes were also constructed and administered, and other questionnaires, completed by pupils, teachers and headmasters, gave sociological and other data.

The tests and questionnaires were machine-scored as far as that was possible, but some of the items were open-ended, and these and the questionnaires had to be coded by workers in the various countries before the replies were transferred to magnetic tape for analysis by the computer in the Department of Education of the University of Chicago. Two main methods of analysis were employed, the first being the testing of hypotheses about the mathematical attainments in the different countries and the factors associated with these attainments. The second used the techniques of multivariate analysis. The Council has now embarked, with other countries in the group, on researches into other subjects of the curriculum.

Co-ordination of research

In educational research it is very easy for an investigator to begin and sometimes even to complete a project in ignorance of the fact that another investigator is engaged on the same problem. It may be that the two approaches are complementary to each other, but this would occur only by chance. The Council therefore maintains a register of research, so that any investigator who wishes to be put in touch with workers on the same problem may be given the necessary information.

Other investigators may wish to obtain access to Scottish schools for research work, and the Council, which has very good relations with administrators and teachers, is often able to help. The Council is able, too, to shield schools from projects that have been badly constructed or make too great demands on pupils or teachers.

Future problems

Now, in 1967, the Council has completed a set of projects and is making plans for research into a new set of problems. These include some aspects of the complex question of examinations, and studies of the effect of environment on educational attainment. Each of these topics is of great importance in the current educational system, and answers to the many questions that can be raised will be welcomed by administrators, teachers, parents and the general public. The Council looks forward to having the co-operation of all of these in its efforts to find at least some of the answers to these questions.

Maurice Chazan

Children's Emotional Development

Introduction

A) PAUCITY OF RESEARCH STUDIES

Although the importance of non-cognitive factors in the educational process has been increasingly recognized, there has been a relative neglect of the study of children's emotional development by educational research workers in Britain (Wiseman 1959). We still depend greatly on American research work in this field, particularly for normative data; but while some of this work is relevant to this country, it cannot be assumed that the results of investigations involving samples of American children are equally applicable to British children.

Many reasons may be suggested for this neglect of the study of emotional development; chief among them may be mentioned the lack of measuring instruments, the failure to establish an acceptable theoretical framework within which research can be carried out, and the complexities of the study of emotional development, which is not easily amenable to laboratory experiment. As the adequate study of children's emotional development demands research lasting over a long period and properly involves a team of research workers, it is not surprising that, with the limited resources of educational research workers in Great Britain, so little has been done in this field.

B) THEORETICAL TRENDS

The insights of psycho-analytic theories have continued to make a contribution to the understanding of child development (De Monchaux 1957). Though few educational research workers now adopt a framework of psycho-analytic theory as a basis for their own inquiries, it has been suggested by Hindley (1957), in the light of American work attempting a synthesis between learning theory and psycho-analytic approaches, that many of Freud's theories are capable of being reformulated in terms of learning principles. Eysenck, in numerous publications, has maintained that most of the emotional reactions and behaviour patterns of children can be understood in terms of learning, without recourse to psycho-analytic theories. Anthony (1956, 1957), Schaffer (1958) and Woodward (1965) have shown that Piaget's system, though mainly concerned with children's cognitive development, has implications for the understanding of children's emotional development and behaviour. The contribution of the ethological approach, which has thrown so much light on animal behaviour (Lorenz 1950, Tinbergen 1951), has been stressed by Bowlby (1957) and Grant (1965), particularly in the identification of critical periods of development.

All these approaches have provided a wealth of ideas and hypotheses for the research worker, and much more controlled experiment and observation is needed to integrate the various theories propounded. It is likely that these theories are less in disagreement over fundamental issues than they would seem to be at first sight.

c) CURRENT LONGITUDINAL STUDIES

American longitudinal studies have provided valuable data on emotional development in childhood and adolescence (Dearborn and Rothney 1941, Gesell 1940, 1946, Jones, H. E., 1943, Macfarlane et al. 1954, Meek 1940, and Terman 1925, 1926, 1930, 1947), but few long-term studies of emotional development have been made in this country. There are, however, three longitudinal studies on children in Britain which are producing valuable data. First, the follow-up investigation of all children born within one week in March 1946, carried out under the auspices of the Population Investigation Committee, has provided information on the attitudes and behaviour of over 5,000 children as well as on their intellectual development and scholastic progress (Douglas 1964, Douglas and Blomfield 1958). The investigation is now continuing as part of the programme of a Medical Research Council Unit at the London School of Economics.

Secondly, at the Centre for Study of Human Development of the University of London Institutes of Education and Child Health, a sample of London children has been studied longitudinally from the pre-natal stage. The project, which was begun in 1949, has been concerned with, among other things, the predictability of personality characteristics at an early age, the incidence of particular kinds of behaviour at different ages, and the relation between behaviour or emotional disturbance and a variety of factors (Moore, T. W., 1959, 1966, Moore *et al.* 1954).

The third longitudinal study is the National Child Development Study, now being administered by the National Bureau for Co-operation in Child Care, which involves 16,000 children all born in Great Britain in the same week of March 1958 (Pringle and Butler 1966). These children are being followed up every three years during their school life, and a report on the physical, educational and psychological development of the children at the age of seven has been published (Pringle *et al.* 1967).

The findings of some aspects of those longitudinal studies in which reports have been published will be discussed below.

In spite of the paucity of studies concerned with children's emotional development, it is impossible, within the compass of a single paper, to do justice to all the recent and current work of psychologists, psychiatrists, sociologists and workers from other disciplines which is significant. In this paper, therefore, I shall confine myself mainly to research of particular relevance to education in four areas:

1. Factors influencing children's emotional development.
2. The relation between personality factors and scholastic achievement.
3. Emotional and behaviour difficulties at school.
4. The emotional development of handicapped children.

1. *Factors influencing emotional development*

The emotional development of children is influenced by a variety of factors, operating in combination. Our knowledge of the effects of these factors comes, in the main, from clinically-based studies of deviant behaviour and emotional disorder rather than from studies of representative samples of the normal population.

A) TEMPERAMENTAL FACTORS

A number of studies have been concerned with the link between temperament and conditionability. Eysenck (1960b, 1964), using a framework of research on personality based upon the two axes or dimensions of introversion–extraversion and stability–instability, has put forward the hypothesis that introverts form conditioned responses more quickly and lastingly than do extraverts. Applying this hypothesis to the study of behaviour disturbance, he has suggested that these differences in conditioning greatly affect the direction disturbed behaviour will take. Characteristically, the introverted unstable child has personality problems such as depression or feelings of inferiority; the extraverted neurotic child tends to show conduct problems, such as temper tantrums and destructive behaviour. Eysenck finds considerable evidence in favour of a strong hereditary predisposition towards extraverted or introverted behaviour and also towards strong or weak emotionality. His work, with its stress on the need for disturbed or delinquent children to learn new ways of behaviour or to unlearn undesirable habits, has interesting implications for treatment (Eysenck and Rachman 1965).

The importance of the influence of heredity has also been emphasized by Shields (1962), who compared forty-four pairs of identical twins brought up separately with forty-four pairs brought up together. He found significant resemblance between twins in both groups in respect of a number of variables, including extraversion, neuroticism and a number of other personality characteristics.

Trasler (1962, 1963, 1966) has examined the process of emotional learning and has attempted to synthesize ideas derived from Eysenck's work and from American contributors to personality theory. He hypothesizes that social training is mediated by conditioning in the child specific anxiety reactions which inhibit proscribed behaviour, and suggests that the differences between introverts and extraverts in their response to such training are worthy of exploration.

Hallworth (1964), using factor analysis to study personality ratings of adolescents, found that teachers' ratings were largely grouped into the two factors stressed by Eysenck: 'sociability' or 'social extraversion' and 'emotional stability' or 'reliability and conscientiousness'.

B) CONGENITAL FACTORS

Stott has suggested, in a number of studies (1957, 1959, 1964, 1966), that the influence of post-natal environmental factors on the emotional development of children has been over-emphasized and that not enough attention has been given to a susceptibility to stress which may be congenital. In particular, he has found a link between stressful pregnancies and subsequent emotional maladjustment in the child (1957). According to this view, congenital damage often takes the form of a disposition to breakdown or malfunction, there being an interaction between congenital impairment and adverse post-natal environmental influences, as Drillien (1964) has shown in her study of children born prematurely.

These studies—though they need confirmation from further work —underline the importance of careful consideration of pre-natal and peri-natal conditions as well as circumstances after birth.

c) PHYSICAL MATURATION

Rate of maturing

Tanner (1961), while admitting that we lack knowledge about the relation between the maturity of the brain and the development of the emotions, points out that maturation of the cortex must play an important role in changes of behaviour. He also stresses the wide range of individual differences in the rate of maturing, in the physiological sense, and points to the possible repercussions on behaviour which result from early or late maturity. Douglas (1964) also discusses the relation between physiological and emotional development. In his survey, girls who mature early were reported by their teachers to be more amenable to discipline and less likely to be shy or aggressive than those who developed more slowly. At home, there was no evidence to suggest that the early developers showed more behaviour problems, or caused their mothers more worry, than the late developers.

Much more detailed and systematic research is needed on the relation between physical and emotional development and its implications for education. For example, as Tanner (1961) observes, the fact that girls are physically and emotionally more advanced than boys throughout most of their school career has important implications for co-educational schools.

Physical changes at puberty

Studies of adolescents have for a long time been concerned with the behavioural and emotional changes associated with physical growth and, in particular, the sudden maturing of the endocrine glands.

Adolescence is no longer thought of as inevitably a period of storm and stress (Hall 1904), though emotional life is intensified then (Wall 1948). Cultural factors have an important influence on emotional development during adolescence, and interact with biological factors (Tanner 1961). There is a great increase in sexual awareness during this period, but, in spite of the obvious importance of this for education, little attention has been given by research workers to the study of sexual attitudes and behaviour during adolescence. Recently, Schofield (1965) has attempted to provide some factual knowledge on this topic by studying the sexual attitudes and behaviour of young people aged 15 to 19. He set out to assess the extent of sexual experience in the age-group, and to identify some of the psychological and sociological factors associated with such experience. 1,873 boys and girls were interviewed at length, and it was found that over half the sample had obtained their sex education from their contemporaries. Few had got information from books, and only half of the sample (mainly the boys) had been given advice by their parents. Fifteen per cent had experienced sexual intercourse, but promiscuity is not, according to Schofield, a prominent feature of teenage life.

The lack of adequate sex education, which this report emphasizes, indicates that schools and parents need to devote much more thought to this aspect of education.

Body-build and personality

Some research work, stimulated by the studies of Kretschmer (1921) and Sheldon *et al.* (1940, 1942), has been carried out in this country on the relation between types of body-build and personality types or characteristics. Parnell (1958) reviews research work on this problem and its implications for education. With Davidson and McInnes (Davidson *et al.* 1957), he reports on a somatotype study of 100 seven-year-old children which formed part of the Child Health Survey of the Institute of Social Medicine in Oxford. The findings of this study suggested that, even at the age of seven, there was a discernible association between behaviour pattern and measurable somatic components. Correlations between body-build and many personality traits were found to be significant, and the general assertion that fat children tend to be easy-going and thin children withdrawn and anxious was both confirmed and expanded.

d) HOME BACKGROUND

There have been numerous studies demonstrating the powerful influence of a child's home background on his emotional development, though much of our knowledge of the child's basic emotional needs is derived from studies of children whose emotional development has been unsatisfactory in some way. A selection of these studies will be referred to here to illustrate the trends in research.

Parent-child relationships

The work of Bowlby (1946, Bowlby et al. 1956), emphasizing the importance of a warm, intimate mother-child relationship in the child's early years and stressing the emotional damage which can be caused by deprivation of maternal care, is very well known. H. Lewis (1954), studying 500 deprived children, found that maternal deprivation was more likely to have ill effects if it occurred in the first two years of life and if it were lasting, but stressed that the child could be considerably helped by good substitute mothering even in circumstances like these. Pringle and Bossio (1958), studying 188 children in institutions, also found that deprivation had worse effects when the first separation from the mother occurred at an early age and when contact with the mother was completely broken off. Ainsworth (1962) reviews the findings of research studies on the effects of maternal deprivation which have been carried out since Bowlby's original work.

Andry (1960) has argued that insufficient attention has been paid to the role of the father in the emotional and social development of children. His study of a sample of eighty delinquent boys and a matched control sample of eighty non-delinquent boys showed that a major feature differentiating the two groups was the delinquents' perception of their fathers' role as being negative.

Parental attitudes and discipline

Faulty parental attitudes and inadequate or inappropriate discipline have been found to affect children's emotional development to a greater extent than adverse material conditions in the home. Bannister and Ravden (1944) showed that a high proportion of 112 children referred to a child guidance clinic for emotional or behaviour difficulties had parents whose attitudes were unsatisfactory or whose discipline was inadequate, and their findings have been confirmed by many subsequent studies (O'Connor and Franks 1960). Children may imitate the personality characteristics of their parents, react to an atmosphere made gloomy or morbid by chronic mental or physical ill health in the parents, or rebel against severe discipline, particularly at adolescence (Chazan 1959). Burt and Howard (1952) factorized the correlations between twenty-four conditions reported among 273 maladjusted children, aged 9 to 13 years, and examined in fuller detail the frequencies of the various conditions occurring in 394 cases of maladjusted children and the same number of normal children, aged 6 to 14 years. The most important conditions in the home affecting emotional development included lack of affection, over-strict discipline, the proneness of the parents to alcoholism, or the presence of a step-mother or foster-mother.

H. Lewis (1954) confirmed the associations found in the United States by Hewitt and Jenkins (1946) between parental rejection and unsocialized aggression in the child, neglect and socialized delinquency, and constraint at home and neurotic symptoms in the child. Brandon (1960), whose study was based on the Newcastle 1,000 Family Study (Spence *et al.* 1954), compared a sample of maladjusted children with a control group developing satisfactorily, and found that a high proportion of the mothers of the maladjusted children suffered from mental ill health. The maladjusted children had younger, more immature and less independent parents. Carney (1963) found that over-demanding parents tended to have children who showed mainly aggressive symptoms, while the maladjusted children whose parents were over-anxious showed symptoms chiefly of a withdrawing kind.

Family cohesion

Carney's study (1963), which investigated the relations between home background and adjustment among 157 junior school children, also showed the effects of a lack of family cohesion on the children's emotional development. He found, *inter alia*, that (1) children from slum-breakdown homes were the most severely maladjusted in the sample, showing disturbance mainly of an aggressive type, and (2) 65 per cent of those children whose homes were broken were considered maladjusted, also mainly in an aggressive way; a higher proportion of children (79 per cent) who had lost a parent by death were considered maladjusted than of those whose homes had been broken by divorce or separation or other circumstances (53 per cent). Whilst the cohesion of the family and the attitudes of the parents were major factors in the causation of emotional maladjustment, other factors—for example, congenital and physical handicap—were also involved.

Brandon (1960) found that more of the parents of the maladjusted children in his sample had a disturbed marital relationship than of the controls.

Social class

Douglas (1964) found only small differences between the number of symptoms of maladjustment, mainly of a psychosomatic nature, reported for middle-class and manual-working-class children of eleven years old. A higher proportion of children from the middle class, however, were reported to have good attitudes towards their school work. Furthermore, in the case of behaviour disorder of the delinquent kind shown by the age of fifteen, there were considerable class differences (Douglas *et al.* 1966). Boys from the lower manual working class were approximately seven times as delinquent as those from the upper middle class.

E) SCHOOL

The influence of the school on the emotional development of children has received much less attention than the influence of the home. Yet, even if the home is the major influence, the school must be considered as having a considerable effect on the emotional development of its pupils. Emotional and behaviour difficulties arising at school will be discussed more fully later on; here we shall be concerned with the studies which have emphasized the positive role of the school in the development of personality.

Effects of nursery school attendance

As great importance has been attached to the first five years of life, inquiries into the effects of going to nursery school are of considerable interest. Douglas and Ross (1964) report on a follow-up study of 130 boys and girls out of their national sample who went to nursery schools and 160 children who went to nursery classes. They found, on the basis of reports on the behaviour of the boys and girls at the ages of thirteen and fifteen, that nursery school attendance was not followed by better than average emotional adjustment or by less delinquency.

However, they point out that the original selection of the children for nursery school attendance was probably a biased one: it is likely that the group included a large proportion of children who were highly vulnerable on entry and who had in fact been given help by going to a nursery school or class.

Teacher-pupil relationships

T. W. Moore (1966), who comments that few studies have been made of the problems faced by children in coping with everyday school life, has surveyed the difficulties of ordinary children in adjusting to the primary school. His sample consisted of 164 children aged 6 to 11 years in 115 primary schools, and it is worthy of note that their mean I.Q. was above average, the boys' mean Stanford-Binet I.Q. being 121·2, that of the girls 111·5. His information was obtained from the mothers of the children, by means of a preliminary questionnaire and subsequent interview. He found that 18 per cent of the pupils did not become thoroughly reconciled to school throughout their six years at the primary school. The commonest and most persistent type of difficulty was a general reluctance to go to school, sometimes attributable to over-dependence. Difficulties with teachers and with school work were relatively frequent.

Adolescent attitudes to school have been studied by E. A. Allen (1959), who individually interviewed sixty-eight fifteen-year-old boys and girls in a Central London secondary modern school and administered attitude tests throughout the school. Although, on the whole, the pupils tended to have favourable attitudes towards school, a large number of unfavourable comments were made by the older pupils, particularly about the quality of the teaching they received, and the methods of discipline used.

Relations between contemporaries

Children are strongly influenced by their contemporaries, and the gangs and groups formed within and outside the school exercise a potent formative influence on their development. Two aspects of the study of this field which have received attention recently are (1) the relation between social adjustment and sociometric status, and (2) the effects of co-education on emotional development (see also the paper by Dale).

Belfield (1963) studied the social adjustment of most-accepted and least-accepted children aged 9 to 11 years in unstreamed classes in junior schools in a small urban community. Using the Bristol Social Adjustment Guides, he found that there was a tendency for the most-accepted children to have good, and the least-accepted children to have poor, social adjustment. About 50 per cent of the least-accepted children and about 5 per cent of the most-accepted, were socially maladjusted. The aggressive pattern of maladjustment was most common among the maladjusted least-accepted children.

The association between low sociometric status and maladjustment has been confirmed by Carney (1963), K. M. Evans (1962) and Lunzer (1960a), though, as Belfield showed, high and low sociometric status is related to factors other than social adjustment. Such studies have demonstrated that the use of sociometric techniques in class can be of value in discovering children with emotional difficulties.

F) MASS MEDIA

Few studies have been made of the effects of mass media on children's emotional development, in spite of their growing importance. The Wheare Report (Ministry of Education 1950) suggested that the cinema could be a contributory factor in delinquency, misbehaviour and nervous strain, though its ill effects were not considered to be far-reaching. Wall and Simson (1950, 1951) investigated the emotional responses of adolescents to the cinema, but found little evidence of enduring fright. They concluded, however, that the cinema provided a powerful stimulus to fantasy life, and that the more serious films could have an effect on emotional development.

Since these studies were carried out, watching television at home has largely replaced going to the cinema. Himmelweit et al. (1958) have made a large-scale inquiry into the effects of television on children. Their sample consisted of over 4,000 children (aged 10 to 11 and 13 to 14 years) in five cities. Using a variety of techniques, they found that certain programmes—for example, detective, murder and crime thrillers—were frightening to adolescents as well as to the younger children studied; fiction made a deeper impact than reality. However, children tended to be more readily frightened when watching television in specific circumstances, such as in the dark or without an adult in the room. They were particularly disturbed by situations with which they could identify themselves. Viewers were not found to be any more aggressive or maladjusted than non-viewers; and it was concluded that television is unlikely to cause aggression, although it could precipitate it in children already emotionally disturbed.

The effects of reading different kinds of books, newspapers, magazines and comics have received very little attention from research workers; this is an important field for further study.

2. *Personality factors and scholastic achievement*

A number of recent studies have been concerned with the relation between anxiety, introversion–extraversion and attainment in ordinary school children. These will be discussed here with reference to (a) primary school children, and (b) secondary school pupils. Studies of the relation between maladjustment and severe learning difficulties will be dealt with in the next section.

A) PRIMARY SCHOOL CHILDREN

Lynn (1957) studying eighty normal children (forty-two boys, thirty-eight girls, mean I.Q. 112·2) from predominantly middle-class backgrounds, found a tendency for anxious children to be better at reading than at arithmetic. Reed and Schonfield (1958), however, examined the evidence put forward by Lynn and suggested that it was inconclusive; and Biggs (1962) has argued that at earlier educational levels stress and neuroticism are inimical to optimum performance in many school subjects. Savage (1966), studying a sample of ninety-three children (average age 7 years 11 months), reports a significant positive relation between extraversion and I.Q., and between extraversion and arithmetic quotient; he concluded that high extraversion was related to a brighter intellectual level and higher academic attainment. The neuroticism scores were negatively related, to a significant degree, to reading quotient, but were not significantly related either to I.Q. or to arithmetic quotient.

B) SECONDARY SCHOOL PUPILS

Astington (1960) obtained teachers', classmates', and self personality ratings on 678 boys in a maintained boys' grammar school. At all age-levels successful boys received significantly higher ratings than unsuccessful boys for persistence, independence and interest. No consistent relation was found between assessment of dominance and academic performance or between emotional stability and scholastic success. Astington's study clearly shows that the results of this kind of investigation depend on the source of the rating.

Hallworth (1961) studied anxiety in 900 secondary modern and grammar school children in twelve single-sex schools, using eight self-rating questionnaires. The groups from the secondary modern schools had significantly higher mean scores on three measures of manifest and separation anxiety, and they also had higher scores on a measure of emotional introversion. The groups from the grammar schools had a significantly higher mean score on a measure of social introversion, and higher mean scores on measures of self-blame and thinking introversion. Hallworth concludes that grammar school pupils have less anxiety and worry than pupils of secondary modern schools and that, at least for pupils of this age, the overall correlation between anxiety and attainment is negative.

Callard and Goodfellow (1962) gave the Junior Maudsley Personality Inventory to 3,559 boys aged 11 years to 14 years 11 months. They established an association between status in the educational hierarchy and scoring for neuroticism: the lower status groups (secondary modern school pupils and the less intelligent groups within all schools) were shown to have higher averages in neuroticism than the higher status groups (grammar schools and the more intelligent groups within schools). At the top of the educational hierarchy there was a tendency for the more intelligent boys to score slightly more highly in neuroticism than their less intelligent contemporaries, whilst, at the bottom of the hierarchy, neuroticism and intelligence were significantly correlated in a negative direction.

Butcher et al. (1963), using Cattell's H.S.P.Q. test, compared samples of British and American children aged 12 to 14 years. They found that British pupils at a secondary modern school were more introverted and anxious than Illinois children; but a second sample, covering the whole range of ability, revealed no significant differences concerning either extraversion or anxiety. The American children, however, were very significantly more sociable, less assertive and more conscientious than either British group. Conscientiousness and self-sufficiency correlated fairly consistently with school attainment.

Child (1964) examined the relations between introversion–extraversion, neuroticism and performance in school examinations. His sample consisted of 138 children from an urban comprehensive school and forty boys from a public school. Using the J.M.P.I. and General Anxiety Scale, he found that extraversion, neuroticism and I.Q. were statistically unrelated. There was a positive correlation between stable introversion and attainment in school examinations; high or even moderate neuroticism or general anxiety were not advantageously related to attainment.

Rushton (1966) used teachers' ratings and Cattell's C.P.Q. test to examine the relation between personality characteristics and scholastic success in 458 eleven-year-old children. Both teachers' ratings and the personality test showed that well-adjusted, extravert children tended to do well at school.

These studies have clearly demonstrated the importance of personality factors in school achievement; and there is general agreement that stability is positively correlated with academic success and that anxiety tends to interfere with scholastic progress. However, as Warburton (1962) points out, the level of difficulty of the tasks performed, the age of the subjects, and the stage of education reached may be important factors. The relation between anxiety and scholastic attainment is complex: at certain levels, anxiety may act as a motivating agent, but it is likely to be a handicap if excessive and if the task to be performed is a difficult one.

There is less agreement about the nature of the relation between extraversion and scholastic attainment. Although most studies show a negative relation, some have suggested that extravert children do better than introverted children in their school work. Again, it is probable that the difference in the findings is, at least partly, due to the nature of the samples and the tests used, and further comprehensive investigations are needed.

3. *Emotional and behaviour difficulties at school*

With the recognition, in the 1944 Education Act, of the category of 'maladjusted' pupils, there has been a growing interest in children who show emotional or behaviour difficulties severe enough to warrant special educational treatment. Research on maladjusted children has tended to be based on fairly small clinical samples, and only very recently have there been attempts to study emotional and behaviour difficulties in representative samples of school children. Although much emotional disturbance is specific to the situation, and a fully comprehensive approach to the study of maladjustment should include both school and home circumstances (Mitchell and Shepherd 1966, Rutter and Graham 1966), the discussion in this section will be largely confined to work on emotional and behaviour difficulties found *in the school*.

A) INCIDENCE

Research on the incidence of emotional and behaviour difficulties in school has been handicapped by the lack of reliable and valid methods of assessment. This is not surprising in view of the varying levels of tolerance of children's behaviour which teachers and parents have, so that what is considered a problem in one case may give no cause for concern in another. Most children show *some* emotional and behaviour difficulties, at least for short periods; and we do not know enough about norms of behaviour at different ages to be able to make precise statements about criteria for regarding certain kinds of behaviour as deviant. Estimates of the incidence of emotional and behaviour difficulties will, therefore, vary according to the criteria used and must be considered as very tentative.

A number of studies of maladjustment in the school situation have been carried out with the aid of the Bristol Social Adjustment Guide (The Child in School), using the number of symptoms of behaviour disturbance marked by the child's teacher as a criterion. Crawford (Stott 1963) found 16 per cent of Liverpool seven-year-old boys, and 14 per cent of the eight-year-old boys, to be maladjusted; 5 per cent of the seven-year-old girls and 11 per cent of the eight-year-old girls also fell into this category. In addition, between 16 per cent and 24 per cent of the sample were 'unsettled' or mildly maladjusted. In a similar study of children in schools in south Wales Chazan (1963) found 20 per cent of a sample of junior school boys aged $9\frac{1}{2}$ to $10\frac{1}{2}$ years, and 8 per cent of a sample of girls of the same age, to be maladjusted. Eleven per cent of a sample of secondary school boys, 7 per cent of secondary school girls, aged $13\frac{1}{2}$ to $14\frac{1}{2}$ years, were maladjusted. A further 19 to 30 per cent of the pupils showed 'unsettled' behaviour at school. Stott (1964) reports that 11·2 per cent of a sample of 429 British children aged 6 to 15 years came within the 'maladjusted' category and 19·1 per cent within the 'unsettled' category. He concludes, on the basis of the studies made with the Bristol Guide, that between 11 and 15 per cent of boys, and 8 per cent of girls, in Britain are maladjusted by the criterion of twenty recorded indications of behaviour disturbance on the Guide. Sampson (1966a), investigating the incidence of maladjustment in 130 boys and 136 girls, a representative sample of a nine-year-old urban population, found 17·6 per cent of the boys and 15·4 per cent of the girls to be maladjusted on the basis of the Bristol Social Adjustment Guide. In a further individual study of a small sub-sample, she found that in 9 per cent of the children the Bristol Guide rating was confirmed by clinical tests and impressions.

Douglas (1964) obtained a rough measure of disturbed behaviour in children at the age of eleven by asking their mothers and teachers how many out of four symptoms or groups of symptoms, mainly of a psychosomatic nature, the children showed. Nearly 14 per cent of the sample showed two or more of the symptoms, and a further 36 per cent had one symptom. The mothers who reported that their children had several symptoms were worried about them in other ways, particularly about their health and educational progress. A high incidence of maladjustment was also found in the sample at ages 13 and 15 (Mulligan et al. 1963). On the basis of teachers' ratings, 31 to 32 per cent of 'non-delinquent' boys at these ages, and 50 per cent of boys with at least one court appearance, fell into one of the three categories of maladjustment used in the survey ('nervous', 'aggressive' and 'mixed').

The surveys made by Brandon (1960) and Ryle et al. (1965) found quite high proportions of children of primary school age showing symptoms of emotional disturbance.

Rutter and Graham (1966) investigated the prevalence of psychiatric disorder in children aged 10 and 11 years who lived in the Isle of Wight. After screening questionnaires had been given to the teachers and parents of 2,193 children, 13 per cent were selected for intensive study. On the basis of information from a variety of sources, it was finally estimated that 6·3 per cent of the total sample suffered from some degree of psychiatric disorder. This estimate, however, did not include children with educational difficulties or mental subnormality, or those showing certain symptoms, such as nocturnal enuresis, in isolation.

All the evidence, therefore, tentative as it is, suggests that far more children have serious emotional and behaviour difficulties than had previously been supposed.

B) TEACHERS' ATTITUDES

The main investigations into teachers' attitudes towards children's behaviour have been by Hollins (1955) and Gabriel (1957). Hollins drew up a form containing forty items of behaviour considered undesirable by teachers, and asked a sample of 100 teachers to rate each item with respect to seriousness or undesirability in children. Four factors were extracted, as follows (in order of seriousness in the eyes of the teachers):

1. Problems mainly concerned with moral offences (e.g. sex misconduct).
2. Problems connected with the teacher's authority (e.g. insolence).
3. Problems concerning the introverted child (e.g. unsociability).
4. Problems concerning classroom offences (e.g. talkativeness).

Hollins, comparing his own findings with those of previous studies (nearly all carried out in other countries), suggests that the way in which the teachers are approached affects the order in which they put children's problems, though there is considerable evidence to show that they do not regard the introverted, unsocial child as much of a problem. Gabriel, who made a questionnaire-based study involving over 900 teachers, also concluded that withdrawn behaviour caused teachers less concern than overt misbehaviour, though Rutter and Graham (1966) did not find that teachers missed the less obtrusive neurotic children.

C) MALADJUSTMENT AND LEARNING DIFFICULTIES

While not all maladjusted children have learning difficulties, the evidence available (reviewed by Biggs 1959, Sampson 1966b and M.D. Vernon 1957) suggests that a considerable number do have quite serious difficulties of this kind, which may be either the cause or the effect of their maladjustment. Among recent studies, Crawford (1961), in a survey of reading attainment in children of 7 and 8 years of age, found that few of the maladjusted children were doing well at school. Chazan (1963), examining the relation between maladjustment and progress in the basic subjects in a sample of primary and secondary modern school children, found that while some children were able in spite of maladjustment to function well at school, few of the disturbed children had satisfactory all-round attainments and most were considerably under-functioning, especially in arithmetic. Data based on six streamed secondary modern schools showed that nearly all the maladjusted children were to be found in the lower streams. Douglas (1964) found that eleven-year-old children showing symptoms of maladjustment tended to have low scores in tests of general ability, arithmetic, reading and vocabulary and to deteriorate in test performance between the ages of eight and eleven. The teachers reported that children with several symptoms were poor workers, lacked concentration, had difficulties with their classmates, and obtained fewer places in grammar schools than children who showed no symptoms. Mitchell and Shepherd (1966) found that academic success at school was negatively associated with deviant behaviour shown by the children at home.

Lunzer (1960b) suggests that there is a marked tendency for aggressive children to do particularly badly in arithmetic. Gregory (1965) reports a significant connection between reading failure and restlessness (as measured by the Bristol Guide) throughout a primary school, and between reading failure and anxiety for the approval of other children among the nine-, ten- and eleven-year-olds. Restlessness seemed to be a contributory *cause of* reading failure, whereas anxiety appeared to have been, at least partly, *caused by* reading failure.

Roe (1965), in a survey of pupils attending special schools and classes for maladjusted children in the London area, found a high proportion of the pupils to be educationally retarded on admission.

D) TRUANCY AND SCHOOL REFUSAL

There has recently been great interest in the problems of children who do not go to school, particularly those whose non-attendance stems from emotional disturbance—cases of 'school phobia' or 'school refusal'. The literature on the subject has been well reviewed by Cooper (1966a) and Clyne (1966).

Although the children who refuse to go to school do not form a homogeneous group, 'school phobia' or 'school refusal' has been distinguished from truancy (Hersov 1960a,b). A comprehensive study of a sample of truants was made by Tyerman (1958), who investigated 137 cases of truancy in a town in south Wales; he found that adverse home conditions and lack of satisfaction in home or school were probably the most important factors in truancy. Few of the truants had a happy and secure home environment; most were from broken homes or homes in open disharmony. The parents were often neglectful and ineffective in their supervision. On the whole, the children were inferior intellectually and academically to the majority of their age-group. Hersov's controlled studies (1960a,b) of school phobia largely agree with those of other writers in this country (Chazan 1962, Cooper 1966a,b, Kahn 1958, Kahn and Nursten 1964, Model and Shepheard 1958, Morgan 1959), though Chazan puts more emphasis on educational factors in both aetiology and treatment. Hersov compared three groups of cases— fifty cases of school phobia, fifty truants and fifty first attenders at a child guidance clinic. He concluded that school refusal is one manifestation of a neurosis, and that children referred for this (1) tend to come from families with a greater incidence of neurosis than the other groups studied; (2) have less experience of both maternal and paternal deprivation; and (3) are passive, dependent and over-protected, but show a high standard of work and behaviour at school. The commonest precipitating factor was either transfer from a junior to a senior school or promotion to a higher class, and the most frequent underlying factor was fear of separation from home.

In general, the emphasis in the treatment of school refusal has been placed on therapy for the mother and child (Clyne 1966, Davidson 1961, Kahn 1958), though Chazan (1962) found that a carefully-planned change of school often helped the child to readjust to the school situation. On the basis of a recently published study, Tyerman (1968) concludes that there is little justification for making a distinction between 'school phobia' and 'truancy' in the treatment of children whose non-attendance at school presents a problem. He stresses that many of the children who are regarded as 'truants' rather than cases of 'school phobia' are emotionally maladjusted, and suggests that the situation of every child who is often absent from school should be carefully investigated and the child treated as an individual rather than an example of a type.

E) TREATMENT

Although a great deal of rehabilitative work with children showing emotional and behaviour difficulties is undertaken by clinics, hospitals and special schools and classes, few evaluative studies of it have been made. American work (Levitt 1957) suggests that about two-thirds to three-quarters of disturbed children who are given psychotherapy of some kind show improvement; but, according to Eysenck (1960c), children suffering from emotional disorders and treated by psychotherapy recover or improve only to approximately the same extent as similar children not receiving psychotherapy.

A similar picture is shown by Shepherd *et al.* (1966), who report on a comparison between a group of fifty children (aged 5 to 15) attending child guidance clinics and another group of children matched by age, sex and behaviour. The matched group was taken from a representative one-in-ten sample of supposedly healthy children attending l.e.a. schools in Buckinghamshire. The results indicated that referral to a child guidance clinic was related as much to parents' reactions as to morbidity, and that about two-thirds of both groups had improved over a two-year period. The writers suggest that many so-called disturbances of behaviour are no more than temporary exaggerations of widely distributed reaction-patterns, and stress the need for knowledge which will help us to discriminate between the kinds of problems which are likely to disappear spontaneously and those which need skilled help.

In the field of special educational treatment for maladjusted children, studies have been made by Petrie (1962) and Roe (1965). Petrie examined factors related to progress in the adjustment of twenty-three children at a special boarding school for maladjusted pupils. He found that the rate of progress of the children tended to be inconsistent. Severity of symptoms and level of intelligence were slightly related to improved adjustment, but a more important factor seemed to be improvement in parents' attitudes. There was a marked tendency for the inhibited children to make better progress than children with other forms of disturbed behaviour. Roe surveyed the progress in behaviour and attitude of 140 maladjusted pupils in special schools and classes over a period of twelve to eighteen months. Using the Bristol Social Adjustment Guides, she found no simple significant trend towards improvement in pupils who went to day and boarding special *schools*. Instead, there was a statistically significant two-way trend wherein children who had originally scored very highly tended to have reduced scores, while children who had originally scored low tended to have increased scores. Children who went to special *classes* for maladjusted pupils did, however, show a simple significant trend in the direction of a reduced score. Roe concludes that there is a need for a deeper understanding of the reactions and feelings of maladjusted children and their parents, and suggests that too much should not be expected from special schools in respect of the most disturbed children.

4. Emotional development of handicapped pupils

In research on the emotional development of handicapped children, the importance of attitudes *towards* a child's handicap has been stressed. Within the limitations imposed by the handicap, most handicapped children can lead a normal emotional life if they are given the opportunity to do so and if they are not additionally handicapped by adverse parental attitudes, rejection by their contemporaries or unsatisfactory school placement. The study of the emotional and social problems of the handicapped is, however, a complex one and many variables are involved. In this section, recent work on four groups of handicapped children will be discussed briefly: (a) visually handicapped children; (b) children with auditory handicaps; (c) educationally subnormal children; and (d) physically handicapped children.

A) VISUALLY HANDICAPPED CHILDREN

Zahran (1965) inquired into the personality differences between blind and sighted children. Examining the literature, he found two differing points of view regarding these differences. One view is that blindness leads to compensatory behaviour possibly accompanied by personality maladjustment or by introversion; the other suggests that the process of adjustment in blind persons is not significantly different from that of the sighted. Zahran compared a group of fifty blind children (aged 9 years to 13 years 11 months) with a control group of fifty sighted children, matched by age, I.Q. and socio-economic background, with regard to a number of personality variables. He found that many of the blind subjects were more introverted than the sighted, and had higher neuroticism scores on the Junior Maudsley Personality Inventory. On the basis of a sentence completion test, the blind subjects were shown to be less adjusted than the sighted. These differences, however, were not statistically significant; and the main conclusion of the study was that there are no distinct personality problems produced by blindness, but problems frequently arise from the reactions of the blind to their social environment.

B) CHILDREN WITH AUDITORY HANDICAPS

Ewing (1958), in a study of behaviour problems shown by 180 deaf and 180 hearing children aged 1½ to 5½ years, found that the deaf children presented difficulties connected with toilet-training, bed-wetting, sleep, play, fears, temper tantrums and withdrawal to a much greater extent than the hearing children.

Johnson (1962), in a study of sixty-eight children (aged 5 to 16 years) who had defective hearing but who were able to profit from education in the ordinary school, assessed 53 per cent of the sample as normally adjusted, 38 per cent as unsettled and 9 per cent as maladjusted, on the basis of interviews and home visits. The most important factors for successful adjustment in the ordinary school were considered to be (1) level of intelligence; (2) type of hearing impairment; (3) the child's temperament; and (4) attitudes of the parents. Behaviour sometimes improved rapidly with special educational treatment. B. Fisher (1966) confirms these findings, estimating that, out of a sample of forty-one boys and forty-two girls, aged 5:4 years to 16 years, with impaired hearing but attending ordinary classes, 53 per cent were normally adjusted and 47 per cent had unsatisfactory adjustment (on the basis of the Bristol Guide). He found that these children were significantly less well adjusted than a control group of children without hearing loss, and further suggests that impaired hearing may affect the adjustment and attainment of girls to a greater extent than boys.

The personality adjustment of severely deaf and partially hearing children has been compared by Bowyer et al. (1963). In a pilot inquiry three groups were studied, each of ten children, aged 8 to 10 years, respectively severely deaf, with partial hearing, and of normal hearing. Adjustment was assessed mainly by Lowenfeld techniques. The severely deaf children were found to be above average in adjustment, while the partially hearing children were below average, though not to a statistically significant degree.

c) EDUCATIONALLY SUBNORMAL CHILDREN

The relation between poor adjustment and low attainment has been discussed above, but attention has been drawn recently to the particular problem of maladjustment among children in special schools for the educationally subnormal. Tansley suggested, in 1951, that the incidence of emotional disturbance in E.S.N. children is considerably higher than that found among children in general. This has been confirmed by Chazan (1964, 1965), who investigated the incidence, nature and aetiology of maladjustment among children in special schools for

E.S.N. children in south Wales. His initial sample consisted of 169 E.S.N. pupils in two age-groups (9 plus to 10 plus, and 13 plus to 14 plus years) and the same number of children in ordinary schools, matched for age, sex and socio-economic background. Assessments on the Bristol Social Adjustment Guides showed that over a third of the E.S.N. children were maladjusted in the school situation, nearly three times as many as in the control group. The E.S.N. children showed considerably more symptoms of depression, hostility towards adults, inhibition and emotional tension than the controls. There was also a higher incidence of speech defects, unsatisfactory attendance at school and delinquency in the E.S.N. sample (see also the paper by Lovell).

D. Evans (1956) has made a contribution to the experimental study of methods of treating maladjusted E.S.N. pupils. He found that appropriate psychotherapy could help even seriously maladjusted E.S.N. children, who were particularly affected by adverse environmental conditions.

d) PHYSICALLY HANDICAPPED CHILDREN

Of the mixed group of physically handicapped children, the problems of children suffering from cerebral palsy have aroused considerable interest in recent years, and Stephen (1965) has reviewed research findings on these children. The emotional adjustment of cerebrally palsied children has been studied by Dunsdon (1952), Floyer (1955) and Cockburn (1960, 1961). All have found a high prevalence of emotional instability among this group of children, who often lack normal reserve, are emotionally immature and tend to be highly distractible. Cockburn found that severe handicap, low intelligence, poor attainment and unsatisfactory adjustment tended to go together and to reinforce one another.

Future needs

This review of research on children's emotional development, which has dealt with selected aspects, has shown that inquiries have been made into a variety of problems. Most of these inquiries, however, are very limited in scope, and perhaps the most pressing need is for investigations in this country which combine both breadth and depth, where adequate representative samples of children are studied without recourse to superficial methods. Such investigations will be of greater value if more attention is given to the construction of instruments for assessing emotional maturity and adjustment. The Bristol Social Adjustment Guides, for example, have proved very useful to research workers, but their value would be enhanced if they were revised in the light of experience and recent statistical work on maladjustment.

We need more work involving experimental situations and controlled observational techniques as well as schedules and questionnaires. Many statements have been made, for example, about the response of children to various kinds and degrees of frustration, but in fact we have little evidence on this question which is firmly based on experiment or observation.

Finally, perhaps there has been, relatively speaking, too great a preoccupation with the negative side of children's emotional development, with an over-emphasis on difficulties of adjustment. There is certainly great scope for studies of the joys of childhood and of the positive effects on children of a well-balanced, highly stimulating home and school environment.

E. A. Lunzer

Children's Thinking

During the last decade and more, research on children's thinking has been largely centred on the theory and findings of Piaget (Flavell 1963, Hunt 1961, Lunzer 1960c, Wallace 1965, Wallach 1963). There are two reasons for this. In the first place, Piaget and his co-workers in Geneva have amassed a body of evidence which is remarkable for its novelty, for its sheer bulk, and for its apparent educational relevance. In the second place, Piaget's theory provides a useful starting-point for scientific inquiry in this field.

The first section in this paper is therefore devoted to a brief summary of the Genevan work in so far as this bears on studies in Britain. Section 2 deals with replications and extensions, more or less closely linked with a Piagetian approach. Section 3 is a discussion of the part of learning in the acquisition of new modes of thinking. The evidence here is by no means unambiguous. In section 4, therefore, some attention is given to the question of how far Piaget's theory of stages requires modification in the light of subsequent evidence. A number of studies to be considered highlight the limitations of an exclusive concern with structural factors in thinking, and at the same time suggest the need to achieve an integration between the psychology of learning and the psychology of thinking.

1. *Concrete and formal reasoning*

Piaget uses the term 'concrete operations' to describe the developments in conceptualization which are achieved between the ages of five and ten. They include the conservation of continuous and discontinuous substance, as well as the conservation of weight and of at least one aspect of volume ('interior volume'). As a typical experiment in conservation one may take the conservation of liquids: a child is first shown two identical glasses filled to the same level, and acknowledges that they contain the same amount of water (or 'lemonade'); the contents of one are then transferred to a tall thin glass; the other glass may be left as it is, or it may be emptied into a much wider container to test the limits of conservation; alternatively, the liquid may be poured into several smaller glasses, etc. The critical question is always the same: are the amounts the same in both containers after the transfer of liquid? (See Piaget and Szeminska 1952.) The child is also asked to justify his answer; Piaget himself lays particular stress on the ability of the child from the age of seven or eight onwards to explain that the quantity remains invariant, despite the deceptiveness of its perceptual appearance, because there is compensation between two perceptual aspects: it is taller but thinner. At younger ages, the situation usually gives rise to judgments of non-conservation, due to the distortion imposed by a single perceptual dimension (more on one side, because it comes higher, etc.). The gradual achievement of conservation is often attested by the appearance of intermediate phases: the child admits conservation in some situations, where the changes are smaller, but not in all.

Just as the conservation of continuous liquid substance was tested in this experiment, so the conservation of solid (plastic) substance was tested in an analogous experiment involving the deformation of a ball of plasticine: two equal balls are shown to the child, and one of them is squeezed out into a different shape (Piaget and Inhelder 1962). Similarly, the conservation of number may be tested by a variety of experiments, one of which consists in constructing two rows of objects parallel with corresponding elements facing each other, and then elongating one of the rows by spacing its elements out (Piaget and Szeminska 1952). Further experiments bear on the conservation of length (of an object), of distance intervals (between objects) and of areas (Piaget *et al.* 1960), as well as on the equality of time intervals (Piaget 1946a). Analogous experiments are brought to bear on the relations between time, movement and speed (Piaget 1946a, b). Verbatim extracts from Piaget's works describing many of these will be found in a recent work by Brearley and Hitchfield (1966).

The importance of these experiments derives largely from the fact that they appear to bear on the appearance of invariants which can serve as elements in the logical conceptualization of the world in terms of its quantifiable spatial and physical properties. In an important sense, number is realized in the first instance as a property of objects which is defined by the action of enumeration and which remains invariant under all transformations involving displacement only. Similarly, length is defined by the action of measurement and, likewise, may be treated as invariant where there is displacement without deformation. More generally, it is argued that in the course of the sensori-motor stage of development (up to eighteen months), the child achieves a complex of behavioural patterns, which amounts to an internalized image of a stable world occupied by objects with more or less clearly definable properties, disposed in a space which may be explored by several means (visual, kinaesthetic, etc.) with congruent results, and subject to consistent causal laws—especially those that relate to the permanence of objects, to the relative stability of their sensible properties, and to the experience of gravitational phenomena and to certain very general aspects of the mechanics of movement and rest (Piaget 1953, 1955). However, although these developments imply awareness of the properties and relations of things as well as the conservation of objects, that awareness remains intuitive; i.e. it is tied to anticipation and imagery, so that the 'pre-concepts' which result (bigger, smaller, the same, a lot, heavy, light, etc.) are lacking in definition (which is why they are termed 'pre-concepts'). A good example is the child's behaviour in arriving at judgments of time and speed. Two dolls travel along parallel lines being set to start and to stop at the same time, but one out-distances the other. Younger children find difficulty even in recognizing that they started and finished at the same time; below the age of five, children are apt to be vague about the distances travelled; they also reason that the doll that went faster and further must have taken more time to a much later age (43 per cent at age 9 in Lovell and Slater's replication study, 1960). It is apparent that their concepts (in this experiment) are global and undifferentiated: further implies faster implies more time implies better all round! The reciprocal relation between movement, time and speed is, of course, a difficult one for children to grasp, but the same tendency to global judgment is apparent in every conservation experiment, e.g. taller level implies more liquid.

According to Piaget, along with the conceptual realization of these physical and mathematical invariants as revealed in the conservation experiments, the child acquires a facility in applying certain logical relations both to objects and to these invariant properties. These logical relations are said to constitute well-defined 'structures' involving the operations of classification and seriation. The structures are termed 'operational' because in performing certain actions the child shows a realization of systematic equivalences between related actions. Operations are actions (or 'moves') within a system. For instance, given $A > B$ and $B > C$, one may deduce $A > C$, although the latter is not directly given; similarly, from the knowledge that a class B includes a sub-class A, one may deduce that $B = A + A'$ (the complementary sub-class under B, e.g. $B =$ birds; $A =$ ducks; $A' =$ other birds) and also that $A = B - A'$, that B is not less than A, etc. The sanction for these deductions does not rest on any empirical test, but on the definition of terms and the rules of the game. Younger children are unable to make such deductions because they are unable to retain the invariance of the terms entering into them. For instance, in inclusion problems, given, say, six blue beads and two red beads, all of which are made of wood, they insist that there are more blue beads than wooden beads, because the basis of categorization shifts from the inclusive term, material, to colour without their being able to control it. Similarly, they cannot systematically seriate a collection of different-sized rods when the differences are small, because to do so implies a realization of the transitivity of size: they are compelled to resort to trial and error, with more empirical controls than are logically necessary (Inhelder and Piaget 1964). A striking instance occurs in the work of Donaldson (1963) to which reference will be made later. Asked to solve the problem: 'Tom is taller than Dick; Dick is taller than John; which of these three boys is the tallest?' several children of ten talk of 'the other Dick', as if there were two Dicks rather than a single Dick who enters into two relations. The instance highlights the greater difficulty in retaining the invariance of terms which results from verbal presentation. In a concrete experiment involving the comparison of three rods, even the child of five or six is unlikely to commit the error of supposing there are four rods; but he fails to retain and compose the two relations into which one term must enter (because, being the link term, these relations are the inverse of each other). It is instructive to note that Donaldson's subjects who showed this confusion were nevertheless very liable to arrive at the correct solution of the problem—by confused reasoning.

As well as being applied to collections of objects defined by arbitrarily chosen properties such as shape, colour, etc., for the purpose of reasoning experiments, Piaget finds that the same structures of classification and seriation are applied to the invariants of number, space, etc. Thus he claims to have shown that the ability to seriate weights and to acknowledge their transitivity develops alongside the conservation of weight. Similarly, number is defined as a synthesis of classificatory and serial structures (every number includes all its predecessors—a classificatory structure, while the classes to which number is applied are defined solely by their susceptibility to the serial operation of taking every element once and once only).

Iterative measurement, whether linear or areal, is likewise regarded as a synthesis of operations: serial displacement on the one hand, and relations of inclusion defined by successive limiting boundaries on the other. The critical experiment here is one that requires a child to compare lengths of lines using a measuring rod which is shorter than what is being measured; in other words, he constructs his own measuring system on the basis of the principles implied in conventional systems of measure.

Since several of the studies to be referred to bear on Piaget's theory of the child's conception of space (Piaget and Inhelder 1956), it is necessary to add a word about this. It is well known that Euclidean geometry holds an honoured place in the history of mathematics as one of the earliest branches to be systematically studied. Other geometries, often of a more general nature, were developed very much later, notably projective geometry, which preserves relations of co-linearity and parallelism but which makes abstraction of angular and linear measurement, and topological geometry, which is more general and elastic still, being concerned exclusively with systems featuring boundaries, enclosure and overlap (see Land 1961 and Sawyer 1955 for descriptions addressed to the non-mathematician). Piaget maintains that the child's conceptualization of space proceeds in the reverse order: he is able to handle topological relations representationally before he can tackle projective and Euclidean relations—for instance, when required to copy figures or to identify a shape which is only felt from a visual array which includes several distractors. While Piaget acknowledges that the child acquires an active appreciation of verticality through postural adjustments at a very early age, he contends that an adequate representation of horizontality and verticality depends on the construction of a (Euclidean) rectangular co-ordinate system, and does not appear until very much later. An experiment which bears on the problem consists in requiring the child to anticipate the plane which will be taken by the surface of a liquid in a half-filled flask when this is tilted at various angles. Another consists in asking him to plant a line of telegraph poles upright on a model hill. Piaget and Inhelder find that correct representations in such experiments are not achieved until an age of nine on average. Similarly, the elaboration of projective co-ordinations is illustrated in an experiment in which the child is asked to indicate the several views which may be had of a model landscape (three distinctive mountains forming a small massif) depending on the position of the observer. Children of six and under remain centred on their own viewpoint: although they are aware that the view changes with the displacement of the observer, they are unable to represent the form of these changes and simply reproduce what they see from their own viewpoint, or in choosing among pictures, they may select those that carry the maximum information ('childish realism'). Here, too, complete co-ordination of the transformations of before-behind, left-right, respecting all the co-linearities preserved in the rotations (which is what the task requires) is not achieved until about the age of nine.

The volume of literature bearing on the subsequent development of reasoning is considerably smaller. Undoubtedly the most seminal work in this field in recent years is Inhelder and Piaget's *The Growth of Logical Thinking* (1958). This work reports fifteen experiments all bearing on the development of hypothetico-deductive thinking with special reference to the changes that may be observed beyond the age of eleven or twelve.

We will mention only two of these, both of which have since been replicated in studies by Lovell (1961) and S. Jackson (1965). In the 'pendulum' experiment, the subject is presented with adjustable lengths of string, which may be suspended from a bar by the attachment of one of several weights and made to oscillate. His task is to ascertain the part played by variations in length, weight, height of drop and the initial impetus given to the apparatus, by freely manipulating the set-up. In effect, he must discover that (within limits) length is the only relevant factor. The part of each variable can only be proved by deliberately varying each factor in turn, keeping all others constant. In this and other similar experiments, it is found that children are unable to engage in systematic experiment and deduction until well into adolescence. In particular, they find it difficult to appreciate the importance of holding some factors constant, because they fail to appreciate that a given result may be due to any of several causes. Although children at the 'concrete' level can classify events and discover lawful relations, they are unable to prove such laws unambiguously by deliberately selecting or constructing those events which will be decisive in assessing alternative hypotheses. The second experiment deals with the equilibrium of a balance. The apparatus consists of a simple balance made of meccano parts. Various weights can be suspended at appropriate distances from the fulcrum, and the subject's task is to discover a principle which will tell him how to achieve an equilibrium. Children at the concrete level (from the age of seven) have no difficulty in establishing that to balance a greater weight with a smaller, the smaller weight needs to be hung further from the pivot. But they do not deduce the law of moments, and, in particular, they do not discover the reciprocal multiplicative relation between weight and distance implied by the formula $L_1 W_1 = L_2 W_2$. Children aged 9 to 11 are particularly liable to try to compensate for an inequality in weight by an additive increment or decrement in distance, oblivious of the fact that the two scales are not commensurate. In this and other experiments, it is found that an adequate insight into the concept of proportionality is a very late achievement (11 to 15, in terms of approximate mental age, depending on the situation in which it is tested). More generally, I have argued elsewhere (Lunzer 1965b) that formal reasoning, or, in Piaget's terms, formal logical operations, implies the ability to handle second-order relations, or relations between relations as opposed to relations between things. The easiest, and earliest, manifestations of this type of thinking seem to include the solution of simple multiple-choice analogies, tackled successfully by perhaps 50 per cent of ten-year-olds. But this is no more than a beginning, for the full effectiveness of formal reasoning is seen only when the child is able to handle the relations among abstract mental constructs as easily as he can deal with relations which correspond to more or less directly intuitable properties of things.

2. Replications and extensions

Even this very brief account of the Genevan work is sufficient to indicate why a considerable portion of studies both in Britain and elsewhere have been devoted either to replications and extensions of Piagetian studies, or to the examination of some of the problems which they raise but leave unresolved. A number of the earlier studies were reviewed in a previous publication (Lunzer 1960c). Since that time, it is reasonable to say that sufficient studies have been carried out both in Britain and elsewhere to establish the essential validity of the phenomena described in Piaget's experimental work. This is of some importance in view of the quite legitimate criticisms that have frequently been levelled both in regard to the lack of controls in the Genevan studies and to the inadequacy of their reporting. (For instance, the exact numbers of subjects involved in each experiment are only given occasionally, chronological ages may be reported, but such variables as sex, measured intelligence, or socio-cultural background are never taken into account, nor does one find even the simplest checks on the statistical significance of the data.) Replicatory studies confirm such phenomena as the near universality of non-conservation at earlier ages and of conservation at later ages. More than this, they often provide a clearer index of the mental age at which the transition from one to the other may be expected to occur in any given situation than what one can glean from the original reports.

Taking first researches which were intended primarily as replications of the Genevan work, special mention must be made of the group of studies conducted by Lovell and his students (Lovell 1959, 1961, Lovell and Ogilvie 1960, 1961a, b, Lovell and Slater 1960, Lovell, Healey and Rowland 1962, Lovell, Kellett and Moorhouse 1962, Lovell, Mitchell and Everett 1962). The three studies by Lovell and Ogilvie deal with the conservation of substance, weight and volume, and report the results obtained from a population consisting of nearly every child in a junior school (approximately 350 children aged 7 to 11). The first illustrates the genuineness of the non-conservation in relation to substance: at seven and a half the children are more or less evenly divided among the categories non-conservers, transitional (or wavering) and conservers; by the age of eight and a half, two-thirds are clear conservers. The reasons given for conservation fall into three categories (with very few exceptions): a reference to the original identity or to the potential reversibility of the deformation; a statement to the effect that nothing has been added or removed; a reference to compensatory changes (longer but thinner). The first type of explanation is substantially more frequent than either of the others. It should be said that in general this is found to be true. It certainly implies that the concept of the identity of something through apparent change is far more important than might appear from some of Piaget's own writings, which is in line with the comments of Bruner, Olver and Greenfield (1966). But it is doubtful whether conservation would be consistently upheld unless the child realized the compensation. The proper way to test for the irrelevance of compensation (argued by Bruner) would be to establish that a significant proportion of consistent conservers could not be brought to make a verbal reference to compensation even when they were pressed. Lovell and Ogilvie demonstrated that the converse implication is false. Several children who were non-conservers could be brought to recognize compensation, but they still failed to conserve. In my opinion, the conservation judgment is essentially an identity strategy which is maintained in the face of perceptual indirection because of the awareness of compensation.

Lovell and Ogilvie's second study bears out Piaget's contention that the conservation of weight is a later acquisition than the conservation of substance, for there was an approximate lag of a year. They also point out that Piaget's discussion of the phenomena is too limited. Children were also asked whether they thought there would be a change in weight when butter, water or clay were cooled. Several associated changes in weight with changes in hardness, and there was a very imperfect correlation between conservation through deformation and conservation through hardening. Doubtless the first is more bound up with logical necessity, but the second is of at least equal importance in elementary science. The last study bears out the distinction drawn by Piaget *et al.* (1960) between interior volume (will a rearrangement of thirty-six cubes from a squat tower $3 \times 3 \times 4$ to a tall tower $2 \times 2 \times 9$ alter the amount of 'room' in the tower?) and displacement volume. The first is a relatively early acquisition (*c.* age 7 in a study by Lunzer 1960d), while the latter is not appreciated until the beginnings of formal reasoning (*c.* age 12). Lovell and Ogilvie note that many children associate displacement with weight, and nearly half of junior school children believe that an identical cube would cause more water to be spilled over from a full pint can than from a full gallon can (as if the larger quantity could somehow accommodate itself a little to receive an insignificant little cube).

Of the studies which replicate Piaget's work on number, that of A. A. Williams (1958), carried out on educationally subnormal children, deserves special mention not only because it was one of the first such replications, but also because its author went on to develop, at St Francis' School in Birmingham, a thoroughly programmed scheme of pre-number training designed to bring about an operational understanding (Tansley and Gulliford 1960). A later study by Hood (1962), involving 125 normal children aged 5 to 8 as well as two groups of subnormals, confirmed Williams' finding that a number of children can achieve a modicum of competence in mechanical arithmetic without a basic understanding of number. Hood's work demonstrates clearly the tie-up between mental age and operativity, every subject having been assessed individually using the Terman-Merrill scale. Although some 50 per cent of subnormal children had achieved operativity on most tests between the mental ages of eight and nine, this was considerably later than the mode for normals. Goodnow and Bethon (1966), using conservation of substance, weight, volume and area, found a more exact correspondence between mental age and performance, but the range of intelligence tested was narrower. Although Woodward (1961, 1962) found significant proportions of adolescents and adults at an operational level even though severely subnormal (with measured I.Q.s sometimes below 50), the balance of evidence indicates that in cases of subnormality in general, whether mild or severe (roughly, I.Q.s below 70), it is unwise to expect that children will automatically perform in accordance with their mental age. Two of Lovell's studies (Lovell and Slater 1960, Lovell, Kellett and Moorhouse 1962) bearing respectively on the child's concept of time and speed, indicate a specific retardation in the subnormal. Although it is less obvious in Lovell's replication of Inhelder and Piaget's studies of classification and seriation (Lovell, Mitchell and Everett 1962), it was considerably more striking in S. Jackson's study of hypothetico-deductive reasoning (1965). Lovell's view that learning in the subnormal is more specific, with less transfer of training (see also the paper by Lovell) is borne out by the greater variability of performance shown in M. B. Kelly's (1967) study (see below).

Perhaps the most ambitious replication project to have been undertaken in Britain is that of Beard, in association with the A.T.C.D.E. The aim is to verify the order of concept attainment in two fields, number and substance, weight and volume, and at the same time to establish norms based on a representative sample of children and to assess the effects of different environments. A preliminary report by Beard (1962) indicates broad agreement with the order of difficulty suggested by Piaget, at least in the field of number. Beard is more sceptical about the relation between conservation of substance and weight, quoting the negative evidence of Hyde (1959). On the other hand, Lovell and Ogilvie's (1960, 1961a) study supports Piaget. The evidence here is conflicting and sufficiently important to warrant separate discussion in section 4.

Anticipating, I share a very general belief that Piaget tends to exaggerate the unitary character of children's thinking, and the connectedness of his conceptual structures. Nevertheless, there are good grounds for examining the psychological co-ordinations involved in any area of understanding in which one is interested, not taking them for granted, but submitting them to experimental test. Such is the rationale underlying a number of recent studies which may be thought of as extensions of Piagetian methods.

Willington and Kelly devised a number of tests to investigate the growth of mathematical understanding in children aged 6 to 10. The situations involved the spontaneous recognition of associativity in addition, the distributive law, commutativity in multiplication, the equalization of groups, and the odd/even relation. Even the most elementary co-ordinations in these areas prove to be appreciably more difficult than the conservation of number. Nevertheless, it was found that by the age of ten a majority of the children studied were able to solve problems involving the distributive law without calculation; likewise they extended the principle of associativity to unknown numbers, and, again with unknown numbers, they were rapidly able to discover the additive and multiplicative structures of odd and even (odd + even = odd; odd + odd = even; odd × odd = odd; odd × even = even; etc.). In most of the practical situations studied, as many as five clearly defined levels could be distinguished. Children of eight or nine could usually solve practical problems involving known numbers, but they generally did so by laborious calculation. Educationally subnormal children were generally inferior to normals at comparable mental ages and also showed far greater variability in performance (Kelly, M. B., 1967, Willington 1967).

G. H. N. Turner (1966) tested the hypothesis that 'moral realism' as shown in the work of Piaget (1932) is basically due to failure to co-ordinate the several judgments involved. Asked to compare the amount of blame attaching to two imaginary children who committed misdemeanours, younger subjects do so in terms of the objective results, ignoring the allegedly good intentions of one of the two.

Turner argued that if the 'results' judgment was due to failure of co-ordination, there should be intermediate cases where the subject is inclined to acknowledge that a child who is trying to please but commits a wrong act is 'on the whole good', taking intentions and results into account, but goes on to judge that he is 'worse' than another whose intentions were 'bad', whose offence was objectively less, and who has previously been judged as 'on the whole bad'. He found very substantial evidence of such an intermediate level of moral judgment, with a peak incidence at ages coinciding with the decline of 'moral realism'.

In the sphere of formal (second-order) operations, Pumfrey showed the difficulty of problems involving proportionality, using a number of different situations (Cuisenaire rods, pantograph, balance). An interesting finding was that children were generally more inclined to devise complex strategies to enable them to solve problems additively instead of applying the equalization of ratios which they failed to grasp (Lunzer and Pumfrey 1966, Pumfrey 1965). Lovell and Butterworth (1966) administered a test of twenty items (some of which involved several questions) to a group of sixty children aged 9 to 15. The majority of the items bore directly on the concepts of ratio and proportion. Several items, however, involved other forms of mathematical reasoning, and one bore on verbal analogies. The results confirmed the difficulty of the proportionality concept and also its unitary nature. Factorial analysis also gave some support for the affinity between proportion and verbal analogies postulated by Lunzer (1965b).

Several of the key features of formal reasoning are brought out in a study by Lunzer (1965a) dealing with false conservations. A series of transformations of a square which preserves the perimeter of the original while producing rectangles of increasing length gives rise to progressive diminution of area. Similarly, if the square is cut by a single section joining two adjacent sides and the parts are transposed, the resulting figures will be greater in perimeter (with constant area). It was predicted and found that children at the concrete level of reasoning would reason falsely that both area and perimeter would be conserved in both situations. Such false conservation proved extremely resistant to perceptual infirmation and counter-suggestion. The pattern of reasoning was that if the area is conserved, then the same must hold of the perimeter, both being essential attributes of the figure—conceived as an invariant object. By contrast, formal reasoning showed itself in the gradual emergence of an ability to consider the lawful changes in area and perimeter, being abstract but nonetheless 'real' thought-objects, the relations between which could be manipulated to construct serial transformations of which the actual figures used were no more than instances. Concrete reasoning is object-bound, not in the sense that the child cannot deal with verbal problems (which he manifestly can), but in the sense that it consists essentially in anticipating what will happen to objects, or groups of objects, if certain systematizable, but none the less intuitable, actions are performed. It was interesting to note that a freeing from the concrete mode of thinking was achieved much more readily when the figure was defined by constant area, apparently because the concept of perimeter is more easily detachable. The kinds of measurement used by subjects of different ages to test the validity of their arguments also brought out the hypothetico-deductive character of formal reasoning and its late development (see Lunzer 1968b for a fuller summary of this study).

The majority of studies in the literature deal with developments in the solution of problems having a mathematical, scientific, or a more or less formal logical content. But there are notable exceptions. An excellent study by G. Jahoda (1963a) concerns the development of a conceptual framework governing ideas of nationality. Ages ranged from six to eleven. The principal questions concerned the understanding of the relations between Glasgow, Scotland and Britain. Jahoda observed four stages, which do not exactly parallel those postulated by Piaget (1928). The first stage represents a geographical awareness which is confined to the child's immediate neighbourhood: Glasgow, his city, is thought of as down the road, etc. At stage 2 there is a realization that he is in Glasgow, but no understanding of what Scotland is, although there may be a verbal formula 'Glasgow is in Scotland'. Stage 3 is transitional: replies about Scotland may be verbally accurate, but there is a haziness about its relation to Britain. At stage 4 replies are correct. From the formal standpoint, this is an inclusion problem, and Jahoda tested understanding further by setting a practical task involving the arrangements of cards representing Britain, England and Scotland, with a counter for Glasgow. The technique revealed very clearly the uncertain grasp that existed even at stage 3. There were marked social class differences: a substantial proportion of middle-class children had reached stage 4 by the age of nine and nearly all by the age of ten or eleven, the proportions in a working-class school being considerably lower. The understanding of national belonging closely paralleled this development. It is apparent that the application of the inclusion schema to this semi-abstract field lags considerably behind the ability to solve concrete inclusion problems, though the problem should be submitted to direct test.

Recent studies of historical understanding are again rare. Coltham (1960) used an unstructured technique, which proved none the less highly revealing. Children were asked to illustrate by means of drawings their notions of 'king', 'ruler', 'early man', 'invasion', 'trade' and 'subject'. It was found possible to categorize these into two or three broad groupings showing successive levels of historical understanding. The drawing scores proved reasonably scaleable and correlated well with results from verbal questioning and model-making. Coltham concludes that historical understanding is often very confused at the primary school level, again as compared with reasoning in relation to concrete objects. G. Jahoda (1963b) reviews the literature on the understanding of history with special reference to historical time, and notes the prevalence of gross structural errors up to the age of eleven or twelve. It is interesting to note that a recent study by Rogers (1967) indicates that the several aspects of physical (Newtonian) time show maximal improvement between the ages of thirteen and fourteen in groups of above average ability, this being a year later than the most significant developments with respect to historical time.

A group of studies initiated by Peel and carried out in Birmingham is directed more to the structural analysis of children's explanations as a measure of the levels of thinking which are realized when handling verbal material in a wide variety of contexts—historical, moral and religious, geographical, literary, etc. (Case and Collinson 1962, Goldman 1965, Lodwick 1958, Loughran 1967, Peel 1959, 1960, 1966, 1968a). To illustrate the type of inquiry, the following item is reproduced from Peel (1966):

Jane is a very clever fifteen-year-old girl who is preparing for her 'O' level examinations. She has homework every evening and she always works at this diligently, but she is a great help to her mother in looking after the younger children and doing errands and jobs about the house.

One evening as Jane was doing her homework her mother asked her to look after her younger brother, Teddy, whilst she went out.

Teddy wandered from the living-room into the kitchen, got hold of a pot of jam, ate a lot of it, covered his clothes with it and spilled it on to some clean, dry washing in a basket so that it was ruined.

Was Jane a careless person?

Why do you think so?

Generally speaking, the answers given to this type of problem may be allocated to one of three categories: (a) irrelevance and misunderstanding (e.g. 'Her brother was careless'); (b) relevant, but limited solution, focusing on one relevant factor in the story and basing a final comment on this alone (e.g. 'Yes, because she let Teddy wander'; 'No, because she was doing her homework'); (c) solutions which take into account all the elements in the situation, weighing one against the other, and sometimes going beyond the data by showing what additional information would be required to arrive at a firm judgment.

Case and Collinson (1962) report very high inter-rater reliability of the three-value marking scale (0·98 and over). Peel (1966) suggests the possibility of a finer gradation, resulting in a five-value scale. On the other hand, it also appears from Case and Collinson's study, which bore on passages taken from geographical, historical and literary contexts, that the reliability of subjects' performance on this type of item is low, with coefficients of reproducibility seldom exceeding 0·8 and often falling considerably lower. It also appears that solutions of type (c) are not absent at any age, even as low as eight, even though they do not constitute a majority until the age of fifteen and over. Doubtless these variations are in part a reflection of the normal spread of ability in the population. However, they also indicate differences between items due to the type of content, the subject's familiarity with it and the consequent availability of solution strategies, and so on. At the same time, it seems to me that this type of study can be extended and sharpened by a greater structurization of the questions (e.g. provision of a set of possible solutions and requiring the subject to state his reasons for agreeing or disagreeing with each, or requiring the subject to specify or to choose among alternatives what additional evidence would be relevant to an unambiguous judgment, etc.). Taken in conjunction with the open-ended type of question, this sort of sharpening would probably reduce some of the variability of response.

Variability of response is an especially prominent feature in a recent study by Loughran (1967) bearing on the development of moral judgment. Loughran's subjects ranged from 11 to 18 years of age. Piaget (1932) suggested that the basis of children's morality shifts from respect for authority, marked by unquestioning acceptance of rules, absolutism of values, an expiatory view of punishment, etc. This is followed (at 7 to 8 years) by judgments based on reciprocity. Finally, from the age of ten onwards, children are increasingly ready to take special circumstances into account—the morality of equity. Loughran found that the incidence of the first of these levels was as high as 35 per cent at eleven to twelve, and was not entirely absent even at the age of fifteen. Similarly, he noted replies indicating objective responsibility ('moral realism') with very great frequency in all age-groups (76 per cent at eleven to twelve; 42 per cent at thirteen to fourteen; and 35 per cent at fifteen to eighteen). However, the verbal situations chosen by Loughran were far more complex than those used by Piaget. This is particularly true of Piaget's 'moral realism' problems, where the simplicity of the presentation tends to throw structural features into sharp relief—as shown by G. H. N. Turner.

When speaking of the structural features of the child's thinking, we are referring to the ability to achieve a systematic co-ordination of his judgments. The basic judgments are taken for granted; they are elements of the structure. Failure of co-ordination then implies a purely logical disability, i.e. an inability to process the data in the ways required for problem-solving. Abstraction is made of content. Piaget tries to achieve an approximation to the assessment of development in logic by using concrete situations (even when studying formal reasoning) and a readily categorizable primary content (longer, heavier, red, square, etc.). Even so, variability from one situation to another is by no means exceptional (see section 4). The studies just considered illustrate that, even supposing that the child possesses the ability to co-ordinate, the availability of the appropriate strategies is apt to be greatly reduced when he is faced with problems in which the content is confused with irrelevant material (as it usually is in real life), where it is unfamiliar, and where it is inadequately symbolized in his vocabulary. An important work by Donaldson (1963) is enlightening in this context. Donaldson's book deals with changes in the patterns of errors found in children's attempts to deal with logico-mathematical problems presented in verbal form, i.e. the kinds of problems which feature prominently in group tests of intelligence. Two groups each consisting of twenty children were interviewed individually. The problems were put on two separate occasions, the second two years later than the first. The younger group were ten on the first occasion, the older group twelve. Problems fell into five categories: matching problems, three-term series (transitivity), series extrapolation, matching series, and verbal syllogisms. In all of these problems Donaldson was able to pin-point the most characteristic types of error and to classify them into three groups: structural errors, arbitrary errors and executive errors. Structural errors include failure to appreciate that the same term may enter into several relations (the two Dicks referred to earlier), failure to co-ordinate direction in series extrapolation, failure to distinguish between the dependent and the independent series in series-matching, and classical errors in syllogisms. Arbitrary errors were more difficult to classify, but included jumping to conclusions from part of the data, the assumption of evidence and of rules which were not given, and reasoning by assimilation to what is known to common sense. Executive errors include especially 'loss of hold': the correct reasoning is initiated, but the subject fails to recall his interim conclusions correctly. Examining each group of problems in turn, Donaldson finds considerable support for the thesis that arbitrary errors are most common at the youngest ages, structural errors increase at first, then decrease, while executive errors are the most common where understanding of the problem is adequate.

Donaldson argues with reason that executive errors are most probably attributable to failures of immediate memory. However, McLaughlin (1963) has argued that the type of co-ordination which a child can achieve is itself a function of the number of bits of information which he can process, since the recognition of a structure entails the co-presence in immediate memory of all its terms. McLaughlin's thesis is an attractive one. Nevertheless, the distinction drawn by Donaldson would appear to be sound. It seems reasonable to argue that factors of experience and of language are more prominent in ensuring freedom from executive errors, i.e. that these are primarily errors due to specific failure in symbolization. However, it is probable that structural processing always implies some symbolization. We must therefore consider studies bearing on the part of cultural and instructional factors in the acquisition of co-ordination in general.

3. *The role of experience and learning*

In so far as it is possible to separate out the structural factors in children's thinking, it is clear that there is development. We have already noted that the set-up of Piagetian experiments in general, and of conservation experiments in particular is such as to maximize structural factors, i.e. the role of co-ordination. However, the mere accumulation of cross-sectional (or even of longitudinal) data cannot shed light on the causes of such development, or on the part of experience in promoting it.

The problem is, of course, a tricky one, and so we may begin by setting up an inherently unlikely hypothesis, one that we can reject. This is that the co-ordination of internalized actions as revealed in operational thinking is attributable entirely to the maturation of the nervous system. If this were true, we should expect no significant differences to appear between individuals raised in widely different cultures, and no differences to occur as a result of different schooling experiences. One of the first cross-cultural studies, that of Hyde (1959), showed a retardation of up to two years in non-European children in Aden using tests of numerical understanding. There was also some indication, although not significant, of a correlation with length of schooling. Recent studies by P. E. Vernon (1965, 1966) show highly significant retardation in groups tested in the West Indies and among Indians and Eskimos in Canada. The rationale of these investigations is to assess the relative standing of various culturally deprived groups as compared with English norms, using a battery of tests which can sample attainment over a wide area, enabling one to discover which abilities are most culture-saturated and which least. It is interesting to note that many of the Piagetian tests, those bearing on conservation in particular, tend to handicap children of all these cultures far more than many other tests, e.g. spelling, reading comprehension, draw-a-man. Also concept formation, a classificatory task, discriminates less across cultures than do tests of conservation. It is true that the evidence is not always easy to interpret. Price-Williams (1961) finds little evidence of retardation among the Tivs in Nigeria on the conservation of liquids, and no differences between schooled and unschooled children. He also (1962) finds few differences due to length of schooling in a classificatory task, although here it would seem that there is some retardation relative to English children. Goodnow and Bethon (1966) found no differences in the proportion of children conserving substance, weight, volume and area as between eleven-year-old American children and unschooled eleven-year-old children in Hong Kong, but substantial differences in the understanding of the combinatorial. The latter is taken by Piaget to be one of the hallmarks of formal reasoning. The evidence on formal reasoning is thinner, but more consistent. Peluffo (1964) found the amount of schooling combined with exposure to the Italian culture to be decisive in groups of Sardinian children from an illiterate environment: two years' schooling were sufficient to wipe out cultural differences. However, schooling also played a considerable role in Greenfield's study of the conservation of liquid in Senegal (1966).

It is not easy to sort out the causes of these very disparate findings. The most promising line of inquiry consists in supposing that the successive bits of information accruing from any experimental test situation are assimilated by the subject to one of a number of information-processing strategies. What these strategies are, and which among them is most resistant to extinction, depends on the specific features of any particular culture chosen, for not all primitive cultures can be lumped together. This is the essence of Greenfield's thesis. The effect of schooling in turn will vary with the type of non-operational strategies of information-processing which it must combat, and also with the character of the schooling itself. Finally, second-order operations of formal reasoning have not been found in the absence of *any* schooling.

However, to say that experience is important does not imply denial of the role of maturation. It is difficult to see how co-ordinated strategies of information-processing can arise except on such a basis, or at least on the basis of very great facility with more elementary strategies for interpreting, retaining and representing information (Lunzer 1968a). Bruner (1966) was able to show a striking increase in judgments of conservation in the conservation of liquids test using a technique devised by Frank, which consists in asking the child to anticipate the height which will be taken by the liquid when poured into a narrower container, using a screen to prevent a perceptual judgment. The technique was highly successful with five-year-olds (although Bruner did not require a verbal justification, and some doubts are raised as to the implications of his results by Inhelder *et al.* 1966). But it made no difference at all to the performance of four-year-olds.

Again, granted that experience aids in the achievement of co-ordination, one may well ask what kind of experience? The researches of Gréco (1959), Smedslund (1959, 1961a), Wohlwill (1959), Wohlwill and Lowe (1962) strongly suggest that the acquisition of co-ordination is not a mere matter of response learning. In other words, there is little differential learning merely as a result of giving a reply (e.g. 'same', 'more') and being told 'right' or 'wrong', or noting the correctness of the response—e.g. in conservation of weight. Children often show some improvement on post-test after training, but usually the improvement is not significantly greater for the trained groups than it is for the untrained controls. The initial exposure to the test itself seems to bring about some improvement. On the other hand, insightful teaching, consisting in the creation of situations broadly similar to the experimental situations but not identical, or of making use of occasions which arise in everyday classroom experience to extend children's understanding, has been shown to yield a significant improvement as compared with normally taught controls by Churchill (1958), based on intensified small-group teaching over a period of four weeks, and by Phemister (1960), based on a year's ordinary classwork by an enlightened class-teacher.

However, these two experiments, important as they are, are insufficient to pin-point accurately the nature of the learning that occurs. Systematic experiments designed to evaluate the relative effectiveness of different kinds of training experiences have been relatively few in Britain, and it is therefore necessary to recall some of the most outstanding findings drawn from research elsewhere. Many of these have been conceived more or less deliberately to test the validity of Piaget's theory of equilibration. Since this, too, is a not very clearly defined group of ideas, a brief explanation is needed. At least three notions are involved. First, that behaviour and learning do not consist merely in responses to stimuli, but in the assimilation of cues to action strategies (which are interrelated in the form of schemata), the inception of such strategies, and their accommodation to the novel features of the present situation. Learning, especially the acquisition of co-ordination, is a matter of the modification of such strategies and the elaboration of new schemata. In other words, it is not some arbitrarily chosen but observable end-term of behaviour, the 'response', which is crucial in learning, but the character of the information processing which gives rise to it (see Lunzer 1968a for an extended discussion of the theoretical and experimental issues involved). Secondly, there is the notion that accommodation inevitably results in the formation and crystallization of co-ordinating schemata which exhibit certain well-defined structures: the structures of classification and seriation, which are semi-lattices, at the concrete level, and the combinatorial and I.N.R.C. propositional four-group at the formal level (see Mays 1953, Peel 1960). Thirdly, movement from one type of co-ordination to another occurs as a result of probabilistic increases in the occurrence of strategies representing different ways of processing input (Piaget 1957).

Piaget's theory of equilibration has been severely criticized by Bruner (1959), mainly on the second and third counts. I believe this criticism to be partly justified. Logical structures, and especially the structure of the group, are too general to be of much value in describing the fine detail of thinking processes (see Mays 1966), and the variability of thinking behaviour is too great to justify its assimilation to these entities (see next section). As to the third thesis, Piaget's 1957 statement is very closely tied to the conservation situation and too closely wedded to the role of compensation. He argues that the child's thinking passes through four successive stages: a perceptual strategy based on the single cue of the leading dimension (e.g. level of liquid); a perceptual strategy based on the non-leading dimension (e.g. cross-section); oscillation between these two; recognition of compensation. This statement neglects the part played by the child's need to reconcile the apparent inequality after transformation (e.g. pouring) with the perceptual equality previously recognized. Similarly glossed over is the need to reconcile the perceptual inequality with the fact that nothing has been added or taken away. However, the central core of the first thesis is that new strategies arise and gain strength in the course of conflicts induced by the application of previous strategies. This is the aspect stressed by Smedslund, who was able to show in several experiments that learning can occur in the absence of reinforcement and even in the absence of feedback, especially when based on conflict between addition and subtraction (1961b, c, conservation of substance and weight, 1963, conservation of length). The role of conflict is also recognized by Bruner, Olver and Greenfield (1966).

It may be added that there is increasingly wide agreement in respect of the first equilibration thesis as given above, if not among psychologists who elect to study 'learning' defined somewhat narrowly, then at least among those interested in thinking.

We have already noted that the inducement of conflict between the fact of non-addition or subtraction and perceptual judgments has been shown experimentally to produce significant gains in conservation. Also mentioned already was the screening procedure. Other methods shown to be effective include strengthening reversibility (Wallach and Sprott 1964) and direct manipulation of material (giving the experience of transformation), especially when combined with verbalization (Sonstroem 1966). Language may be used in two ways; one is by verbalization of relevant features of the situation, e.g. the separate properties of things that need to be reconciled, as in Sonstroem's work, in studies reported by Inhelder *et al.* (1966), and in a recent investigation reported by Sigel, Roeper and Hooper (1966). The other is to use language as a means of direct instruction of the strategy to be applied. The last method is, perhaps not surprisingly, the most effective of all (Beilin 1965, Kohnstamm 1967). Pascual Leone and Bovet (1966) questioned whether Kohnstamm's results based on the teaching of inclusion (appearing in a preliminary report) represented a true gain in co-ordination or merely a mechanically acquired routine. It is true that experimental gains are not accompanied by operational reasoning in a wide range of related fields: as Beilin indicates, there may be transfer to very similar tasks, 'near transfer', but not to broadly related tasks, 'far transfer', e.g. from conservation of length and number to conservation of area. But, as we see in section 4, variability is characteristic of spontaneous co-ordination, too. There are also good theoretical grounds for suspecting the generalizing efficaciousness of training which consists merely in giving the child a routine strategy to carry out without bringing this into conflict with established strategies. But Kohnstamm's description of his training sessions on class inclusion indicate that conflict was often quite marked, but that it was overcome. There was also the notable finding that thirty-three out of forty subjects who had been taught the class-inclusion problem were able to turn the problem round and frame appropriate questions to the experimenter when they were shown a suitable array. On the other hand, they were far less successful than spontaneous solvers of the original problem when they were required to choose an appropriate array as well as frame the question.

Lest it be thought that any method of teaching is successful in Piaget-type problems, it should be stressed that the relative gains are often quite small, and no method is successful with all children, especially very young children. In an unpublished study I tested the effectiveness of a variety of methods in inducing conservation in five-year-olds. The methods included addition/subtraction, experience designed to stress continuity of one-to-one correspondence, and experiences emphasizing compensation. None of these methods yielded greater gains than those found in the untreated controls—although several had been shown to be effective in one previous study or another, usually with older subjects.

Far more research is needed before one can say anything with confidence about the cumulative effects of training. Even if training in small doses leads only to 'near transfer', it is perfectly possible that training in a variety of problems will promote superior co-ordination all round. It would be a higher-order learning-set. It would not be a learning-set of the sort studied by Harlow (1949). Lunzer and Astin examined the formation of an oddity learning-set (choosing the one that is different among three objects of which two are the same) in children aged 4 to 10, and found a very steady decrease in trials to criterion with increase in age. Having solved the problem, the subjects were required to make their own problems for the experimenter (cf. Kohnstamm's counter-test): here the development was quite sharp; hardly any of the four- to seven-year-olds were successful, and nearly all the eight-year-olds and over were (Lunzer 1968a).

Finally, there is a need for more studies of the effectiveness of teaching in the promotion of formal reasoning. Lunzer and Coombes are at present evaluating the results of an experiment in which children of various ages were trained in problems based on Inhelder and Piaget (1958). A preliminary glance suggests that significant improvements did occur in comparison with untaught controls. A clearly related question is whether young children can be taught formal logic, and whether such teaching produces more effective thinking. Such an attempt has been undertaken by Mays (1965), who devised a method of teaching syllogisms based on Lewis Carroll's Game of Logic, and tested its feasibility in a class of nine- and ten-year-olds in Blackpool. The lessons were later given for three months at the rate of one hour a week to a group of ten-year-olds in Manchester. Apart from the finding that logic can be taught to juniors, Mays was able to show that the less able boys showed relatively greater improvement in a test of reasoning when compared with matched controls. No differences appeared in the results of the more able. Mays (1966) doubts whether what he taught was 'intelligence' as he would define it, which would include inventive thinking, but he argues that it is 'intelligence' as measured by tests.

4. *Limitations to the theory of stages*

Piaget's theory of stages derives from the logical analysis of behaviour. How valuable is such an analysis in explanation and prediction? Put in its strongest form, one might suggest (i) that any test situation that we select or devise can be analysed to reveal the exact pattern of co-ordinations which its successful solution would imply; (ii) as a result of such analysis, the item can be located on a perfectly scaleable continuum, representing the universe of all possible situations with which the subject might be faced: such a continuum would be governed by a transitive law in that a subject who passed a more difficult item would necessarily be successful in solving all easier situations, while no predictions could be made in the reverse direction; (iii) progress along this continuum is a function of intellectual development; (iv) the gaps of difficulty which separate adjacent items from one another are not equal: within a stage there will be many 'tied' items, and progress along the continuum to adjacent items will be relatively rapid, while adjacent items representing successive stages will be separated by a larger gap. Even in this strong form, there would be no absolute link with age, since all the statements refer only to the ordering of items and their relative separation. This is the point of Inhelder's oft-quoted remark: 'The order of succession of stages is constant, but the age at which structures appear is relative to the environment, which can either provoke or impede their appearance' (Inhelder 1956).

Many of the studies reviewed in previous sections indicate that this formulation is much too strong: there is a great deal of inter-individual variation. At least one study was undertaken with the direct aim of testing the idea of constant order, using Piaget's own tasks: Smedslund (1964), which is a careful analysis of the interrelations of nine well-chosen tasks in a group of 160 children. Smedslund's results indicate clearly that, although some tasks are solved more frequently than others, there is considerable variation in order. On the other hand, Inhelder's remark refers only to the principal stages of cognitive development: sensori-motor organization, concrete operations, formal operations. Now it looks as if the achievements characteristic of these do in fact occur in invariant order. But the statement could easily become trivial, for there is nothing startling about the fact that no one has ever found a child who lacks the conservation of objects but who nevertheless can classify in terms of two dimensions, etc. Similarly, unless a child can classify in two dimensions, it is inconceivable that he should be able to sort out the relative merits of conflicting hypotheses.

In point of fact, the Genevan formulation is more subtle, and relies heavily on the notion of 'ties': that kinds of behaviour which represent similar co-ordinations are achieved at *approximately* the same time. A second notion which is often prominent is that careful logical analysis can indicate relations which might otherwise be missed—e.g. between classification, seriation and number.

To complete Inhelder's formulation from which we quoted earlier, we must add two further propositions: viz. that each stage is defined by structured wholes—ways of processing experience characterized by the recognition of clearly definable logical relations resulting from the classification of input, enabling generalizations to be made from particular pieces of behaviour to others of the same type; and, secondly, that each successive stage marks a new integration of the acquisitions of the preceding stages.

b) To begin with the first: much of the evidence clearly refutes the proposition that one can predict success on one task from success in another, supposedly related task. It will be recalled that Piaget argues that the operational construction of number is closely linked with the development of classificatory and serial structures. Dodwell (1962) found that a majority of the correlations between success on inclusion problems (more B or more A, where $B = A + A'$ and $A > A'$) and two number conservation tasks were insignificant in a group of sixty children aged 5 to 8, and none was high.

Although Mannix (1959) obtained a high coefficient of reproducibility (0·94) in applying a scalogram analysis to the results of eight number tests to a population of forty-eight educationally subnormal pupils, even this constitutes very doubtful support for the Piagetian thesis, for the inclusion problem turns out to be appreciably more difficult than the conservation of number. Woodward (1961) found conservation of number considerably more frequent in a group of subnormals than seriation or conservation of liquids or equalization of groups. Similarly, Lunzer (1960c) found no support for the argument that the conservation of displacement volume depends on the elaboration of a complex structure involving the interaction of three linear dimensions and an understanding of the notions of continuity and infinity. On the other hand, P. E. Vernon (1965) did find a tendency for Piagetian tests of operativity to factor reasonably coherently, with 'inclusion' grouping near tests of conversation, these two being distinct tests having a strong arithmetical flavour, and others having a strong visualization component.

Taken as a whole, the results of research fail to confirm the notion that one can select a concept in mathematics or in science, analyse the concept to discover its logical implications, and, after devising suitable tests to ascertain the degree to which our child subjects understand each of these taken separately, predict that if they have the major concept, as defined, say, by a test of conservation, they will also prove successful in tests which bear on its logical underpinnings. And this is certainly one of Piaget's contentions. As a matter of fact, it has proved a valuable starting-point for research, since it was this that led him to devise the experiments which he used. The results of these are still enlightening, since a full appreciation of elementary number, measurement, etc., does imply an avoidance of confusions of all sorts. Piaget's tests pin-point the nature of these confusions, and at the same time suggest very strongly that each of them is primarily due to a failure of co-ordination of one sort or another, or, as one might say, to inadequate processing of the perceptual input. Just the same, it appears that the acquisition of these ways of processing experience is much less coherent than Piaget would have us believe.

There are even paradoxes. Lunzer (1965a) found in a group of fifty-seven children aged 5 to 9 no less than eleven who could spontaneously measure a line to compare it with another by marking off its length on a plain ruler but who failed to conserve length, with only two instances of the reverse. Yet why construct a length equivalent if you cannot conserve it? The point is that they do conserve it in the measuring situation. Success in this or that problem depends on a great many factors, most of which are psychological rather than logical.

Probably the least successful of Piaget's *a priori* assumptions concerning the necessary order of conceptual development is his suggestion that topological relations are mastered before projective and Euclidean relations. The haptic exploration experiment has been repeated in studies by Lovell (1959), E. I. Page (1959) and G. H. Fisher (1965). All these studies agree onfirming the inadequacy of exploration in young children: they feel the objects passively instead of exploring them for significant cues. (One may add that the psychological and epistemological relevance of this type of experiment is now widely recognized, cf. Birch and Lefford 1963.) Moreover, all agree that, using Piaget's array of models, those which exhibit mainly topological features prove easier to identify. But Lovell also finds that it is no more difficult for young children to discriminate curves from straight lines (a projective property). Fisher was able to establish, first, that haptic identification of familiar objects relies more on textural cues than on topological spatial cues: identification of wooden models of complex familiar objects proved no better than that of regular geometrical shapes; and, secondly, that although topological shapes were better recognized than shapes with Euclidean features by a group of children who had merely learnt to point at them in a preliminary training session, a group who learned to name them by assigning to them a nonsense syllable actually proved more successful with the regular shapes. Thus it looks as if symbolic mediation plays an important part in tasks of this sort.

It is, of course, clear that the co-ordination of relations between objects in several dimensions, as in the three mountains problem, is very much more difficult than, say, the reproduction of an inverse serial order (in a string of beads). But this is because of the complexity of the task rather than because it involves Euclidean geometry. This is not to gainsay Piaget and Inhelder's remarkable proof that the appreciation of the omnipresence of a uniform horizontal and vertical is a conceptual achievement and not a self-evident perceptual datum (in the mountain, posts and water level experiments). The fact is supported by the difficulty of achieving learning by simple confrontation with the relevant perceptual facts (Beilin et al. 1966, Smedslund 1963). Yet, even here, the child's pattern of replies to related questions may be far from consistent (Dodwell 1963). The truth with regard to geometry is that we do not know whether there are innate perceptual mechanisms for recognizing straight lines; we do not know how easy or difficult it is to acquire recognition patterns of one sort (e.g. acuteness of angle) relative to another (e.g. presence of a twist in a Moebius ring); yet it is by no means improbable that most of the theorems of topological geometry would prove at least as difficult to master as Euclid, precisely because of their great generality, which brings them closer to algebra.

...Reverting to the question of necessary order, there are instances of related problems where the factors favouring an operational co-ordination are heavily weighted on one side. This is clearly the case in regard to the earlier appearance of conservation of discontinuous compared with continuous substance. Similarly, all studies agree that if a small increment is added to one of two equal piles and the same piece is then removed, or if a piece is removed and then replaced, the conservation of the original is established earlier than in the case of deformation, and also that − + is easier than + − (presumably because the collection is seen as a 'compound object' which is mutilated and then restored) (Lovell and Ogilvie 1960, Smedslund 1961c, 1966, etc.). A knowledge of such sequences may be suggestive of suitable training procedures for accelerating all-round co-ordination (Inhelder et al. 1966, Smedslund 1961b, Wohlwill and Lowe 1962).

The conservation of substance, weight and volume also forms the subject of a recent study by Guyler (1966), specifically designed to verify the question whether there is an invariant order in the attainment of solution to the various problems posed. The inquiry arose directly out of Piaget's contention that a '*décalage*' (consistent time-lag) exists in the acquisition of conservation of substance, weight and volume (Piaget and Inhelder 1962), taken in conjunction with Smedslund's (1961c) observation that conservation is acquired in relation to dis-continuous material before the same schema is applied to continuous material. Also investigated was the relation between conservation of weight and transitivity of weight, concerning which the evidence was a little more ambiguous (Smedslund 1961a). The results confirm the greater difficulty of conservation of volume. On the other hand, Guyler (unlike Piaget and Lovell) finds no significant difference be-tween conservation of substance and of weight, nor did success in one imply success in another. The relation between discontinuous and continuous substance is confirmed, however. Guyler also finds a signi-ficantly greater difficulty in the test of transitivity of weight when compared with its conservation—but little evidence of a necessary order.

To sum up: many of the specific dependencies suggested by Piaget are not borne out by the evidence. On the other hand, within any given class of experiments, one can often find strong suggestions of a constant order of difficulty, usually governed by psychological factors rather than logical ones, such as the degree to which the perceptual and imaginal input hinders or facilitates the availability of co-ordinating strategies.

c) In spite of the variations and inconsistencies that have been revealed, the evidence does not permit us to wholly abandon the notion that each of the three stages represents a successive 'equilibrium'.

In the first place, taking the concrete operational stage in particular, one cannot but be struck by the fact that, relatively speaking, the average age-span over which the child achieves operational co-ordination in so many disparate areas (classification, seriation, conservation and operational definition) is quite short relative to the course of cognitive development as a whole. The time-lags involved may even be found to be smaller when a sufficient body of longitudinal evidence has been accumulated, allowing us to compare each child with his own previous performances instead of with cross-sectional averages.

In the second place, there are the remarkable resistances to understanding or perceptual infirmation, which manifest themselves when we require a subject to solve problems which imply higher-order co-ordinations than those of which he is capable. Thus the experiments reviewed in section 3 show that various forms of teaching, ranging from the most indirect to the most direct, may all be successful in bringing about gains in co-ordination in children aged 5, 6 and 7; but they also suggest that such teaching is easier in six- and seven-year-olds than it is in five-year-olds, and even Kohnstamm (whose position is probably more extreme than that of most other investigators) is prepared to recognize that little can be achieved in most four-year-olds —confirmed by Bruner in the screening study. It is important to remember in this respect that these gains cannot easily be explained away by a simple 'mediating response' theory of language. As Bruner points out very clearly, the semantic and syntactic structures of language imply both classification and causal implication, yet children aged 3 to 4 show a remarkable facility with the linguistic structures themselves combined with an equally remarkable imperviousness to the relations which they imply. Bruner quotes an instructive simile from Sapir (1921): 'It is somewhat as though a dynamo capable of generating enough power to run an elevator were run almost exclusively to feed an electric doorbell' (Bruner, Olver and Greenfield 1966, ch. 2). Inhelder et al. (1966) claim to have found a strong relation between spontaneous advances in the adequacy of linguistic description and the solution of conservation problems, while both Gréco (1962) and

Hood (1962) found that insistence on correct usage often precipitated paradoxical behaviour: in the conservation of number problem, the child counts the same number in two collections and repeats, 'There's six here and six there, but there's more here.' As to the transition to formal reasoning, I have been particularly struck by the resistances shown in the false conservation situation. Why do nine- and ten-year-old children insist that a rectangle measuring 5 cm. × 45 cm. has the same area as a 25 cm. square, when both younger children and adults recognize the discrepancy at once (Lunzer 1965a)? Clearly because they are impressed by the need for *logical* consistency between perimeter and area.

This brings us to the second of Inhelder's additional propositions noted in section 1. The co-ordinations achieved at each of the first two stages form the necessary material for their integration within a higher stage. From a logical point of view, this would seem self-evident, always providing that our logical analysis of the various co-ordinations is psychologically correct. However, the test of this is in experiment and counter-experiment. I am myself impressed by the cogency of the evidence so far accumulated favouring the notion that the strategies which one may use for processing input are classifiable in terms of a very restricted number of *orders* of structure (cf. McLaughlin 1963), and that an examination of these is a necessary, but not a sufficient, instrument for describing the complexity of this or that cognitive task for any subject. At the same time, it is important to recognize that far too much of this evidence rests on a single type of experiment—that initiated by Piaget and his school.

Considerable interest therefore attaches to attempts at tackling these same problems, using quite different experimental techniques. Three recent British studies are of some relevance. Forrest (1961) investigated development in the adequacy of strategies used by children in concept attainment, basing his techniques and analysis on the work of Bruner, Goodnow and Austin (1956). The essentials of the task can best be illustrated by means of a concrete example. Suppose a display featuring eight geometrical figures: large red circle, large blue circle, large red and blue squares, and smaller versions of each. The experimenter chooses a concept, which, in Forrest's research, was always one of the values of one of the attributes taken singly, e.g. 'red'. The subject is shown one diagram which instances the concept, and his task is to discover the concept in as few moves as possible by selecting appropriate figures from the array and ascertaining whether or not these are instances. While the studies of Bruner *et al.* extended to conjunctive and disjunctive concepts (e.g. 'red square', 'red or square'), and covered more complex arrays, Forrest limited himself to a consideration of two-attribute, three-attribute and four-attribute arrays, with two values for each attribute. His main group of subjects were seven, ten and thirteen years old. He predicted and found that there would be considerable gains in the adequacy of concept-attainment behaviour with increase in age. Perfectly systematic strategies, assuring concept discovery with no redundant choices, would seem to argue formal reasoning (a combinatorial). Such strategies were few at seven, and increased gradually. They were far more common with the simple 'two-attribute' array than with the more complex displays. Boote (1967) argued that a true combinatorial must allow for conjunctive concepts, and tested the hypothesis by comparing two sixteen-instance arrays, one being Forrest's four-attribute array, and the other a random arrangement of only four different diagrams, each appearing four times. The first array was used for single attribute tasks only, while the second allowed of conjunctive concepts also. Boote's prediction that the second task would prove harder was not confirmed. Many more choices were required for the first at all ages. On the other hand, consistently perfect strategies were achieved for the second task at fifteen and not at twelve or nine. It is very apparent that many subjects use what Bruner terms a strategy of 'successive scanning', i.e. testing one hypothesis at a time, and retaining it until it is infirmed; if it is wrong, they try another, and so on. This, as Forrest remarks, is clearly not formal reasoning. But it is a strategy which rapidly proves effective in Boote's second task. More work is needed, extending the criteria of performance from the number of choices made to include an analysis of what leads the child to change hypotheses.

Peel (1968b) has investigated children's understanding of logical connectives using a number of techniques. One of these, the game technique, consists in requiring the subject to select either a red counter or one of another colour, depending on the experimenter's choice and the rule he is given—implication, incompatibility or disjunction. Thus, the implication rule is, 'If I draw a red you must draw a red'; the incompatibility rule is, 'If I draw a red you must not draw a red', while the disjunction rule is, 'You must make your draw so that there is always one red counter drawn'. Two of the most salient findings of this study were: (a) the disjunction rule is not understood at five or eight, but it is at eleven, while there is good understanding of the other rules at all ages; (b) both in implication and in incompatibility younger children tend to apply symmetrical interpretations, as if the rule dictated their choice whatever the experimenter's choice: for instance, 'If I draw a red you must draw a red' does not dictate the choice if red is not drawn first, yet younger children tend to simply match the experimenter's choice. Peel's technique, which he is developing further, has the merits both of objectivity and of elasticity.

While the results of Peel's work are not inconsistent with the stage theory, we are bound to conclude on a note of caution. In view of the established fact that operational co-ordinations can be learned for individual tasks, it seems to me that the notion that each of the two operational stages constitutes an 'equilibrium' has little more than descriptive value unless it can be shown (a) that learning a number of different problems representing the same level of co-ordination (e.g. especially concrete operations) leads to increasingly rapid learning of new tasks—a 'super learning-set'; (b) that such learning has little effect on the acquisition of behaviour representing higher co-ordinations (formal level), requiring a new kind of learning-set; (c) that similar results are obtainable using a wide variety of methods.

It is important to point out that a number of recent studies report considerable success in teaching what amounts to formal or abstract logic to quite young children. Mays' experiment is one. Among other examples one may cite L. E. Allen (1965), Suppes (1965), and the algebraic approach to primary mathematics in Soviet experimental schools (Davydov 1965). It is possible to argue that this amounts to no more than the learning of first-order co-ordinations which are applied to symbols instead of objects, rather than genuine second-order co-ordinations in which appropriate symbolic translations are discovered, and appropriately general transformations are applied. But this has not been proved.

Taking all the evidence into account, there is no warrant for simply waiting until the child spontaneously reaches the appropriate level for assimilating any new body of knowledge. The better our grasp of the kinds of co-ordinations which it involves and the kinds of symbolic facility that it requires, the better equipped we are to experiment with new ways of preparing for it and introducing it, to facilitate understanding.

D. Graham

Children's Moral Development

This paper deals with research carried out in Britain into general or, if we may use the word, 'normal' aspects of moral development; it is not concerned with the background of delinquency, nor with the development of delinquent tendencies. Although the question of moral development is an important one, and although there has been over the past few years a considerable volume of work in this field in the United States, research in Britain has not been on a large scale. The earliest study in the field appears to be that by Barnes (1902); this is not unlike some of the more recent work, and is of special interest in that Barnes compared British with American children. He presented hypothetical situations to children, and asked them to write answers indicating what punishments for wrong-doing they thought just and what unjust. He concluded that English children were more mature in their judgments and more frequently favoured 'restitutional' than 'punitive' correction.

Most of the more recent studies have been influenced by Piaget's famous book (1932), either directly or indirectly, and most have been concerned with moral thinking, judgment or attitudes rather than with moral behaviour. The reasons for this, no doubt, lie at least partly in the practical difficulty of investigating moral behaviour under controlled conditions, and the relative ease with which attitudes or judgments can be studied. Since Piaget has had such widespread influence, it may be appropriate here to indicate briefly what seem to be the most influential aspects of his work. According to him, development takes place through a number of stages, from an egocentric to a co-operative orientation, from acceptance of adult constraint to more or less autonomous, 'rational' morality, from a view of responsibility as objectively determined by the consequences of one's actions ('moral realism') to a view of it as subjectively determined by the actor's intention, from a view of punishment as the automatic consequence of infringement of rules (including the belief in 'immanent justice' or the idea that retribution is built into the order of nature), through a stage of equalitarianism, where the punishment fits the crime and everyone must be treated alike, to a stage of equity, where due account is to be taken of the particular situation in which each individual actor is placed. The idea of more or less 'natural' stages of development through which children pass (or fail to pass) on the way to maturity is central to Piaget's thought, as also is the insistence on the importance of the peer-group for adequate development. Although Piaget locates his stages of development in terms of age, these age-boundaries would appear to be rather flexible and to be influenced by cultural factors.

Studies based on Piaget and similar work

Piaget's views were derived from observations of Swiss children, and some critics have claimed that he does not attribute sufficient importance to the socio-cultural environment as a force shaping development. A study by Harrower (1934) is relevant. Harrower repeated, with slight modifications, Piaget's procedures in a study of children's attitudes to punishment and cheating. She used groups of younger children (ages 5, 6 and 7 years) and older children (ages 8, 9 and 10 years), and took these from two different kinds of school, one an L.C.C. school, with predominantly working-class children, the other a private school with children predominantly from the upper middle class. Among the L.C.C. children, the results were similar to those reported by Piaget: almost all the younger children favoured 'retributive' punishment, while more of the older children favoured 'reciprocity' punishments. Among the middle-class children, however, an appreciable number of the younger children favoured reciprocity, and the number of older children favouring reciprocity was no greater. Thus Harrower's findings provide some limited support for Piaget, but suggest that cultural and subcultural differences in experience may play an important part. In a discussion of her findings, Harrower considers the possibility that her middle-class children had passed through Piaget's stages by the time they were examined; but she rejects this as unlikely. Harrower did not control for differences in intelligence, but a few years later an American investigator, E. Lerner (1937), found that children of higher socioeconomic status gave more mature answers to similar questions, even when age and intelligence were controlled. He thought that this was probably due to working-class parents being more authoritarian and giving their children less opportunity to learn more autonomous attitudes. Other more recent workers in the U.S.A. have also reported class differences, e.g. Macrae (1954) and Havighurst and Taba (1949). The question of class differences is an interesting and important one, and there is a need for more thorough research in this direction.

An article by J. F. Morris (1958) is concerned with changes in moral judgments in late childhood and adolescence. His subjects were ninety-four pupils selected at random from the boys and girls attending a London co-educational grammar school. Fourteen situations involving moral problems were presented, and the subjects were interviewed individually and asked to say for each situation what *should* be done and what probably *would* be done. Morris found that, with increasing age, there was a decline in the use of self-interest as a criterion, a decline in dependence upon authority, subject to fluctuations around puberty, an increasing complexity in the basis of judgment, and a relatively rapid growth of 'normative' elements (involving a principle) for the 'should' questions, with a much slower growth of such elements for the 'would' questions. Sex differences were slight. Morris viewed his research as providing general support for Piaget's views, but emphasized the extent of individual differences which he considered that Piaget had neglected.

Magowan's (1966) research was specifically concerned with 'immanent justice'. His hypothesis was that children would give more 'immanent justice' responses to stories involving unfamiliar situations than to stories involving familiar situations, and this was clearly borne out with children of between nine and twelve years of age. An interesting feature of this research was that 'projective facility' (or fluency) was controlled on the basis of a picture projective test. In addition to his findings on the effect of familiarity, Magowan also found that with the unfamiliar stories the children gave more 'immanent justice' responses in an open-ended test, and were more likely to select the 'rational' alternatives offered in a multiple-choice test. Both boys and girls gave more 'immanent justice' responses to stories in which the principal character was male. Magowan thinks this is because the children believed that boys ought to be punished more severely than girls. A further finding was that girls gave more 'immanent justice' responses to male stories than boys did. Magowan hazards an explanation in terms of identification. If girls generally identify themselves more with their mothers, then when they *do* identify themselves with their fathers, they do so less perfectly, with the result that they are less realistic than boys and make fathers punish their sons more than in fact they do. This explanation, however, must be regarded as extremely tentative. In my view, the concept of identification is a very awkward one, and often raises nearly as many problems as it casts light upon—perhaps more.

Not many studies of very young children have been made in Britain, but Valerie Pearson (1963) carried out an investigation with children of six years of age. An implication of Piaget's view is that young children will regard offences as more serious if they are punished. Pearson used four stories, two involving stealing, one laziness and one lying. The stories were told twice; on one occasion the offender was punished, on the other he was not. The children were asked to say which offence was the worse. Stealing was regarded as worse when punished, but not laziness or lying. The number of children involved was small, but a similar study carried out by a group of undergraduates gave similar results.

Following earlier work by Macaulay and Watkins (1926), Bray (1962) was interested in exploring the values of children as indicated by the persons they admired and the reasons they gave for admiring them. His data were taken from essays written by eleven-year-old boys and girls. Bray found that children's choices of 'admired persons' were more frequently of remote persons than of relatives or friends. Recognition and success seemed to be the principal criteria. There were distinct sex differences, boys more frequently choosing people associated with war, politics, adventure and sport, girls more frequently choosing religious and humanitarian leaders. Fifty per cent of the girls' choices were of male figures, it is interesting to find. This, no doubt, reflects the fact that our world is still to a large extent a man's world. Bray concluded that children's attention should be drawn to great persons of both sexes. It may well be, of course, that the choices of Bray's children were influenced by the setting in which the essays were written at school.

Edwards (1965a) took up Bray's 'ideal person' test with boys of eleven to fifteen, and added two further measures. He asked his pupils to describe what they regarded as the most wicked things a person could do; and he presented them with six hypothetical situations concerned with honesty, loyalty, responsibility and punishment, asking them to select one of three methods of dealing with each problem. He found substantial confirmation of Bray's results on the choices of ideal persons and the reasons for the choices, but he also found some tendency for older boys to attach more importance to materialistic criteria than younger boys.

In his moral wickedness test, Edwards found that the more intelligent of the older boys more frequently named *general* crimes, such as bigamy or perjury, as against *particular* misdeeds like cruelty or stealing. In the moral incidents test, Edwards found that more of the younger boys assigned blame according to the extent of the damage done, thus supporting Piaget's view of 'moral realism'; but he also found that more of the younger boys blamed the boy who was most guilty in terms of intentions or motive. More of the older boys felt that those who did the more damage and those with the worse intentions should be blamed equally. This introduces a new degree of complexity. Edwards thinks that his findings may be due to a sense of fairness or group loyalty, and this would be in keeping with his further observation that the older boys were less influenced by extenuating circumstances. He also comments that many of the duller older boys had difficulty in thinking out the issues involved. The main conclusion to which one may come is perhaps that there is some confusion and the situation is complex, but that these boys possessed quite a well-developed sense of fairness. There is no support for the contention of Macaulay and Watkins (1926) that from the age of nine until adolescence, children do not express their own opinions but accept the judgment of society on what is right and wrong. Edwards' findings seem to give support for the view, stressed by Piaget, that the peer-group is an important source of influence.

In a further article, Edwards (1965b) used an attitude scale, teachers' ratings and a 'guess who' test for four moral concepts, honesty, responsibility, moral rightness and friendliness. He found that the older boys (age 14 and 15) showed *less favourable* moral attitude scores than the younger boys (age 11) on all concepts except friendliness; and he suggests that this might be due to the uncertainties of adolescence and to 'unilateral constraint' (unthinking acceptance of authority) being replaced by a more co-operative attitude in which authority is questioned and one's contemporaries become more important. Although there is some confusion of detail, such findings, interpreted in this way, are not really greatly at variance with the main aspects of Piaget's account.

E.R.B.—4*

Finally, Edwards also reports correlations of attitude scores with intelligence as measured by Raven's Matrices to be positive but rather small.

Yet another study, by Pringle and Edwards (1964), used the same three tests, 'ideal person', 'moral wickedness' and 'moral incidents', with eleven-year-old children. There were three groups of differing intelligence as measured by the Stanford-Binet test—able, average and dull. The dull children gave fewer wicked actions, and their thinking was less subtle and abstract. A relatively large number of the young children gave 'good' in the sense of 'kind' as a reason for their ideal choices. Pringle and Edwards wonder if this is because they receive less kindness and are more in need of it. This study also reports that for stealing, the able children tended to discriminate in terms of the wrongfulness of the behaviour—i.e. to give weight to intentions—whereas the dull children tended to assign blame according to the amount stolen. As Pringle and Edwards remark, 'the duller child's moral judgment is prone to become confused or blurred in the face of complexity'. The duller children were more inclined to give the offender another chance, while the able children were the most punitive.

Maureen Lee (1965), basing her work loosely on that of the Americans Allinsmith (1960) and Aronfreed (1961), studied boys and girls of nine, twelve and fourteen years of age. She used a story completion test and was interested in the *types* of response to transgression revealed by this semi-projective technique. She found that the commonest response was expectation of discovery and punishment, even at the highest age-level. This might well be taken to reflect a pragmatic, self-interested view. Mrs Lee also observed, like J. F. Morris, that individual responses became less consistent and more complex with increasing age. In the higher age-groups, but not in the lower, girls used confession, apology and reparation significantly more frequently than boys. Considerable individual differences were noted at all ages. Lee considered that her results indicated a greater degree of 'internalization' of standards among the older girls; but it is possible that this is relatively superficial, and she suggests that since the older girls were in girls' schools, there may have been more emphasis on the use of apology, confession and reparative action. It is, however, also possible that the observed differences reflect more than specific training in the nature of acceptable responses; this would be in line with other research which suggests that girls may 'internalize' more than boys. The question of the possible effect of single-sex or mixed schools is an interesting one, which so far does not appear to have received much attention, although Wright and Cox (1967) did look at the question in their research; we shall refer to this again presently.

Brennan (1962) studied the relation between age and intelligence and certain 'moral' variables. He used a test of moral judgment similar to Piaget's, Lunzer's Vineland-Manchester Scale of Social Adaptation, and the Bristol Social Adjustment Guides as a measure of emotional adjustment. He found 'perspective' or the cognitive aspect of social adaptation to be positively related to mental age, and 'responsibility' or the executive aspect to be positively related to chronological age. Moral judgment was related to chronological age and mental age up to the age of nine and a half, but from nine and a half until eleven, mental age became of less importance and chronological age became insignificant. This might suggest that there is some minimum of mental capacity necessary, beyond which differences are of limited importance, and there may well be something in this idea. But it may also be that in this case the decline in the importance of mental age is related to the particular problems used.

Brennan also found that high 'perspective' was associated with low 'moral realism', as one would expect. There was no relation between emotional adjustment on the one hand and perspective, responsibility and moral judgment on the other, and no relation between moral judgment and responsibility. An interesting feature of Brennan's research is that he found seven of his questions on moral judgment to be 'scalable', with an increasing total score on the scale indicating a movement away from moral realism. The possibility of applying scaling techniques in this field has been little exploited, although there is an article by Ekman (1962) which discusses this.

Two British studies have applied factor analysis to the field of moral development. Nesbitt (1962) used quite a number and range of tests, including intelligence tests, tests of honesty, persistence, ascendance-submission, suggestion, level of aspiration, and measures of reputation and self-rating. His most important factors he interpreted as (1) a dishonesty factor loading mainly the honesty and intelligence tests, (2) a 'general moral' factor, reflecting socially approved behaviour and relative absence of anxiety, and (3) level of aspiration. Nesbitt found that the major factors, especially the general moral factor, increased in importance with age from ten to fourteen years of age. This suggests an increase in the understanding and observation of general principles as children become more matuie. I myself feel, however, that there is not yet a wide enough range of sufficiently reliable and significant measures of the relevant variables to promise much advance from the further extension of factorial methods as used by Nesbitt.

A different kind of factorial study was carried out by Hallworth and Waite (1966). They used Osgood's semantic differential, with thirteen scales applied to forty-eight concepts from areas considered to be important in adolescent life. A factor analysis indicated considerable similarities in values for boys and girls, with some differences. This study is perhaps most important in suggesting the use of methods which have proved fruitful in other fields.

Moral development and religion

Studies of religious development do not necessarily have much to say about moral development, but some are either directly or tangentially pertinent. Moreton (1944) found some tendency for adolescents and adults to regard religion as essential to leading a good life, and Forrester (1946) found confirmatory evidence with adolescents. This does not, of course, demonstrate that it *is* essential, and, indeed, Forrester observed that one half of his subjects regarded religion as *unessential* to a virtuous life. Hilliard (1959), in a study of 220 university and training college students, reports very similar findings. A more interesting study is that by Goldman (1964). His sections on children's concepts of divine justice and group moral judgments are of particular interest here. Goldman asked children whether it was fair that all the men in the Egyptian army should be drowned, and if God could treat people unfairly. He found that elements of authority and constraint entered into nearly all the children's answers to the first of these questions; but he did find advance from a retributive or expiatory view of justice (youngest children) through an intermediate stage about the age of ten, to a more distributive (impartial) view of justice after the age of about eleven and a half. Thus Goldman's findings here support Piaget, though Goldman's children reached the 'stages' rather later than Piaget's. Goldman suggests that this might be due to one or more of three factors: (1) sampling and/or cultural differences, (2) differences in the stories—this seems very reasonable in view of the findings of Magowan (1966) already discussed—(3) the possibility that religious stories of the kind used require transfer of thought to a situation remote from the children's lives.

For the second question, Goldman found a comparable progression from the view of God as arbitrary and unpredictable (young children) through a stage when children think that God is kind and does his best, but sometimes cannot help being unfair (about age 10) to the view that God *cannot* be unfair, since that would be contrary to his very nature.

In dealing with group moral judgments, Goldman again asked two questions: whether all the Egyptian soldiers were bad, and whether all the Israelites were good. For the first question, there were again three stages: (1) in which no differentiation within the group was made (up to age 8), (2) in which there was some differentiation but not the concept of degree of responsibility for evil actions (age 8 to 13), (3) in which realistic differentiations were made (after about age 13). The second question gave results almost exactly corresponding to the first question. Thus Goldman's findings again provide general support for Piaget, although the age-boundaries may not be quite the same.

Hilliard (1965) comments on Goldman's work that a *longitudinal* study of the same children would have been better than the cross-sectional sampling which Goldman used, criticizes the material used and the manner of presentation, and suggests that factors like the quality of the home and the quality of the teaching may be relevant. Hilliard's criticism of the cross-sectional method does not seem very serious, although it would certainly be useful to have confirmation by a longitudinal study, and individual case histories of development would almost certainly add to our understanding. His criticism of the stories and their presentation again underlines the caution that results may be sensitive to the specific experimental procedures used. And if Goldman does not stress possible differential contributing factors, it is simply that he has not included them in his study. He nowhere suggests that they may not be important.

More recently, Wright and Cox (1967) have investigated the relation between various indices of religious belief and practice and items of moral judgment involving gambling, drunkenness, smoking, lying, stealing, premarital sexual intercourse, suicide and the colour bar. Their subjects were sixth-form pupils in maintained grammar schools. They were required to rate each item on a five-point scale of degree of 'wrongness', and to give reasons for their choices. Wright and Cox found a fair degree of *generality* in severity of judgment, and found that girls tended to be more severe than boys, except over stealing and smoking. The more religious also strongly tended to be more severe, especially over the more 'ascetic' questions (those in which the consequences primarily involved the individual, compared with the more 'social' questions, in which the consequences caused distress to others). In their comments on the items, the non-religious subjects tended to argue that if behaviour does not harm others, it should not be subject to moral judgment by other people, while the religious subjects argued that *all* behaviour is of concern to God and may properly be the subject of evaluation. Wright and Cox further comment that for some religious subjects, moral beliefs seem to fulfil some degree of defensive function, but that at the same time, other religious subjects regard moral rules as conditions for the development of self-respect and responsibility.

Another recent study, by Barbara Reid (1966), compared boys and girls, and Protestants and Catholics with respect to events regarded as important, and qualities valued, by children. She found that Catholic girls included many more religious events as the most important thing which had ever happened than did Protestant girls, but that there were no differences between Catholic boys and Protestant boys. As the most highly-valued quality, honesty was given most frequently, especially by Protestant girls. The relevance of these findings to questions of moral development may seem remote, and one may well suspect that such differences are comparatively superficial. At least one American study (Boehm 1962), however, found significant differences in moral judgment between children in Catholic schools and children in public (state) schools. It seems likely not only that these differences reflect the somewhat different experience of Protestants and Catholics, but that their importance also depends upon the more general social context within which the two religious groups function.

Social class and family

The work of John and Elizabeth Newson (1965, 1967) is particularly relevant to any discussion of the possible influence of social class and family factors. They have been occupied with a long-term study designed to provide information on patterns of child-rearing in general. They used the interview method, and their work differs from most of

the investigations already referred to in that, as far as moral development is concerned, they were interested in finding out ways in which
children were brought up which might have a bearing on their moral
development, rather than in studying the children's development itself.
Their information was gathered mainly by interviews with the mothers,
conducted when the children were one, four and seven years old. These
authors observe that nearly all the mothers are 'warm' towards their
children, and nearly all parents of all classes are concerned with giving
their children long-term moral training which will influence the child's
character; but they find certain fairly well-marked differences in the
behaviour of the 'middle-class' (white collar) and 'working-class'
(manual) families. The most significant of these differences are perhaps
that the middle-class parents are more likely to use verbal reasoning,
more likely to give weight to the child's *own* reasons (e.g. for not obey-
ing immediately), and also to encourage the child to learn habits of
verbal self-justification. Middle-class parents tend to be more concerned to show the nature and general applicability of moral principles and
to emphasize fairness and reciprocity. They also tend to provide better
'models' of the 'correct' pattern of behaviour for their children to
imitate. The Newsons rightly stress that since linguistic emphasis is
likely to promote the transmission of values from parents to children,
middle-class parents are likely to be more successful. Whether this
lower level of verbal communication in working-class families is due to
lack of verbal skill, or to other factors impeding the *application* of the
appropriate verbal interaction, as the Newsons believe, is something
about which we may reserve judgment. The discussion of the role of
verbal skills does, however, draw attention to a point which may be
relevant to many researches. It is the question how far studies in which
the essential data are records of verbal behaviour of one kind or another
reveal any more than that the child has learned the appropriate verbal
expressions. This is, of course, always a danger; but it seems likely that
at least in interview techniques (such as that of Kohlberg), the 'correct'
verbal behaviour implies at any rate an understanding of the concepts
involved, although the child may not be very good at applying them in
his own behaviour.

Stephenson (1966) used a fairly elaborate interview technique. His
material yielded assessments for 'conscience motive' (active concern for
the welfare of others), 'intropunitive guilt' and 'other-directed anxiety'.
Stephenson compared twenty psychopaths with twenty normals of

comparable social class and intelligence, and found that the psychopaths scored lower than normals on all his measures. More detailed analysis of responses also indicated that the psychopaths were more externally and pragmatically oriented, while normals showed more regard for personal and social obligation. In a more general study of conscience and factors related to its development in fifteen-year-old boys, Stephenson used a revised version of the same interview form and also Shaefer's Child Perception of Parent Behaviour Inventory and Stott's Delinquency Prediction Instrument. He developed eight 'types of conscience' and found these to be related to scores on the Delinquency Prediction Instrument, i.e. the more developed the conscience, the less the probable anti-social behaviour. Stephenson also thinks that guilt tends to decrease and 'conscience motive' to increase with increasing age. Most interesting of all his findings is perhaps that 'conscience motive' was notably related to all measures of social status and education. Although this might to some extent have been due to differences in intelligence, the relation between class variables and conscience was still marked when intelligence, as measured by a vocabulary test, was partialled out, although, of course, a vocabulary test itself tends to be socially biased. It seems likely, according to Stephenson's findings, that intelligence is important mainly at the lower end of the distribution of intelligence. Parental discipline and conduct also appeared to be significant factors; and, in particular, conscience motive tended to increase as maternal punishment increased. Stephenson's book is full of useful observations, comments, suggestions and speculations, and is necessary reading for anyone interested in this field.

Studies of 'moral training'

Comparatively few investigators have attempted an experimental approach to the possibility of influencing moral development. In the United States, Hartshorne and May (1930, 1931) gave character training inside and outside the classroom. They concluded that effective training was possible, but that for it to be effective, schools should be reorganized so that satisfactory character development resulted from experience in school as a whole. Vernon Jones (1936), also in the United States, suggested that moral instruction should not obviously appear as such to the pupils, and that immediate experience plus discussion was likely to be most successful. Two relatively recent studies have been made in Britain, by McPherson (1950) and by Bradburn (1964). McPherson, working at a simple level, found that eight fifteen-minute periods of instruction on alternate days produced a significant improvement in the level of moral judgments, but left behaviour as measured by cheating and performance on a 'confession test' unaffected. There was also some evidence that when the children from a school attended mainly by 'above-average' children in terms of their parents' socio-economic status were compared with those from a school attended mainly by 'below-average' children, the ideas of the below-average children on punishment tended to be more primitive, but that some values such as kindness, sympathy and self-respect showed no such differences. McPherson did not attempt to control for differences in intelligence.

Bradburn's investigation was much more elaborate. She used questionnaires, rating scales, records of the number of co-operative and uncooperative actions performed by children of ten in 600-minute time samples, and observational records of teachers and children. A comparison was made between children taught by a teacher with an exceptionally good reputation for developing sound moral attitudes, and a teacher not highly regarded in this respect. Her general findings showed that more boys than girls valued personal success, while more girls valued kindness to old people and animals; but they revealed little else by way of sex differences. Poor children more often mentioned stealing, children from wealthier homes more frequently referred to damage to property and irresponsible behaviour. These results seem to be a clear reflection of socio-economic reality. When the two schools were compared, the children with the 'better' teacher showed up distinctly better. This teacher gave more 'positive' moral training (praise, encouragement), while the other teacher used more 'negative' techniques (criticism, punishment, forbidding). But a year after both groups of children had gone to the same secondary modern school, the differences between them were much less. Bradburn interprets this as meaning that the 'worse' children were 'worse' because of their less satisfactory teacher, and that they responded favourably to the more effective treatment in their new school. Her general conclusion is that the teacher and the 'climate' in the school may have important effects.

A similar study is that of Staines (1958), who was concerned with the 'self-picture'. Staines shows that teaching methods may be important in the development of the self-picture or self-concepts of the children, and stresses that a change in the self-picture may be reflected in subsequent learning. Staines distinguishes between the cognized self, the other self and the ideal self, but does not indicate what relation these bear to moral development.

Work in progress and in prospect

Among very recent work, work in progress and work likely to be undertaken in the near future, several projects deserve mention. John and Elizabeth Newson, in Nottingham, are still engaged upon their investigations, and may be expected to provide further data with a bearing on moral development. Derek Wright, in Leicester, may also be expected to extend his investigations. The Farmington Trust Research Unit in Oxford is specifically concerned to study the problems of moral development and moral education. John Wilson, the director of the Unit, has written a book, not yet published, which, although it does not itself report the results of research, provides a general framework for research in various aspects of moral education. More specifically, Norman Williams (1966), also of the Unit, has suggested certain lines for a research project. Basing his approach on the idea of 'stages' of development, each of which develops out of but does not wholly replace the previous stage, he provisionally posits six stages or types of morality: (a) morality based on obedience to external constraints, (b) morality based on irrational introjected values, (c) group-oriented morality, (d) empathic morality, (e) morality based on the ego-ideal, and (f) rational morality. Although the designation of the stages or types of morality is different, this scheme reminds one of Stephenson's and also, as we shall see, of Kohlberg's (1963). Williams proposes to cover a very wide age-range, from pre-school to sixth-form level. He suggests the use of semi-structured interviews, in which the children would be asked to explain why certain things are wrong. These would involve four main areas: (a) general ideas of right, wrong and fair, (b) deceit, (c) stealing, and (d) bullying. The initial purpose of such an investigation would be to provide justification for and clarification of the types of morality suggested. Presumably these types could then be used as tools for the examination of detailed hypotheses, possibly arising from the initial investigation. The very wide age-range which Williams suggests should be covered, if it is practicable, would immediately give this kind of study an interest and significance which more limited studies cannot attain; but the practical problems are, of course, formidable.

The similarity between Williams' suggestions and Kohlberg's approach in the United States is remarkable, especially since they were conceived independently. Kohlberg proposes six 'types' of moral thinking, grouped in pairs into three 'levels', the pre-moral level (hedonistic), the level of conventional role conformity, and the level of self-accepted principles. Each type is claimed to represent a restructuring of the previous type, with higher modes of thought replacing or inhibiting lower modes as development proceeds in the social matrix. Kohlberg defines thirty different 'aspects' of moral thinking, such as one's conception of rights, one's orientation to punitive justice, the extent to which intentions or consequences of actions are taken into consideration. His method of investigation is to interview subjects individually, telling them a number of stories, each posing a moral dilemma, and questioning them on how they would resolve the dilemma and for what reasons. Each response is then classified in one of 180 categories corresponding to the six types and thirty aspects. These data may be treated in several ways, the most direct of which is the obtaining of a total score for each 'type' of response for each subject from the percentage of all his responses falling in each type. Kohlberg argues that if his six types reflect progressive moral development, there ought to be a progressive change in the number of responses of each type with increasing age; and he suggests the use of Guttman's 'quasi-simplex' correlation matrix technique here, the argument being that the more any two types of thought are separated in developmental sequence, the lower should be the correlation between them. Kohlberg produces some evidence that his types behave in this way.

Not the least difficulty with Kohlberg's method is the amount of labour which has to be expended in scoring even a small number of scripts, and some experience is necessary if the scoring is to be reasonably reliable. Nevertheless, it does seem to be a promising technique, offering a more thorough way of studying moral thinking than most. Kohlberg himself suggests four purposes to which his method might be put: (a) the empirical isolation of sequential stages of development, (b) the study of the relation between moral thinking on the one hand, and conduct and emotion on the other, (c) the application of 'type' analysis to sub-cultural and pathological deviations, and (d) the isolation of the social conditions required for sequential development. Of

Kohlberg's suggestions, (b) and (d) would appear to be the most difficult: (b) would require adequate measures of conduct and emotion, while (d) would require the largest amount of resources for its implementation.

Kohlberg's method has been used in at least two studies in Britain. Critchley (1963) compared delinquent and non-delinquent boys, with rather disappointing results; but only small numbers were involved, and lack of experience may well have vitiated the scoring. Simpson, Graham and Ward, in Durham, used the technique on a sample of about 300 children of twelve and fifteen years old with a view to making comparisons of age, sex, school and particularly social class. It was hypothesized that, even with intelligence controlled, one might expect differences in moral 'perspective' corresponding to differences in social position. Not all the data in this investigation have been fully analysed; but a preliminary examination suggests that, as far as overall 'level' of maturity of judgment is concerned, differences in age and intelligence are important, but that differences between social classes are slight when groups come from the same kind of schools and are matched for intelligence. In addition to the Kohlberg stories and two measures of intelligence, a number of other measures were also given, including an academic cheating test and a modified version of Allinsmith's (1960) story completion technique. Cheating (which admittedly may have been highly specific to the situation) was significantly and inversely related to intelligence. The least intelligent children, in particular, were the most likely to cheat. Children from social classes I and II cheated significantly less frequently than children from social classes IV and V. When, however, selected groups matched for intelligence were compared, class differences appeared slight. It would therefore appear that intelligence is the important factor; but we must be extremely cautious here, since several variables are confounded. If we match children from social classes I and II with children from social classes IV and V for intelligence, as was done in the present case, it is likely that we shall get an atypical sample. Inter-school differences as such may well be significant, and the investigation did not cover a wide enough range of schools.

In one part of the story completion test, the stories were broken off at a point which allowed the child to complete the story either by transgressing or by not transgressing. Older children transgress significantly less frequently than younger children, and older girls less frequently than older boys. This fits quite well with the findings of Maureen Lee (1965) which have been discussed.

In the second part of the story completion test, the boy or girl in the story had already transgressed, and here the endings were classified according to the type of ending, e.g. showing self-criticism. Self-critical responses increased markedly with age for both boys and girls, with the girls showing rather more tendency to give self-critical endings. Self-criticism did not appear to be related directly to intelligence at either age, but this point requires more careful examination. There was a marked relation between self-criticism and social class, and it appeared that this could not be accounted for entirely in terms of intelligence. The general picture is that children develop noticeably in their attitude between the ages of eleven and fifteen, acquiring an orientation of greater self-criticism and responsibility, and that this may be related to social class. It is hoped that further analysis, especially of Kohlberg's material may throw more light on the factors involved. Two small-scale extensions of this work, involving the application of the Kohlberg or a similar technique to backward children and to children at a preparatory school are also being planned.

Conclusion

The general impression of research on moral development in Britain is of a number of uncoordinated studies bearing, with few exceptions, little direct relation to one another. There has been a fair amount of support for Piaget's ideas, although with some variability in detail. R. S. Peters (1960), after criticizing Piaget on various grounds, indicates the importance of finding out what *causes* the transition from conventional morality and what may prevent it. As we have seen, Kohlberg has also expressed an immediate interest in this question, and more widespread application of Kohlberg's or similar methods, together with studies of the 'feeling' aspects of morality and of background conditions, along lines similar to Stephenson's, would appear to offer promise. Such a programme would include studies of the possible effects of early learning and experience. Peters suggests that psycho-analytic theory plays a part. Perhaps the development of ego-psychology may prove of value.

Writing in the same symposium as Peters, Eysenck (1960a) suggests that conscience is to be regarded as a conditioned reflex. If this is so, what is needed is a vigorous application of conditioning and learning theory. This has to some extent been done (see Eysenck 1964, Trasler 1962), but mainly in relation to crime and delinquency. There appear to have been in Britain few, if any, experiments with young children along the lines of Bandura and Walters (1963), and this also would appear to be a promising line, although we need not expect it to provide all the answers. The very piecemeal nature of research to date, and the nature and limitations of the investigations carried out, strongly indicate that much larger, methodically programmed research undertakings, with better co-ordination of efforts, are urgently needed.

Kenneth Lovell

Backwardness and Retardation

The work under review in this paper covers the period 1962–6 inclusive.

Concepts of backwardness and retardation

No new conceptualizations concerning backwardness have arisen during this period; but two papers have been published which bear on the concept of retardation. Levy (1962) entered the argument that had raged in earlier years over the relation between general ability and scholastic attainment. He presented a new psychometric formulation of the problem, but in order to apply his model, it would be necessary to standardize available tests in a new way. Even if this was done, however—and it would involve a great deal of labour—it seems as if the retardation scores, calculated by the 'prediction' method described below, would agree almost perfectly with the measure of retardation proposed by Levy. In contrast, Curr and Hallworth (1965) made an empirical study of the concept of retardation in complete age-groups of nine- and thirteen-year-old children. Three criteria of retardation were used: (a) a 'difference' retardation score obtained by subtracting non-verbal reasoning scores from reading scores and adding 100; (b) a 'ratio' retardation score obtained by dividing reading scores by non-verbal reasoning scores and multiplying by 100; and (c) a 'prediction' retardation score obtained by subtracting predicted reading scores from observed reading scores and adding 100. These indices were, of course, indices of 'forwardness', not of 'retardation'.

This study clearly revealed that backwardness is associated with adverse environmental and social conditions, but that the various measures of 'retardation' or 'forwardness' have no significant or consistent association with the many other psychological or sociological variables involved. The authors point out that, while their evidence does not prove that the concept of retardation is a statistical artifact, it certainly fails to provide evidence that it is anything more. They also point out that it is possible that other measures could be assessed which might have a closer connection with reading, and in my own judgment this is certainly likely to be the case.

Educationally subnormal children

A) INTELLECTUAL STRUCTURES

A number of studies have been carried out within the conceptual framework of Piaget's developmental system. Woodward (1962) supplied evidence relating to the performance of moderately subnormal children and moderately to mildly subnormal adults. She used a sample of forty-four of the former aged 8 to 15 years, with I.Q.s on the Revised Stanford-Binet test ranging from 25 to 55, and fifty adults whose I.Q.s ranged from 44 to 73 on W.A.I.S. On a test of drawing twenty-one figures, only one subject was reported at the stage of concrete operations, while on the test of axes of reference three adults reached this stage of thought. Woodward's evidence suggests that the moderately subnormal rarely reach the stage of development where first-order operational schemata become available to them. While it is heartening to know that all laboratory and workshop experience shows clearly that many of these people are capable of learning a great deal, and may become partly self-supporting, there is no evidence from the point of view of the growth of thought that it involves anything other than a linear sequence of actions which is at a level within the range of pre-operational thought. There may well be considerable transfer of training at that level of schema complexity—as Harlow's apes showed transfer of training at their own level—but there is little evidence of a simultaneous apprehension of successive schemata by a first-order operational schema, so the co-ordinations within the mind remain linear.

Lovell (1965) and his colleagues have studied many groups of E.S.N. special school pupils with I.Q.s in the range 50 to about 75, and it has been repeatedly shown that it is between thirteen and fifteen years of age that a proportion reach the stage of concrete operational thinking. These studies cover the growth of logical structures, and the concepts of time, speed, space and geometry. Like ordinary pupils, pupils from E.S.N. special schools show great variation in the developmental stage they reach in specific situations. Content, familiarity of the materials and situations, expectations based on past experience, and other variables, affect the frequency with which these pupils display first-order operational schemata. Thus it is not possible to say what proportion of them reach this stage of thinking. Evidence suggests that somewhere between 30 and 50 per cent of thirteen- to fifteen-year-olds reach the stage of concrete logical thought in a number of varied situations. But the figure is much higher in respect of classification, seriation and number, and much lower in respect of the infra-logical groupings. Thus the concepts that develop early in normal pupils are the ones that are easiest for E.S.N. special school pupils; this confirms the view proposed by Inhelder that the order of stages and development of particular concepts in the subnormal is the same as in normal children. But there is not the increase in plasticity of concrete operational thought among the subnormal children that one finds in normal eight- to ten-year-olds. Moreover, those who do not attain the stage of first-order operational schemata, seem to possess schemata whose structure is less complex than those of normal five- to six-year-olds, since their capacity for transfer is so inferior to normal children. They seem to have to learn everything afresh each time.

S. Jackson (1965) tested E.S.N. special school pupils in the I.Q. range 60 to 80 on six tasks taken from Inhelder and Piaget's *The Growth of Logical Thinking*, and found not a single pupil at the stage of formal operational thought even at 15 years of age. Indeed, 95 per cent of the replies were of a quality no higher than the first stage of concrete operational thought. For a good deal of these pupils' school lives, learning consists of a linear series of actions at the level of pre-operational thought, and it is only in the later school years that first-order operational schemata develop; and this in only a proportion of these pupils.

B) LANGUAGE GROWTH

Lovell and Bradbury (1967) studied the growth of English morphology in 160 E.S.N. special school pupils aged 8 to 15 years, following the general lines of Berko's earlier study, but with extensions. The following are the main findings. These had all been predicted from our knowledge of the growth of mental structures in these pupils:

1. At 14 to 15 years of age the ability to inflect nonsense words is below that of Berko's first-grade children; but the ability to

derive and analyse compound words is at about the same level, since first-order operational schemata seem necessary for the latter skills.

2. A limited increase in the ability to inflect, derive and analyse compound words between 8 and 15 years of age.

3. A positive and significant relation between I.Q. and the number of correct responses when nonsense words have to be inflected.

4. A positive and significant correlation between reading age and the number of correct responses when lexicon words have to be inflected.

5. A low and non-significant correlation between reading age and the number of correct responses when nonsense words have to be inflected.

These findings indicate the great need for language experience in school for these pupils, although it must be realized that the ability to inflect lexicon words is learnt more by usage than is the case in abler pupils. The evidence strongly suggests that the ability to inflect, in a generative sense, is dependent upon the structure of the schemata or the quality of thought, and is consonant with Piaget's general view that the level of understanding modifies the language that is used rather than the other way around.

Lovell and Dixon (1967) studied the growth of the control of grammar in imitation, comprehension and production among six- and seven-year-old E.S.N. special school pupils as well as among normal children from 2 to 6 years of age inclusive. The test used had been earlier developed by Fraser, Bellugi and Brown. It was found that in both kinds of subjects imitation was ahead of comprehension, and comprehension ahead of production. The order of difficulty of the various grammatical contrasts was found to be almost constant across the age-groups, both in respect of the normal subjects and between the normal and subnormal children. The performance of the six-year-old subnormal pupils was much the same as that of a normal three-year-old, while that of the seven-year-olds was close to that of an average four-year-old. For the subnormal, as for the normal child, the affirmative/ negative item is the easiest grammatical contrast of those tested for, and the subject/object in the passive voice and the indirect object/direct object items the most difficult ones. These findings are entirely con-sonant with the position of the Geneva school in respect of the relation between language and thought.

c) EMOTIONAL ADJUSTMENT

An important study in this field was carried out by Chazan (1964, 1965) among two complete age-groups (9 to 10 and 13 to 14 years) in eight special schools. On the basis of the Bristol Social Adjustment Guides, over one-third of the subjects were found to be maladjusted. They showed more symptoms of hostility to adults, depression, inhibition and emotional tension than did control groups of ordinary pupils in the same age-range attending junior and secondary schools. Further, there was a higher incidence of speech defects, poor school attendance and delinquency in the E.S.N. sample. When thirty of the most maladjusted E.S.N. pupils were matched with thirty of the best adjusted for age, sex and school, it was found that significantly more of the most maladjusted pupils (a) gave evidence of some physical weakness or defect, (b) were subjected to adverse psychological pressures and unsatisfactory discipline at home which was related to parental instability, and (c) had had interrupted or incomplete relationships with their parents. But there were no significant differences between the two groups in respect of the incidence of adverse congenital factors, difficulties in early development and poor material conditions at home. Maladjustment was, in many instances, associated with lack of progress in the basic subjects, although this was more often true in the case of number than in the case of reading.

The overall findings of the study by Chazan suggest the importance of paying attention to the emotional and social needs of E.S.N. children and of providing guidance for their parents.

d) CHANGES IN I.Q.

Rushton and Stockwin (1963) studied the question of I.Q. changes in E.S.N. pupils during their school years. Previous evidence on this issue had been conflicting. They examined the test results on the 1937 Terman-Merrill revision of the Stanford-Binet Intelligence Scale (Form L) for 111 boys in an E.S.N. special residential school. When the results obtained on entry at 7 years of age or older were compared with those obtained by the same pupils when they left school between 14 and 16 years of age, there was a deterioration in mean I.Q. in spite of the fact that Roberts-Mellone corrections were applied. The proportion of non-verbal sub-tests was consistently higher than the proportion of verbal sub-tests passed at all age-levels, and it was concluded that part of the deterioration in mean I.Q. scores between the chronological ages of $9\frac{1}{2}$ and $15\frac{1}{2}$ years was due to the increased verbal weighting on this test at higher age-levels. This suggests that the test is not altogether suitable for the testing of these pupils.

Stein and Stores (1965) compared the I.Q.s obtained before admission with those obtained just before leaving, for a mixed group of seventy-five children attending special school for E.S.N. pupils. The average age of the children at initial testing was 11:2 years, and that on final testing 16:0 years. At the initial testing, Terman-Merrill I.Q.s (with Roberts–Mellone corrections) were obtained, whereas at the final testing the Wechsler Full Scale was used. When Terman-Merrill and Wechsler I.Q.s for mentally subnormal children of this age-range are obtained, the Wechsler score is, on the average, about two points higher than the Terman-Merrill. After allowing for this difference, it was found that roughly one-third of the pupils made gains of between 4 and 22 points of I.Q., a third had I.Q.s which remained unchanged within ± 3 points, and the remainder deteriorated with I.Q. decrements of from 4 to 18 points. The authors conclude that the score obtained on the Terman-Merrill test is of limited predictive value in the case of these children. It seems likely, in my view, that these children with considerable upward changes in I.Q. may well be those who rise into the stage of concrete operational thought.

E) READING ABILITIES IN E.S.N. PUPILS

C. J. Phillips (1966) has reported research relating to reading abilities among senior E.S.N. boys and girls. The original research sample consisted of ninety-nine boys and sixty-six girls admitted to the school over three successive years, although some of the pupils were not available for successive testings. On a number of cognitive and perceptual tests the boys were, on the average, superior to the girls, although this superiority was not maintained in respect of reading and spelling. For example, on the W.I.S.C. Full Scale the mean scores for the boys and girls were 73·3 and 69·1, and on Progressive Matrices the corresponding figures were 23·7 and 21·7; whereas the mean scores for boys and girls on the Schonell Graded Word Test were 31·5 and 31·2 respectively and on Schonell's Spelling Test 24·3 and 25·8.

Sixty children were also tested annually for four years. Among the main findings were:

1. Comprehension of passages read was, on the average, at the same level relative to reading skill (accuracy) as in a general population.
2. The correlation between w.i.s.c. I.Q.s and reading comprehension is significantly higher than the correlation with reading accuracy.
3. The correlations between w.i.s.c. Verbal and Performance I.Q.s and successive reading tests increase year by year. For example, the correlation coefficient between the w.i.s.c. Full Scale and accuracy on the Neale Analysis of Reading Ability test increases from 0·18 to 0·39 between the first and fourth years. The corresponding figures for the Schonell Graded Word Test were 0·22 and 0·39.
4. On the Schonell Graded Word Reading Test at a mean chronological age of 12 years 3 months, the mean reading age was 7 years 1 month; three years later the mean reading age was 9 years 4 months.

Research under the direction of Mr Phillips continues into brain injury among e.s.n. special school pupils, into its cognitive, perceptual and behavioural aspects, and into its aetiology and its neurological concomitants.

F) DATE OF BIRTH AND INCIDENCE OF PUPILS NEEDING SPECIAL EDUCATIONAL TREATMENT

P. Williams (1964) gave details of the dates of birth of 265 pupils in e.s.n. special schools. He found that their birthdays fell more frequently in the spring and summer than in the autumn; but he was unable to establish if this greater degree of gross backwardness was due to a differential entry into the infant school, or whether summer-born children usually remain the youngest in the class and hence suffer from the fact that the teaching tends to be harder for the youngest pupils. In any case, as Williams points out, there is a case for more flexible forms of school organization, and more attention should be given in ordinary schools to the problems of summer-born children. Armstrong (1965) also concludes from a study of pupils recommended for special educational treatment in ordinary schools, that spring- and summer-born pupils are more likely to become serious learning failures than are winter-born children. He also pleads for greater flexibility in educational organization to help in this problem.

g) POST-SCHOOL ADAPTATION OF E.S.N. BOYS

Matthew (1963) studied sixty-two ex-pupils of an E.S.N. special school with an average age of almost 20 years and compared them with a similar size group of ex-secondary modern school boys of the same mean age, but with a mean I.Q. of 99. While there was no difference between the groups in respect of size of family or type of house, there was a greater number of broken homes among the ex-E.S.N. school pupils and fewer of their fathers were skilled workers. The data from the E.S.N. sample showed that some 60 per cent of the ex-pupils gave satisfaction in their work, that when employed they could earn a standard wage, and that they were less gregarious and had fewer friends than the control group, a number of them being completely friendless and unable or unwilling to organize their leisure time. On the other hand, measured intelligence and level of attainment reached in the basic subjects (within the limits of the range of the group) did not seem to be associated with success or failure in employment. Murray points out that the partial failures and failures are potential social problems and it is doubtful if existing social services can cope adequately with these.

h) MISCELLANEOUS STUDIES

Lewis and Green (1965) showed that an auditory distraction did not impair the performance of E.S.N. special school pupils when engaged in simple sensori-motor and short writing tasks. It is true that the pupils were highly motivated in this study, and that in a more usual classroom situation the distracting effect might have been greater. But it does show that under suitable conditions, and given simple tasks, the findings in respect of E.S.N. special school pupils are much the same as those that have been found in respect of normal pupils.

M. B. Kelly (1967) investigated the ability of E.S.N. special school pupils to handle money in practical situations in relation to their mathematical understanding. Four types of test were used: oral problems, mechanical exercises, practical exercises in the handling of money, and tests of understanding of number based on the work of Piaget. A close relation was found between the ability to handle money in practical situations and an understanding of number concepts. She also claimed that the E.S.N. pupils performed no better in practical money situations than did younger normal children of the same mental age.

Backwardness among pupils in ordinary schools

A) BACKWARDNESS IN READING

J. M. Morris (1964), reporting the preliminary findings of a large-scale study carried out by the N.F.E.R., claims that it is reasonable to conclude that a good deal of reading backwardness can be attributed to conditions within the school. Her thesis is that the persistence of much backwardness in reading, although not its origin, is frequently due to the fact that pupils who make slow progress in the early years and who need much skilled help and good facilities and encouragement, often in fact get the least.

Alongside this point of view one must place the views of Ingram (1964). His evidence suggests that failure in reading and writing is commonly found in children suffering from brain damage. Such failure has also been found in children suffering from 'minimal brain dysfunction' described by Williams, Ingram and Prechtl. Other child patients have no history suggesting brain damage and give normal neurological findings. In most of these patients there is some family history of slow speech development and of difficulty in learning to read, which suggests that the reading and writing failure may be genetically determined. In those without a family history, there may be a minor brain injury which is not detectable. (Other aspects of the work of J. M. Morris and of Ingram are discussed in the paper by Reid.)

Lovell, Shapton and Warren (1964) showed among junior school pupils that when backward readers (reading quotient <80) were matched with average to good readers for social class, sex, school and non-verbal reasoning scores, the backward readers showed a poorer performance on a variety of tests involving spatial relations and left–right discrimination; a greater 'rotation effect' on a test involving the copying of abstract designs; a poorer performance on a vocabulary test in spite of the fact that backward readers came close to normal readers in formulating, orally, the basic varieties of the English sentence. There was, of course, a great difference in the incidence of reading failure among boys and girls. In further studies, but using somewhat different test batteries, among both fourteen- to fifteen-year-olds in secondary modern schools (Lovell, Gray and Oliver 1964) and among 'good' and 'poor' readers in senior E.S.N. special schools (Lovell, White and Whiteley 1965), results generally consonant with those obtained above were found. The overall evidence suggests that a number of cases of serious reading disability could be due to some dysfunction of the central nervous system with boys being more frequently afflicted than girls.

Kinsbourne and Warrington (1966a) produced evidence which suggests that the group of backward readers and writers whose difficulties are due to developmental cerebral deficit may be divided into two groups. In one group, where the performance I.Q. was considerably below the verbal I.Q., there were no language disorders reflected in word choices, syntax and articulation, but difficulty in telling which finger has been touched (finger differentiation and order) and in identifying by vision the shape that is clutched in the hand. In the other group with verbal I.Q. well in advance of performance I.Q., there were language disorders but no difficulties with the other tests. Each syndrome may give way to a characteristic delay in learning to read and write.

Walker (1965) gave details of a pilot study involving perceptual, coding, visuo-motor and spatial difficulties and their neurological correlates—a study of relevance to reading and spelling difficulties. Using twenty-six primary school children aged 6 years 11 months to 9 years 4 months, plus seven pupils who had severe learning problems but who were neither educationally subnormal nor maladjusted, Walker found perceptual, coding, visuo-motor and spatial difficulties scattered sporadically throughout the group. There was no consistent association of any particular difficulty with finger agnosia, poor motor ability, etc.; but where the specific disabilities were extensive, the neurological disabilities were marked and in every case there were associated reading and spelling problems. No direct relation between general intellectual ability as measured by Matrices and this physiological-neurological continuum was found.

B) REMEDIAL TEACHING

Lovell et al. (1962, 1963) have provided data on some 500 backward readers whose progress was traced during the period of remedial teaching and afterwards. The principal findings may be summarized as follows:

1. Children who are failing in reading at 7 years of age often make rapid and sustained progress. But pupils who are still

markedly backward (R.Q. < 80) at the time of their ninth birthday tend to make only limited progress thereafter, regardless of I.Q. Two or three per cent of these will pull out of their backwardness and be found among the abler pupils in the secondary school; the remainder rarely reach the standard of their age-group.

2. The correlation coefficient between I.Q. and reading progress under special teaching over the I.Q. range 80–120 is around 0·2. The effects of remedial teaching varied greatly. Some pupils made marked progress, others made little or none.

3. There is no evidence that pupils who are taken out of their classes or schools to a child guidance centre or remedial centre make more progress, in the long run, than pupils who remain within their regular classroom under the tuition of a competent teacher.

Two other studies carried out at Leeds are relevant. Lovell (1963) compared the reading attainments of pupils in formal junior schools with the reading attainments of pupils in informal schools—the division of the schools into formal and informal groups being made by the local education authority concerned. More than 1,200 pupils in each of the age-groups 9 to 10 and 10 to 11 years were tested; they were drawn from eleven pairs of matched schools. After allowance had been made for social class, there was no significant difference in the incidence of reading backwardness in the two groups of schools. In an investigation involving backwardness and non-verbal I.Q., Lovell and Woolsey (1964) showed that 303 out of 610 backward readers (R.Q. < 80) or 49·7 per cent had non-verbal reasoning scores ≥90. Furthermore, 21·6 per cent of the backward readers had a non-verbal reasoning score ≥100. While the ability to reason reflects to some degree the individual's capacity for co-ordinating mental operations or for being intelligent, such capacity does not ensure good reading. Lovell and Woolsey also showed that roughly half of backward readers come from homes in social classes II and III. Thus, whatever is responsible for poor reading skills is operating in all social classes. Low social class *per se* does not appear to be a cause of reading failure, although it may contribute to its persistence.

Shearer (Personal communication 1966), investigating the effects of remedial education in County Durham among fairly small groups of children, claims:

1. Three and a half years after remedial education in junior departments ceased, the group which had received this had better reading attainment than a group which had been recommended for remedial teaching but had not received it.
2. Within the experimental group, children who had also received remedial education in their modern school were at a higher level of attainment than those who had not.
3. The progress of individual children varied greatly both during the period of remedial education and after it had ceased.

A follow-up study of 1,227 junior-age children—all the pupils in a county borough who received remedial education in 1964—is reported by Cashdan, Pumfrey and Lunzer (1967). Data was collected on ten variables. At the time of reporting, the results showed clearly that there was very little relation between measured intelligence and improvement in reading under remedial teaching, thus confirming Lovell's earlier results. Moreover, little relation was found between lateral dominance and either the degree of reading disability or the progress made under remedial instruction.

In another study of the effects of remedial teaching, Lytton (1967) reported that two years after remedial teaching ended, many children did maintain a large part of the gains made in reading, although in some instances the gains were lost. However, the losses in arithmetic were greater. Selection of children by tests or by teachers' judgments did not produce significantly different long-term results. But long-term gains were related to good emotional adjustment.

Ongoing researches or researches which have just been completed

1. Shearer (Personal communication 1966) is studying the development of finger discrimination, handedness and left-right discrimination among normal and retarded readers using three batteries based on Benton's and Harris' tests. It is hoped to establish batteries for ages 5 to 12 and to relate the performance of backward readers to these norms. The tests are also being administered to children in a day E.S.N. special school to find out if (a) these pupils have more difficulties with these tests than normal children of similar mental age, and (b) whether the tests discriminate between children who make progress in reading in an E.S.N. school and those who do not.

2. Rofeh (Personal communication 1966) in studying backward readers has used an experimental paradigm based on the 'vanishing technique' described by Skinner and others. Skinner used this technique in, for example, experiments on memorizing verse, where the material is written on the blackboard and small portions are successively rubbed off each time the subject has read it through. Thus he is gradually left to 'read' the material without visual support.

In the present experiment single words are presented successively on a screen, each word being 'said' by a tape recorder as it appears. The child is then asked to say the word. The volume of the tape recorder sound is reduced after each time the word list is presented in random order; in this way each child is left to read each word in absence of sound support. Using this basic technique, Rofeh has investigated the effect on learning of such variables as inter-item interval, duration of visual and auditory structure, optimal list length and session duration. The findings to date indicate that there is no significant difference in learning rate and in retention of learnt items (after an interval of two weeks) between 'backward' and 'normal' (control) children—both groups, in fact, learn equally well. To date the experiments have been carried out among seven- to ten-year-olds, and they have been taught word lists taken from readers for eleven-year-old pupils. There may well be a number of explanations for these results.

3. Waddon (Personal communication 1966) is currently studying, over a two-year period, a small group of five- to seven-year-old children. The basic idea is to study the way in which the ability to use directional attack in reading develops, this tendency having arisen out of the reversal tendency in very backward readers. The Schonell test R6 is being administered at bi-monthly intervals to 'normal' children, and the ways in which reversals occur is being measured. At the same time, a wide-ranging test battery is being administered to these children in order to obtain a full clinical picture of them.

4. Miles (Personal communication 1966) is studying by 'natural history' methods children reported to be dyslexic.

5. Bannatyne (1964) describes two suggested projects:
a) A psycho-neurological research into the aetiology of specific developmental dyslexia in children.
b) The evaluation of remedial techniques for use with dyslexic children.

No information is yet available on the progress of these projects.

6. Two studies just carried out, and completed, under my general direction:

a) A. Gorton selected an experimental sample of backward readers from a normal school population, aged 9 to 10 years, who had a Terman-Merrill I.Q. >85 and a reading quotient <85. A control group consisted of fifty normal readers matched for sex, age, I.Q., socio-economic status and school experience. Tests given to the two groups included Illinois test of psycho-linguistic abilities, Birch-Belmont test of auditory-visual integration, Monroe tests of sound symbol association, a test of auditory blending and discrimination, visuo-motor Gestalt test, Shapiro test of rotation, Semmes-Weinstein test of spatial orientation, tests of right–left discrimination, Stott's version of the Göllintz revision of the Oseretsky test of motor development. The test scores were intercorrelated separately for the two groups. A principal components analysis clearly showed that within the group of backward readers, reading age was linked to neural integrity. In the case of the normal readers there was no general factor of neural integrity–impairment, and test performance showed greater specificity. Moreover, when factor scores were calculated for individual backward readers for the factor of neural integrity–impairment, those with the lowest scores also failed on the Prechtl test. Altogether the evidence strongly suggests that in the case of some backward readers the disability is linked with neural impairment. Such pupils could probably now be identified.

b) J. R. Milner has worked with the Usage Test developed by Berko and Brown (with some amendments), among normal pupils aged 6, 7 and 15 years, and among E.S.N. special school pupils at each age-level from 9 to 15 inclusive. It was shown that the order of difficulty in using count noun, mass noun, transitive and intransitive verbs, adverb and adjective remains remarkably constant with age within the normal pupils, the E.S.N. special school pupils, and within the combined groups. Kendall's coefficient of concordance was respectively 0·86, 0·83 and 0·80 in the three instances. Analysis of variance showed that within the E.S.N. special school pupils there was a significant but small increase in the use of these parts of speech over the age-range 9 to 15. But within the limited range of intelligence, I.Q. did not seem to affect usage—at least within the 12 to 15 age-range.

Jessie F. Reid

Reading

The following account is not an exhaustive survey of all the research into reading carried on in Britain during the last six years. It does not deal, for one thing, with various experimental innovations (such as Gattegno's Words in Colour) which, although tried out and 'evaluated', have not been the subject of more rigorous study. Moreover, some of the studies which might be included are described elsewhere in the book. The aim of this paper, then, is to indicate some of the main areas in which important work has been done, and to relate results to one another as meaningfully as possible.

General surveys

Research into reading has always had, in addition to the preoccupation with backwardness and retardation, two other main sources of motivation: an abiding interest in the nature of the process of reading itself; and a concern with improving overall standards of instruction in reading, and thence overall standards of literacy. But these three areas of interest overlap, interact with one another, and have mutual implications.

Concern with general standards of literacy characteristically results in one of two types of research undertaking: either a large-scale 'fact-finding' survey, or a 'methods' experiment. The trend towards the former of these was set by the first post-war survey carried out in England and Wales in 1948 by the Inter-departmental Illiteracy Committee. This not only became the first of a series of such government-sponsored surveys, but presumably acted as the stimulus for a crop of regional surveys conducted by local authorities.

As often happens, however, it appears that a great deal of the effort spent on these local surveys was not very fruitful, mostly because of discrepancies in criteria used and in test standards, in the definition of 'backwardness' and 'retardation', and in the way the data were presented. B. S. Cane (1966), who has examined these local reports in detail, gives a critical evaluation of them with which my own judgment, based on a sample of them, would concur. Mention must be made, however, of *Progress in Reading, 1948–1964* (Department of Education and Science 1966b), which gathers together the results of the national surveys conducted in 1948, 1952, 1956, 1961 and 1964. In terms of comprehensiveness and of statistical rigour in sampling, nothing like this had been done before, and the credit for these merits must go not only to the Government departments and other bodies (such as the Newsom Committee) who authorized the surveys, but also to G. F. Peaker, who has given elsewhere (Peaker 1953) a detailed account of the sampling principles involved, and who was responsible for presenting the results.

The measuring instrument for this survey was a short reading comprehension test, lasting ten minutes, devised by A. F. Watts and P. E. Vernon. Being designed to take in a range from at least backward ten-year-olds to competent fifteen-year-olds, the test is of necessity very steeply graded in difficulty of items—that is to say, one point of score represents a sizable increment of reading age—five months at age 11, and seven months at age 15. As far as the assessment of individuals goes, therefore, much depends on the stability of the test. J. M. Morris, who used the same test in her surveys (1966), obtained a stability coefficient of 0·89 on a sample of 2,253 children. The standard error of an obtained score would thus be about 5, and the corresponding 95 per cent confidence limits $\pm$ 10. But for large groups, these variations should to a great extent cancel out. Peaker's results show a steady upward trend at all parts of the range equivalent to an overall advance of seventeen months of reading age for eleven-year-olds and twenty to twenty-three months of reading age for fifteen-year-olds. The pamphlet itself is predominantly statistical, concerned with a brief justification of the sampling procedures, with certain estimating that had to be done to compensate for omissions in some of the samples, and with producing final results incorporating 95 per cent confidence limits. One result which is very noticeable to the educationist, however, is the continued existence, in the presence of overall improvement, of an enormous range of achievement. The table for eleven-year-olds (p. 3) shows that this range has even increased slightly—from 14·5 to 15·3 points of raw score over the sixteen-year period—that is to say, the improvement, though general, was if anything greater towards the upper end of the ability scale. The fact that the test remains unpublished makes it impossible to discuss in detail the limitations of the lowest 10 per cent of eleven-year-olds, who even in 1964 scored 7 or less; but as the early questions are said by Peaker to be so simple that almost any pupil could answer them if they were put to him orally, the conclusion is that these 10 per cent constitute a continuing core of almost illiterate children leaving the primary school. Furthermore, as has been pointed out by Latham and Georgiades (1967), the base from which the improvement has been measured probably represented a decline from standards prevailing in 1938. If this is so, then the measured improvement is barely more than a recovery from the set-back resulting from the Second World War.

Evidence on a nation-wide basis about the progress in reading of seven-year-old children comes from the first report of the National Child Development Study, 1958 Cohort (Pringle et al. 1967). The subjects are 11,000 of the 17,000 children born between 3 and 9 March 1958, and reading progress has been assessed by the Southgate Group Reading Test (word recognition) and by teachers' ratings. Results show that 40 per cent of the group are classifiable as 'good' readers (scoring 28–30), while 18 per cent are 'poor' readers (scoring 15 or less). Teachers rate 30 per cent as above average or superior readers, and 26 per cent below average, including some 3 per cent of non-readers. It should be noted, however, that the results of the Southgate test have a marked negative skew, indicating that the test had insufficient ceiling for the ability level of the better readers, and that the lowest 18 per cent are actually achieving very little. On the other hand, the instructions to teachers on filling up the rating scale indicated that in a normal population, around 30 per cent would come in the two highest (and two lowest) groups. But the figures do suggest a proportion of around 20 per of children with poor attainment in reading on leaving the infant stage (cf. Morris, J. M., 1959). The report also gives some breakdown of scores by sex, father's occupation, and age of starting school. Girls do significantly better than boys, socio-economic level correlates highly with progress, and early starters do better than late starters. More detailed analyses of the data are due to follow in subsequent reports.

It is fitting that these observations should lead to a discussion of the other substantial pieces of published research during the period under discussion, because although some are fact-finding investigations and some are experiments, all bear on some of the concomitants of success and failure, and therefore on the influences underlying the figures quoted above. Other researches which seem to be relevant will be mentioned at appropriate points. Some of these are smaller investigations, and some are researches still in progress the results of which are not yet available.

The Initial Teaching Alphabet

The innovation which has undoubtedly attracted most attention during the last six years has been i.t.a.—the Initial Teaching Alphabet. Several descriptions of this are available, such as those by Downing (1961, 1964b). The alphabet consists of forty-four characters, developed by Sir James Pitman from augmented alphabets like that devised by his grandfather, Isaac Pitman. These characters produce a method of writing English which is almost entirely free of ambiguities and redundancies, and yet which in its 'upper coastline' bears a close resemblance to standard spelling. The definitive account of the first i.t.a. experiment, begun in 1961, appears in *The i.t.a. Symposium* (Downing 1967b). So much has been written about this event, and about i.t.a., that it is difficult to select in a paper of this kind the facts which are not already very well known and which ought to be recorded. The definitive report was preceded by a number of other publications (e.g. Downing 1964b, Pitman 1961). These dealt with (a) the history of this alphabet; (b) the history of previous attempts to regularize English spelling for beginners learning to read; (c) the rationale of the system as a teaching medium; and (d) the conduct and progress of the actual experiment. The report appeared accompanied by an introduction by H. L. Elvin, eleven evaluative comments, and a final summary by W. D. Wall. The whole experiment is therefore very well documented, and is an extremely interesting example, unique in this country's educational history, of the confluence of a number of different interests and the resulting dependence of an educational experiment, conducted by a university institute of education, on substantial financial support from non-government sources.

The plan of the experiment was that two groups of children (matched as well as possible by manipulation, because random sampling was thought to be unattainable in the circumstances and so was not tried) learned to read from the same scheme ('Janet and John') by their teachers' usual methods; but the books of the experimental group were printed in i.t.a., and all the writing to which they were exposed in the classroom (except for some reference books) was in i.t.a. also. The hypotheses being tested were that children who learned by i.t.a. would progress faster through their initial reading scheme, would learn 'lower-order decoding skills' faster, and would show better results in reading, spelling and free writing after transfer, than children who learned in traditional orthography ('t.o.'). It was also predicted that there would be no loss of skill at transfer. The results showed, on average, much faster progress for the i.t.a. group through the initial reading scheme, and much higher results before transfer, on both Schonell's Graded Word Reading Test (Test R1, Schonell 1949) and the Neale Analysis of Reading Ability. Transfer to t.o., however, produced a marked set-back, especially in accuracy; but there was then a pattern of slow recovery and eventual superiority—though of a lesser order—on the t.o. version of the Neale test, and in spelling (Schonell's Graded Word Spelling Test). An assessment of free writing showed greater fluency and more extensive vocabulary than in the t.o. group. On a test of silent reading, on the other hand (Standish NS 45), there was little or no difference at all at the end of four years. Moreover, there apparently remained a 'hard core' of children with whom i.t.a. had failed. On the negative side, the evaluations stressed (though not without recognition of the difficulties) the shortcomings of an experiment which failed to select subjects by some kind of sampling procedure, and which did not randomly allot teachers to experimental or control classes but allowed them to be self-selecting. They also pointed to weaknesses in the drawing of sub-samples from the main sample, in the control of the effect of the i.t.a. medium on teachers' methods, in the management of the transfer procedure, and in the analysis of errors. On the positive side, however, there was general praise for the overall management of the experiment and enthusiasm for the impressiveness of the results before transfer. There was also universal eagerness to see further research done, particularly in the region of better exploitation of i.t.a. through specially designed material, careful study of transfer, especially in children of lesser ability, intensive study of errors over a period, and trial against other schemes in t.o., particularly those which seek to maximize existing regularities, or to alleviate confusion by other means.

A second experiment was begun by Downing in September 1963.

It aimed to meet many of the criticisms levelled at the design of the first one, and preliminary results (Downing and Jones 1966) suggest that the introduction of new controls may produce a somewhat different picture. These changes include the teaching of both experimental and control classes by the same teacher, and therefore the control of socio-economic and school variables too, since the children are in pairs of parallel classes in the same schools. Publicity has been restricted, and parents' meetings for both experimental and control groups have been arranged. In the results before transfer (i.e. experimental groups tested in i.t.a., control in t.o.) the Schonell test (R1) has shown highly significant superiority for the i.t.a. group, though inter-school differences are very marked. Less highly significant overall differences appear in the Neale test, and in some schools the t.o. results are actually better. A comparison (in t.o. to both groups) at a point when 17 per cent of the experimental children have been transferred shows slight overall superiority in favour of t.o. This is, of course, in line with the finding of falling-off in attainment at transfer so noticeable in the first experiment. Mention must also be made of another experiment being conducted in Scotland by Milne (Personal communication 1967). In this investigation i.t.a. is being compared not only with t.o. incorporating a standardized phonic approach, but also with t.o. supplemented by Stott's Programmed Reading Kit (Downing 1964a). The basic scheme for all groups is 'Janet and John', as in Downing's experiments, with a 'Look and say' approach in the initial stages. Teachers have been allocated at random to the three groups (twenty-one classes, mostly—though not all—in groups of three in the same school). Regular meetings have been held for all the teachers taking part. Control results for 'Hawthorne effect' are being gathered from schools using similar media throughout Scotland who do not regard themselves as being 'in an experiment' at all. The results of these two experiments, both much more carefully designed than the first, should throw a great deal of further light on the many questions which the first experiment left unanswered. Valuable information can also be expected from other studies conducted by the Reading Research Unit and not yet available. A comprehensive account of this work is due to be published by Downing soon (1967a). Two relevant reports have, however, appeared recently, one by Sceats (1967), and one by Downing (1967c). Sceats' account is descriptive and qualitative, and therefore impossible to summarize without crucial loss; but it fills in the picture of what was actually happening in the schools who used i.t.a., especially in the area of teachers' views, and makes—as do almost all evaluations—constructive suggestions about further research. Downing's results, based on an analysis of errors, cast doubt on one of the principles underlying the prediction of success after transfer to t.o. —namely that similarity of 'upper coastline' will compensate for changes in spelling. He reports that errors in the Neale test after transfer occurred in some words where overall outline was very similar, but in which letters had different sound values in i.t.a. and t.o. It would seem, therefore, that there is a logical inconsistency to be resolved, in that while the rationale of i.t.a. rests on a belief in the initial advantages of contrived regularity in phoneme-grapheme correspondence, transfer has to rely on the abandonment of many of these learned associations in favour of other visual and semantic clues. Failure to achieve this switch is evidence of what Downing describes as 'proactive interference' and calls for a revision of the symbol forms and their combinations.

There may well be a correlation between these observations and the results of an investigation into the usefulness of i.t.a. in remedial instruction (Georgiades 1967). In a report submitted to the Department of Education and Science, Georgiades gives an account of an experiment carried out while he was attached to the Reading Research Unit of the University of London Institute of Education. Using a design which attempted a compromise between the complete control of variables and the minimum of interference with normal conditions, Georgiades examined the progress of two groups of backward readers, using the same material in i.t.a. and t.o. respectively. All the teachers involved were experienced remedial teachers. All taught children in both groups, though some teachers spent more time altogether than others. The groups were well balanced for urban/rural environment, peripatetic/centre organization, and geographical dispersion. The subjects were selected on closely defined criteria—C.A. between 8 and 9 years; I.Q. (w.i.s.c.) 85–115; R.A. (Burt-Vernon) 5·5–6·5. Analysis of variance performed on the results (assessed by Schonell's Reading and Spelling Lists and the Neale Analysis) showed no significant differences between groups, except a slight superiority in speed for the i.t.a. group half-way through the experiment. It did, however, show a great many significant differences between teacher-sets (a 'teacher-set' being all the children taught by any one teacher) at the final testing session. A repetition of the analysis using gain scores showed a similar pattern. Georgiades suggests, however, that a remedial programme in which the children using i.t.a. did not also have to deal with t.o. at other times of the day might have proved more beneficial. The differences between teacher-sets in terms of progress correlated fairly highly with the amount of teaching time given, but Georgiades points out that this cannot be taken as accounting for all the variation between teacher-sets. The results, in fact, point yet again to the highly individual nature of the teaching situation, and to the difficulty of arriving at 'generally-true' statements about a medium or a method. But the experiment commends itself as an example in procedural and statistical care, and ought to be repeated and built on. In particular, the effect of taking i.t.a. subjects off all instruction in t.o., and of planning and supervising their subsequent transfer in great detail, should be investigated.

Other studies of early learning

Just before the initiation of the i.t.a. experiment, Daniels and Diack (1960) produced support for the belief that regularity in spelling—exploited in ways which make the material meaningful (phonically and semantically)—improves early learning of reading. They published a report of a comparison between a school using their own Phonic Word method and control schools using other methods. The control schools were, however, not treated as a homogeneous group, but were graded subjectively in respect of the degree to which their approach approximated to the Phonic Word method. The results confirmed those previously arrived at in a study conducted by the same workers (Daniels and Diack 1956) with non-reading seven-year-olds. The Phonic Word method gave significantly superior results in tests of both regular and irregular words, and there was a high correlation between degree of approximation to this method and test scores in the control schools. Pupils taught by it had, in addition, much higher scores than would be predicted from their socio-economic status and their I.Q. The superiority extended to reading comprehension and was not restricted to tests of word recognition. In the same year Diack (1960) expounded further in *Reading and the Psychology of Perception* the rationale of this method.

There is, therefore, in general at the present moment a substantial body of evidence suggesting that, in the earliest encounter with print, regularity in spelling, combined with some of the advantages of 'naturalness' and 'interest' on which the rationale of the 'Look and say' approach partly rests, can greatly accelerate initial learning. The degree to which children expect regularity and endeavour to fit their reading experiences into their slowly developing schemata of classification, order, and regular pattern has been shown in a longitudinal study by J. F. Reid (1966) in which five-year-old children were interviewed throughout their first year at school. Children were seen to go through a process of differentiating symbols from pictures, numbers from letters, and letters from words. Later they came to realize that there were different kinds of letter (capitals and lower-case) and different kinds of word (e.g. 'names'). They were seen to be in difficulty when talking about these notions because they did not know the appropriate terms by which to make distinctions. In addition, they showed early tendencies to expect words to be regularly spelt, and were conscious of the problems posed by irregularities and by attempting to synthesize sounds. The findings suggest that the acquisition of the ability to talk—and think—about what is happening to them as they learn to read may be an important constituent in children's progress, and that the result of more deliberate attempts to cultivate this competence should be investigated. It may, for instance, be connected with the ability to transfer from i.t.a. to t.o.

A study of the visual discrimination of letter and word patterns was carried out by J. K. Jones (1965). Basing his material on his own Colour Story Reading system, he investigated the role of colour cues in the matching of letters and of words in an unfamiliar script. His subjects were nursery school children (mean C.A. 4 years 3·4 months). The material was so designed that matching by colour alone would not lead to full scores, but would narrow the range of choice. Jones found that colour greatly facilitated correct matching, and concludes that it has a role to play in aiding visual discrimination in learning to read.

The topic of the efficient learning of spelling has, of course, been highlighted once again by the i.t.a. experiments. Among those who were doubtful of the wisdom of using a transitional writing system, many expressed doubts about the difficulties which would be encountered when t.o. spelling had to be adopted, because what is involved there is not so much 'transfer' on the basis of visual and semantic redundancy as unlearning and relearning. Reading may indeed become 'part-seeing' in the sophisticated reader, but spelling must be *whole-recall*. The results of the first i.t.a. experiment went a considerable way towards allaying the fears expressed earlier, though the reason for the superior spelling of the i.t.a. group is not clear. The graphs in the report suggest that they are partly to be explained by the very good spelling of the best children. However, a recent investigation by M. Peters (1967a, b) provides interesting additional analytical data, of the kind which, incidentally, one wishes appeared more frequently. Using a standardized spelling test and a diagnostic dictation test, and submitting the kinds of error made to detailed analysis, she compared the spelling attainments of groups of children taught by a rigorous phonic method, by i.t.a., and by whole-word methods. Two comparisons were made, one between whole-word methods and the phonic method, and one between t.o. methods and i.t.a. In the first comparison, the overall incidence of errors in spelling was similar, but the kinds of error differed markedly, in that children taught by the phonic method made significantly more 'good attempts' and produced fewer unrecognizable words. In the second comparison she found no overall difference between the groups in terms of average score on standardized tests, but an analysis of the errors made showed that children taught in i.t.a. attacked spelling more economically—that is, they made fewer errors of redundancy and syllable repetition, and made a more rational attempt at spelling words they did not know—but they made more wrong choices in, for instance, double versus single consonants and homophonic groups (like 'ane' and 'ain'). In the higher ranges of I.Q., in both investigations, these contrasts disappeared. Peters concludes that a reading method which encourages analytic seeing and the use of cues derived from regular spelling patterns makes a better basis for the subsequent systematic learning of spelling than does a whole-word method, though 'visual referral' may need to be encouraged at a later stage, and she points out the implications for remedial teaching.

That correct spelling of a word does not necessarily indicate complete mastery of 'phonic analysis' of it was shown by D. J. Bruce (1964). He investigated the ability of children aged 5 to 9 to omit initial, medial and final sounds from words presented orally. He found a developing pattern, from complete inability at average age of five, through various kinds of 'substitution' response, to faulty (though genuine) attempts at the analytic task, to fairly high levels of success. A mental age of seven seemed to be the point at which real analysis (as defined by the task set) began to emerge. At the same time the children were asked to spell some of the words aloud. A distribution of right/wrong spelling by right/wrong analysis showed no significant departure from chance; that is to say, the two abilities were hardly correlated at all. The reconciliation of this finding with those of Downing, Daniels and Diack, and Peters would seem to lie first in the distinction between auditory and visual analysis—and between auditory analysis and phonic synthesis—and secondly in the difference between operating in one stimulus mode alone and operating in two. Children who are reading regularly-spelt material can use the regularities to perform visual analysis and phonic synthesis—they 'take the word to pieces' visually, and 'build it up' phonically and the visual stimulus persists in time—it is present throughout and can be consulted over and over again. In writing, they have certainly to do some auditory analysis of unfamiliar words which they want to write, but as soon as they have begun to write a word, that part of it is then visually present, too. These tasks are not the same as being presented with a complete spoken word, having to hold it in mind while analysing it and subtracting a sound from it, and then synthesizing the remainder, all in the absence of any visual help. It is known that children of five—and younger—can play 'I spy', and the training of five-year-olds in the *hearing* of sounds in words is common classroom practice. It seems probable that the 'subtracting' task employed by Bruce called on the ability to hold stimuli in mind, and to deal with the whole and the parts at the same time in a way which made it different from the skills demanded in the early stages of learning to read and write with the help of 'phonics'.

Linguistics and reading

Recently there have been, as a result of the development of linguistic and psycho-linguistic theory, suggestions that the teaching of reading has in the past been tackled in ways which ignored important aspects of the structure of language and the development in children of an understanding of syntax. In a discussion of theories of reading Dakin (1967) points out how direct evidence that children are structuring what they read can be obtained by noting their selection (when reading aloud) of a particular intonation pattern at the beginning of a sentence, and their success in following it through. This involves prediction and anticipation of what is coming next, and if their prediction is found to be wrong, they may stop and go back to the beginning to correct the faulty intonation pattern. The altering of word order (to make it more 'natural') is also evidence that the child is anticipating structure and imposing his predicted pattern on what he sees. Dakin quotes as a reference for these findings unpublished results obtained by Bradley (1966), who investigated the reading performance of a group of children in Glasgow. Bradley set out to discover what happened when children aged around 7:6 to 8:0 were presented with various recognition and recall tasks using (a) misspelt familiar words, (b) nonsense and 'part'-nonsense words, (c) unfamiliar scripts (for example, i.t.a.), (d) four scrabble letter cards to form words with (e) 'right-branching' sentences, (f) unpunctuated sentence strings, (g) stylistically reordered sentences like 'so off went Chicken Licken', and (h) sentences in the passive. Bradley found strong evidence that as long as children are presented with single words only, perception of the details of the word can be the chief component of the process of recognition; but as soon as groups of words have to be structured, this is no longer true. He concludes that in reading 'the structuring process dictates to a very great extent what we see'. Dakin develops further the question of the relationship of structuring to interpretation, pointing out that (a) we cannot interpret sentences which we cannot structure, though the converse is not true (e.g. 'Jabberwocky'), and (b) we often interpret ambiguous sentences (like 'The detective looked hard') without consciously choosing between two possible structurings. The interaction between structuring and interpretation is therefore complex; but he suggests that those who produce class readers ought to take much more account of these complexities and incorporate the results of research on syntax as well as on vocabulary. A similar suggestion is made by J. F. Reid (1967) on the basis of some earlier research observations (1958).

Roberts (Personal communication 1967) is now engaged on rather similar research into the mental processes which are involved in reading. He is studying the effect of previously induced set or expectation on children's word perception, and their attempts (a) to discriminate between words which are alike, and (b) to read words which are too difficult for them. He is also studying the effect of 'context', that is, the expectations about structure and interpretation which the child forms as he reads and the relation of this to the reading of 'difficult' words. The relative roles of word perception and structuring are being investigated. These researches constitute a promising breakaway from what he (Roberts, G., 1967) has elsewhere described as an over-preoccupation on the part of research workers with the lexical and mechanical aspects of learning to read.

Environment and reading

The researches conducted in Kent by J. M. Morris (1966) have already been referred to in the paper by Lovell. They represent one major publication concerned solely with reading, in that area of research which is (a) fact-finding as opposed to experimental and (b) concerned primarily with the environmental concomitants of reading success and failure. Morris selected from the sixty Kent schools which had formed the basis of her earlier book (Morris, J. M., 1959) ten schools for intensive study. At the same time she obtained further data on the major part of the original sample, and followed up certain selected 'poor readers' until they left school. The amount of material so gathered is impossible to summarize briefly and has relevance in a great variety of contexts (such as the relationship of non-verbal ability to reading). Perhaps the most important single effect of the study is its extension of the emphasis on environment—already made in wider educational contexts by Wiseman (1964) and Douglas (1964)—beyond the home and the community to include the school itself. The 'school variables' associated in Kent with good reading were found to be large classes, urban catchment areas, separate infant school, homogeneous classes, good school buildings and well-equipped classrooms, good libraries, and good teachers. Details of the scales by which these judgments were quantified were given in the text. These characteristics are not, however, independent, as inspection alone shows, and Morris points out very rightly that, for instance, small classes cannot be presumed to have a direct bearing on poor progress, but merely constitute an incidental circumstance associated with other powerful adverse circumstances. One of the results to which great prominence is given is the conclusion that 'after the attributes of their child population and material circumstances had been considered, each school's success or failure in promoting good reading standards and/or progress depended mainly on the quality of its head and staff in that order'.

The evidence for this comes mainly from intensive study of the ten schools selected to maximize contrasts—three at each extreme of the sample, and two at each extreme of 'improvement' or 'deterioration' over the years 1955–7 (relative to the observed national improvement on the same tests). From these schools also came the two groups of 'good readers' (R.Q. 119+) and 'poor readers' (R.Q. 85—). (The appendix explains why these figures were not selected to be symmetrical about a mean of 100.) The two groups provided sharp contrasts not only in the number of unfavourable school conditions but also in the incidence of maladjustment and unsettledness (as measured by the Bristol Social Adjustment Guides). Poor readers showed higher incidence of withdrawal, aggression, tension and nervous symptoms. Boys reacted more than girls with aggression, attention-getting and restlessness. This is a picture already familiar to teachers and clinicians, and reported frequently in previous studies (see Sampson 1966b for a review of the literature, and also the paper by Chazan), but the important point is that to the complex of handicaps usually sub-sumed under 'cultural deprivation' and 'emotional disturbance' Morris has shown that we must often add those of a cramped or dilapidated classroom, devoid of stimulating material or even of adequate cup-board space, and the ministrations of a teacher who (especially at the 8-plus level) has not been specially trained to teach reading, may not regard it as part of her task, and may therefore do little or nothing towards providing help for the backward readers in her charge. On the other hand, Morris noted that most of even the poorest readers im-proved to some degree when specific remedial work was undertaken with them; and she concluded from this that her study therefore lent 'but little support to the idea that "specific developmental dyslexia" is an identifiable syndrome distinct from "reading backwardness" '.

Specific dyslexia

The inclusion of this comment arises presumably from the resurgence of interest in the concept of 'specific dyslexia' which has occurred in many quarters since the war, and which has produced, in the last six years, a good deal of writing at the level of theoretical argument and description of case histories, though not a great deal of systematic research (Critchley, M., 1964, Franklin 1962). The revival of interest has been mainly among neurologists, and psychologists working in medically-oriented settings; and there is a continuing controversy as to whether a condition describable as 'specific dyslexia' exists, or whether it is (to quote one reviewer of Morris' book) a 'reading myth' which 'is often the result of not seeing bad school conditions'.

The various sources of disagreement (and sometimes of misunder-standing) are much too complex to be examined in detail here, but one of them is the difference between the large-scale survey conducted in earch of correlations, and the detailed study of a smaller number of anomalous cases. Group means and correlations can obscure important individual deviations from an overall pattern. This point is made emphatically by M. D. Vernon (1960, 1962), who pleads for more case studies of suspected 'dyslexics' especially with regard to their response to remedial treatment. Such study of the twenty 'poor readers' (R.Q. 85—) in the 'good' schools in Morris' sample, and of those in the same reading category with non-verbal I.Q.s of, say, 110+ would have been a worth-while addition to her report. Page 334 does contain a reference to the fact that some poor readers had very few adverse characteristics; but their poor performance is tentatively explained in terms of the 'complex interaction' of those they did have, without any attempt at further investigation of their disabilities.

Recent British research on dyslexia has taken several forms. Hibbert (1961) described twenty-seven cases of suspected dyslexia referred to him as consulting ophthalmological surgeon to the Local Education Authority of Swansea during 1960. Fifteen of these cases (one girl and fourteen boys), all of whom had been receiving remedial treatment, were subsequently followed up by D. J. Williams (1965). Taking the criteria of the 1961 report, he re-examined each child in an effort to discover whether the clinical picture had changed, and to what extent remedial tuition had been successful. He found that over the five intervening years there was a marked tendency for subjects to outgrow the symptoms (only 47 per cent being retained overall), but that the four subjects making least progress in reading had retained most of the 'criterion factors'. Eleven of the fifteen had changed their handedness pattern, but none from right to left. Seven showed persistent directional confusion, nine were left-eyed but not left-handed, eight had a history of delayed speech, seven were still mispronouncing 'th' (this being one of the principal signs used in the original description), and twelve showed a breakdown in the ability to write numbers to dictation beyond three digits. But only two out of the fifteen were now presenting a sufficient number of factors and a sufficient degree of backwardness to qualify by Hibbert's 1961 criteria as 'dyslexic'. Williams concludes that a classification such as that suggested by Rabinowitch (1962) seems to fit these findings, and advocates that the term 'dyslexia' should not be used in an educational context, but that 'reading retardation' be used instead, with subdivision into 'primary' retardation due to overt brain damage, 'primary' retardation due to cerebral dysfunction of a kind which tends to lessen with age and 'secondary' retardation due to exogenous factors and/or emotional disturbance.

Zangwill (1960) reported on twenty cases of retardation in reading and spelling referred to the Psychological Department at the National Hospital, Queen Square. The sample consisted of fourteen boys and six girls. In addition to poor reading and spelling, anomalies of various kinds were present, including right-to-left scanning and mirror-writing, poor ability in copying and drawing, selective defect on performance tests, and temperamental instability. Evidence of some sinistral tendency (i.e. left-handedness or ambidexterity) was present in twelve of the cases and in the families of three others. This is a high proportion and must have some significance; but Zangwill goes on to point out that the question as to why many left-handed and ambidexterous children have no educational difficulties remains to be answered. His tentative theory is that people who are not right-dominant are (a) less strongly lateralized than those who are, and (b) relatively unstable and vulnerable to stress, and that reading and writing disability may result from the interaction of perceptual and emotional difficulties. Later (Zangwill 1962) he suggests that there may be two types of specific dyslexia, one involving general language disability, and one not.

Shankweiler (1964) studied intensively twelve children (ten boys and two girls, mean C.A. 10 years 6 months, mean I.Q. 96, range 83–101), all severely backward in reading (R.A. < 7 years 6 months in each case). The table of associated disabilities on sixteen criteria shows a great deal of individual variation, one child presenting only one (vocabulary), while two presented disability in eleven of the tests and one in ten. The most prevalent defects were reversals in reading and writing, difficulty in copying a drawing of a cube, in drawing the human figure, in doing the Porteus Maze test, in making right-left discrimination, in doing sums, and in distinguishing one letter from another apart from reversals. Six of the cases had evidence of brain damage as shown by case history and E.E.G., and a further one had an isolated E.E.G. abnormality. Reading disability, sinistrality, speech disorders and mental abnormality in the families of the subjects were assessed. Shankweiler sees the twelve cases as falling into three patterns, (1) 'pure' dyslexia, (2) dyslexia accompanied by spatial and constructional disabilities, and (3) dyslexia as an expression of disturbance of language development; and concludes that it may be that delayed maturation s more commonly the cause of dyslexia than actual brain damage. The condition is not, at any rate, according to Shankweiler, a unitary clinical entity (cf. Zangwill 1962).

The existence of more than one pattern of disability has also been stressed by Ingram (1960) and by Kinsbourne and Warrington (1966a). In an effort to examine the relation between language development and later reading ability, Ingram and Mason (Mason 1966) have been following up a group of seventy-six children who were referrals during the year 1962 to the speech clinic at the Royal Hospital for Sick Children, Edinburgh. The group comprised nineteen girls and fifty-seven boys, again demonstrating the preponderance of boys so often found in studies of retarded speech and in studies of clinic referrals (Ingram and Reid 1956, Shankweiler 1964, Williams, D. J., 1965, Zangwill 1960). Most of the children in Ingram and Mason's group are from social classes I and II, and therefore many of the adverse school conditions discussed by Morris may be presumed to be absent. A control group of matched children with normal speech has been formed, and the subsequent progress of the two groups is being followed. So far, of the twenty children who by 1965 had finished their first school year, the controls could read significantly better than the experimental group, while arithmetic progress showed no difference. In another group (ten girls and forty boys) referred for reading/writing difficulties, a history of retarded acquisition of speech was elicited retrospectively in thirty-two cases. The picture presented here is somewhat in contrast to that shown by Shankweiler's group, all of whom, with one exception, showed normal oral-language competence. But it should be noted that (a) Shankweiler's numbers are small, and (b) their average age is such that we could expect, in the light of Williams' findings, that many of the clinical signs would have diminished or disappeared. Kinsbourne and Warrington (1966a), studying two groups of retarded readers with selective impairment ($>$ 20 points of difference) on the Verbal and Performance scales of the w.i.s.c. and w.a.i.s., found a correlation between impairment in verbal tests and language disability outside reading and writing, and impairment in performance tests and difficulty in finger differentiation and arithmetic. They conclude that there is evidence of two types of disability, both connected with reading and writing: one is concerned with sequential ordering, and the other with language. A further study (Kinsbourne and Warrington 1966b) of the spelling errors made by two groups of adult patients showed a difference in the type of error. Extraneous letters were typical of those with language impairment, while errors of letter order characterized those with finger agnosia.

There is therefore an increasing body of evidence and opinion tending to the discrimination of sub-types of dyslexic disorder.

In an attempt to resolve some of the current controversy, Clark (Personal communication 1967) is now engaged on a two-year investigation into 'the nature and magnitude of specific reading disability'. The subjects are a complete age-group (seven-year-olds) in a single county (1,500 children in all), and all those who have failed to read will undergo intensive individual investigation to discover what patterns of retardation emerge. On the remedial side, Meredith (1966) is investigating principles and methods of analytical programming for the treatment of dyslexia. Analytical programming is a type of programme construction which replaces single frames by displays of related items, and the investigation is aimed at producing programmes which will 'establish an adequate network of micro-skills covering all the essential operations involved in reading and writing'. The work of the recently established Word Blind Centre in London, directed by Bannatyne, should also be mentioned. At this centre, special methods for teaching children with severe disabilities are being evolved, and an account of some of these has recently been published (Bannatyne 1966).

Deprivation and reading

Another area in which the close connection between language development and reading has recently been shown is in the work with deprived children reported by Pringle (1965). For 142 deprived children in three age-groups (8, 11 and 14) she obtained 'language quotients' (L.Q.s) in addition to reading quotient. She found the mean L.Q. was 75 and that more than two-thirds of the sample had L.Q.s below 85, while just under two-thirds had R.Q.s below that level. Forty per cent of the group were judged to be retarded relative to their I.Q. on w.i.s.c. (Full Scale). By contrast, the mean performance scale I.Q. for the group was 95·6. She concludes that this state of affairs is 'the end product of a chain of adverse conditions which interact and reinforce one another'. Prominent among these, however, is the stultification in linguistic development which is the normal concomitant of deprivation.

In the last analysis, all this research, if it is not to remain of purely academic interest, must feed back into the classroom; and it is significant that the problem of achieving adequate feedback has of late become a subject of research in its own right. Perhaps, as J. M. Morris (1966) and Daniels (1967) suggest, the solution lies with those responsible for the training of primary school teachers, both in making them sympathetic to innovation and to research findings, and in training them much more specifically to teach reading. In this setting, work on the normal and the deviant child must be brought together, for, as was remarked at the beginning of this paper, researches in these different areas have mutual implications. Influences that affect reading as a whole will affect *a fortiori* those who start off with more than their share of handicaps; and study of the extremes—of children in severe difficulty, or children with outstanding facility—may give important insights into the complexities of the reading process.

Harry Kay

Programmed Instruction

Introduction

Once a discovery or invention has been made, it is only too easy to find antecedents for it and to arrive at the conclusion that it has 'all been done before'. One wishes that the pundits who indulge in this *post hoc* reasoning would change their strategy and tell us what are the antecedents for the 'discoveries' that have not yet been made. It has become customary since the arrival of programmed learning in the educational field to find that many of its principles have long been part of educational folk-lore, and that the best teachers have always followed its procedures. There is some truth in this; but it is nevertheless accurate to pin-point the beginnings of programmed learning as marking a new departure in teaching methods, and, most significantly, a point from which it was obvious that further advances could be made.

Programmed learning cuts through the verbal morass of defining educational aims and insists that we measure what we are doing. It begins by asking for a precise answer to the question, 'What is the behaviour we are trying to teach?' and it ends by measuring how far this has been achieved. In this sense it is the beginning of an educational technology, which does not mean, as so many people seem to think (for example, *The Times* 1967), an extension of visual aids and hardware, but a change in our attitude to what is expected from teaching methods. It is basically a demand for educational efficiency. This issue has always been clouded because so much learning is accidental. Man, as a biologically adaptive system, spends most of his formative years in acquiring information in a haphazard and fortuitous way. So little of his learning is a result of directed teaching, but rather the results of spatial and temporal contiguities that serve to condition him to his environment. The same random influences continue in the classroom, with the result that some learning occurs—though how far this should be ascribed to any one influence, such as the teacher, it is often difficult to say. We will consider how far programmed learning succeeds in its attempts to assess its own progress; but the aims may become clearer if we consider the beginnings of this work. It is still a very short history.

The beginnings of programmed learning and the work of Professor Skinner

There have been many forms of early teaching machines, of which the ordinary textbook is still the most elegant and successful example. In more recent times (the 1920s) Sidney Pressey designed a testing box which taught successfully, and during the Second World War the American services made wide use of machines to teach their staff such tasks as diagnosing faults in electrical equipment. But it was left to Burrhus Skinner of Harvard to look at teaching as a whole and to put forward proposals that were based not on classroom procedures but on his laboratory experiments. Skinner (1938) conducted some of the most detailed animal experiments in psychology and was able to state precisely the conditions under which an animal would learn. His technique of operant conditioning is one of the most powerful tools ever devised for controlling the behaviour of an animal. It depends upon knowing precisely the response that you wish the animal to make, in rewarding (reinforcing) that response immediately it is evoked, and in repeating the procedure often enough for the animal to retain the behaviour.

When Skinner turned to the usual classroom situation, he found the negation of all the principles he knew to be essential in the laboratory. Pupils made responses, but might wait a day or more before being told whether they were correct. Lessons proceeded at a set pace that might be too slow for some and too fast for others; whilst often the aim was so badly identified that no effort had been made to divide the material into an appropriate number of steps by which a pupil might reach the prescribed goal. Skinner's solution was to provide individual teaching machines for each student, and to write a teaching programme such that each step was within the intellectual capabilities of every member of the class. As soon as a student responded, he was informed of the correct answer; and since the programme was written so that his response could be correct, Skinner argued that this would serve as reinforcement. Thus the characteristic features of a programme were born—the break-up of the material into a sequence of short statements known as 'frames', the constant responding by the student, the immediate confirmation or knowledge of results, and an individual rate of progress being set by the student. These features required a new lay-out for printed material and new presentation devices leading to a variety of teaching machines, with the result that the novelties tended to obscure the more radical principles underlying their adoption. These features are only the means to an end; but often the means have been identified as the end. The whole paraphernalia of programmes and frames and responding are means to provide a self-correcting system with clearly defined teaching objectives, where both pupil and teacher know how far these aims have been achieved.

These basic aims are common to most of the teaching machine procedures that have been proposed, and are much more significant than the ostensible differences that were originally stressed as distinguishing one system from another. For example, linear and branching programmes follow different formats; some programmes use constructed responses, others multi-choice, and much current research has been devoted to ascertaining their effects. We shall look at these variables, but first we will consider the underlying principles of programmed learning.

Programmed learning as a contribution to educational technology

A surprising thing about programmed learning is the extent to which it now embodies a number of principles from different scientific disciplines. Skinner, as we saw, deliberately designed the linear programme to meet the requirements of his own studies of operant conditioning, but scientists from subjects such as cybernetics and communication theory have become interested in applying these principles to teaching. Pre-eminent in their philosophy is the idea of feedback. There is no point in transmitting signals into a void without some indication of where they are going, who is receiving them, and how much has been understood. This is the beginning of their approach and from that follows the central tenet: where the message has not been received and understood, it must be modified in the light of the feedback received before being sent again.

Let us consider what this implies. In order to modify a teaching programme, the aim of the lesson has to be precisely defined. This is usually achieved in terms of some criterion behaviour. For example, if a student had completed a programme on logarithms, we should know the exact operations he can now carry out. It is not enough to leave it vaguely as 'use logarithms'; for, as we know, some pupils may be able to multiply with them but have no notion of how to use them to find square roots. When students are asked to carry out such operations and are unable to do so, the reasons for their failure are sought in the programme, which is then modified. The orientation of communication scientists is to put the emphasis upon the intelligibility of the message in terms of how the recipient responds to it. The student is the key figure in the system. This point is sometimes difficult to get across to educationists, who are accustomed to expressing opinions and to stating that one test is good and another is bad merely in terms of their own judgment. (It seems amazing how little has been done over the years to evalute textbooks; it is symptomatic of the lack of inquiry in the field.) It is, of course, somewhat disturbing to be told that your opinion is not relevant and that the criterion is provided by the student. If the programme teaches him what it set out to teach, then it is satisfactory; if it does not, it is a failure, and any judgment which results from inspection only is entirely irrelevant. The significance of this was brought home in an American study in which the effectiveness of a programme in terms of how well it taught and the teacher's prior judgment of the programme were shown to be *negatively* correlated.

We have, then, a student in the centre of the stage, and we try to specify precisely what we wish to teach him. It is appreciated that the nature of education is such that this is not always easy and that the higher reaches cannot always be rigorously defined. This familiar line of argument is fair enough; but there is still so much in education that can be so defined that the programmer is not likely to feel the limitations for a long time. What, in fact, has happened is that in spite of all the efforts that have been made over the last ten years, there is still a serious shortage of programmes. It takes a long time to produce and evaluate a programme, and it will be many years before we have enough for our present needs. In these circumstances, research has been concentrated mainly upon immediate issues. At first the emphasis was upon comparing the effectiveness of programmes against conventional classroom instruction. In general, the early studies were very much in favour of programming, and the results from many experiments are given by Kay and Warr (1962) and Hartley (1963). But is should be stressed that many of these experiments used only short programmes with relatively few students, and that the whole basis of comparing programming with teachers is suspect. A good or bad representative of either party can so easily invalidate the findings. For this reason we shall not put any weight on these findings; we shall, instead, suggest that the more appropriate test is whether the programme has met its criterion behaviour.

Again in the early days of teaching machines, it was popular practice to examine whether a programme was presented more successfully by a machine than in book form. Results on the whole favoured the machine, but here again they are contaminated by the effects of novelty and the kinds of students who were using them. It would seem that there is no general answer, but that the results depend upon the students, their background and training, and the nature of the material. Perhaps the more interesting feature here is the more varied use of programmes, as in the practical laboratory or workshop situation (Dodd 1964). Here the emphasis is less upon a dichotomy between book and machine, and more upon how it may be used in conjunction with existing equipment and conditions.

We shall be returning to this point when we consider the integrated classroom experiments, but we will divide our review of present research under two heads. On the one hand, there is a series of studies which investigate the effectiveness of specific features of programmed learning, such as the speed/rate of presentation, the response mode, the effect of making any overt response, the presentation to an individual student, or to pairs, or to a whole class. We can think of these studies as attempts to examine the effects of the variables that have often been cited as important features of programmed learning. On the other hand, there have been developments of the ideas behind programmed systems. If we are to create a technology of teaching, then the central question is likely to be, 'How far can we produce a teaching system that will provide each student with the precise instruction he requires to meet his individual needs?' This will appear idealistic; at present it is. No system comes anywhere near meeting such a specification. The older universities with their tutorial system of one student–one tutor may have come near to it; but now they often give more than one student at a time to a tutor, and this is a long way from the comprehensive school with its class of thirty to forty. Again, it should be noted that at the research level, even the laboratory rat is trained on a predetermined schedule; the system does not allow for variation of reinforcement to meet the requirements and progress of the individual animal. We shall examine some ideas where the aim is to meet the individual's changing demands during the course of learning.

Examination of variables that influence programmed learning

A) RATE OF PRESENTATION

One of the widely accepted advantages of programmed instruction is that it allows a student to set his own pace. The advantages to the student seem obvious enough, but the difficulties for any large class where each individual is progressing at a different rate are also apparent. It is pertinent, therefore, to inquire how successful programmed learning might be when the rate of instruction is imposed upon the subject and not left to his own discretion. To support such a line of inquiry it can be argued that programmes aim to control the tuition of a student. Every care has been devoted to the analysis of the subject matter and the unambiguous presentation of material. Why, then, should programmes stop short at the variable that is so flexible—time? If material has been put together in such a way that the programmer expects a student to take a particular time over his learning, it can be argued that it would be wiser to ensure that he does in fact spend that time. When the time he takes differs considerably from the time expected by the programmer, then the nature of the task is radically changed. Again, some experiments in psychology suggest that students do not always select a learning time that is most advantageous to themselves. Why, indeed, should they? Learning means going from the known to the unknown, and the student by definition is denied exact knowledge of where he is going and the difficulties he will meet. In one sense, he is the last person who should be plotting his rate of progress. On the other hand, the programmer has planned the whole course, he appreciates—or should do—the nature of the difficulties that will arise, and allocates the appropriate time to them.

In the United States thinking along these lines produced a series of papers which examined the effect of pacing upon student performance (Frye 1963, Kress and Gropper 1964, Lottes *et al.* 1963, Silverman and Alter 1961). Results showed that the pace at which a student works through a programme can be equally non-adaptive, whether it is self- or externally imposed. Kress and Gropper argue that some students set a pace that is too fast to be compatible with high achievement, whilst others set a pace too slow to be compatible with learning efficiency. Rate of progress aims to maximize both learning achievement and learning efficiency, and their results suggest that this can be accomplished by an externally imposed pace as much as by a self-adopted rate.

b) PACING AND GROUP INSTRUCTION

The subject of paced presentation becomes of paramount interest when we try to present programmes to a group, rather than to individuals. I am thinking of systems where the same frame is shown to all members of the group, but each individual has the facilities to make his own response (Holling 1964). He does so without communicating to other members of the class. It is possible with such methods of group presentation to ensure that all members have time to respond; but this means that the rate of presentation is determined by the slowest student in the group. If we have a heterogeneous group, this may be a most uneconomical way of allocating learning time to the group. If, then, a rate of presentation is externally imposed, we must face the question, 'How can we best determine such a pace?' Studies reported by the Programmed Learning Research Unit at Birmingham (Leith 1966) show that group presentation may produce results equal to or better than those of individual presentation. In one study junior school children were taught to measure time either by individual programmed texts or by groups using an overhead projector. Under each condition one group worked at a fixed pace and another was self-paced. There was no difference in test scores, but the forced-pace method was significantly more highly approved. Again in a physics course involving practical work mixed-ability groups of four children, age 10, gained more than children who worked individually at the programme.

In the Sheffield University Department of Psychology interest in pacing arose primarily through research into group methods of presenting programmes. A fully automatic programmed classroom system was developed by M. E. Sime (1964). The interesting feature here is the flexible manner in which the time per frame is assessed. In theory it is possible for a system to present the next frame to a student after a fixed interval per frame, or by some predetermined interval for each individual frame, or when all the students or some percentage of them have responded. It will be noted that the first two procedures put the onus of decision upon the programmer, the second two on the students. The objections to the different procedures are fairly clear. Predetermined intervals do not allow for much variation between student groups, and measures which automatically cut off some percentage of students from making a response can be unfair—all of the group may be responding in adequate time if given the opportunity. A system was therefore devised that assessed the response time on each frame for a sample of the students and then by extrapolation fixed the total exposure time for that frame. For example, suppose that 50 per cent of the students take x seconds to respond to the frame; the machine may then set the time for that frame to $2x$. In practice the system is more sophisticated: it is found more reliable to sample in the range between 20 and 60 per cent of responses, and, since it is not being argued that responses are normally distributed in time, it is possible to add to or subtract from the total frame time according to the kind of material and the students making up the group.

D. L. Moore (1967) has carried out a series of studies comparing group and individual instruction with different age-groups of school children and different levels of ability. In several instances a machine-taught group scored more highly on subsequent tests than students who had been taught by individual booklets. Even in groups with wide ranges of I.Q., where the natural working speeds would be expected to vary, comparable results to self-paced booklet methods were obtained. The actual strategy that is being followed here is of some interest. The students, as a group, are determining their pace of progress by their individual responses. But each member is also being influenced by the group in so far as he is aware when other members have responded. He does not know the actual responses that have been made, but he is subject to the group 'pressure' if he delays his own too long.

The reduced costs of using a single presentation device are obvious enough, and where programmed instruction is being integrated into a teaching syllabus, the advantage of a class progressing at the same rate throughout an academic session may be highly important. In view of the above results further research on this method of presentation is imperative.

c) PROGRAMMED LEARNING IN PAIRS

In this method of instruction the pair of students are expected to discuss a frame and produce an agreed response. Several arguments have been put forward in its favour: students help each other over difficulties, it is less boring than working alone, retention scores show improvement, and it is more economical (Leedham and Unwin 1965). Hartley (1967) has, however, listed the available evidence and has demonstrated that so far neither test scores nor time results favour either the individual or paired procedure. Hartley stresses that there is no convincing evidence yet that retention is better in students working in pairs. British work has concentrated upon the relative standing of the pupils who make up the pairs, and has used pupils paired at random, or deliberately paired so as to produce either a heterogeneous or homogeneous group. A study by Amaria *et al.* (1966) claimed that the poorer member of a heterogeneous pair gained significantly more from a programme than did students in homogeneous pairs. But more recent work by Hartley and Cook (1967) and Amaria (1967) did not support this finding. In her recent experiment, Amaria not only found homogeneous pairing to be superior to individual instruction, but where she examined pairings of introverts and extraverts it appeared that the findings were related to personality variables. At this stage it would appear that working in pairs is often equal to students working on their own, and that personality interactions are playing their part in these results.

d) RESPONDING—OVERT OR COVERT

One of the most quoted qualities of programmed instruction is that it is an active form of learning. This may not be saying what it seems to be saying, but rather that a student is kept active whilst he is supposed to be learning. It is claimed that making a response, such as writing a particular word, will help a student to keep his attention on the task. Of course, such writing will take a little longer than a covert response, and this extra time may be beneficial in learning.

The practical advantages of overt responses are clear enough. We cannot always say when a student is or is not paying attention; but where many responses are demanded of him, a failure to give and keep making them is immediately apparent. Hence it may be argued that the effects of overt responding will be most apparent in a long programme which requires many sessions from a student. It keeps him going when he is inclined to nod, and ensures that he has responded to the information in a frame and not merely turned the page. But the examination of a long programme of many thousands of frames is painstaking research, and few such studies have been conducted. Experiments on response made with short programmes have yielded varied results: studies by Cummings and Goldstein (1962), Eigen and Margulies (1963) and J. P. Williams (1963) favour overt responses, whilst those by Lambert *et al.* (1962), Stolurow and Walker (1962) and Widlake (1964) did not find any significant difference between response modes. In contrast, Goldbeck and Campbell (1962) found that a test of retention favoured the covert (i.e. reading) responders.

Leith and Buckle (1965) bring out the practical importance of the question, and argue that a succession of similar overt responses may produce boredom. They consider that overt responding will be more successful than covert responding when (a) new, unfamiliar responses are to be acquired; (b) difficult discriminations are required; (c) learners are likely to be distracted; and (d) the sequence of materials is confusing. On the other hand, the authors claim that when responses have already been learned and are now being used in a different context, or when the materials have a clearly perceived structure which overcomes interference, covert responding will be as effective as overt. In their own experiment Leith and Buckle used a 739-frame linear programme on electronics with college students whose background knowledge of physics was classified into one of three grades. Both the post-test and the retention test showed that the scores for students with some knowledge of physics did not differ significantly whether the students used an overt or covert response programme, but the scores for students with the least knowledge of physics were significantly better with the overt response programmes.

It may seem surprising that overt responses were not definitely superior to other procedures, as confirmed by P. Wright's (1966) results, but we should bear in mind that the nature of overt responses in this kind of learning has never been clearly defined. Why should we expect a student to learn more about, say, a logical problem when he has to write down his solution at the end of his deliberations than when he has only to think about the problem without writing anything down? How does the written response contribute to learning? One possibility is that it makes the student commit himself to a definite answer. If he does not have to formulate the response in some overt fashion, he may

be vacillating without coming to any conclusion. This would certainly
be a sound reason for supporting overt responses and in some respect
is on the same lines as the reason previously mentioned of permitting
the programmer to know that the learner is still engaged in carrying ou
the task. On the other hand, overt responses do slow down the rate
at which a student 'reads' a programme, so that we would expect an
interaction between the total number of responses required and the
difficulty of the material.

We might express this another way with reference to Skinner'
original view that by confirming the response we were providing
immediate reinforcement. It is clear enough that what is reinforced i
not the actual written response so that overt or covert responses could
in theory, be equally reinforced. But the practical difficulties of reinforcing a covert response should not be minimized. How do we decide tha
a subject has made a covert response? An even more provoking issue
is whether too frequent confirmation is reinforcing. The rough analogy
is where the constant reward of food is no longer reinforcing to the
animal that is not hungry. When a student's responses are being constantly confirmed and he already knows that the response is correct
it seems plausible to argue that the reinforcing effect of the confirmation
will be diminished (Kay 1964). We can put this in the language of
communication theory by saying that in a situation where a student
is making constant responses and is always correct, the confirmation
no longer carries any information. Technically speaking, such confirmation is redundant. It would seem, therefore, that there are good
grounds for arguing that the rate of overt responding should not always
be rapid and the possibility of being correct should be varied. Hence
the difficulty, and perhaps the length of the frames within a programme
should not be uniform.

E) INTEGRATION OF PROGRAMMED INSTRUCTION

A key problem in the use of programmed instruction is how it may be
integrated within an existing syllabus and within the physical constraints
of our present educational buildings. This issue is often in the minds of
those who see programmed instruction, not as a threat to the teacher,
but as an important instrument to help him in his work. From this
point of view programmes will be used in conjunction with ordinary
teaching methods. They will supplement the normal curriculum, per-

haps supporting it at the points where it is weakest either through lack of staff or inadequacy of their experience.

Some of the most interesting work in examining how far programmed instruction can be integrated into a conventional syllabus has been conducted by the Services. The scale of British work has been small compared with that of the American forces, but some particularly well-conducted studies have been carried out (Wallis *et al.* 1966). Studies by the Services demonstrated that programmed instruction could successfully teach a variety of students and subject matters such as electronics, book-keeping, trigonometry, algebra and map-reading. The Navy then examined how far it was possible to integrate human and programmed instruction within the same course. A programme for radio-electrical mechanics covering the basic material was used for 40 per cent of the total time, practical work was distributed for 40 per cent, and the remaining 20 per cent was used by the instructor. The overall responsibility for the course belonged to the instructor, but the programmes relieved him of much of the routine teaching, so that he had more time to give to individual students and to the class tutorials which were arranged.

The results were very encouraging. The students taught by the integrated procedure were far superior to students who had received conventional classroom instruction; and these in turn were superior to classes that had been taught by a fully automated method without supervision. An even more significant finding with the integrated method was that one instructor had been responsible for twice as many students as in the conventional classroom method, and yet the attitude of both students and instructors was very favourable to the integrated method.

This kind of research seems most promising. If we are to use programmed learning within the conventional curriculum, then it would appear that here are pointers as to how it could be introduced. Programmes are on the one hand giving some variety of teaching methods and on the other providing soundly-based expository courses.

Future developments in programmed learning

In the main, research in Britain upon the significant variables in programmed learning has followed similar lines to that in the United States; by contrast some of the developmental work has followed a more individual line. Much of British investigators' early interest in this field was in exploiting a self-correcting system that offered the possibility of gradually improving upon its initial performances (Pask 1960). Many programmers were prepared to accept the position that in a teaching system we did not know enough to lay down the ideal programme, but here we had a method that would at least tell us when and where we had failed (Sime 1964). If we could not guarantee success, we could detect mistakes and in a world where so much learning is of an accidental—if not an incidental—nature, this assessment of progress was no mean achievement.

Evaluation studies have certainly gone a long way towards furthering the idea of measuring teaching efficiency. It is now expected that programmes should state what evaluation has taken place and what level of success has been achieved by the particular programme. It is fair to say that techniques of evaluation provide one straightforward method of improving the teaching level of a programme in that they raise the post-test performance of groups of students (Hartley 1966.)

But how far will it be possible to develop this feature and adapt the programme to meet the needs of an individual student as he actually works through the programme? This is a much more ambitious undertaking, and the usual branching programme only meets this requirement in a limited way: it caters for individual variation within two or three choices. Let us consider a different type of programme.

We may think of a teaching system as containing a body of knowledge which is available to a student. It is left to a student to indicate by his performance what part of that information he requires. In some learning tasks the different items are independent of one another, and here it is relatively easy to design the system so that a subject can practise an item until he achieves a designated level of performance. In learning a vocabulary or new alphabet, for example, or in training for a key-board skill where the subject is trying to make a binary-coded response to letter or numeric symbols, the items can be taught independently and the amount of practice on each one may be governed by the relative progress of a subject on those items. Sime has carried out such experiments and shown that two features are immediately obvious —the variance between subjects is reduced, and the overall standard of performance is raised. In some studies the improvement was such that the mean scores for the group were equal to those of the highest individual scores where teaching had been by the conventional methods (Kay *et al.* 1968).

In order to design efficient adaptive teaching systems, it is clear that we have to state the *decision rules* which determine the selection of material from the body of knowledge. In cases where items are independent we may not know all the necessary decision rules, but we can at least be confident of some. For example, we can decide to practise those items where a student is performing at a rate below his own average for that particular series, or below the mean for his group. We can certainly practise any items where mistakes are being made. But once we move beyond these first stages, the decision rules become complex even for independent items. For example, what is the most efficient way of practising a response? Should we repeat an exercise at once, or should we delay repetition as long as possible? How long is 'as long as possible'? One hypothesis is that the optimal interval is the longest that is compatible with a student's being able to respond correctly. In other words, we repeat the item at the moment when a subject may have begun to forget but when he still retains enough to make a correct response.

The order of complexity of the decision rules where material is interrelated is increased. We need to subdivide material, so that a student works within and achieves mastery of one set of material before he embarks on the next. But this practice on one sub-set of material is only the beginning, and provision has to be made so that all related material can be retrieved. This takes us into computer-controlled systems where British investigations (e.g. Lewis and Pask 1965, Pask 1960) have been conspicuous in ideas but, with one or two exceptions, inconspicuous with computer hardware. There is no immediate indication of a change in this position, and yet the whole field of computers has been transformed in the last decade. It is clear to workers in the field, and should be much more widely appreciated, that computer-controlled teaching systems can already offer us all the hardware that is required. Such systems are no longer merely pipe dreams, but are rapidly becoming an economic proposition. What is more significant, the limitations and deficiencies are not on the side of the computer but on the side of teaching. As soon as we try to operate with systems like these, where we have to stipulate precisely the decisions we wish to take, we are brought up against our lack of knowledge of teaching. What criteria do we accept for learning? For retention? How does it differ from one subject matter to another? From one class of students to another? We need not be ashamed of our ignorance. The problem is complex and the interaction between variables is great. Fortunately, we can use a large store of subject matter and by studying how a student interrogates the machine we can gain some insight into how he builds up his knowledge, what information he has to have, and how quickly he forgets it under such circumstances. There is no doubt that computer-controlled studies will provide us with significant contributions to our understanding of teaching procedures.

We have concluded our brief review with this mention of computer systems because it is the brightest hope for further advances. The more the problem is examined in terms of the rapidly increasing knowledge we have to impart and the rapidly rising numbers to whom it has to be imparted, the more it becomes apparent that the way to redress the balance is to call in machines and above all the most sophisticated and adaptive machine we possess, the computer. The technological advance has created the imbalance by bringing about this sensational rise in man's knowledge; it must now be used in its turn to supply the means to transmit this information. It is ironical to find we already know enough to build the machine, but not enough about teaching to know what we want the machine to do.

A. E. G. Pilliner

Examinations

Examinations of one sort or another are characteristic features of all stages of British education. They include individually administered tests of intelligence or reading ability; group tests and examinations, traditional and 'objective', internal and external, which characterize both primary and secondary education; the various examinations of universities and colleges, and of professional bodies; the 'country house' selection procedures of the Civil Service and big business; and the tests of proficiency in English administered to foreign students who wish to study in Britain.

Despite their diversity in standard, degree of sophistication and method, they have certain common features. In terms of outcome, all attempt to assess what a person can do in relation to what other persons can do. In terms of basic theory, general principles exist which are relevant, whatever the particular style or level of the examination. It is convenient, therefore, to use a single term, 'examination procedures', to embrace all the modes of assessment hitherto employed or yet to be devised for that purpose.

Purposes of examination procedures

Examination procedures serve a number of functions. To the student they are a stimulus and a goal. To the teacher they feed back information about the effectiveness of his teaching and hence serve as feedback. To society at large they furnish a guarantee of competence in those examined to perform the tasks demanded of them by the jobs or professions they take up (Oppenheim *et al.* 1967). It cannot be assumed that the stimulus to the student is the most appropriate, or that the feedback to the teacher is necessarily desirable. But it would be idle to deny the effectiveness of examination procedures in these respects. This point will be returned to later. Nor can it be assumed that the guarantee they offer to society is infallible. But whether right or wrong, decisions must be made on behalf of society which most of its members have to take on trust.

N. Morris (1961, p. 1) classifies the purpose of examination procedures under four headings: (a) to maintain standards; (b) to act as an incentive to effort; (c) to serve as an administrative device; and (d) to provide a tool for social engineering. The first and second of these clearly include the stimulus and feedback functions and the guarantee of quality referred to above.

One example, by now historical, of the third (administrative) use of examination procedures was for determining school grants, the system of 'payment by results'. A second is the use of examination results to select children, at the end of the primary stage, for the most 'appropriate' type of secondary education. With the development of the comprehensive school, the 11-plus examination, as originally conceived, is becoming increasingly irrelevant. A third example is the use of 'A' level results to select university entrants—a use which, though still current, is giving rise to increasing disquiet.

An example of the use of an examination procedure as a tool for social engineering was the substitution in the twenties by Thomson (1921, p. 102) of 'objective' tests for almost all children in Northumberland in place of the secondary school 'free-place' examination for which many schools in that area did not present candidates. This was the precursor of the 11-plus examination. It is ironical that a device which was intended by its originator to give (and which, indeed, did give) educational opportunity to children who would otherwise have been deprived of it should be seen in its later development as a chief obstacle to the democratization of education.

From a still different (though again related) point of view, examination procedures are 'backward-looking' in that they provide evidence of achievement to date, or 'forward-looking' in that they predict what the examinee is likely to be able to do in the future. Much confusion has arisen through unclear specification of intention in these respects, and through the use of procedures primarily intended to be 'backward-looking' for essentially 'forward-looking' purposes.

Requirements of a good examination procedure

Whatever the purpose of the examination procedure, ideally it should conform to the following requirements:

1. The content should consist of a representative sample of every aspect of the domain in which achievement or potential is to be assessed.
2. The procedure should be organized to impose as little stress on the candidate as possible so that each should 'do himself justice'.
3. The content and organization should make possible the consistent evaluation of the achievement or potential of each candidate.
4. The final outcome of the procedure should be the placing of candidates in a rank order, or in ordered categories, valid in respect of some acceptable criterion. Frequently the criterion is present achievement or potential success, or both, as defined explicitly, or accepted implicity in a given culture.
5. The influence of the procedure on the work of pupils or students preparing for it, and on their teachers, should be educationally beneficial.

Discussion of these requirements

These requirements are seldom, if ever, completely achieved.

1. It is rarely possible to examine or test comprehensively every aspect of the domain concerned. Some kind of selection is necessary. The degree of arbitrariness, inevitable in the selection of material, can be reduced by the application of a good sampling procedure. This presupposes that the extent of the domain in question has been mapped and stated. The preparation of such a statement is a salutary exercise for the compiler of the examination in his capacity as educator.

2. In any examination procedure some degree of stress is inevitable, and it is improbable that every candidate will 'do himself justice'. Pre-examination stress at the university level and its medical and psychological treatment have been discussed by Malleson (1957). Hallwork (1964) found a slight tendency for anxiety measurement and the performance of secondary school children to be negatively correlated. The effect of the 11-plus on children in primary schools has been summarized by P. E. Vernon et al. (1957, ch. 7). They report that despite a few authenticated cases of individuals for whom stress appeared directly

linked to the examination, the anxiety for which this procedure was alleged to be responsible had been much exaggerated.

Well before the date of the examination, all candidates should know quite explicitly the form it will take, the number of questions they will be required to answer, and in particular the qualities the procedure aims to assess. By these means, not only will stress be reduced, but also whatever educational ends the procedure is capable of serving will be given fuller scope (Himmelweit 1967, p. 365).

Within the examination room, stress on the candidate should be combated by making the occasion as informal as possible. More important still is absolute clarity in the paper itself, so that every candidate knows precisely and without ambiguity what he must do. A 'pilot' try-out would be the best way to detect and eliminate ambiguities, but it is frequently impracticable. This being so, considerable foresight and imagination, backed by experience of difficulties encountered by candidates in previous examinations, are required of those compiling the papers. Misprints in the paper itself often disconcert candidates, so that impeccable editing and proof-reading are essential.

Experiments in new procedural techniques, conducted so far mainly at the university level, might be extended to other educational levels. These experiments include: (a) procedures in which papers consist of a selection from a larger number of questions made available to the candidates well beforehand; (b) 'open-book' procedures in which the candidates can take texts into the examination room. These may or may not be prescribed (Cox 1966, p. 23); (c) procedures in which performance in course-work as well as the examination proper is taken into account.* Again, in addition to a possible reduction of stress, important educational ends might be served.

3. The problems involved in the consistent evaluation of each candidate's work are notorious and formidable. They will be more fully described later in this paper under the heading of 'Reliability'. Meanwhile, it is suggested that where the nature of the domain examined allows of it, 'objective' questions which require no evaluative judgment in their marking should be used. Where the nature of the domain calls for extended writing, the attendant difficulties of marking consistently have to be accepted.

* In recent years, the University of Edinburgh Education Department has awarded its Diploma in Education on the total of equally weighted course and examination marks. The correlation between them is about 0·6–0·7.

4. Placing candidates in an order of merit or in ordered categories perfectly valid in respect of some acceptable criterion must probably remain an aspiration. Difficulties arise when the criterion against which examination performance is to be validated is not made sufficiently explicit, or cannot be agreed on. Since the nature of the criterion delimits the content of the examination, no finality can be reached as to this content either. This is discussed further under the heading of 'Validity'.

Certainly, however, stress on the candidates and ambiguity in the questions reduce validity, a further reason for minimizing the first and eliminating the second.

5. The fifth requirement is at once the most important and the most difficult. There is a large measure of truth in the statement that those who control the examination dictate the work of the institutions preparing for it. The pejorative connotation of the expression 'backwash effect' implies the conviction of those who use it that the influence of examinations cannot be for good. These critics argue that an external examination imposes on many schools a common syllabus which may stifle initiative and militate against the diversity among schools which they consider natural and right. They further argue that the examination, by its very nature, must depress the status of the aesthetic and creative aspects of education—which, they would maintain, are non-examinable—while exalting the status of memorizing and factual knowledge.

Few would deny the force of these arguments. Yet not all would share the critics' pessimism. The aim should be to improve rather than abolish examination procedures. Among teachers at all levels and in every official report from Robbins to Plowden, there is now a flow of discussion, probably unprecedented, of wide and important issues with implications for examination procedures. More specifically, this is a time of positive criticism of the procedures themselves, of research and experiment, of active modification, and the introduction of hitherto untried techniques. It is significant that universities, traditionally resistant to change, are now discovering researches into examination procedures conducted elsewhere and adding their own contributions (Jahoda, M. et al. 1967). It is significant, too, that the newest school examination, the Certificate of Secondary Education, is more flexible than its predecessors. The schools presenting candidates for the c.s.e. have three options available to them: external examinations on a syllabus provided by the local Regional Board; external examinations on a syllabus devised by a school or group of schools to take account of special local conditions; and examinations internally set and externally moderated. The schools are free to mix these options, if they choose, for different groups of candidates or different subjects. Another major difference between this and previous school examinations is the much greater degree of control of the C.S.E. by the teachers themselves.

The efficiency of examination procedures

As Morris points out, 'examinations are tools, designed for various purposes and to perform various operations' (Morris, N., 1961, p. 1). The purposes examinations serve were discussed earlier. But, as with other tools, examination procedures cannot serve such purposes unless they are technically efficient. The criterion of efficiency may be stated as follows: an examination procedure must discriminate among the persons examined both reliably and validly.

A) DISCRIMINATION

The examination procedure must reflect differences in the attribute concerned which are presumed to exist among the persons examined. The extent to which a single person manifests the attribute becomes meaningful only in relation to the corresponding manifestations of others. We are impressed when told that someone can run a mile in under four minutes because we already know that such a feat is beyond most of us. But if we are told that someone has achieved 75 per cent in a geography examination, we withhold (or ought to withhold) judgment until we know how others have done in the same examination.

B) RELIABILITY

But discrimination, though a necessary, is not a sufficient condition of a good examination. The procedure must be consistent in the discriminations it makes. Scores, that is, must be reliable.

The direct method usually available in the physical sciences, in which a number of observations of an attribute (weight, chemical composition, stellar distance) are made on the same individual, is inappropriate for estimating the reliability of an examination procedure. Since the attribute to be measured is itself subject to modification by the very process of measuring it, an alternative method must be employed. Independent measurements are made on the attribute (essay, discussion) for each of a number of individuals (persons), and the number on each is reduced to two. If the same scale is used* for both sets of measurements, the correlation coefficient between them furnishes an index of their consistency—the 'reliability' coefficient—and from it can be inferred the 'standard error' of measurement.

The general model sketched above—two measurements on each of a number of individuals—is applicable to several different situations. The first and second sets of measurements may be derived from the same examination repeated, or from two different examinations purporting to measure the same attribute. The period of time between the two administrations may be short or long. Alternatively, the second set of measurements may be hypothetical. From the internal relations of the marks assigned on a single administration of an examination it is frequently possible to infer the hypothetical correlation between scores on this examination and scores on a similar ('parallel') examination that might have been substituted for it on the single occasion of examining. Though hypothetical, this last form of reliability coefficient corresponds to a situation which for the candidate at all events is highly realistic. Obviously the paper actually set is not the only possible one. It may be admirable in content and conform to the best canons of constructional technique. But no one (except, perhaps, the compiler) would seriously maintain that no other paper, equally excellent and *equally acceptable for the purpose in hand*, might have been set in its place. It is improbable, to say the least, that for individual candidates the outcome with this other paper would have been identical to that with the paper actually set.

Similar considerations apply to the other forms of 'reliability coefficient', based on the administration of the same or a different examination on two occasions separated by an interval of time. These forms, too, are realistic in that they relate to the possibility of choosing a different date for the examination. While not entirely fortuitous, the

---

* It is obvious, though insufficiently recognized, that if the scales are *not* the same, the reliability coefficient and the inferred standard error of measurement will be misleading. It is conceivable (though unlikely) that for two examiners A and B, marking the same set of scripts, the correlation coefficient is unity. But if A is a severe and B a lenient marker, or if A spreads his marks out more than B, then individual examinees will receive different marks, despite this perfect correlation.

choice of date is nevertheless to some extent arbitrary. For individual candidates it is unlikely that the outcome, whether with the same or a different examination, would have been identical if for the sake of administrative convenience a different date had been chosen. The point to note is that the scores candidates obtain will be accepted as measures of their relative performances, whatever date is chosen.

So far the discussion has related to the variability arising from the choice of one examination paper or another, or of one administration date or another. When the candidates have sat the chosen paper on the appointed day, another problem of variability arises. Cox (1966, p. 2) records a number of studies of the extent of marker unreliability; the best known in Britain is that of Hartog and Rhodes (1935). Using scripts written for examinations at university level in various subjects including English essays, mathematics and history, they found that the marks awarded to the same script varied over a disturbingly wide range from one marker to another. Intercorrelations among markers were in the main low and variable; in history, a typical example, they averaged 0·44 and ranged from 0·8 to −0·4. Other studies, notably the French Carnegie inquiry, showed similar results. With medical examinations, Bull (1956) found a correlation of 0·3 when the same examiner re-marked the same scripts after an interval of several weeks. In Israel, papers set in the Bagrut (matriculation) examination are marked independently by two examiners as a matter of routine. Pilliner (1961) found that the inter-marker correlation in Hebrew composition ranged in a sample of eleven schools from 0·83 for one school to −0·05 for another with an average value of 0·39; in Hebrew language the corresponding range for the same schools was 0·66 to 0·36, averaging 0·45. Moreover, although in Hebrew composition the *overall* average marks awarded were practically identical, there were highly significant discrepancies among the school averages. In Hebrew language a similar interaction was observed, and in addition the overall averages were significantly different.

H. J. Taylor (1964) investigated the difference in standard from one marker to another in the matriculation examination conducted by the Indian University of Gauhati. For each of a number of school subjects the scripts were thoroughly mixed before they were sent in batches of about 250 to the numerous examiners employed. Because of this randomization, the expectation of average quality was the same for all batches, and the effect of sampling error could be allowed for. Taylor found startlingly different batch averages with different markers. In English, the highest of twenty median marks was 46 and the lowest 18. In Indian, the highest of eighteen median marks was 51 and the lowest 34. Moreover, foreknowledge of the passmark by the examiners affected the distribution of marks. On or just above the known passmark the concentration of marks was unduly high. Immediately below the passmark a gap occurred.

In short, in studies of this sort with examinations of the traditional type, inter-marker inconsistency is the normal finding. Inevitably the question comes to mind: how consistent is the marking in public examinations in Britain? Evidence is hard to come by. Though they presumably conduct trials of consistency, the examining boards do not make the results generally available. An exception is a recent publication of one of the boards reporting reliabilities of 0·97 and above between the marks awarded by examiners from different boards to the same set of 'A' level history scripts. Unfortunately, the fact that marks and comments from the first examiner were left on the scripts for the second examiner to see totally invalidates the inquiry (Pilliner 1965).

Much research effort has gone into the attempt to raise marker consistency in essay-type examinations. In Britain, Cast (1939) was responsible for the definitive studies of 'analytic' marking, and Wiseman (1949) and Finlayson (1951) for those of 'impression' marking. Using the analytic procedure, the American Stalnaker (1951, pp. 495–530) found that marker reliability decreased as the level of sophistication of the essay increased. Though it is hazardous to generalize, the evidence suggests that, marker for marker, the impression procedure is slightly less reliable than the analytic. However, the analytic method is the more laborious and time-consuming. In terms of marker hours, several impression markers are no more expensive than one analytic marker. With short essays written by eleven-year-old schoolchildren, Wiseman obtained a reliability of about 0·9 for the total or average over a group of four markers. Finlayson reported similar results with children one year older, and showed in addition the unreliability of a single essay as a measure of a child's 'essay-writing' ability. In an unpublished study, in which he also used a team of markers, Wilkinson (1952) found marker reliabilities of the same order with essays written by children aged 14. He also investigated the effect of fatigue on marking standards. With initially randomized scripts his average mark per hour tended to increase and the scatter of the marks he awarded per hour to decrease.

Pilliner (1968) made a comparative study of the two methods, using English essays written by Israeli pupils aged 16 to 17 and marked by Israeli teachers of English. Again the pool of four impression markers was superior in reliability to a single analytic marker. This study also showed that the pooled marks of several analytic markers correlated about 0·9 with the pooled marks of several impression markers. This suggests that basically, when individual idiosyncrasies are ironed out, the two different procedures are measuring similar qualities. Probably 'impression' and 'analytic' marking are best thought of as two extremes on a continuum. Different markers operate at different points along the continuum and so does even the same marker at different times or for different purposes.

Cox has recently criticized the use of several markers on the ground that reliability may be increased at the expense of meaning. 'The improvement does not represent greater agreement on the value of essays, it is merely a device for getting the same mark every time' (Cox 1966, p. 8). There is some substance to this criticism if each marker is highly self-consistent and if at the same time each agrees poorly with everyone else. Under these conditions, the mark re-mark correlation, of the total (or average) of them all will be both positive and high. But this correspondence will be independent of the differences which presumably exist in the merits of the scripts. Instead, it will express the obduracy with which each marker maintains his own judgments, a reflection of enduring personal idiosyncrasies, an agreement to disagree. On the other hand, if there is a fair measure of initial agreement among the individual markers about merits of the scripts, the aggregated marks from a team of markers will be a valid expression of the team's consensus of opinion. Cox's criticism is then invalid.

A feature common to both methods is the attempt to improve marker consistency by increasing the number of measures. With the analytic procedure the scheme can be summarized as 'so much for this aspect, so much for that'. With Wiseman's adaptation of the impression method the increase is in the number of markers.

An obvious extension of the same principle is to increase the number of questions asked. The examining boards have for long employed this method for some parts of the papers they set, particularly at 'O' level, and at the university level there has been some experiment with the method, particularly in the medical schools (Hubbard and Clemans 1961).

The logical extreme of the method of increasing the number of questions is the so-called 'objective' test. Before embarking on a discussion of objective methods of examining, it is perhaps worth pointing out that by 'subjective' in the present context most people mean 'requiring judgment' and by 'objective' they mean 'automatic'. In this sense, of the three aspects common to all examination procedures, setting, sitting and assessing, the first two are inevitably subjective. Only the third can be either subjective or objective.

Historically, it is not entirely clear whether the original intention of objective forms of examining was to reduce the labour of marking, as, for example, when the United States faced the problem of building an army at short notice when she entered the First World War, and made extensive use of the Army Alpha and Beta tests for selection purposes; or to reduce marker inconsistency, as with the 11-plus and similar procedures; or to serve psychological ends, as with the Binet-Simon test. The history of objective tests is well discussed by P. E. Vernon (1961, ch. 1). Certainly they serve all three purposes. Provided that the group to be tested is large enough, the decrease in the labour of marking more than offsets the considerable increase in labour involved in the production of a well-constructed objective test. Because the process of marking is automatic, marker reliability is—or ought to be—perfect. Psychological tests employing objective marking procedures proliferate, particularly in the United States where, it is interesting to note, there is an increasing volume of protest against the invasions of 'personal privacy' by tests of this nature (*American Psychologist* 1967). The United States is also the scene of the most extensive development and the widest use of objective tests for educational purposes at all levels. In Britain, development has been slower and more cautious, though a great deal of research has been done: in England especially by the National Foundation for Industrial Psychology and the National Foundation for Educational Research; in Scotland by the Scottish Council for Research in Education and the Education Department of the University of Edinburgh. The use made of objective tests has been restricted in the main to the primary and secondary levels of education. At the tertiary level their use has hitherto been minimal: university teachers in general remain sceptical or even antipathetic, though it is fair to say that even at this level there is now greater interest than hitherto in the potentialities of this form of examining.

Whatever the attitude to objective techniques may be, it is a fact that the technical principles of examination construction have been worked out in the context of these techniques. Though of general application, the use made in Britain of these principles in other examination procedures is inadequate. Oliver castigates the examining boards for their neglect: 'A fundamental concept in measurement—and examining is a form of measurement—is the "standard error of score". What is known about the standard error of a mark in any G.C.E. subject examined by any examining body?' (Oliver 1961, p. 178).

That these principles can be usefully applied in the study of high-level examinations of subjective type is evident from the work of Parkyn in New Zealand (1959, vol. 1).

As examples of the technical quality of objective tests, it may be stated that the correlation between two N.F.E.R. or two Moray House reasoning or attainment tests administered up to forty days apart, is typically 0·95 or above; and that the coefficient of equivalence (based on the notion of substituting one test for another on the single occasion of testing) is rarely below 0·98. It is not suggested that the traditional form of examination can ever achieve this degree of technical excellence. Rather is it suggested that those concerned with other types of examination should make it their business to know *something* of their technical quality—and of the implications of this knowledge. We might then be spared the criticism of a distinguished American educator: 'The illusion that a grade of C on an "A" level examination is a C, is a C, is a C when it is probably a case of a B or a C or a D, is a cruel illusion for students, and a foolish illusion for the universities that make distinctions between grades of C and B' (Valentine 1967, p. 14).

c) VALIDITY

Though the discussion of validity has been left till last, in order of importance it undoubtedly comes first.

As with the psychologists' 'intelligence' or the chemists' 'affinity', so the psychometrists have appropriated the term 'validity' from common usage and employed it—some would say sterilized it—to convey special restricted meanings. 'Predictive' validity, 'concurrent' validity, 'construct' validity—all have essentially statistical connotations. In contrast, 'content' validity has more regard for educational considerations. To encompass all these meanings, a rather broad definition is required: the validity of an examination procedure is the extent to which it does what it is designed to do.

Predictive validity will be discussed first. Recognition that this is one overriding requirement has sometimes been taken to mean that reliability is of minor importance. Interpreted broadly, this could mean that if two alternative examination procedures correlate equally well with the criterion, they will do equally well, even though they place candidates in quite different orders. Candidates might be excused for disagreeing. Although improbable, it is not inconceivable that a validity of 0·70 may be associated with a predictor reliability as low as 0·49—quite inadequate for most purposes.

Reliability is, in fact, a necessary though not a sufficient condition. Spearman wrote: 'The relations of reliability and validity are one-sided. Low reliability necessarily involves low validity, but the converse is not true' (Spearman 1936). More recently, Cronbach has commented: 'Even those investigators who regard reliability as a pale shadow of the more vital matter of validity cannot avoid considering the reliability of their measures. No validity coefficient and no factor analysis can be interpreted without some appropriate estimate of the magnitude of the error of measurement' (Cronbach 1951, p. 297).

If reliability has been neglected by many compilers of examinations, validity has fared even worse. This is partly because the criterion in a predictive study is often years away. With a definable criterion at the end of that period, and with a 'captive' population, a follow-up study is not difficult. It is otherwise when the criterion is more nebulous and the population tends to 'escape'. Probably this is why there is a descending order of frequency of such studies from 11-plus to 'O' or 'A' level; from 'O' or 'A' level to university degree; and from degree to some later criterion of 'success'—by this time extremely difficult to define. This is also why the corresponding validity coefficients tend to be in descending order of magnitude. Matters are made worse by increase in predictor as well as criterion unreliability at the secondary and tertiary levels; and, worse still, by narrowing in the spread of ability following increasingly stringent selection. Eventually a point is reached at which errors of measurement inherent in both predictor and criterion are comparable with or even exceed in size the discriminations both attempt to make. As yet the educationist has nothing corresponding to the physicist's electron microscope to fall back on.

Because of the time-lag in predictive validation, test constructors often substitute 'concurrent' procedures. If an existing test is known to be a good predictor of some criterion, then a second test correlating highly with the first should serve about as well. But the limits are surprisingly wide. Given that two tests correlate 0·96 with each other, and given that one of them has a validity coefficient of 0·80 in respect of some criterion, then that of the other must lie between 0·94 and 0·60. With examinations instead of tests, both reliability and validity are likely to be lower, and the limits correspondingly wider. If 0·70 is substituted for both the 0·96 and the 0·80 in the previous example, the limits widen to approximately +1 and zero! In addition, more often than not it would be impracticable in the first place to arrange two allegedly comparable examinations and to have the same candidates sit both. Altogether, 'concurrent' validation for examinations is scarcely a viable procedure.

Earlier a distinction was made between definable and nebulous criteria. From a statistical standpoint, the more definite and the more quantifiable the criterion, the better it is. From this point of view, G.C.E. 'O' level marks are superior as a criterion to some vague measure of post-university success. But a further distinction can be made from an educational standpoint. A criterion, though statistically convenient, may be educationally undesirable.

This brings us to the concept of 'content' validity. In an excellent discussion Wiseman (1961, ch. 6) distinguishes between two ways in which a criterion may possess content validity; (a) it may sample and measure what has been taught, that is, it may be geared to the syllabus; (b) it may measure the degree of achievement of aims and purposes, that is, it may be geared to educational objectives in the area concerned. Wiseman chooses the second. The syllabus is to be regarded 'merely as a means to an end, as a way in which the teacher tries to achieve certain specific aims or goals'. The criterion is valid to the extent that it measures 'the degree to which these aims have been attained'. He goes on: 'The syllabus-content approach tends to perpetuate ineffective educational practices: it is a reactionary instrument helping to encapsulate method within the shell of tradition and accepted practice.' In contrast, 'The goal-orientated test is exactly the opposite: it evaluates learning—and teaching—in terms of the aims of the curriculum, and so fosters critical awareness, good method and functional content.'

Wiseman recognizes explicitly the influence any examination procedure exerts on the work done in preparation for it, and challenges the compiler to 'analyse and clarify the aims of the curriculum being tested'. He points out the inadequacy of blanket-phrases such as 'the fostering of aesthetic sensibility' and 'the inculcation of the critical faculty'. Difficult though it is, the task must be undertaken of analysing phrases of this sort in search of the underlying skills or attitudes and of expressing these as observable and measurable elements of behaviour. Cureton (1951, p. 652) makes the same point. After discussing command of fundamental processes as one aim, he says: 'Those educators who insist (and rightly, we believe) that other aims are at least equally important, and in the aggregate more important, could advance their cause most rapidly and effectively by setting about the task of specifying the materials, actions, situations and scoring criteria implied by the abstract terms which define these other aims. They will find the task difficult but in most cases possible. When they have accomplished it, they will find that teachers will use the materials, set up appropriate school situations, and teach the desired acts.'

The swing away from the syllabus-geared to the goal-oriented approach is increasingly observable. Bloom's *Taxonomy of Educational Objectives* (1956) is becoming better known in this country. Oppenheim *et al.* (1967, pp. 341–51) have laid the groundwork for further discussion of objectives at the university level. Himmelweit (1967, p. 362) has pointed out the tendency of predictive validity studies to turn into analyses of the content validities of the examination procedures themselves. Universities and colleges of education conduct courses on curriculum study.

'Forward-looking' and 'backward-looking'

The distinction between predictive and content validity corresponds broadly to the distinction between 'forward-looking' and 'backward-looking' examination procedures. An example of a procedure that is 'forward-looking' in intention is the now disappearing 11-plus. Examples of procedures intentionally 'backward-looking' are the G.C.E. 'O' and 'A' level examinations. But whatever the intention, in practice examination procedures have a way of playing both roles. As well as an indicator of potential, the 11-plus is a record of present performance based on earlier learning. As well as records of achievement to date, high or low marks in G.C.E. examinations are accepted as pointers to the probability of more or less success in institutions of higher education.

This dual role is not only as it should be, but as it must be. Bronowski sums up the situation exactly (1960, p. 114): 'The human predictor interprets the signal by an act of recognition which puts it into some general category. We then assume that the future will have some general likeness with futures we have met before which followed this kind of signal, and this is the kind of future we prepare for.' He continues (p. 115): 'The predictor . . . makes no larger claim than that the future can in general be predicted, within defined limits of uncertainty. And since there are uncertainties the prediction will sometimes be wrong.'

Concluding discussion

Earlier it was stated that examinations, in common with other aspects of the British educational system, are now being subjected to critical reappraisal. The ferment is wide-spread. A complete issue of *Universities Quarterly* (June 1967) has been devoted to the problems of examining in universities. It raises many issues, answers some questions, and suggests many others to which answers are desirable. The emphasis throughout is on the research now in progress and on the necessity for its extension. Research is also under way at other levels. In Scotland a large inquiry is now being carried out into the relative efficiency for university selection of the traditional Scottish Leaving Certificate examination and a completely objective examination made available by the Educational Testing Service, Princeton (see also the paper by Butcher). Also in Scotland an experimental form of geography test, completely objective, has been administered alongside the traditional form to a sample of 1,000 candidates in the Scottish Education Department's 'O' level examination. Results are still awaited. In England, Miller is experimenting with high-level aptitude tests. In England, too, the new General Certificate of Education is characterized by a degree of flexibility without precedent in the field of public examinations. Even its predecessors in this field are becoming infected with the new spirit of inquiry. The 'Use of English' tests associated with Oliver are now employed by several examining boards. There are indeed signs of increasing awareness in several directions on the part of the boards: the possibility of using new procedures; the necessity to bring methods of evaluation up to date; and the desirability of better public relations.

The common thread in all of this is the increasing realization at all levels of the positive role of examinations in the educational system. In the past the tendency has been to see them as isolated to some extent from the system, rather like industrial quality control tests occurring at various points in a production line. Up to a point, the analogy serves. But in the educational process, not only is a rather large proportion of the product tested, but also the effects of the test on the product are considerable and apt to spread to the untested remainder. More and more it is accepted that for the feedback of examinations to be educationally beneficial they must be geared to objectives, clearly defined and educationally acceptable, and not merely reflect and perpetuate existing syllabuses. The hard thinking and discussion required in the explicit formulation of these objectives is itself a valuable by-product. To quote Wiseman once more: 'No teacher who attempts such an analysis is ever quite the same again' (1961, p. 147).

An increase is predictable in the volume of experiment directed at improving examinations in this direction. Various new techniques will be tried, some subjective, others objective. Recent advances in the second category are remarkable. After studying the examples provided, for example, in Bloom's *Taxonomy* and weighing up their potentialities, only the most prejudiced critic could still maintain 'the myth of the multiple-choice question as a superficial exercise—one that requires little thought, less insight, and no understanding' (Educational Testing Service *et al.* 1963, p. 1). The unprejudiced and original thinker will be impressed by what has already been achieved in this area and will wish to go on from there.

This does not mean that subjective procedures will be elbowed out. It does mean that in attempting to measure the achievement of educational objectives, which may well be composite, subjective methods will be more appropriate for some purposes, and objective methods for others. 'Render unto Caesar . . .'

One final question remains. It is implicit in the following comment from Montgomery (1965, p. 12): 'A considerable amount of research has been carried out . . . into the actual mechanics of . . . examinations, but perhaps less has been done to probe the fundamental reasons for having them.' After reviewing the multitude of research reports, mainly of a technical nature, few would deny the existence of the imbalance Montgomery indicates. In the area of examinations, as in other areas, it is easier to answer—or to seek answers to—the question 'How?' than the question 'Why?'

It is difficult to envisage a highly developed society without examinations of some sort. 'Whether we like it or not,' says Himmelweit, 'society will continue to use the degree as a predictor device' (1967, p. 364). If this is accepted, the 'Why?' question changes its impact. It is to be answered by the development and specification of sound educational objectives. The present climate of inquiry gives reason to hope that in this highly important sense the balance will be redressed.

John Williams

The Curriculum: Some Patterns of Development and Designs for Evaluation

In this paper I shall try to give an impression of the general lines along which curriculum research seems to be progressing in Britain. I shall mention several of the major curricular projects, but cannot hope to give anything like an adequate picture of them. Particular projects will be cited only as instances of general trends.

The paper falls into two sections: in the first, curriculum *developments* will be examined in the light of seven general features that would seem to characterize curricular innovation; in the second, curriculum *evaluations* will be analysed with a view to the eduction of some directives for further activity in this relatively neglected area of research. In structuring the survey in this way, the intention is to introduce some representative researches, and, in addition, to highlight their significance in relation to a broader framework.

It might be argued that many of those projects concerned with curriculum development incorporate an unofficial evaluative component—in that they allow for the weeding-out of items that prove 'unsuccessful'—and that the distinction between the two kinds of research which is implied by the organization of this paper is therefore artificial. Certainly some developmental projects do embody an evaluative component; in such projects the initial versions of a curriculum are subjected to trial runs, and, where these trials indicate that the curriculum is lacking in some respect, steps are taken to modify it in the direction of better functioning.

In principle, such an ameliorative process could be carried out to great effect. Usually, however, the evaluative procedure adopted in such cases, although better than nothing, and, in its way, quite plausible, is unsystematic and lacks objectivity. Teachers will edit trial texts 'in the light of their experience' and make alterations where these seem to be needed; they will also meet one another and specialists for detailed discussions of ways of improving a curriculum. Thus they will proceed, by a series of acts of faith, conjecture, and—we might hope—reason, to seek out, and then to 'iron out' the faults in a curriculum. At the very worst, the result of this procedure will be a course of learning the parts of which will not be glaringly incompatible and the whole of which will be vaguely 'viable'.

Unfortunately, where evaluation has been carried out with so little guarantee of objectivity, there will be very little to prove that the curriculum has exceeded these minimal standards, and, if it has exceeded them, in which ways and to what extent it has done so. If we are to obtain information of this more precise and communicable kind, we must resort to the use of systematic and objective techniques of evaluation, some of the characteristics of which are exemplified in the second section of this paper.

Some patterns of curriculum development

In this section I shall consider curriculum development from the point of view of seven features that tend to characterize it. Each of these I shall illustrate by reference to projects that are being carried out in Great Britain. Usually projects will embody more than one of these features, but frequently a project can be seen to take most of its shape from one of them.

A) IMPROVING THE STRUCTURE OF CURRICULAR CONTENT

In many areas it can be seen that a curriculum could be improved if its content were structured in a way that would facilitate learning. In certain areas, such as those of mathematics and the physical sciences, it is possible to make great improvements in the coherence and sequencing of a curriculum on grounds that are largely logical. It is in such areas as these that the most convincing changes in structure have been made; but there have also been attempts to effect such changes in other areas.

Perhaps the need for careful structuring of a curriculum is most apparent in the case of primary school mathematics. At this stage decisions must be made about the foundations upon which subsequent learning in this highly sequential subject must be built.

A project in which a great deal of attention has been given to these questions of structure is the Nuffield Mathematics Teaching Project (Sealey 1967). The objective of this project has been to devise a contemporary approach to the teaching of mathematics to children between the ages of five and thirteen. Guides for teachers have been produced for three main categories of subject matter: (a) relating computation and structure; (b) relating shape to size; (c) relating graphs, algebra and statistics. Apart from guides leading from stage to stage in each of the main categories, 'weaving' guides are produced, crossing the boundaries of these categories, where appropriate.

A project that aims to restructure subject matter in a field in which it is less obvious how to do so than in mathematics is the Nuffield Programme in Linguistics and English Teaching. This is based at the Communication Research Centre of the Department of General Linguistics at University College, London. The project is manned by school-teachers trained in linguistics, together with three research linguists. This team is devoting itself to the investigation of the possibilities of improving our ways of presenting the English language in school work. It is hoped that the outcome will be sets of materials that will help teachers to overcome the difficulties to the learner that are posed, for example, by traditional grammar.

The representation of academic experts in this latter project perhaps emphasizes the importance of the basic reorientation that is necessary for the restructuring of curricula.

B) REORGANIZING CURRICULAR CONTENT IN ACCORDANCE WITH PSYCHOLOGICAL PRINCIPLES

As in the case of other bases for curricular reform, the use of psychological principles as a criterion is more or less universal—but in some projects their use is more marked than in others.

A project in which the influence of such principles is crucial is the Psychology and Mathematics Project (Skemp 1962, 1963a, b). This provides a five-year course up to 'O' level consisting of a blend of modern and traditional mathematics, which has been devised in accordance with Dr Skemp's theories on schematic learning and reflective intelligence, which are essentially Piagetian in origin. Care has been taken to analyse components of the curriculum in terms of kinds of knowledge and psychological abilities that they presuppose, and to ensure that the manner and timing of their presentation are suitable to the readiness of the learner to assimilate them.

Another approach to the teaching of mathematics that is heavily laced with a well worked-out system of psychological principles is that of Z. P. Dienes (1963, 1965). This has not been sponsored as a 'project' yet; but it is reaching the schools through several sets of books and other materials, and is likely to exercise a considerable influence on the primary school curriculum. Dienes has formulated and tested several principles of mathematical learning, including his better known cyclic theory of learning and principle of multi-embodiment. Using these as guides to an approach to teaching, and, in some cases, to the selection of curricular content, he is developing ways of teaching primary school children sets, relations, propositional logic, vectors, groups and many other mathematically important topics.

Hitherto, it seems that it is the mathematics curriculum that has received the greatest amount of attention from theorists with a clear psychological position; but it is no doubt only a matter of time before some of the more appropriate of the available principles of learning (such as those of Piaget) are taken as guide-lines for the development of curricula in other content areas—particularly in that of primary school science.

c) THE INFLUENCE OF TEACHING METHODS AND MATERIALS UPON THE CURRICULUM

It is difficult to say in which direction influence between, on the one hand, methods and materials, and, on the other, curricular content, has passed. No doubt each has to some extent determined the other.

An obvious factor in the influence of methods and materials upon curricula is that pupil-centred methods and materials permit diversity of lesson content. Programmed instruction and language laboratories obviously permit pupils in the same learning-group to study different topics at the same time. Another such factor takes the form of the facilities that are available for concrete presentation of material to be learned. The use of films and television makes possible a much more realistic, less formalized presentation of the content of geography, applied science, etc. The use of tape-recorders makes possible the employment of oral approaches to the learning of languages—which is likely to result in an emphasis on the spoken use of a language instead of the traditional emphasis on its grammatical and written characteristics.

The Nuffield Language Teaching Materials Project provides an example of the way in which new techniques have facilitated the use of a new approach to teaching. This project is concerned with the preparation of courses in French (for pupils between the ages of eight and thirteen), and in German, Spanish and Russian (for pupils between the ages of eleven and thirteen). In this project the emphasis is placed upon the use of language for communicating, and each course is introduced by a purely oral phase, which is later followed by reading and writing. Wherever possible new teaching techniques are used, and a great deal of use is made of audio-visual aids. As part of the work of this project a survey of children between the ages of eight and thirteen is being carried out, in an attempt to gather information on their linguistic performance and main centres of interest.

Another Nuffield project—the 'Resources for learning' project—is devoted especially to the study of the use that can be made of new techniques and methods in the school. No doubt this will demonstrate clearly how the implements of education can influence the subject matter with which it works. Among the questions being investigated are: In which ways can programmed instruction, television and other media best be used? How can timetables be rearranged, children be grouped, and staff be deployed so as to make the best use of these resources? What are the architectural, social and economic repercussions? How can we ensure that these changes bring about real benefit to the pupil's learning?

d) THE BREAKING DOWN OF SUBJECT MATTER BOUNDARIES

Sometimes the factor that prompts curricular change is the obsolescence of boundary-lines between subject matter areas. As more basic ways of conceiving different subject matters are adopted, continuity can be seen where little existed before. For example, in many courses in modern mathematics it is sometimes difficult to distinguish among geometry, algebra and arithmetic, for many parts of these may be approached by means of a single unifying set of concepts. Again, as greater emphasis is placed upon the illustration or application of academic subject matters in real situations, the interrelation of the corresponding subject areas becomes more important. This has been acknowledged for some time in the case of history and geography, for many of the more realistic applications of which it is better to think in terms of the single discipline of 'social studies'.

A good illustration of an explicit attempt to effect such an amalgamation of different school subjects is the Nuffield Combined Science Project. This was initiated because of the clear educational demand that biology, chemistry and physics should be taught as a single subject. It embodies material already developed for the Nuffield 'O' level courses, and is suitable for children of the age-range 11 to 13 years.

An extreme illustration is to be found in the form of the Interdisciplinary Enquiry project (I.D.E.). This is a project based at Goldsmith's College. Its aims are well expressed in the following excerpt from one of the publications of the Goldsmith Curriculum Laboratory (University of London, Goldsmith's College Curriculum Laboratory 1965):

'Our first pillar is . . . *enquiry*, enquiry which is active in process and often leads to action. Secondly we believe that once one starts to enquire into and attempt to solve fundamental problems, the barriers between subjects, which seem formidable when they are dividing up a fixed body of knowledge, seem less relevant, and the work necessarily becomes *interdisciplinary*: we have to use a variety of disciplines in formulating the problem, creating hypotheses as to its solution, working on and communicating our findings . . . Our concern can therefore be identified as being with *interdisciplinary enquiry in the secondary school*, which we shorten into I.D.E.'

E) THE INTEGRATION OF THE WHOLE
SCHOOL CURRICULUM

Occasionally, the necessity to change the structure of the school has led to quite basic reorganizations of the curriculum. In some cases such reorganization has brought with it a careful reconsideration of how subject areas relate to one another and to the goals of teaching. In many cases, the change-over to comprehensive schooling can be seen to have affected the curriculum in this kind of way. Similarly, the Nuffield Foundation and the Schools Council are collaborating on a project ('Society and the young school-leaver') which aims to plan changes in the curriculum that will be appropriate to the raising of the school leaving age to sixteen. The aim is to redesign the curriculum for the early school-leaver along the general lines recommended in the Newsom Report. An attempt is being made to reorganize teaching in such a way that its relevance to the present interests and future life of the early school-leaver will become more apparent.

F) THE INTEGRATION OF SCHOOL TEACHING WITH SPECIFIC SOCIAL DEMANDS

To a certain extent this can be said to be an objective for which most curriculum reform must aim. An almost invariable outcome of the streamlining process of planning a curriculum in relation to specified objectives is the alignment of teaching with the subsequent functioning of pupils in society. However, in some cases the objective is sought more explicitly than in others. The 'Society and the young school-leaver' project mentioned in the last section is one example of a project that is largely geared towards the achievement of this objective.

Another project with this objective in view is the 'Mathematics in education and industry' project which has been organized by the Industrial Committee of the Mathematics Association. Among the activities of this project, which has been organized primarily in an attempt to effect a liaison between education and industry, are: attempts to modernize the structure of advanced school mathematics examinations; the introduction into the school syllabus of a great deal more statistics; the introduction of computers and computing into the schools.

G) CHANGES OF THE CURRICULUM IN RELATION TO THE PUPIL'S AGE

In many cases the most prominent characteristic of curriculum change has been that topics and subjects that have hitherto been taught at a later stage in the pupil's education are now introduced at an earlier stage. The arguments for doing this are various, but some of them are the following:

1. There may be subjects that are better learned at an earlier age. It is fairly obvious that subjects involving physical skills, such as playing the piano, should be introduced at an early age; but it has been suggested that certain skills that are usually regarded as more 'conceptual' in nature, such as speaking foreign languages, are more readily learned

at an earlier stage in the child's education than at a later stage. The Nuffield Foreign Languages Project, which we have mentioned above, is a good example of the introduction at an early stage in the child's education of topics that have formerly been reserved for later stages.

2. In the case of mathematics, a great many of the more basic aspects of the teaching content consist of very simple notions. It is both necessary and feasible for the child to become acquainted with these notions at an early age, for they constitute very powerful interpretive tools—which will help him to understand the mathematics that he encounters later—and are ideally simple for introduction at an early age.

3. The obvious argument for introducing topics at an early age is that we can thus enable the child to cover more material during the course of his 'educational life'.

In addition to the Nuffield Language Teaching and Mathematics Projects, the Nuffield General Science Teaching Project is an interesting example of the advancement to the primary school stage of a subject that has traditionally been confined to the secondary school. Much success is being achieved in attempts to introduce young children to some of the procedures and ideas of science.*

Designs for curriculum evaluation

INTRODUCTION

It is not inconceivable that a new curriculum, while giving everyone the impression that it is excellent, should be inferior to an alternative, or inferior to what it might be. For this reason we are prompted to look for objective proof of a curriculum's worth. How do we obtain such proof? The obvious steps to take would be first to state clearly and in objective terms the details of the outcomes we demand of the curriculum, and then to construct instruments and procedures that we might apply to the task of establishing whether these outcomes have been achieved.

It is becoming usual to talk of two kinds of evaluation:

* Further information about the Nuffield projects can be obtained from Nuffield Lodge, Regents Park, London N W 1.

1. *Summative evaluation*

This consists of the assessment of the final effects of a curriculum. It enables us to compare the effectiveness of one curriculum with the effectiveness of another, or with that required by standards that we have set, and thus to make decisions concerning either whether we should use it or in what form we should use it.

2. *Formative evaluation*

This consists of the assessment of the effectiveness of a curriculum during the course of its development. It enables us to detect how the curriculum might be improved in such a way that its parts become more compatible both with one another and with the objectives that we have set for the curriculum.

It may appear that there are insurmountable obstacles to evaluation of these kinds. Obstacles there certainly are, but there are also ways of surmounting them. In the following presentation of some of the kinds of curriculum evaluation that have been and are being carried out in Great Britain, I shall first list some of the difficulties of curriculum evaluation, then examine the ways in which various attempts at evaluation have coped with these, and, finally, list some of the features of such attempts that might usefully serve as pointers of the directions that future evaluative studies might take.

THE PROBLEMS OF CURRICULUM EVALUATION

1. *Which criteria should we use?*

Let us first consider this at the level of the actual tests that we might use in evaluating a curriculum. Suppose that we wished to choose or construct a test for comparing the effectiveness of two mathematics curricula, in one of which traditional topics were taught and in the other of which modern mathematical topics were taught. Of what should our test consist? If it covered only traditional topics it would favour one curriculum, while if it covered only modern topics it would favour the other. Presumably it might also cover only those topics that the two curricula shared, or topics that appeared in neither curriculum but for which both might be expected to prepare the pupil indirectly; but, even in this case, the danger of bias is not avoided.

An apparent way out would be for us to state clearly what we wanted from *any* curriculum and then to devise a test which was appropriate for the measurement of this *whether or not* the particular curricula under evaluation catered for it. That a curriculum did *not* cater for it would be a criticism of the curriculum.

Clearly, before we are able to take any of these courses, we must be very sure of our educational objectives. The task of sorting these out is by no means a simple one, for decisions about objectives depend upon a complex of factors ranging from what is feasible in terms of our teaching resources to what is desirable in terms of our basic social values. However, it would seem that this is a task that we must face. We must specify precisely what it is that we wish to evaluate—right down to the very items of behaviour we expect to be able to extract from the pupil—before we can meaningfully begin to construct our instruments of evaluation.

It will be appreciated from the above that it is only too easy to obtain just about any result imaginable by loading our tests appropriately. In a world of unformulated objectives, it is difficult not to do this—either randomly, out of blindness to our purposes, or systematically, out of blindness to our prejudices. But where a detailed analysis of objectives has been carried out, we at least know what our criteria are and can offer them to others for approval—even if it remains debatable that, in relation to ultimate values that all would accept, they are the correct criteria. Perhaps one can go further than this, and argue that the selection or construction of instruments of evaluation—or, indeed, the evaluation in its entirety—should be carried out by a body that is independent of those innovators that have invested so much in the development of a new curriculum. In a case such as this—where fairness in the selection of criteria is pivotal—prejudice is fatal.

2. *At which level should we judge a curriculum?*

Should a new curriculum in the junior school be assessed for the effects it produces at the end of the junior stage, or should we assess it in terms of its effects at a later stage—say, when the pupil takes his G.C.E. or his degree, or when he actually has to use his education to earn a living in the adult world? Obviously we are not interested only in the *immediate* effects of a curriculum, but obviously, on the other hand, the further we get from the impact that the curriculum has on the pupil, the more likely it is that these effects will have become diluted by intervening influences.

Two means of surmounting this problem have been used. The obvious means is that of assessing the products of the curriculum both immediately and then subsequently through a series of follow-up evaluations. A less obvious means is to use, in the immediate assessment of a curriculum, instruments whose relation to the long-term effects in which we are interested is known. Interesting examples of the employment of both of these strategies are to be found in the evaluations described below.

3. *The problem of change*

As the world changes, so do our educational needs. As these change, so should our teaching—and so it does to some extent. If teaching, and our educational needs, change, our evaluative criteria are liable to become out of date and our evaluations are liable to become irrelevant.

What should be our response to these difficulties? Three solutions suggest themselves and find illustration in some of the evaluative work that has been carried out in Britain. First, since evaluative criteria can assess more, or less general features of the pupil's performance, we should perhaps concentrate upon those features of performance that are more general and thus more likely to be relevant to changed criteria. Secondly, since evaluations can extend over longer or shorter periods of time, we should perhaps favour those that are rapid enough for their results to be relevant to decisions about situations that still exist by the time that the evaluation is completed. Thirdly, where the results of an evaluation that has taken place some time ago are to be used as a basis for decisions about present-day teaching, measures should be taken to establish the relevance to present-day teaching objectives and practices of both the practices that obtained at the time of the evaluation and the criteria that were used.

4. *The atypicality of the conditions of innovation*

Unless we wish to close the stable door after the horses have bolted, we wish also to evaluate a curriculum before it has become established. But our need is for information about what the curriculum will be like *once it has become* established. Moreover, in an evaluation we frequently judge such a curriculum by comparing it with an established curriculum that it might replace. But consider some of the obstacles which might prevent us from obtaining information that is relevant to our purposes, and some of the difficulties in making a fair comparison of two curricula under these circumstances.

If we use those instances of the employment of the new curriculum that already exist, we are likely to find that these 'pioneer cases' have occurred in circumstances that are by no means representative of the circumstances under which the curriculum will eventually need to be implemented if it is generally adopted. For example, the teacher who adopts a new and relatively untried curriculum is likely to be exceptionally talented or exceptionally keen.

If, on the other hand, we introduce the curriculum anew to teachers and classes that we have chosen for their representativeness, we are faced with other problems: the new curriculum may be at a disadvantage because the teacher who uses it is inexperienced in its use, or it may be at an advantage because the teacher and pupils who use it are fired with great enthusiasm over its novelty.

Is there a way out of this dilemma? A means of escaping from some of the difficulties—and one that is illustrated in two of the studies described below—may be, on the one hand, to concentrate our evaluation on those aspects of the curriculum that are unlikely to be affected by its novelty and, on the other, to assess the effect of increasing the teacher's familiarity with the new curriculum.

SOME EXAMPLES OF CURRICULUM EVALUATION

This section will include an account of four of the evaluative studies that have been or are being carried out by the N.F.E.R., together with a study that could well be adapted to the purposes of curriculum evaluation. While the first four of these studies are cases primarily of summative evaluation, it will be seen that they serve also to evaluate in the formative sense. The aim will be partly to acquaint the reader with the investigations, but also to use them as illustrations of the problems outlined above and as points of departure for some of the recommendations that will appear in the concluding section.

A survey of methods of teaching arithmetic

The N.F.E.R. has recently published an account of a survey of methods of teaching arithmetic (Biggs 1967). This can be considered to be a curriculum evaluation. This study was primarily concerned with the effects of the *method* used in teaching, rather than the particular kind of curricular content that was taught; but the method of teaching used has, in many cases, influenced both the emphasis placed upon particular topics within similar curriculum areas and the actual choice of topics taught.

In this survey a battery of tests—covering problem arithmetic, computational skills, mathematical concepts, anxieties about and attitudes towards arithmetic, and general intelligence in the form of verbal reasoning—was administered in the third junior year of eighty-seven schools selected for this purpose from a total of some 7,000 schools that had initially been circularized.

This comprehensive battery was used to compare teaching methods that had been found empirically to fall into five categories: traditional methods; 'uni-model' structural methods, like the Stern and the Cuisenaire, in which only one representation of mathematical situations is used; a 'multi-model' structural method, in the form of the Dienes method, in which a variety of representations of mathematical situations are used; 'motivational' or 'activity' methods; a mixture of motivational and traditional methods.

From a complex analysis of the data obtained by means of the tests, together with data about pupils and schools obtained by means of questionnaires, some highly qualified findings were obtained. For example: uni-model methods were effective only with boys of high intelligence; these methods, together with motivational methods, were more useful where applied remedially than were traditional methods; the abstractive method favoured especially the dull and backward, and although girls taught by it performed poorly and became highly anxious about number work when they were first introduced to it, they later reached a level of attainment higher than that reached by children in other method groups.

This study can be regarded as a case of summative evaluation—for it could be said that its main object was to decide which of several general approaches the teacher should adopt. However, it provides us with information about a variety of different aspects of each approach, and indicates to us how approaches might be improved and how their use might be directed towards particular kinds of pupil. Because the study thus indicates lines of improvement of teaching methods and their application, it can also be regarded as 'formative' in function.

Since it is a simple survey, involving only one testing, and not requiring the pursuit of the pupil's course of learning over a period of time, this study is, in principle, of a kind which could be carried out very rapidly, and which therefore could be expected to produce results that were pertinent to the contemporary educational scene. Again, it involved for the most part methods that had become well established at the time at which it was carried out, so that its results were not threatened by bias from the atypical conditions that usually accompany curricular innovation; it is therefore likely that the results of this study would be representative of results obtaining in the usual teaching circumstances of most of the methods examined. However, for these two advantages the study has had to pay a price. Since it did not set up conditions for investigation, but limited itself to the examination of conditions that already existed, it suffered certain handicaps to which a contrived experiment would not have been subject: frequently the numbers of children being taught by one particular approach were too few for conclusions of great validity to be drawn about it, and frequently the conditions of operation of an approach varied so widely that it would have been difficult to detect any steady effect due to this approach.

An important feature of this study is that it includes within its test battery a test of basic mathematical concepts and a questionnaire concerning attitudes towards mathematics. The test of mathematical concepts helps it to weather the criticisms included in points 2 and 3 above. A high level of performance on a test of basic concepts suggests that a pupil is well equipped for later mathematical learning, and thus such a test has implications for performance at later stages in the pupil's learning career. An instrument that measures basic attitudes towards a subject has similar implications. Again, mathematical concepts are *general* benefits of a pupil's learning, which are likely to serve him well in his future even in circumstances in which the curriculum and our criteria of excellence have changed considerably.

An experimental comparison of methods of teaching arithmetic

Following the above survey the N.F.E.R. has carried out an experiment (Williams, J. D., 1965) in which certain methods of teaching arithmetic—the Cuisenaire, the Stern, the Dienes, and the traditional— were studied under carefully controlled conditions.

In this experiment, a battery of tests similar to that described above was used—although there were certain differences of some importance. The main difference between the tests used in the experiment and those used in the survey was that the former admitted of much more detailed scoring. Scores for several kinds of mathematical understanding and problem-solving were given, and attitudes towards mathematics along several different dimensions were examined. The test of computational skills was particularly refined in its analysis of performance. This included several 'contrast scores' which facilitated comparisons of such aspects of performance as power $v.$ accuracy, relative performance in different denominations, performance in denominate $v.$ performance in non-denominate number operations, timed $v.$ untimed performance, etc.

For the most part, the experiment was concentrated upon children in the first and second year of the junior school.

Two complementary experimental designs were used: an 'external' design and an 'internal' design. In the case of the external design children were tested at the beginning of the junior school and again after two years had passed. In this way it was possible to assess differences in progress that might be attributed to different methods of teaching. It proved both difficult, and in some ways undesirable from an experimental point of view to compare groups of children at the same school, so children were compared *across* schools. In the case of the internal design, children of a generation which had used one method were compared with children of a generation which had used another method. Thus, children were compared across generations— although these children were taught in the same school.

An interesting feature of this experiment was an 'up-dating survey', which was carried out some years after the experiment had taken place in order to establish that teaching methods had not changed to such an extent in the intervening period that results obtained at the time of the experiment would no longer be applicable at the time at which they became available. The report of the results of this experiment has not yet appeared.

A difficulty that immediately becomes apparent in the case of a longitudinal study of this kind is that results might take too long to obtain for them to remain relevant to contemporary educational practice. A feature of the study designed to overcome this difficulty is the up-dating survey. Perhaps it should become general practice for longitudinal experiments of this kind to be supplemented in this fashion.

As in the case of the survey of methods of teaching arithmetic, the criteria used in the experiment for assessing performance were ver varied. In this case they were particularly varied for the followin reasons:

a) An attempt was made, on the one hand, to do justice to speci features of the methods examined as well as to those areas in whic their objectives might have been expected to overlap, and, on the othe hand, to include among the criteria tests of outcomes which, althoug not especially catered for by the methods, would be deemed desirabl as the consequences of any method of teaching mathematics at th stage in the pupil's career.

b) It was hoped to obtain not so much an overall statement of th relative merits of the teaching methods as a profile of the relativel strong or weak points of each of these methods. Thus it could be saic as it could in the case of the survey, that, while the study was primaril 'summative', its results would give us information of a 'formative evaluational kind.

The policy adopted in this study was that of avoiding 'pioneer case by introducing methods into schools in which they had not previousl been used. As pointed out in the introduction to this section, thi policy brings with it the difficulties attaching to experimental stimula tion and teacher inexperience. Attempts of two kinds have been mad to cope with these factors:

a) Methods are being compared in terms of differences in pattern of scores along dimensions of pupil performance that could be expecte to be depressed equally by teacher inexperience or boosted equally b experimental stimulation.

b) The effectiveness of teachers (in terms of pupil performance after one year of using a method is being compared with their effective ness after two years of using the method. Thus it should be possible to obtain an indication of which aspects of performance are affected b either experimental stimulation or teacher inexperience.

An experimental evaluation of French teaching in primary schools

This is another longitudinal experiment (Burstall 1967). In it th effect of introducing French in the second year of the primary schoo is being studied over a period that extends to the second year of th secondary school. French is taught predominantly by oral methods and in the initial stages very little attention is given to reading an writing skills.

The following aspects of French learning are receiving particular attention:

a) The effect of the introduction of French in the primary school upon other aspects of the pupil's education. To this end pupils are being assessed for intelligence, and attainment in English, reading, problem arithmetic and mechanical arithmetic.

b) The organizational and teaching problems that arise. An assessment by H.M.I.s will provide information on these.

c) The question of whether there are levels of ability below which French teaching might be of dubious value.

d) Possible advantages for French learning that derive from beginning to learn it in the second year of the junior school.

e) The methods, attitudes and incentives that best promote French learning.

Since, in the early stages, teaching is largely for *oral* skills in French, there have been constructed oral tests of listening comprehension, ability to reproduce the sounds of spoken French, and ability to respond appropriately to an oral stimulus.

Several experimental designs are being used, but, as in the case of the mathematics experiment, the two main designs involve a comparison of different generations (one taught French, the other not) within the same school, and a comparison across schools in some of which French has been taught and in some of which (the controls) it has not. In this experiment, since the general attainment tests are standardized, the norms for these will provide further controls.

This is another study that serves both as a summative and as a formative evaluation. On the one hand, the effect of introducing French into the curriculum is being compared with that of not doing so, while, on the other, the problems concerned with doing this effectively are being studied.

In this case, the problems of criteria do not yet present themselves in the same way as they do in that of the other studies we have considered. Since one main set of criteria is solely concerned with the effect that French learning has on the learning of other school subjects and on general verbal ability, it can be said that this set of criteria would be assumed to have a justification, irrespective of the course being evaluated. Nobody would challenge the importance of the effect that one course might have on others. Since, at the present stage of the project, it would be meaningless to apply to the control group the other main set of criteria—the oral French tests—problems of fairness of comparison in terms of this set of criteria do not arise. However, in the later stages of the study, where comparisons on French tests between sets of pupils who have been subjected to different kinds of French teaching will be made, the problems of loading the tests fairly will demand attention.

An important feature of this study is that intensive investigations of one kind or another will be carried out on limited parts of the main sample. In this way it will be possible to extract a greater variety of kinds of information from the sample for a given expenditure of energy and money.

This is a longitudinal study which covers a considerable period of time. While this fact helps to settle questions of the point at which the teaching venture should be appraised (obviously at *several* points over the duration of the experiment), it at the same time *raises* questions relating to the possibility that the terminal findings will be obsolete by the time they are obtained. Since the conditions just do not exist for a briefer study of the eventual effects of learning French in the primary school by oral methods, this possibility must be accepted. However, it should be pointed out that evaluative information will become available at several intermediate stages during the course of the study.

As in the case of the arithmetic experiment, this study will pose problems of teacher inexperience and experimental stimulation. However, its design permits an assessment of the effects of these factors, for, as in part of the arithmetic experiment, two generations of pupils are being tested—and a comparison of these will give an indication of whether the inexperience of teachers in the experimental group has depressed performance and of whether the stimulus of experimental conditions has boosted it.

The modern mathematics study

The N.F.E.R. has just launched a pilot study preparatory to an evaluation of modern mathematics learning situations as operated in the primary school (Williams, J. D., 1967). So far these situations are those devised by Z. P. Dienes (1965), but it is intended to expand the study to cover other instances of modern mathematics learning in the primary school. Although this study has barely been launched, it has certain methodological characteristics that entitle it to our consideration.

Like the other studies so far examined, this is primarily a summative evaluation, but it serves also to provide us with evaluative information of a formative kind. Its basic design is similar to that of the experimental studies considered above—this consists of both internal and external components. For the most part, the experiment is being carried out on children in their first three years of the junior school. At present, most of the schools included in the experiment are in Quebec, but more English schools are expected to join the experiment as it emerges from its pilot phase.

The evaluative instruments in this experiment include three rather interesting kinds.

a) Intelligence tests. It is expected that the learning of modern mathematics at an early age will raise performance on intelligence tests. For this reason intelligence tests are being used as one of the main criteria.

b) Programmed instructional tests of learning-sets. Since one of the main functions of a learning situation at an early stage in the child's career is to prepare the child for subsequent learning, it has been deemed important to assess the effect that modern mathematics learning at this age has on subsequent ability to learn particular items in the curriculum. It has been thought suitable to use modified programmed instructional sequences as standardized situations in which the ability to learn particular parts of the curriculum can be assessed.

c) Tests of various basic aspects of conceptual performance. Some experimental tests of such aspects of conceptual performance as the ability to break habits of thought and the ability to engage in 'second-order conceptualization' have been devised. It is thought that the rather basic kinds of thinking required for the tackling of modern mathematics learning situations will be likely to affect such basic aspects of conceptual performance.

Instruments of a more conventional kind, like those used in the arithmetic studies, will also play a part. Since the battery of tests used will thus be massive, a strategy that will spread the testing load in such a way that any one pupil or teacher is not overburdened will be used. Within each part of the experiment, randomly selected pupils will take some of the tests, while the remaining pupils will take others. As Cronbach (1963) has pointed out, since in curriculum evaluation our main interest in the pupil's test results is not in what they tell us about the pupil, but rather in what they tell us about the curriculum by which he has been learning, it is less important in this kind of evaluation to interrelate test results obtained by particular pupils.

At the same time as this attempt at evaluating the 'product' of modern mathematical learning experiences is going on, several 'process' investigations will be carried out on limited sections of the experimental sample. Among these process investigations are investigations into the dynamics of group learning, and the experimental manipulation of 'learning cycles'. It should be possible by means of these process investigations to find ways of improving the learning situations and of increasing our understanding of the basic factors underlying them.

Considered in terms of our four critical points, this investigation embodies some interesting characteristics. The evaluative criteria would seem to require very little in the way of justification, for few would doubt that the improvement of the pupil's performance on intelligence tests—bringing with it the possibility that we are improving the pupil's 'intelligence'—is an objective to be desired. Again, while the fairness of a test of learning-sets would depend on the content of the particular test used, it is of importance to know that *any* learning-set can be improved by a course of a certain kind. Part of the justification for the use of this kind of test is that it will constitute an 'existence theorem' for the validity of this kind of testing. Finally, we can justify the use of tests of various basic aspects of conceptual performance by the same argument as that which is used in the case of intelligence tests.

This study acquits itself particularly well when we question it from the point of view of the level in the pupil's career at which we should place the 'pay-off' of an educational course. We could summarize the strength of its position in relation to such questions as follows:

a) The use of standard intelligence tests as one of its major criteria automatically relates the results of the investigation to later stages in the pupil's career, for a great deal of information has been amassed about the degree to which performance on such tests can be used in the prediction of subsequent performance of various kinds.

b) The tests of learning-sets have direct implications for the next stage in the child's learning, and can be designed to cover a topic that would inevitably be included in the curriculum to which the child would afterwards be subjected.

c) It can be assumed that where a pupil's basic conceptual skills have been improved, he will be in a better position to perform in subsequent learning situations.

To the threat of change this study again responds with a certain degree of success. The use of very general criteria, such as tests of intelligence and of basic conceptual skills, would give the results of this investigation relevance to a great variety of situations, while, since the topics contained in the curriculum are of wide generality, they would be likely to prepare the pupil for a wide variety of **new** learning situations. The inclusion in the investigation of 'basic' research into the learning process is also an investment against obsolescence. The very purpose of such basic studies is to obtain general rules that would hold in a variety of different kinds of situation—even perhaps in situations in which the curriculum content differed completely from that of the situation in which the basic generalization had been obtained.

To some extent it can be said that challenges on the grounds of either the inexperience of teachers or the stimulus of the experimental setting can be regarded as irrelevant to the main purpose of this experiment. Although it might be difficult to get an accurate idea of the extent to which intelligence, etc., are affected by the new mathematics learning situation, rather than by its very novelty, it will be of great interest that these characteristics are affected *at all*.

The N.F.E.R. 'Item bank' project

The aim of this project (Wood 1967) is to devise a system for the calibration of attainment in the c.s.e. examination, and thus it has the purpose of providing a means of assessing pupils rather than curricula. However, I include a description of it here because it embodies many characteristics that could be shared by a similar scheme devised for the purpose of curriculum evaluation.

The scheme works in this way:

a) Teachers are asked to state with great precision and operational detail their teaching objectives and the subject matter to which they apply these objectives in teaching. This statement is described as a 'blueprint' of their examination requirements.

b) The blueprint is then submitted for relation to the 'item bank', which consists of test items, which have been contributed from a great variety of sources, and which are suitable for testing the achievement of specified teaching objectives within specified content areas.

c) A selection of items suiting the requirements of each particular blueprint is made, and these items are used by teachers for purposes of constructing a test that will be appropriate to their particular curriculum composition and their particular teaching objectives.

d) The implications of scores on such tests can be known by those who use them, for each item that goes to make up a test has indices of for example, difficulty, which enable us to characterize the test.

For curriculum evaluation the possibilities of such a system are considerable. The advantages of its use include at least the following

a) It would permit the assessment of a variety of curricula and at the same time enable us to compare particular components and aspects of different curricula in order to assess the effectiveness of these components and aspects.

b) Since it provides opportunity for the assessment of components of a curriculum, it would be of great use in formative evaluation. By means of such a scheme, it would be possible to assess whether a particular component of a curriculum was being taught effectively in comparison not only with other components of the curriculum, but also with the effectiveness with which it is being taught in other curricula.

c) The problem of unfairness of criteria would be unlikely to arise with the severity with which it occurs in the case of the 'blanket evaluation'. The item bank enables us to particularize our assessment and thus to ensure that the composition of a test corresponds to the objectives of any particular curriculum.

d) Finally, since the choice of the test items used in such a scheme is directly dependent upon curricular components and teaching objectives, the scheme could provide evaluative instruments that were as flexible as these components and objectives turned out to be changeable By means of such a flexible test system, curricula could be continuously monitored as they developed, and, where comparison between curricula was relevant, could be compared fairly and in great detail.

The 'Item bank' project is only in its pilot stages at present, and so far it has been in operation only in the area of mathematics. Moreover, its objective has not been that of curriculum evaluation. However, it would seem to offer us an extremely important lead in tackling the problems of both summative and formative evaluation. Perhaps it could be said that such a scheme shows great potential in doing justice simultaneously to the requirements of both formative and summative curriculum evaluation and that, to some extent, it could enable each to help the other.

SUMMARY OF SOME INTERESTING FEATURES OF THE DESIGN OF THESE STUDIES

It makes little sense to hope for a prescription for *the* perfect technique of curriculum evaluation, for, to a great extent, the ideal design of any evaluation will depend upon our interests in carrying out this evaluation. On the other hand, it should be stressed that while there is no simple solution to *all* evaluative problems, there are *several* solutions to *particular* problems. Where the problem is stated clearly, it is likely that the research worker will be able to go some way towards providing a satisfactory solution. In the above survey of some of the curriculum evaluations that have been and are being carried out in Britain we have encountered some of the research strategies that are available for the solution of certain kinds of evaluative problem. I shall end this paper with a summary of these.

a) In comparing curricula we should recognize that our criteria should take into account: the special outcomes of each curriculum as well as common outcomes; the possibility of using indirect as well as direct measures of these special outcomes; the possibility of choosing criteria for their relevance to our teaching objectives rather than to the outcomes to be predicted of the curricula being evaluated. If we formulate clearly our expectations of curricula, many of the problems of criterion selection dissolve.

b) One way of overcoming the difficulty of deciding when, in the pupil's career, to evaluate the effects of using a curriculum, and, partly, also of reducing the likelihood that one's results will have become obsolete by the time one obtains them, is to use, in testing the immediate effects of a curriculum, instruments that have implications for the pupil's performance at later stages in his career.

c) Other ways of coping with the dangers of obsolescence are: to concentrate on the more *general* features of the pupil's performance; to concentrate on short-term studies; to use 'up-dating' devices; to concentrate, as far as is possible, on research of the more 'basic' kind, which will yield generalizations that are relatively independent of the specific circumstances of an investigation; to obtain information about the *components* of a curriculum rather than about the curriculum as a whole, for it is less likely that *all* of these will change than that *some* will.

d) Where it is necessary to evaluate a curriculum soon after it has been introduced, the evaluation should recur after a period of time for the measurement of effects due to teacher inexperience or experimental stimulation. Where, in such cases, we have evaluated particular *components* of a curriculum, or *aspects* of its effects, it may be possible to detect *patterns* of effects which cannot be attributed to these factors.

e) In addition to helping us to solve some of the problems of change and atypicality of the conditions of innovation, the evaluation of particular components of the curriculum enables us to perform formative evaluations and a much more discriminating kind of summative evaluation.

f) By distributing the testing in such a way that the full test battery is shared by representative and equivalent samples of the pupils involved in an evaluation, it is possible to assess a great variety of aspects of the effect of a curriculum while minimizing both the expense of testing and the testing-load placed on any one pupil.

T. *Gordon Monks*

Comprehensive Education

The development of the comprehensive school may be traced through
the bilateral organization recommended by the Hadow Report (Board
of Education 1926) and the tripartite system recommended by the Spens
Report (Board of Education 1938b). The Hadow Report proposed the
abolition of the old sequence of standards from one to seven in the then
elementary schools, children being transferred at about the age of eleven
to secondary schools suited to their individual needs and attainments.
This, of course, necessitated different types of secondary schools, which
were to be grammar schools, providing academic courses, and modern
schools, providing more general courses.

In accordance with the recommendations of the Spens Report, this
separatism was continued and extended, with the addition of a second
kind of selective school, the technical high school. Parity of conditions
and esteem for all types of schools was advocated, and equality of
opportunity for all children implied.

The multilateral school (providing all types of secondary education
'by means of separate streams') was recognized in the Spens Report,
though not advocated. Experiments in this kind of organization,
however, were given guarded encouragement, and this type of school
was seen as suitable for certain areas. The report states: 'The multilateral
idea, though it may not be expressed by means of the multilateral
school, should permeate the system of secondary education as we see it.'

The provisions of the 1944 Act allowed, if not encouraged, the
further development of a tripartite system. This fitted to a large extent
existing buildings and organizations, and continued the practice of
segregation. To satisfy the criterion of education suited to a pupil's age,
ability and aptitude, a test of intelligence, generally accompanied by
tests in English and mathematics, was used in the selection procedure.
At this time the standardized intelligence test was generally accepted as

a satisfactory instrument for separating children suited to an academi course from those suited to a more general course.

Throughout this period, however, social and political pressure were bringing the principle of the comprehensive school with its idea of 'equality' nearer to practical implementation, and as early as 194 one local authority at least was advocating this type of provision. Thi pressure, reinforced by a growing body of evidence about the effects o environment on the development of intelligence and about the falli bility of selection procedures, made it increasingly apparent during th last decade that some form of reorganization was inevitable.

Government policy is, as proclaimed in Circular 10/65 (July 1965) 'to end selection at 11 plus and to eliminate separatism in secondar education'. The circular requested all local education authorities to prepare plans for reorganization on comprehensive lines.

Varieties of comprehensive secondary education

A comprehensive school has been officially defined as '. . . intended to cater for all the secondary education of all the children in a given are without an organization in three sides' (Ministry of Education 1947).

Circular 10/65 describes six forms of comprehensive organization which have 'emerged from experience and discussion'. It maintains however, that only four of these are fully comprehensive. These are:

1. The orthodox comprehensive school with an age-range o eleven to eighteen.
2. A two-tier system whereby *all* pupils transfer at the age of eleven to a junior comprehensive school and *all* go on at thirteen or fourteen to a senior comprehensive school.
3. Comprehensive schools with an age-range of eleven to sixteen combined with sixth form colleges for pupils over sixteen.
4. A system of middle schools which straddle the primary/second-ary age-ranges. Under this system pupils transfer from a primary school at the age of eight or nine to a comprehensive school with an age-range of eight to twelve or nine to thirteen. From this middle school they move on to a comprehensive school with an age-range of twelve or thirteen to eighteen.

The circular describes the two other types of organization, given below, as being acceptable only as interim stages in development towards a fully comprehensive secondary organization.

1. A two-tier system under which *all* pupils on leaving primary school transfer to a junior comprehensive school, but at the age of thirteen or fourteen *some* pupils move on to a senior school, while the *remainder* stay on in the same school. There are two main variations: in one, the comprehensive school which all pupils enter after leaving primary school provides no course which ends with a public examination, and normally keeps pupils only until fifteen; in the other, the school provides G.C.E. and C.S.E. courses, keeps pupils at least until the age of sixteen, and encourages transfer at the appropriate stage to the sixth form of the senior school.

2. A two-tier system in which *all* pupils on leaving primary school transfer to a junior comprehensive school. At the age of thirteen or fourteen *all* pupils have a choice between a senior school catering for those who expect to stay at school well beyond the compulsory age, and a senior school catering for those who do not.

At the time of writing (September 1966) the Department of Education and Science recognizes 342 schools in England and Wales as comprehensive. Since, however, most areas retain some form of alternative provision, few function truly as such, and with all local education authorities in the throes of reorganization the position is one of flux.

Studies of the history and organization of comprehensive education

Research into comprehensive schools has meant in the past, and still means, research into those schools where it is intended to provide for the full range of social and intellectual variation but operating within the limits of local organization.

The history and evolution of comprehensive schools is discussed from different aspects by Koshe (1957), Miller (1958), Currie (1962), and Hind (1964).

Miller divides his study of the 'emergence, development and significance of the comprehensive secondary school in England' into three 'strands', historical, philosophical and experimental.

Historically, the political aspects of the emergence of the comprehensive school are traced through the Labour Party's early policy of a

'provision of a variety of types of secondary education, equal in stat
to suit the differing needs and abilities of all children', and its increasi
support of the multilateral school for 'a combination of socio-politic
and strictly educational motives'. Of the experimental strand Mill
states: 'Certain assumptions implicit in many of the arguments for a
against the comprehensive school are formulated as hypotheses a
then tested. Of major interest are those assumptions concerning t
more or less intangible features of school morale, parity of esteem, soci
and cultural homogeneity, and cultural standards. Specifically
attempt is made to assess the effect of the comprehensive seconda
school situation, as compared with that of segregated schools, on boy
attitudes, opinions and activities in respect of certain school, social a
cultural phenomena.' In this section the findings suggest that t
comprehensive school 'may well contribute to the development
greater cultural unity and to an improvement in general cultur
standards'. More obviously, it may also 'help to overcome the proble
of disparity of esteem between different types of secondary educatio

In regard to the secondary modern type of child Miller states: 'T
beneficial effects of the comprehensive school may be due to one
more of the following:

1. The greater variety of facilities available.
2. The fact that the children concerned consider that their school
   held in high esteem by the community.
3. The stimulus afforded by the presence of the more able pupil
4. The opportunity (on the surface at least) which the compreher
   sive school offers for them to gain a nationally recognize
   examination qualification.
5. The possibility that the occupational futures of the children a
   not as definitely determined as those of their counterparts in th
   secondary modern schools.'

Compared with the secondary modern school Miller finds that th
comprehensive school offers an education which is more purposeful
well as encouraging boys to stay at school longer (see the discussion
Dixon 1962 and Egglestone 1965 below). He states: ' "Secondar
modern" children in a comprehensive school have higher regard for th
school, the value of its courses and its place in the community tha
secondary modern children in a bipartite system.' He also finds that th
comprehensive school is equally effective as the grammar school in thes
matters as far as the more able boys are concerned.

Regarding cultural unity, Miller points out that this is not achieved by merely bringing children of all abilities together in one type of school; 'complete cultural unity is not, by any means, an inevitable outcome of comprehensive secondary education'. Social maturity seemed to be allied to ability and/or home conditions rather than to school environment.

In general, Miller's findings indicate that comprehensive schools have beneficial results in regard to certain cultural, social and educational phenomena. It must, however, be borne in mind that the schools in his survey had a respect for academic achievement which affected their internal organization. They were also well equipped, housed and staffed and still 'experimental'. Miller reminds us that findings in a limited number of schools do not necessarily apply throughout the country.

Hill (1959) examines various methods of internal organization and tentatively assesses their relative strengths and weaknesses. He states: 'The purpose of comprehensive schools has become clearly apparent:

First: to provide an education for all children at secondary school age suited to their varying ages, aptitudes and ability.

Secondly: to provide this education in the common environment of a single school.'

Hill considered that in the schools he studied the children were gaining a 'richer' education by the schools serving representative communities of children both socially and intellectually and through the provision of wide ranges of courses combining liberal and technical studies. However, he sees problems of size and confusion of social purpose with educational aims as two inherent dangers to educational standards in the comprehensive school.

The results of comprehensive education

Different aspects and effects of school organization are discussed by Currie (1962), Sinha (1963), and Hind (1964).

As well as discussing the 'English comprehensive school system', Currie is concerned with the educational, social and cultural effects of the single-sex and co-educational types of school. Comparing single-sex with co-educational schools, he finds:

'The co-educational boys and girls exhibited less "academic" motivation, less desire to continue with school or further education, but their parents preferred them to remain at school longer.

'Co-educational girls were more orientated towards being future wives and mothers than the girls in the single-sex schools, who were more interested in their school progress, appearance and character development. Co-educational boys were interested in being popular with members of the opposite sex and wished to obtain a status symbol, a beautiful girl friend. Boys in the single-sex schools were more interested in success and popularity with their boy friends, with wealth and the difficulty of mixing socially.

'The comprehensive schools, however, were less extreme in the display of the above marked differences.'

Currie's studies covered comprehensive, grammar and modern schools, and he states in general that the main problems associated with co-educational and single-sex schools (family restrictions and controls, sibling rivalry, sociability, physical-sexual relationships) were less marked in the comprehensive schools sample. His findings suggest that by catering for a wider range of needs and interests, the comprehensive school provides more compensations and satisfactions for its pupils. The evidence for this Currie finds in the fewer emotional upsets, tensions and problems. Tensions associated with learning and development were generally less severe in the comprehensive schools. Similarly, a 'purpose is given to education expressed by greater interest in school subjects, stronger feelings of success and closer integration between school and future employment.

In Currie's view, 'Comprehensive school pupils have a very strong desire to leave school to be employed and become economically independent of their home; this was not due to lack of interest or to feelings of resentment of school controls and restrictions.'

Further, the 'comprehensive boys expressed stronger overall evaluation of their school subjects, particularly of the practical subjects, woodwork, metalwork and technical drawing with the emphasis being placed on usefulness, interest and appreciation of teaching methods'.

Regarding secondary provision generally Currie states: 'Finally this study indicates that it would be wrong to evaluate the relative success or failure of the various secondary school systems by using the same criteria. It can be justifiably claimed that the grammar and comprehensive schools are providing different functions within the English secondary educational system and therefore should not be considered as rivals in status or efficiency.'

In a smaller investigation carried out in one school involving two groups of about 400 children, one group entering the school in 1957 and the other in 1959, Holly (1965) inquired into 'the relationship (if any) between social class background of the pupils, their sex, their measured ability on entry and the extent to which they profited from the opportunities, cultural and academic, offered by the school'. The study extended over six years.

He found that 'In terms of attendance, scholastic performance over the first three years of school, choice of a full secondary course, performance in public examinations, sixth form membership, reported involvement in school activities and selection for prefectship, girls and boys, middle-class and working-class pupils, pupils of high and low measured ability at 11 plus, derive differential benefit from a common secondary school environment. In general terms boys tend to choose more readily to complete five years and have a wider range of examination qualifications at the end than girls; girls take more interest in school activities than boys; middle-class pupils derive especially more scholastic and social benefit from the school than pupils from the homes of less-skilled workers; pupils of low academic ability at entry continue to show less interest in either the scholastic or social opportunities provided by the school.'

Hind (1964) investigates the comprehensive school with 'special reference to the house system'. From a survey involving 235 schools he states that the majority use a house system and though great value is placed upon it for its 'personal' qualities, much more use could be made of the house and few schools fully recognize its value for social service, careers, parental contact, leadership, welfare, and moral/ spiritual guidance.

Using a personal questionnaire approach, Hind inquired into pupils' ideas on the function of the house. Competitive aspects occur most frequently, sport being mentioned by 85 per cent of the pupils. Social service and welfare are mentioned by only 9 per cent and 5 per cent respectively. Improved provision of facilities, such as lockers (69 per cent) and toilets (52 per cent) was considered by the pupils to be an important purpose and function of the house.

Among points emerging from his study, Hind lists:

'A different and "better" parent-teacher-pupil relationship can be developed through the house.

Children think about their houses, regard them with some affection/ loyalty without loss of school pride.

Children need to be brought more into accepting responsibility and sharing discipline and school organization.'

Another aspect of the effect of the house system is commented on by Pape (1961) in a small study involving third-year children in one comprehensive and one grammar school. His results indicate that the pupils of the comprehensive school tended to mix socially, irrespective of level of ability or form membership, whereas those in the grammar school 'already creamed off as the top fifth of the ability range are ... seen to separate themselves off within the school, both within the classroom and outside, into still finer ability groupings corresponding to the graded forms'.

Streaming, intelligence and social class

In one London comprehensive school, Dixon (1962) finds that 'The predominantly working-class origin of most of the pupils restricted the possibility of contacts with middle-class children, but despite this limitation, social mixing of pupils of varying abilities and poor home background did occur both in classroom and extra-curricular activities.'

In a more technical thesis Sinha (1963) sets out three aims:

1. To investigate the importance of general and special abilities at the ages of thirteen and fourteen with special reference to verbal, numerical, practical, and spatial and mechanical abilities.
2. To compare specialized streaming in three comprehensive schools with 11-plus estimates of intelligence and with measures of general and special abilities assessed later by objective tests.
3. To find how closely related are the results of Moray House tests of intelligence given in the 11-plus examination and then at the ages of thirteen and fourteen.

Sinha finds a clear indication of verbal, numerical, spatial and practical abilities in all three samples and of mechanical ability in one. Verbal and numerical abilities showed fairly clearly in 'grammar' forms, practical-mechanical or spatial in technical streams.

Streaming in the schools appeared to be based on general ability, since Sinha found a high correlation between streams arranged in order of merit according to the schools and '(a) the general factor measurement obtained and (b) the 11-plus estimates of intelligence'.

Sinha points out that the developing abolition of 11-plus selection and the increase in comprehensive provision means that the schools have no guidance in organizing streams for the diversified courses they provide and will necessarily have to conduct their own examinations. She accepts the usefulness of teachers' ideas, but reiterates the value of standardized tests in selection and guidance work, especially for those pupils outside the normal. Her findings indicate an overall gain of 6 points of I.Q. from the age of eleven to the age of thirteen or fourteen. The average increase was the same for the two age-groups and for the three schools. The correlation between the 11-plus I.Q. and the I.Q.s obtained in her investigation ranged between 0·83 and 0·91.

Sinha also states that general education does not provide wide enough scope for the differentiation of specific abilities, and that specialization could begin at an earlier age in comprehensive schools.

Internal organization of pupils is studied by Dixon (1962), Holly (1963), and Thompson (1966). Holly's findings support the general criticism that streaming discriminates against children of lower socio-economic background who are less well equipped to display ability in any selection tests—'middle-class pupils being consistently over-represented in the A streams and youngsters from less-skilled working-class homes considerably over-represented in the C streams'. He further states that 'This, no doubt, reflected the well-known social bias of the 11-plus tests, since streaming at entry was largely based on the tests taken by nearly all London school children at the time of transfer to secondary schools.' As far as promotion between streams was concerned, Holly found that this occurred more frequently with pupils from middle-class backgrounds.

Dixon (1962) also finds that 'children from better home backgrounds had more chance of initial selection for higher streams and also of obtaining promotion. The belated working of measured intelligence did not appear to be the chief factor in transfers.'

Thompson (1966) argues against any form of rigid streaming during the first three years of secondary school. In a small study involving 129 boys from one year who were examined in six subjects after one term and one year, and seven subjects after three years, he states: 'Of those thirty boys who came top in the school after one term, using the evidence of six subjects, only nineteen of them came in the top thirty places in the examination taken six months later at the end of one year, and only sixteen of the original group came in the top thirty places two years later at the end of the third year . . . Only eleven of them were consistently in the top thirty places after one term, one year and thr years.' Thompson considers the concept of innate ability to be tl greatest hindrance to the acceptance of non-streaming. 'Streaming itself is a conditioning process which on the whole is favourable as f as pupils in the top stream are concerned, but unfavourable to all the in the other streams because it conditions them to a level of respon below that of which they are capable.'

Using one grammar, two comprehensive and two modern schoo Koshe (1957) made a 'comparative study of the attainments and inte ligence of children in certain comprehensive, modern and gramm schools'.

In his conclusions, attempting to answer the two questions— there a lowering down in the comprehensive school in the case children whose I.Q. is comparable to a grammar school?' and 'Do tl children of comparable I.Q. progress better in a comprehensive scho than in a modern one?'—Koshe states: 'The answer to the first questic seems to be that in I.Q. and English, girls profit by entering a gramm school. Boys did better in the arithmetic/mathematics tests when the were in one of the comprehensive schools.' Regarding the secor question, Koshe's results generally show that the attainment in Engli and arithmetic of a comparable group of pupils in a comprehensi school is superior to that of the group in a modern school. Hence l says: 'If it is admitted that it is possible to provide a better environme in a comprehensive school than in a modern school, the argument f a comprehensive school can be said to be supported by these finding The tentative conclusions, based mainly on the I.Q. comparisons, the subject results are not entirely consistent for the two schools ai must depend to some extent on the quality of the teaching, is th girls seem to have been more susceptible to the influence of the ty| of school than boys.

In an investigation involving 337 maintained secondary schools five county boroughs and three county local education authorities the Midlands, Egglestone (1965) explored the hypothesis that 'volunta extension of schooling is associated not only with variables in soci economic background but also with distinct administrative and con munity variables in school environment'. His sample included a numb of comprehensive schools. In comparing comprehensive schools wi others in the provision and holding power of extended cours Egglestone found that comprehensive schools emerged superior, thou<

he pointed out that this is partly due to the socio-economic attributes of the areas where most of the comprehensive schools were situated and the 'climate of expectation' of extended education of local education authorities involved. Some evidence emerged, however, of less complete holding power in the 'open 'comprehensive school over its most able pupils than that of selective schools.

Miller (1958) found evidence that the comprehensive school showed some superiority in holding power, especially for those who would normally have left school at the age of fifteen. Dixon (1962) states: 'There were some indications of the school's success in catering for different ability groups: "premature leaving" was at a low level, well over half the intake remained at school after reaching the age of fifteen, whilst candidates for external examinations included some from the lower ranges of ability in the 11-plus selection.'

Current large-scale research

A major research project into comprehensive education in all its aspects, sponsored by the Department of Education and Science, was announced by the Secretary of State in September 1965, following the Government's policy decision proclaimed in Circular 10/65 (July 1965). Earlier, a working party of educationists had been commissioned to advise on the feasibility of such a project.

The work will be carried out by the National Foundation for Educational Research and is planned to extend over at least six years, proceeding by a series of stages. It will be kept under review by a Consultative Committee representing comprehensive schools, local education authorities, universities, H.M. Inspectorate and the N.F.E.R. (see also the paper by Wall).

Stage 1 is concerned with fact-finding and consists of two surveys, the first of which is now complete. This has been designed to give an overall picture of comprehensiveness in secondary education as it now stands. For this reason, in selecting the population of schools the net has been cast widely and a broad criterion of inclusion adopted, bearing in mind the limitations mentioned earlier (i.e. that most areas retain some form of alternative provision, few function truly as comprehensive, and the position is one of flux). A general breakdown of the 385 schools involved, under their designations on the Department of Education and Science's lists, is given in the table below.

TABLE I

Derivation of schools involved in first survey from the D.E.S. lists of schools County councils (42 L.E.A.s)

	Comprehensive		Grammar		Bi/multilat.		Sec. mod.		Other		Total	
	No.	%	No.	%	No.	%	No.	%	No.	%	No.	%
Boys	26	14·1							1	2·1	27	9·9
Girls	25	13·6	1	6·3	2	10·0			4	8·3	32	11·8
Mixed	133	72·3	15	93·7	18	90·0	3	100	43	89·6	212	78·3
Total	184(67·9%)		16(5·9%)		20(7·4%)		3(1·1%)		48(17·7%)		271(100%)	

County borough councils (22 L.E.A.s)

	Comprehensive		Grammar		Bi/multilat.		Sec. mod.		Other		Total	
	No.	%	No.	%	No.	%	No.	%	No.	%	No.	%
Boys	15	16·0	1	33·0	1	10·0					17	15·0
Girls	15	16·0			1	10·0					16	14·2
Mixed	64	68·0	2	67·0	8	80·0	3	100	4	100	81	70·8
Total	94(82·5%)		3(2·6%)		10(8·8%)		3(2·6%)		4(3·5%)		114(100%)	

Reprinted from Report on Education no. 36, H.M. Stationery Office, 1967, by permission of the National Foundation for Educational Research in England and Wales, the Department of Education and Science, and the publishers.

Questionnaires were sent in February 1966 to all these schools and the data from these formed the body of the first report, published in May 1967 (Department of Education and Science 1967b).

The questionnaires are in two parts, part 1 referring to the school and completed by the head, part 2 being personal to the teachers in the schools.

Part 1 inquired into all aspects of the school, its organization, derivation and stage of development.

Specifically, the topics covered include:
Derivation and stage of development
Size, age and ability range
Staffing
General organization

Mobility of children between groups or streams
Examination courses provided
Subject curricula
Choice of subjects available
Social organization (houses, tutor groups, etc.)
Involvement of the school with community
Voluntary extra-curricular activities
Involvement of the school with research in progress
Parents' occupations

Part 2 of the questionnaire covered such topics as:
Educational background
Type and length of training
Subject and type of pupils taught
Regular duties other than teaching
Experience
Weekly timetable
Current studies being undertaken
Present involvement with any research project

The inquiry produced a response rate of 86 per cent on part 1, 331 questionnaires being returned. Of these schools, 222 (67 per cent) were fully developed by September 1965, including 182 'all through' schools.

By September 1965, five comprehensive systems were operative either as interim or long-term solutions. However, only two of these systems are described in Circular 10/65 as producing schools which are fully comprehensive in character. The system of middle schools straddling the primary/secondary age-ranges was not represented in the survey. Of the 331 schools which responded, 262 were co-educational, the remainder dividing into thirty-four boys' schools and thirty-five girls' schools. The size of the schools ranged from less than 400 pupils to over 2,000, with 58 per cent having less than 1,000 pupils and 13 per cent more than 1,600. Only two schools had more than 2,000 pupils. Most schools were organized into smaller units such as houses, tutor groups or lower, middle and upper schools.

The predominant feature in pupil intake was the number of pupils average in general educational ability. Taking this as the middle 60 per cent of a normal national distribution, 117 schools (34 per cent) received more of these pupils than might have been expected, yet in only thirty-six (12 per cent) were similar proportions of children in the locality. Thirty-nine per cent of the heads state that their schools are involved in on-going research projects covering a variety of topics including local history, traffic surveys, c.s.e. comparability and juvenile delinquency. Many mention Nuffield mathematics, science and language projects.

Only six schools, however, mention topics directly concerned to investigate comprehensive schools. The topics are :

The factors in the organization and life of the school which may affect the attitude, behaviour and attainments of its pupils

The development of comprehensive schools

The Bradford scheme

A survey of social opportunities within the house system

The relationship of school sponsored extra-curricular activities to leisure habits of pupils in secondary schools in Pembroke

The validity of the 11-plus and the percentage of transfer within a comprehensive school following on the number of 'O' levels, c.s.e. or 'A' levels attained by various groups, i.e. those that were in A streams from the start and those that were transferred later

Of the 11,291 teachers involved in the first survey, 11·4 per cent state that they are actively engaged in research, and of these 25 per cent intend to submit their work for a further qualification.

The topics given cover a wide field, the main broad categories being:

Subject topics
Example: Possibility of c.s.e. papers in Latin and classical studies, and programmed learning with various teaching machines as applied to Latin

Wider educational topics
Example: Career motivation at 14 plus

Topics in special education
Example: Team teaching of remedial pupils

Topics relating to the school
Example: The role of the housemaster in the comprehensive school

Social topics
Example: The development of social groupings in the youth centre on the school campus and group pressures

Other topics
Example: The conflict of science and religion in the Renaissance with special reference to Kepler and Spinoza

The part 2 questionnaire (61 per cent response) yielded information on the teaching force identified within five categories, namely:

1. Qualified, trained, with graduate addition to salary.
2. Qualified, untrained, with graduate addition to salary.
3. Qualified, trained non-graduate.
4. Qualified, not trained (recognized by some special qualification).
5. Unqualified.

Graduates and non-graduates were about equal in numbers, with the balance slightly in favour of the non-graduates. Of the graduates, 80 per cent had had professional training and four or more years of full-time further education. Aspects of the teaching force covered in the report are age-ranges, marital status, levels of appointment, and length and type of experience.

The second survey in stage 1 is intended to supplement the first and to inquire more profoundly into the working of the schools, particularly with reference to those aspects of comprehensiveness which could not be studied adequately in the first survey. In particular, it is intended to seek insight into the relation of the schools to the surrounding community, the problems posed by size, the ways in which the needs of special pupils are met, the sociological structure of the school, the attitudes of teachers and pupils to comprehensiveness, and so on. This will be carried out on a smaller number of representative schools, and will involve field work and more direct methods than postal questionnaires. It is intended that evaluative studies shall follow the factual surveys. To this end a research group, working in co-operation with the National Foundation, has been set up in the University of Manchester under the direction of Professor Warburton.

From a consideration of the aims and objectives of comprehensive education, it is the task of the group to develop techniques of assessment which can be used to discover whether, or to what extent, such aims are being realized in the different types of comprehensive provision. To consider and classify the objectives, two groups of educationists have been established. One group consists of philosophers, psychologists and sociologists, concerned more with the theory of education, the other of practitioners in the field, heads, teachers, directors of education and inspectors.

Later it is hoped that action research might be carried out in limited number of schools to investigate the effects of changes in organization. Important aspects in the growth of comprehensive education are the ways in which changes are implemented and how individual schools react and reorganize themselves. To get first-hand knowledge of this emerging pattern, liaison has been established with a number of local authorities which have either recently begun to reorganize their schools along comprehensive lines, or are on the point of doing so. Throughout the period of the research, this liaison will be maintained so that data in the form of longitudinal studies will result.

When the research is complete, it should provide the first large-scale factual statement on one of the most important and controversial aspects of the education system.

T. Christie

The Sixth Form

'In the past, sixth form work was understood to be work of a certain standard; or, to put the same idea differently, the sixth form was open only to pupils of a certain kind and degree of ability, such as suited them for a university career. That would no longer be true as a general statement about the sixth form today' (Board of Education 1938a, p. 7).

'Allusion may be made to examinations for open scholarships at universities . . . they have in the past tended to encourage rather than discourage a close specialization' (ibid., p. 9). 'For example, it is still by no means unknown for a sixth form group to devote some four-fifths of its time to science and mathematics' (ibid., p. 11). 'The complaint is frequently made in the schools that the standard set in open scholarship papers in mathematics and science at the older universities—both for boys and girls—can only be reached by indulgence in precisely this kind of premature specialization' (ibid., p. 12).

Misgivings about the intellectual calibre of sixth-formers and resentment against the supposed determination of the curriculum by university entrance requirements—the sixth form may be a developing institution, but the character of its plaints shows remarkable stability over a period encompassing the 1944 Act, Crowther and Robbins; so much so, in fact, that the worries take on the guise of assumptions and the assumptions demand investigation.

Such investigation, however, is difficult to find and exists only in piecemeal fashion. It was in response to this situation that Professor R. A. C. Oliver of the University of Manchester Department of Education applied successfully to the Department of Education and Science in 1963 for financial aid in setting up a large-scale survey of the present situation.

Two units of analysis have been used: a questionnaire survey of a schools with sixth forms taking the Northern Universities Joint Matriculation Board examinations has elicited information on the salient administrative features of 570 sixth forms, while in a stratified sub-sample of twenty-eight schools a comprehensive psychometric assessment of over 2,000 sixth-formers has been made.

The sample is thus affected by one serious truncation, the almost complete absence of schools south of the Birmingham conurbation—serious in that attitudes to early leaving, for instance, vary between the north and south of England. On the other hand, there is considerable variety of type of institution within this geographical area. Of the schools in the survey, 406 are wholly maintained, forty-six are independent, and the others either aided or direct grant; furthermore while the majority are grammar schools, there are forty bilateral, thirty-nine technical, twenty-seven comprehensive and twenty secondary modern, all with sixth forms. This diversity has been retained in the sub-sample, which also contains a wide range of location, from city centre to extreme rural with children travelling by taxi and school bus, and of size from a dozen sixth-formers to over 200.

The data collected from both sources are still being analysed, mostly by computerized techniques; this means that there is little in the way of interim results, and only the scope of the project and the problems it seeks to illumine can be reported here.

The link with university

The Crowther Report saw the first mark of the sixth form in its close link with the universities, and it is this aspect of its activities which has received the closest attention in recent years. Furneaux in *The Chosen Few* makes the point that during the period of his investigation much of the effective selection for university entrance has taken place before the sixth form stage, at 11 plus and in early leaving, or as he would have it 'leakage', from the grammar school. Only 52 per cent of boys and 35 per cent of girls who gained five 'O' level passes in 195 went into sixth forms (Furneaux 1961, p. 10) at a time when 75 per cent of grammar school sixth-formers could expect to gain two or more 'A' levels and qualify for entry to a university (ibid., p. 164 About 89 per cent of qualified male school-leavers and 59 per cent of females then went on to make an application to a university (ibid

p. 37). The significant figures are those for the transition to the sixth form. Furneaux ventured the prognosis that 'an increase in the size of sixth forms might in itself result in an increase in the proportion of qualified leavers who could be persuaded to apply for admission to universities' (ibid., p. 42).

Such an increase has certainly occurred. In 1936 there were 39,000 sixth-formers (Board of Education 1938a). The next twenty-two years saw an 80 per cent increase to 70,000 in 1958; but it took only another six years for an increase of the same order to take place, bringing the number of sixth-formers to 128,000 in 1964 (Schools Council 1966). And the expansion appears to have had the effect which Furneaux hypothesized. Although in the post-war period the number of university students doubled to 120,000 in the early 1960s (King, E., 1965), pressure from schools has built up to an alarming degree, and one of the most striking concomitants of this pressure has been an increase in the attractiveness of the sixth form itself. In the Manchester survey only about 1 per cent of schools report a wastage rate (defined as pupils leaving who were in the headmaster's eyes capable of two 'A' level passes) in the transition from fifth to sixth form of the size which Furneaux accepted as normal in the mid-fifties, and over 5 per cent claim that no suitable candidates left prematurely. Analysis of reasons for leaving is not yet complete, but a small number of head-teachers still report that in their area, usually a heavily industrialized one, there is no tradition of staying to the sixth form. Such areas, however, now appear as pockets of resistance to the accepted trend.

Once in the sixth form, 89 per cent of those who stayed in 1958 took 'A' level examinations; by 1964 the figure had risen to 96 per cent (Schools Council 1966). This picture of an increasing number of sixth-formers increasingly preoccupied with 'A' levels inevitably raises the 'more means worse' argument which Sir Eric Ashby deprived of much of its persuasiveness at university level by showing that the standard of degrees awarded in the decade beginning 1952 actually rose (Ashby 1963).

This question of student calibre is still open at sixth form level. In 1964, 17·4 per cent of those who sat N.U.J.M.B. papers at 'A' level failed in all the subjects they attempted, ranging in number from one to five; and the Board reports that this percentage is slowly increasing over the years (Northern Universities Joint Matriculation Board 1964). More means worse perhaps, and yet such a rate of failure in relation to the percentage presenting suggests that a sixth-former had, if anything, better chance of gaining at least some 'A' level qualification in 196 than he would have had, judging from Furneaux's data (1961, p. 162 of gaining Higher School Certificate in 1950. Indeed, the pressure of university places does not seem to be —as E. King, for instance, sugges —the direct result of a greater number of candidates of border-lin ability ignoring the publicity given in the early 1960s to unsuccessf applicants with good qualifications. Lawrence has shown that in fac the proportion of well-qualified candidates who were unable to con tinue full-time education did not rise between 1961 and 1963. Instea the pressure was created by a larger proportion of these candidat applying for university places rather than starting work; 'this facto coupled with the increase in the number of applicants arising from th growth in the size of the sixth forms, made it more difficult for margin candidates to gain admission in 1963 than in 1961' (Lawrence 1964 It seems plausible that the pressure which is by tradition attributed t the universities and is amply demonstrated by the drop from a fou fifths to a two-thirds intake of qualified applicants reported by Robbin (Ministry of Education 1963b, Appendix 1, p. 119) has actually bee created not by their becoming more exclusive, but by their becomin more attractive to the sixth-formers themselves.

The problem of transition from sixth form to university has re ceived specific attention in the psychometric part of the Manchest survey. Each sixth-former was asked about his career aspirations an his destination on leaving school is now known. As well as his 'A level record, there are available the candidate's score on Miller Analogies test and on a scholastic aptitude test which was constructe especially for this project on the model of the test of the Colleg Entrance Examination Board which is used by over 900 America colleges and universities as part of their selection batteries. While i the Manchester survey this test is used as a moderating variable i studying achievement at 'A' level in relation to school, home an personality, it was originally intended to examine its predictive validi by following the successful university candidates from the samp through their courses in response to the following paragraph in th Robbins Report. 'In recommending investigation into methods o testing aptitude, we are not suggesting that such tests should repla academic examinations. These, with school records, must continu to play an essential part in selection procedure. But if some of th predictive load could be shifted from examinations, the pressure upon candidates to cram for them would be less; and selection is likely to be more efficient if based on performance in more than one type of test. We recommend experiment and investigation here, rather than a frontal attack on the present system of selection' (Ministry of Education 1963b, p. 84).

In the interim, however, the Committee of Vice-Chancellors and Principals have instigated an 'investigation into supplementary predictive information for university admission' with the steering committee under the chairmanship of Lord James of Rusholme. This aspect of the Manchester investigation has now been subsumed in this much more extensive project, and the Oliver s.a.t. will be the first in an experimental series of parallel forms of the test to be administered to samples of about 30,000 sixth-formers from successive year-groups. Thus, while the Manchester survey itself in taking a still photograph, so to speak, of the sixth form, is not in a position to examine directly changes in the calibre of sixth-formers, this information will eventually become available for the period 1967–71.

The social background of sixth-formers

It is hoped, in the meantime, that some germane inferences about the 'more means worse' allegation will be made possible by a close examination of social class representation in sixth forms. Furneaux in his calculations uses the *Early Leaving* report figure of sixth-formers as 10 per cent of all grammar school pupils (1961, p. 158) and shows the massive discrepancies between social classes in their representation at that level. He concludes: 'If it should be possible to raise the output of sixth form students per unit grammar school intake to the same value in *all* occupational groups as is now found for the professional and managerial one, then this by itself would increase the number of sixth form students by some 70 to 80 per cent . . .' (ibid., p. 50). The Northern Division of Her Majesty's Inspectorate for England and Wales report (1967) that in 1964 sixth-formers accounted for 15·2 per cent of the total population of pupils at 100 maintained grammar schools in their area, and that by 1966 the figure had risen to 16·3 per cent. The situation in 1966 is complicated by the arrival of the 'bulge', but the increase in 1964 of 50 per cent coupled with the fact that this region is below the national average in the numbers of pupils staying at school beyond the statutory leaving age (Department of Education and Science 1966d, pt 1, p. 56) suggests that Furneaux's projection of 70 per cent is already a reality. Obviously there is considerable interest in seeking to establish in what ways, if any, the social class distribution of sixth-formers has changed in the decade since Furneaux's 1953 survey, as, should the dramatic increase have come about in the way he outlines and should there be no striking mean differences in ability between social classes at this level, the implication will be that a more effective use is being made of the 'pool of ability' rather than that its banks are being artificially eroded.

Social class is also being examined in the wider context of its interrelations with creativity and personality as well as aptitude and achievement and, as the basic method of analysis is correlational, the expected skewness of data relating to this variable was rather undesirable. Furthermore, it is more than likely that those children categorized as R.G.IV and R.G.V who do enter the sixth form are hardly representative of their class. In an attempt to examine this hypothesis and to provide data more readily amenable to correlational analysis, three instruments were constructed, each of which attempted to go beyond what are essentially indications of the content of incidental learning to what has in fact been learned.

Two of these were multiple-choice tests of information, which was hypothesized was more likely to be available to high and to low socio-economic groups respectively. Here are some sample items.

Information, high

1. 'Gilts' is a term characteristic of
   a) painting
   b) sculpture
   c) the furniture trade
   d) the law courts
   e) the Stock Exchange

2. Which is the 'odd man out'?
   a) Clifton
   b) Marlborough
   c) Roedean
   d) Rugby
   e) Winchester

3. Which of the following is most likely to be produced at Glyndebourne?
   a) *As You Like It*
   b) *The Marriage of Figaro*
   c) *Messiah*
   d) The 'Pastoral' Symphony
   e) *Swan Lake*

Information, low

1. 'Getting a Yankee up' involves a knowledge of
   a) distance   b) form   c) height
   d) space   e) time

2. Which is the 'odd man out'?
   a) Barbara Kelly   b) Hughie Green   c) Jean Armstrong
   d) Michael Miles   e) Mike Sahn

3. Which is the 'odd man out'?
   a) bird   b) doll   c) judy
   d) punch   e) scrubber

The construction of the second test was bedevilled by the essentially local nature of working-class customs and vocabulary, with the result that it tends to draw to a greater extent upon 'pop' culture than is desirable.

The third test attempted to sample the value system of the testee. Merely by being in the sixth form the pupil has espoused middle-class values; this is the essence of William F. Whyte's (1937) distinction between 'corner boys' and 'college boys'. Both types are products of working-class families and neighbourhoods, but the college boy has assumed middle-class values and behaviour. The interesting question is whether there has been a wholesale or a selective switch. The test was constructed on the basis of the eight socially differentiating values described by A. K. Cohen (1955), and each was represented by two items in the test. Some sample items follow.

1. Bill and John sit together in a Latin class. Bill is conscientious and always prepares proses. John, although clever, does not do so, with the result that his teacher becomes increasingly annoyed. When John is having his 'last chance', he is in a position to copy from Bill's open notebook. Bill closes it. Later they have an argument about this. Whose side are you on?
   a) Bill's   b) John's

2. *Tom*   Come and help me canvass for the local elections.
   Paul   What on earth are you doing that for?
   Tom   These people deserve our support. They give up their spare time to protect our interests.
   Paul   Go on! What's your real reason for canvassing?
   Whose side are you on?
   a) Tom's   b) Paul's

3. *Mike* Come camping for a week at Easter.
Jim No. We have an exam just after and we need a fortnight to prepare.
Mike Don't be daft. We can spot five questions, prepare them in five nights, and four of them are sure to be there. We'll get a better mark that way.
Whose side are you on?
a) Mike's   b) Jim's

An initial study of the relations between these three tests and various conventional indicators of social class has been made in an effort to establish their validity as sociological variables at this level. The results, reported in tables 1 and 2, are based on the responses of 493 sixth-formers, who provided this information:

Variable 1 Father's occupation coded on an amended form of the Registrar General's classification of occupations whereby R.G.II manual = 3, R.G.III *nm* = 4, and so on, to yield an eight-point scale.
Variables 2 and 3 The age at which father and mother each ceased full-time education used in raw score form.
Variables 4 and 5 The number of books in the home, fiction and non-fiction respectively. Several respondents appeared to live in book-shops.
Variable 6 Ownership of house: council house = 2, private = 1
Variable 7 Type of house: detached = 1, semi-detached = 2 terraced = 3, flat = 4, cottage = 5. This variable was suggested by Professor Alan Blyth.
Variable 8 Social values: 'corner boy' values are coded high.
Variable 9 Information pertaining to low socio-economic status (37 items).
Variable 10 Information relating to high socio-economic status (60 items).

The means and standard deviations of each variable and a varimax rotated factor solution are reported separately for boys and girls, since there are mean differences for sex on almost all variables, always in the direction of a more exclusively professional and managerial background amongst girls.

It will be seen from the tables that at least among boys the values test appears to be a worth-while variable; it is certainly the one of the

TABLE I

Boys (n = 279)

Variable	Mean	S.D.	Varimax		
			I	II	III
1. Father's occupation	3·652	1·826	—0·053	0·076	—0·704
2. Education (father)	16·004	2·600	0·311	—0·022	0·610
3. Education (mother)	15·477	1·771	0·426	—0·087	0·535
4. Fiction	146·8	440·6	0·933	0·045	0·003
5. Non-fiction	94·1	166·8	0·930	—0·008	0·137
6. Council house	1·265	0·458	—0·032	—0·143	—0·438
7. Type of house	2·100	0·821	0·074	—0·074	—0·540
8. 'Corner boy'	4·545	2·047	—0·067	0·280	—0·431
9. Information, low	23·624	5·915	—0·072	0·849	—0·096
10. Information, high	37·591	8·417	0·102	0·821	0·187
	Percentage variance		20·44	15·16	18·85

TABLE 2

Girls (n = 214)

Variable	Mean	S.D.	Varimax			
			I	II	III	IV
1. Father's occupation	3·061	1·882	—0·277	—0·036	—0·779	—0·064
2. Education (father)	16·435	2·895	0·581	0·020	0·408	—0·238
3. Education (mother)	15·981	2·272	0·540	0·112	0·288	—0·181
4. Fiction	169·2	161·6	0·858	0·014	0·048	—0·043
5. Non-fiction	139·3	226·2	0·815	—0·077	0·005	0·170
6. Council house	1·117	0·376	—0·008	0·173	—0·709	—0·333
7. Type of house	1·981	1·002	—0·060	—0·024	—0·638	0·265
8. 'Corner boy'	3·280	1·959	0·058	—0·088	—0·016	—0·872
9. Information, low	20·523	5·805	—0·170	0·809	—0·113	—0·046
10. Information, high	33·093	9·726	0·253	0·796	0·056	0·138
	Percentage variance		22·06	13·47	17·85	10·86

three which is most saturated with social-class variance. Corner boys tend to have fathers from the lower socio-economic groups, to come from lower status housing and to be first generation sixth-formers. Among girls the picture is not nearly so clear-cut. The values test relates to neither of the conventional social-class factors, but instead appears as a fourth vehicle factor which has picked up variance in a rather confused way.

As among boys there is a positive relation with council housing which suggests that the espousal of such values may well be an indication of an ecological rather than a school-based reference group. However, in the analysis of girls' responses there is a second source of variance, a slight tendency for 'corner boy' girls to have mothers or fathers who themselves continued their education beyond the school leaving age and now have status housing to show for it. This result throws light upon the lack of relation to father's occupation. An inspection of table 3 reveals that the relation is non-linear.

TABLE 3

Registrar General Category	n	'Corner boy' values Mean	Median
I	42	3·6	3·6
II	92	3·1	2·9
III *nm*	11	2·9	1·4
III *m*	52	3·2	3·0
IV and V	17	3·6	3·4

In effect, whereas boys with lower social status give the impression of reacting aggressively against the middle-class mores of the sixth form, among girls those on that delicate border-line R.G.III react by becoming more 'middle class' than the middle class themselves, who exercise the freedom to feel as they please. In the light of the complexity of the relation to the Registrar General's scale, it is hoped that the 'corner boy' values test will prove to be a fruitful variable.

The two information tests do not present such a promising picture. It is immediately obvious from a consideration of either table that they are flawed by their very rationale in that amount of information or 'well-informedness' seems to be a more or less independent source of variance, which affects both tests equally in spite of their subject matter. The varimax solution presents perhaps a more emphatic picture than need necessarily be the case. The actual correlations between the two tests are 0·465 for boys and 0·327 for girls, not of a large absolute magnitude, but large relative to the average inter-correlation of about 0·25 among the criteria. When these intercorrelations are considered along with the regular bipolarity of the subsidiary loadings of the tests, it appears that a single score indicative of bias in information area which would be independent of the general level of information might be a more fruitful variable.

On this general point of information it is anomalous that among boys there is a slight tendency for the well-informed to come from private homes, while among the girls the opposite is true and there is a minimal difference in favour of those from council estates. Whether this is a function of availability of information the new bias score should help to clarify. Certainly girls tend to lead slightly more sheltered lives than boys, and these are only slight differences. But a second hypothesis of more directly educational relevance and greater plausibility in the light of the values test results must also be investigated: it is possible that this is a reflection of the greater social exclusiveness of girls' sixth forms, making greater demands of achievement from girls of a non-professional background. That question, important in connection with the calibre problem already raised, will be better answered with reference to an information scale covering literature and the arts, the biological and the physical sciences constructed by Dr D. G. Lewis for use in this research.

It should be made clear at this point that the research as a whole is not primarily a sociological exercise. Indeed, the foregoing instruments are not even *primi inter pares*: at least as much work has gone into, for instance, Professor F. W. Warburton's investigation into the personality of sixth-formers which makes use of objective as well as questionnaire techniques on a Cattellian model. Effectively the research is designed around two or three main problem areas which the individual areas of investigation are intended to clarify from a multiplicity of angles.

The problem of specialization

A second major problem area in sixth form study centres round the place of specialization in education. Of the twin functions of the sixth form proposed in the Crowther Report, preparation for university (Ministry of Education 1959–60, para. 331) appears in many eyes to have taken precedence over the obligation to give an education which is 'good in its own right' (ibid., para. 332). Although in 1943 the Norwood Report had declared that secondary education had reached maturity and no longer needed the control of external examinations (Secondary Schools Examination Council 1943), although in 1951 the

Ministry of Education in introducing the new G.C.E. challenged the schools to abandon their previous pattern of examinations and embrace the freedom of seven consecutive unexamined years of secondary education for their pupils (Ministry of Education 1951), Stevens' survey revealed that the more representative headmasters expected prospective entrants to take some subjects at 'O' level, and even then would only allow those who seriously aimed at three 'A' levels into the sixth form (Stevens 1960, p. 200). There they would find teachers of whom 44 per cent made 'much' use of published examination questions and 41 per cent used them 'moderately' (ibid., p. 232). In the more recent Manchester survey, of 445 grammar schools, two-thirds had two or more 'O' levels timetabled 'primarily to broaden the sixth-former's education', and only three spontaneously volunteered comments to the effect that they did not approve of using examinations for this purpose. Stevens' conclusion may still be warranted that 'the whole body of grammar school teachers . . . has turned to find its source of curricular authority in the syllabuses and question papers of the public examining bodies' (ibid., p. 232).

Change is taking place in the content of that curriculum, especially on the science side. The reforms advocated in the Crowther Report (Ministry of Education 1959–60, para. 393) are being undertaken in a series of projects sponsored by the Nuffield Foundation. But it is with structure rather than content that the greatest unease is felt. The concentration on specialized preparation for a narrow group of examination papers within either arts or science, which Pheasant in a survey of fifth-year pupils in eight schools claims prevented pupils from studying subjects in which they were interested (Pheasant 1961) has led to various approaches to reform of the curricular structure. Of these the most worthy of note in the eyes of the Schools Council are Peterson's proposals, the ABC agreement and the rise of the General Studies Association (Schools Council 1966).

Peterson has made a devastating attack on Crowther's first premise (ibid., para. 387) which he calls the 'myth of subject-mindedness' (Peterson 1960). This phenomenon appears among bright sixteen-year-olds and the ablest fifteen-year-olds, and leads to two years of deep immersion in their own subject during which they show no inclination to question what relation it bears to other people's interests. There is some support for this analysis in a study by Hashim of the subject interests of twelve- to fourteen-year-old children, which revealed that their interests tended towards either the arts or the sciences and that the tendency grew stronger with age. But the correlation between interest and ability in a subject was only 0·25, which is rather more tenuous than the Crowther description suggests (Hashim 1948). Furthermore, Lewis' evidence that 45 per cent of sixth-formers in Belfast had most enjoyed a group of 'O' level subjects drawn from both the arts and the sciences (Lewis, D.G., 1961) when taken in conjunction with Peterson's own finding that, given free choice, 40 per cent of a sample of English sixth-formers preferred a 'mixed' group of three 'A' levels (ibid.) and Roe's finding that 27 per cent of schoolboys and 42 per cent of girls favoured broad university courses (Roe 1963–4), confirms that this is only a tendency and that 'subject-mindedness' is less than endemic in the grammar school population.

In fact, the sixties are already producing a swing away from this emphasis in the shape of a growing compromise. In spite of Crowther's rejection of a mixed pattern of 'A' levels (ibid., para. 419) the percentage of boys who gained such a combination has increased from 6·4 per cent in 1962 to 10·2 per cent in 1965, of girls from 10·5 to 12·4; and these percentages are even higher in maintained grammar schools (Department of Education and Science 1965c). This is not to say that Peterson's alternative proposal (Oxford University Department of Education 1960) has been endorsed; no school in the Manchester questionnaire survey presented all pupils for the mixed group of subjects which the scheme entails. One reason is not far to seek. Peterson's curriculum involves the loss of any provision for independent study, one of Crowther's 'marks of the sixth form' which is widely accepted (cf. Incorporated Association of Assistant Masters in Secondary Schools 1962).

Stevens found that her sample of teachers were in agreement with Crowther on the attitude of the able sixth-former to specialization. On the other hand, the Agreement to Broaden the Curriculum endorsed by over 1,000 headmasters, while recommending the retention of the specialist curriculum, set aside one-third of school time for non-specialist studies. It is the major function of the Manchester questionnaire survey to present a picture of the current emphases of the sixth form timetable and of how the degree of specialization bespoken therein relates to such variables as school type, size of sixth and destination of sixth-formers.

These physical arrangements are of especial importance in view of the well-authenticated finding that 'Grammar school pupils are less consciously influenced by parents, friends and out of school activities in general than by their teachers and their performance in relevant school subjects' (Oxford University Department of Education 1963). As well as interviews with a sub-sample of sixth-formers which largely confirm this finding, various aspects of the psychometric study are directly oriented to the investigation of arts/science differences.

Sixth-formers have been asked to nominate the subject combinations they would have chosen had all combinations been possible, and from this information an index of 'subject-mindedness' and one of 'job-satisfaction' can be derived. These two variables will be related to school organizations as well as to individual characteristics in both the cognitive and the affective domain.

Hudson in his recent book *Contrary Imaginations* advances the view that 'subject-mindedness' can be defined in terms of cognitive styles. Arts students are 'divergers' (that is, they score more highly on open-ended 'creativity' tests than on conventional intelligence tests), while science students are 'convergers' (they exhibit the opposite bias). Absolute level of either score separately is not as efficient a discriminator between subject choices as is bias (Hudson 1966, p. 155). On the other hand, Hudson's use of a five-point scale of intelligence on which the physical scientists, the largest group, average 'high' (ibid., p. 155), thus rendering it inherently improbable that they will be other than 'convergers' or 'all-rounders' on a bias scoring, introduces an element of doubt about the validity of his conclusions, since in practice only just over 50 per cent fell into the convergent category (ibid., p. 157).

The Manchester study includes a wide range of 'creativity tests' selected from those used by the major workers in the field and including questionnaires as well as cognitive exercises. These last are intended as part of a battery to throw some light on the modes of thinking demanded by the more popular 'A' level subjects, and also as predictors of achievement in their own right. They are being combined with intelligence in the four sub-groups suggested by Wallach and Kogan (1965); 'all-rounders', split up into high/high and low/low rather than excluded, as well as convergers and divergers. The 'subject-mindedness' and the personality characteristics of each group will be investigated and should throw more light on Hudson's thesis.

The most interesting of the four groups in this respect should be those who are equally proficient in both types of test. Do they, above all, go for mixed subject groupings at 'A' level, or do they get enough satisfaction from minority time?

Several surveys suggest that the latter possibility is fairly remote. Iliffe, interviewing first-year students at Keele University, found that 90 per cent of the students were overwhelmingly critical of their general studies course, their disaffection stemming from the low prestige which attaches to the subject in many schools (Iliffe 1968). Cotgrove and Friend (1965) found the same attitudes among freshmen at the London School of Economics. A survey by *New Society* (1964) suggests one reason for this state of affairs: they missed in the replies 'any widespread sense that the social sciences were vigorous disciplines demanding the same sort of time, attention and accuracy as the more traditional school subjects', just such a fate as Cannon (1964), in her perceptive analysis of the history and rationale of school social studies, predicts for a subject which through its flowering in the secondary modern school in the early fifties became identified with the younger, less academic pupil.

The problem of minority time is seen first and last as one of status. The time allocation stressed by the A B C may well be irrelevant in those schools in which, as Crowther realized, 'some sort of adventitious incentive is probably essential'. What effect, if any, the general studies examination at 'A' level of the N.U.J.M.B. has had upon the use made of minority time is another major facet of the questionnaire survey. In spite of Crowther's rejection of examined minority time, reaffirmed by the Secondary Schools Examinations Council in 1962, this 'A' level paper attracted in 1966 the third largest number of entries, exceeded only by English literature and physics (North Universities Joint Matriculation Board 1966).

Sixth form morale

Status through examination may be the answer to the problem of minority time, but those who attribute qualitative changes to the quantitative growth of the sixth form may be right in proposing the rethinking of the entire internal organization of the sixth form. Certainly what research there is suggests widespread disaffection among both teachers and pupils.

Bernbaum draws attention to the decreasing attractiveness of teaching to the good honours graduate. Even among those who do

join the profession there is a wastage rate which was running at 6 p⟨
cent in 1961–2. He points out that the sixth form master 'identifi⟨
himself very closely with his subject', and that 'the growth of tertiar
education has created opportunities for teachers to perform academ⟨
roles which never previously existed, to achieve status through wor
which is of a high standard' (Bernbaum 1967). His particular solutio
is the sixth form centre, a topic without the scope of the Manchest⟨
survey, as is the whole question of teacher satisfaction.

Some attempt has been made, however, to assess the prevailin⟨
sixth form climate as it is seen by the students. Dale (1966b) and Chil
(1965) both report sixth form discontent, even among intendin⟨
teachers, especially with opportunities for social learning, a spher⟨
which grammar school teachers reject (Musgrove and Taylor 1965⟩
The most extensive recent research in this field, using sentence com⟨
pletion techniques, concludes that 'the grammar school, particularly i⟨
its higher reaches, may often be failing to promote the self-confiden⟨
and assured maturity which is often supposed to develop from sixt⟨
form experience', although it 'measures up to the considerable deman⟨
for intellectual development and personal advancement. But it is see⟨
as a largely restrictive institution, and many pupils appear to find staff⟨
student relationships remote and chilling even in the sixth' (Musgrov⟨
1966).

The approach to these perceptions in the Manchester survey i⟨
through an anglicization made by the author of the High Schoo⟨
Characteristics Index (Stern 1968), a thirty-scale test consisting of 30⟨
true/false statements about the school. 'You soon get to know who th⟨
distinguished former pupils are' and 'you need permission to d⟨
anything around here' are typical examples. The scales are based upor
Henry Murray's need-press model, and were retained as separat⟨
variables in the item analysis of the rewritten test with the exceptior
of p sex, which was dropped in its entirety as the items tended to the
sensational in the context of the single-sex school. A varimax analysi⟨
of the scale totals, derived from 226 first-year training college student⟨
each retrospectively rating a different sixth form, revealed eight signi⟨
ficant factors of which the major four, two instrumental and two
expressive, take out 42 per cent of the variance from the test as a⟨
whole.

They appear to be the same factors as the five described by Pace as⟨
constituting his College and University Scales (Pace 1963) with the

exception that 'awareness', the degree to which interest in philosophy, the arts, and national and international affairs give evidence of personal awareness in relation to society, and 'scholarship', the degree to which the pursuit of knowledge and ideas and the attainment of scholarly achievement are highly valued, have collapsed into one factor, a tendency which is apparent in Pace's normative data. The other three factors of some dimensionality are 'practicality', the degree to which the environment is structured and orderly and emphasis is placed on achievement rather than understanding, 'community', the degree to which a warm, cohesive atmosphere is emphasized and where there are close relationships between staff and students, and 'propriety', the degree to which proper forms and conventions are emphasized, where good manners are evident, and where there tends to be an absence of unconventional behaviour. The C.U.E.S. is intended to yield only institutional not individual scores, and this was originally the sole function of the H.S.C.I. in the Manchester survey.

There is good reason in the literature on creativity to guess that highly creative pupils will be unhappy at school, a hypothesis since confirmed for 'divergers' by Hudson (1966, p. 159), and so an attempt is being made through the H.S.C.I. to establish which climates are most conducive to creativity as the tests measure it. In practice, however, sixth-formers rating the same institution use the whole range of possible scores, each goes to his own school in a very real sense, and this has led to the use of individual scores.

These have been found to relate separately to creativity, to personality, and to home background; but the way in which the whole situation gels seems to vary from school to school, and further analysis of the scales into institutional and peer group press is being undertaken in an attempt to clarify the situation. The nub of the problem is that the test is an interaction, which is a function not only of the pupil's perception of the institution but also of the institution's perception of the pupil.

It is just such an interaction that tends to be left out of account, especially in the context of prediction, although one would expect its effects to be far-reaching. For instance, mention has already been made of the influence of teachers upon the subject choices, and by implication adult careers, of their pupils. Who is it then who is providing the impetus which may well alleviate the two cultures problem of the sixth form? With a 465 per cent increase in 'A' level passes during the last decade (Department of Education and Science 1965c) economics is now second only to medicine in the number of university applications which go through the u.c.c.a. system (Universities Central Council on Admissions 1966). The socio-economic subjects, economics, economic history and British government, have now so increased in importance that the Council for Scientific Policy feel that the statistics of the Ministry of Education cannot be truly meaningful until this is recognized as a new category (Department of Education and Science 1966a). Such recognition would bring sixth form studies into line with the conclusions of the Harvard Report, *General Education in a Free Society*, that there are different modes of experience in the arts, the natural sciences and the social sciences—the general studies pattern but on the macrocosmic scale such that specialism is retained as a mark of the sixth form.

If the questionnaire study can throw any light on the provision made for this tripartite grouping, or the psychometric study on the characteristics of the students who espouse it, then discussion of the problem of the proper nature of the sixth form curriculum, as well as of the problem of sixth form calibre, may go forward on a slightly surer footing.

R. R. *Dale*

Co-education*

Many books have been written on the aims and methods of education. Prominent themes have been 'the education of the whole man', 'preparing the child to take his place in the adult world', and 'the need for right social and emotional development'; yet in all this consideration of fundamental principles mention is rarely made of one of the most powerful factors in social and emotional growth—the influence of male on female and female on male. The authors of the studies have failed to see that one of their first tasks should have been to consider whether this influence ought to be used in education, or deliberately excluded on the ground that it is detrimental. As a subject strangely 'apart' from the main theories, it was, however, debated with much heat, abysmal prejudice and a deplorable lack of facts. Co-educational schools like Bedales claimed notable achievement; so, too, did some single-sex public and direct grant grammar schools, and the success of these last in preparing their intellectually superior entrants for the universities clouded the issue by associating, in the public mind, single-sex grammar schools and high academic attainment, as if one were a specific cause of the other.

In this country in the nineteenth century there were the old-established grammar and public schools for the education of boys; girls, when educated at all, were taught to be useful about the house and ornamental. When the era of the 'finishing' of young ladies passed insensibly into that of academic emulation of the male sex, the Victorian era was in full spate; this ensured that the new schools were for girls only, except in rural areas, where economic considerations were stronger than Victorian fears. Since then, though the attitude to co-education has varied a little, the single-sex tradition has continued its self-perpetuating course; it has been founded not on educational

* The subject is fully discussed in Dale (1968).

theory but on historical evolution, and has derived strength from th
public image of a few schools where an *élite*, educated by an *élite*, ha
produced future scholars for the ancient universities. Yet there is littl
research evidence to evaluate the achievement of these schools, es
pecially in areas other than the academic. There must have been mucl
solid worth; but it is not easy to determine where the worth ended anc
the myth began, nor to what extent the achievement and prestige are
due to the special clientele, the 'upper crust' of academic success, wel
qualified staff, or tradition. Certainly there is no reliable evidence tha
the single-sex nature of the education produced better academie
progress.

Co-education is now rarely challenged at the primary school level
and is increasingly accepted in higher education; but its value is stil
debated at the secondary level. Recently the re-examination of educational aims has led to a sharp increase in the proportion of co-educational secondary schools, and it looks as if this movement will continue.
Can it be justified?

In this paper we shall examine research work related to the problem,
and shall endeavour to provide some concrete evidence on which to
base the discussion. Unfortunately, most of the research has been
limited to grammar schools, so that this paper will necessarily have the
same restrictions. Whether the findings are applicable to other secondary schools is left to the judgment of educationists. The sections of the
paper will be on attainment, pupils' attitudes and emotions, including
teacher-pupil relationship, and the verdict of teachers. In each of them
the sexes will be treated separately.

Attainment in co-educational and single-sex schools

Almost all the research on the effects of co-education on academic
attainment has taken as criterion the examination results of pupils
taking the first external examination at 16 plus. This is a ready-to-use
measuring rod, which is reasonably accurate for comparing large groups
of pupils. It is by no means easy, however, to assess the reasons for the
differences between groups in average marks. So many factors affect
the academic attainment of pupils that it would be highly dangerous to
base a conclusion on one single piece of research. Some of these factors
are age, social class, academic aptitude, number of subjects taken, and
teachers' ability and qualifications. Only after an intensive and critical

analysis of the results of a number of researches, allowing for all these variables (some of which were not noticed in the original work) and often recalculating from the original data, was it possible to see a consistent pattern emerging. A fuller account of this whole subject is given in *Educational Research*, June 1962, November 1962 and June 1964.

A) THE RAW RESULTS

It is convenient first to give the raw results, and then to discuss the nature of the co-educational and single-sex populations and the related variables. The findings based on the raw results will naturally be modified by the analysis of the samples, and this should be borne in mind. The researches examined are those carried out by Tyson (1928) at Manchester and Clark (1937) at Liverpool, with the thousands of pupils taking the N.U.J.M.B. examinations, by Gott (1928) and Walton (*c.* 1934) in all the Middlesex grammar schools, by W. H. King (1949, 1966) with large numbers taking the London General Schools examination, by Sutherland (1961) and Dale in Northern Ireland, and by Douglas and Ross (1966) with a small national sample, and by A. E. Cameron (1923) studying the attainment in mathematics of girls in a small sample of schools. All these produced rather similar findings, and the only studies yielding results that are partly discrepant are those of King (1966) and Douglas and Ross (1966) in mathematics and reading. These dealt with much smaller numbers than the other researchers, and their findings are debatable. Reasons for this statement are presented later.

With boys, the general picture is that those educated in co-educational grammar schools reach a higher average standard of attainment in the first external schools examination, in almost all subjects, than do boys educated in boys' schools. This is so in the researches of Tyson, Clark (by inference), Gott, Walton, King (1949) (by inference), and Sutherland. King (1966), comparing the schools in mathematics only, does not confirm this trend, but neither can he be said to refute it. There is a tendency, occasionally, for boys' schools to have a slight superiority in French. In Northern Ireland, analysis by Sutherland (1961) and Dale gave the boys' schools a slight lead in English language, which may well be due to the influences of social class. Here there were only nine boys' schools, so that the smallness of the sample might make it unrepresentative of boys' schools in general.

Douglas and Ross (1966), unlike almost all the other research workers, found a slightly lower standard in English and mathematic among boys in co-educational grammar schools; this needs special comment. They themselves state that the pupils who entered the boys schools at 11 plus were abler and of higher social class; it is therefore understandable from these facts alone that they should increase their lead by the age of fifteen, though surprising that the working-class boys from boys' schools, when taken separately, should lose a little of their lead over the co-educated boys of the same class, on the mathematics side. An additional reason why these findings do not conform to the general pattern may be because their national sample was rather small for reliability when broken down into its component parts: there are about 130 boys in mixed grammar schools, divided into two social class groups, one of which must be sixty-five or less in number. The two social classes into which their pupils are divided are also too rough a classification to ensure a proper equating of the groups e.g. it is probable that the 'middle-class' sample from the single-sex schools contains an appreciably larger proportion of 'upper middle class' than the co-educational sample, and that the 'working-class' samples, though the same in name, may have similar inequalities. In addition, the survey was carried out at a time when many rural co-educational grammar schools were becoming bilateral, and the research workers must have had serious difficulties in classifying schools, so that one could not be quite sure that like schools were being compared. Finally, whereas all children of agricultural labourers were in the sample (their lower standard penalizing the co-educational schools, as there is a greater proportion of them in rural areas), only one quarter of the children of unskilled and semi-skilled workers were included—thus raising the apparent average standard of attainment of the single-sex schools, which are mostly urban.

In the case of girls, the consensus of the findings is not as clear. In the survey of all Middlesex schools made by Gott over a period of seven years, girls in co-educational schools had a clear overall lead over girls' schools; but in those of Tyson, Clark, Walton, Sutherland (and Dale in English only) the opposite is the case, though the pattern which emerges shows the difference in favour of the co-educated boys to be greater than that in favour of girls in girls' schools.

Mathematics, however, does not conform to the general pattern, the girls in co-educational schools usually being superior (Dale 1962b). This is supported by the work of A. E. Cameron (1923), even though her sample of schools seems on examination to be biased against co-education. Douglas and Ross (1966) agree with this part of the finding, so that the only exception is the work of W. H. King (1966)—and as he was using a sample of only five co-educational schools, his results cannot be considered as reliable as those of other workers, nor were his co-educational and girls' schools entries equivalent in 'academic aptitude' as measured by a non-verbal test. The slight superiority of the girls' schools in mathematics in this single case may therefore be due to a more selective academic intake or to pupils of higher social class. There is also evidence that he had difficulty in securing a correct classification of schools as 'grammar' or 'modern'.

B) THE VARIABLES

The above picture presents the raw results. There are a number of unwanted variables, however, which should be taken into account in any comparison of the effects on attainment of co-educational and single-sex schooling. Most of them spring either from the comparatively rural situation of many of the co-educational schools in contrast with the largely urban single-sex schools, or from the greater age and tradition of the single-sex schools, which is sometimes accompanied by superior status. With only two exceptions they are serious handicaps to the co-educational school, though they are not inevitable concomitants of co-education, having merely arisen historically. Perhaps the most important is the contrast between the two types of school in the percentage of the 11-plus age-group which is admitted. Co-educational grammar schools tend to take in a larger percentage of the 11-plus age-group (partly because of movement of population to large towns and cities) than do the single-sex city schools. For example, in Wales, where the proportion of co-educational schools is greater than in other areas, the average percentage intake is now 29 per cent; and this figure embraces country areas where the intake has been 40 per cent or more for many years, and coastal town and city areas (with single-sex grammar schools) where it has been lower than the Welsh average. In southern England, with its increasing population and preponderance of single-sex grammar schools, only some 13 per cent of the 11-plus population are selected. In general this picture holds good for the whole of the country.

The social class variables are perhaps next in importance. We know from the report *Early Leaving* (Ministry of Education 1954), and from research by Floud, Halsey and Martin (1956), Dale and Griffith (1965), and others, that there is a strong association between social class factors and the standard of attainment of pupils in the grammar school. An example which highlights this trend is provided by Dale and Griffith. They examined twenty-nine cases of severe academic deterioration in one grammar school and found that none of them came from the professional, executive and inspectional classes, whereas thirteen out of thirty-six who improved came from these classes; thirty-seven out of the thirty-nine were from the skilled, semi-skilled and unskilled classes. For various reasons, such as city position, direct grant or similar status and low percentage entry, the single-sex grammar schools have pupils of a rather higher social class than the co-educational schools. This is confirmed by my own surveys and by that of Douglas and Ross (1966). The difference is therefore a considerable handicap to the co-educational schools when they are compared in academic attainment with single-sex schools.

Age is another variable which needs to be considered. Whereas the average age of the two groups of boys when taking the first external examination is usually the same, the co-educated girls tend to be about three months younger than their counterparts in the girls' schools. In Northern Ireland in 1957 this difference arose because 29 per cent of the co-educated girls took a five-year course instead of the usual six-year, whereas in girls' schools the figure was only some 12 per cent. If the other 17 per cent of the co-educated girls had spent an extra year on their studies, they would undoubtedly have raised their group's average. In other investigations the difference in age was probably produced by divergent policies in the two types of school, e.g. possibly because the girls' schools held back weaker pupils until they were more ready to take the examination.

One other factor relating to the samples of pupils must be mentioned. In all the inquiries the co-educated girls took appreciably more subjects at 'O' level than did the girls from girls' schools. In King's inquiry, for example, it was 9·3 subjects per pupil for 'mixed pupils', 9·2 for boys' schools, and 8·6 for girls' schools. Other surveys support the interpretation that the difference found here is due to the girls and not the boys. The raw results in such terms as average mark or percentage of passes can therefore be very misleading, as one is comparing schools where many pupils have been allowed to drop their weaker subjects with schools where this practice is less extensive. The comparison here is one of policy as well as of the level of attainment reached. The 'refinement of the sample' in girls' schools has been most pronounced in mathematics, physics and chemistry.

Comparison at 'O' level could also be affected by the incidence of premature leaving. The term 'premature leavers' is applied to pupils who neither completed a five-year course nor obtained a School Certificate or any subject at 'O' level. The report *Early Leaving* (in table 4) gave 20·2 per cent for girls' schools and 23·9 per cent for girls in mixed schools; as there is a tendency for the greater proportion of premature leavers to be of lower social class, and also of low academic standard, the slightly greater percentage leaving from the mixed schools would result in increasing the average standard of the remaining girls when they took the 'O' level examination. The very small difference between the percentages of leavers would, however, still leave girls' schools with a big social class advantage. The true figure for boys in mixed schools in the same year (1954) is 23·4 per cent, while for boys' schools it was only 14·6 per cent, and the comparison of boys', girls' and mixed schools shows little change over a long period. Although a greater percentage of leavers from co-educated schools than of leavers from boys' schools were of higher academic standards, this factor, operating as in the case of the girls, would materially reduce the boys' schools' social class advantage at 16 plus, and partly offset the more restricted intake of boys' schools, but it seems improbable that it would cancel these out. This illustrates the difficulty of assessing working situations where a number of variables cannot be controlled; they should, however, be shown to exist, even where the extent of their influence cannot be measured exactly.

So far attention has been concentrated on the pupils, but attainment is also influenced by the quality of the teaching. It is generally agreed—though without precise evidence—that single-sex grammar schools, because of their urban location and sometimes direct grant or similar status, have probably been rather better staffed than the rural co-educational schools. At present, however, girls' schools may be less well staffed in mathematics, physics and chemistry. There is little specific evidence, but in 1962 I made a survey of the qualifications of teachers of mathematics in three contrasted areas, Northern Ireland, Yorkshire and Hertfordshire. This is given fully elsewhere (Dale 1965a, 1966a); here it can only be said, briefly, that by far the best staffed schools were those for boys, with the mixed schools appreciably behind, and those for girls rather more closely behind the mixed. This situation arises because of the scarcity of good women graduates in mathematics, the mixed schools having the advantage that they can appoint either a man or a woman, though this does not put them on an equality with the boys' schools.

c) SUMMARY AND COMMENT ON THE EVIDENCE ABOUT ATTAINMENT

With boys there is a consistent trend of superiority in co-educational schools in spite of their lower social class intake, less restricted entry and probably rather less well-qualified staff. The only variable helping them is the higher incidence of premature leaving in co-educational schools, and this is scarcely likely to balance the others. It therefore seems likely, though it cannot be said to be proved, that co-educational schooling benefits the grammar school boy, though some individual may not conform to the general pattern. There is no evidence whatsoever for the hoary argument that a mixed school is bad for boys because the presence of girls distracts them from their work. If such a distraction exists, it appears to be more than compensated for by other forces, perhaps friendly rivalry between the sexes and the example set by the greater conscientiousness of girls.

For girls the trend is not so clear. In raw scores the co-educated girls are slightly inferior in a majority of subjects (except in the researches of Gott and of Douglas and Ross), but against this has to be set their age handicap, their lower social class, their less selective entry to grammar schools, their greater subject load in the examinations, and—much more doubtfully—their less highly qualified staff (except in mathematics and perhaps physical sciences). Attempting to balance these factors is not easy and leads only to very general conclusions; but it would be safe to say that there is no evidence to justify any claim that single-sex education for girls produces *per se* a higher standard of attainment than co-education. If results for the two sexes are taken into account, the balance of the argument is in favour of co-education, though much more rigorous evidence is required.

This paper is about the 'average school'. There will be some co-educational schools where the attainment level is high, and some where it is low, and similarly for single-sex schools. The sex of the school is only one factor in a complex situation. Finally, let no one think that this study is even slightly critical of the often dedicated work of the headmasters, headmistresses and staffs of single-sex schools. When we remember some of these people, and consider the greatness of their service to the community, we cannot but recognize that it is not in the statistics of examinations but in the spirit by which men and women serve that the highest values lie.

Pupils' attitudes and emotions

Until recently there had been little research on the attitudes of pupils, excepting attitudes towards school subjects. Some of this work is connected with that on co-education because it examines sex differences in the interest shown towards various aspects of subjects (cf. Dale and Jones, I., 1957, Dale and Jones, J. A., 1964). This section, however, will concentrate on new evidence about the happiness of pupils at school, their attitude to their teachers, to their schools and to the other sex. Lack of space excludes other available evidence, but more detailed accounts of these topics can be found in Dale (1966b, c, d).

A) HAPPINESS

Though we have all heard of the 'whining schoolboy . . . creeping like snail unwillingly to school', we like to think that such creatures are scarcer now than in the days when the lines were written. We should dearly wish our own children to be happy at school. One of the questions we might ask is whether John or Mary would be happier in a co-educational or in a single-sex school. This problem was first approached by asking 935 male and 1,047 female student teachers, as ex-pupils of grammar schools, 'Was your life at school, viewed as a whole, very happy/happy/jogging along/rather unhappy/very unhappy?' This will be termed the 'Second college' survey, since the first was concerned only with general attitude to school. The questionnaire was administered to large groups, and 100 per cent of the forms were completed. The results are given in table 1.

The most noticeable feature of the results is that few of these pupils were unhappy at school. Though the co-educated men had been slightly happier than those who went to boys' schools, the differences are not large enough to be reliable. On the other hand, the co-educated women reported a much higher level of happiness than did those from girls' schools—a difference which is statistically highly significant. The comments invited from the students showed that the co-educated women (like the men) were more positive than their opposites about the 'good atmosphere', and they made far more frequent mention of happy pupil-staff relationships. There was a strong tendency for both men and women from single-sex schools to say their happiness changed from junior to senior school. This was absent in the co-educated.

TABLE I

Happiness at school

School education	Men		Women	
	Single-sex	Co-ed.	Single-sex	Co-ed.
Very happy	166 (28·5%)	113 (32·2%)	145 (22·7%)	154 (37·8%)
Happy	280 (48·1%)	171 (48·8%)	352 (55·2%)	213 (52·4%)
Jogging along	113 (19·4%)	55 (15·7%)	123 (19·3%)	34 (8·4%)
Rather unhappy	22 (3·8%)	9 (2·6%)	17 (2·7%)	5 (1·2%)
Very unhappy	1 (0·2%)	2 (0·6%)	1 (0·1%)	1 (0·2%)
Totals	582 (100%)	350 (100%)	638 (100%)	407 (100%)

These students were also asked, 'Do you think the school atmosphere was very pleasant/pleasant/neutral/rather unpleasant/very unpleasant?' Few estimated the atmosphere to be rather unpleasant or worse. The co-educated men gave more favourable answers than those from boys' schools, particularly in the 'very pleasant' category, the difference being statistically reliable. The difference between the women's groups was greater, a third of the co-educated, but only a seventh of those from girls' schools, estimating 'very pleasant'. Only five of the co-educated (1·2 per cent) thought the atmosphere 'rather unpleasant' contrasted with thirty-seven (5·8 per cent) of the opposing group. In all these results the differences were not due to the different social class composition of the samples.

It might be objected that in some way the sample from the co-educational schools might not be equivalent to the single-sex schools sample. To meet this a questionnaire was administered to 175 men and 620 women, from colleges of education, who had attended both a co-educational and a single-sex secondary school (excluding secondary modern). They were from seventy-one institutions throughout England and Wales, and are representative of hundreds of schools. This will be called the 'Both schools' survey. It is not often that research results can be termed dramatic, but these were. They are given in table 2.

Nine-tenths of the men said they were happy at the mixed school, but less than 60 per cent at their boys' school. Ten out of 186 said they were only 'jogging along' when attending their mixed schools; but

TABLE 2

Happiness at school
Estimates of students who attended both mixed and single-sex schools

	Men		Women	
School life in	Single-sex	Co-ed.	Single-sex	Co-ed.
Very happy	47 (25·1%)	82 (44·1%)	169 (25·5%)	358 (54·4%)
Fairly happy	63 (33·7%)	87 (46·7%)	245 (36·9%)	224 (34·0%)
Jogging along	34 (18·2%)	10 (5·4%)	132 (19·9%)	38 (5·8%)
Rather unhappy	37 (19·8%)	7 (3·8%)	104 (15·7%)	34 (5·2%)
Very unhappy	6 (3·2%)	0	13 (2·0%)	4 (0·6%)
Totals	187 (100%)	186 (100%)	663 (100%)	658 (100%)

The totals in table 2 exceed the number of students because any student who attended two schools of the same type gave two estimates.

this became nearly one in five when they were at boys' schools. The table shows a similar difference in the 'unhappy' section. The women were equally emphatic. Three times as many of them were unhappy at their girls' than at their mixed school, whereas more than twice as many were very happy in their mixed schools as were very happy in their girls' schools.

As these samples were not representative of all types of pupil, a survey was made among 2,240 pupils in fourteen boys', fourteen girls' and fourteen mixed grammar schools in the West Riding and south Wales. The returns are available for only half of the pupils—those aged 15 plus—at their first testing. The results from the 560 boys, on the happiness question, were much as expected, the difference in favour of the co-educated boys being not quite statistically significant. Whereas about four in every ten co-educated boys gave a 'happy' estimate (the category 'very happy' was in this survey changed to 'happy'), compared with three in ten for boys' schools; this was rather more than reversed in the 'fairly happy' section. Both groups had an identical tiny minority in the unhappy categories.

The girls' results were frankly puzzling—though in this work there are so many unwanted variables to control that it is not surprising if an occasional result falls out of line. In these attitude surveys the difference between the girls' groups has usually been found to be greater than that between the boys'. Here, though still in favour of the co-educated, it is appreciably smaller and not reliable; almost 43 per cent of both groups were 'happy', but 4 per cent more in the mixed schools were 'fairly happy'; only six girls from the girls' schools and one from the mixed said they were 'very unhappy'. The reason for the narrowing of the difference is under close examination. The rather small sample of schools may not be sufficiently typical of schools of each kind; but as the change is due almost entirely to one social class in one region, it may be caused by something in the selection of the pupil sample.

B) PUPIL-TEACHER RELATIONSHIP

The 'Second college' survey included several questions on pupil-teacher relationship. In reply to a question on the friendliness of teachers (on a five-point scale), the co-educated men thought their teachers were slightly more friendly than did those from boys' schools; but the difference was not statistically significant. Only some 3 to 4 per cent of the ex-pupils of both groups thought their teachers 'rather unfriendly' or worse. On the other hand, rather more than 20 per cent answered 'neutral'. In table 3 the women's groups show a greater divergence.

TABLE 3

Friendliness of teachers

Teachers in	Men		Women	
	Single-sex	Co-ed.	Single-sex	Co-ed.
Very friendly	84 (14·5%)	63 (18·1%)	52 (8·2%)	94 (23·2%)
Friendly	345 (59·6%)	199 (57·2%)	379 (59·4%)	248 (61·2%)
Neutral	129 (22·3%)	76 (21·8%)	181 (28·4%)	59 (14·3%)
Rather unfriendly	19 (3·3%)	9 (2·6%)	22 (3·4%)	5 (1·2%)
Very unfriendly	2 (0·3%)	1 (0·3%)	4 (0·6%)	0
Totals	579 (100%)	348 (100%)	638 (100%)	406 (100%)

It will be seen that the difference is more in the positive friendliness categories than in the unfriendly ones, and, as in the case of the men, only a small minority is to be found in the 'rather unfriendly' category, or worse. The results from a question on the *helpfulness* of teachers produced a closely similar pattern to that in table 3, for both men and women, though rather more teachers were put into the unhelpful categories than were put into the unfriendly ones! The co-educated women gave a higher rating to their teachers; it should be noted that many of these teachers would be men.

Students were also asked whether one or more of their teachers had had a powerful influence for good or for bad. The men's groups had identical results, both for good and for bad. One-third of both endorsed 'powerful influence for good', and one-tenth the opposite. The difference between the women's groups was statistically significant for both 'good' and 'bad' aspects, favouring the co-educated, but it was not as large as in other replies.

These results need confirmation from other samples, but they are not unsupported, since they fall into the same pattern as that which has evolved from the remainder of the work. We now need to ask why the co-educated women recorded their teachers as more friendly, more helpful, with a somewhat greater influence for good and rather less 'influence for bad' than did the women who were educated in girls' schools. It may be that this is a true picture. On the other hand, the co-educated women may have preferred, consciously or unconsciously, being taught by men; this emotional outlook might therefore lead them to give a higher estimate of their teachers' friendliness, even though the teachers were no more friendly than those in a girls' school. Yet even if this is so, the pupils would presumably be benefited by thinking that their teachers were friendlier. Such a belief might, of course, influence the conduct of the girls towards their teachers and make the teachers themselves more inclined to be friendly. The attitude of teachers towards co-education, outlined later, gives strong support to the conclusions in this section.

c) ATTITUDE TO SCHOOL

This section concentrates on the preference of pupils for mixed or single-sex schools. As the results from three large-scale surveys closely resemble each other, only the most important of them—the 'Both schools' sample—is given here. Students in seventy-one colleges of

education, who had gone to both a mixed and a single-sex secondary
school, were asked, 'Which did you prefer, the mixed or single-sex
school?' The results were as follows.

TABLE 4

School preferences

	Men	Women
Single-sex school much	25 (15·1%)	68 (11·6%)
Single-sex school a little	15 (9·0%)	46 (7·9%)
No preference	13 (7·8%)	33 (5·7%)
Mixed school a little	13 (7·8%)	75 (12·8%)
Mixed school much	100 (60·3%)	362 (62·0%)
Totals	166 (100%)	584 (100%)

Whereas 60 out of every 100 men *much* preferred the mixed school
the figure for the boys' school was 15 in 100. The women's verdict
was a little more strongly in favour of the mixed school—62 in 100
as opposed to nearly 12 in 100 for the girls' school.

A more detailed analysis shows that the order in which the schools
were attended has some influence. Men who finished up in the sixth
form of a boys' school showed only a moderate preference for co-
education; but if they finished in a co-educational sixth, the proportion
in favour rose to 80 per cent. Sixty-five per cent of the women preferred their mixed school, even if they attended it first, and this rose
to 81 per cent if they attended it last. This is in spite of the built-in
advantages of many single-sex schools, some of them direct grant and
taking the scholastic cream of wide areas.

D) ATTITUDE TO THE OPPOSITE SEX

One of the advantages claimed by protagonists of co-education is
that conditions for social development are enhanced by the presence
of both sexes in the same school. In the 'Second college' survey this
was examined by asking the students a number of questions about their
attitude to the opposite sex; for example, 'Did your school life help
or hinder you in your relations with the opposite sex?' Over 40 per
cent of men from boys' schools and 5·5 per cent from mixed schools
thought that their education had been a hindrance, the corresponding

figures for women being 39 and 1·4 per cent. As one might have expected, both men and women from co-educational schools found it appreciably easier *to work with* members of the other sex than did ex-pupils of single-sex schools. Men from boys' schools found it more difficult than did co-educated men *to work under the direction of* a woman, but there was little difference between women's groups.* This change in the direction of the findings is probably due to the prevalence of a social attitude which regards it as normal for a woman to work under the direction of a man, but not vice versa. Whereas the education of boys with girls helps to break down the traditional resistance of the male sex to working under a woman, in the case of girls there is no need for such corrective education, as it is customary in our society for women to work under the supervision of a man. Moreover, judging by the comments made in the above study, they prefer to do so.

A further analysis of the data was undertaken to see whether social class factors were affecting the results. No such influence was apparent in the samples; but the sampling of social classes in the schools themselves is not on an equal basis for all classes, the manual-working-class pupils being more finely selected for academic ability than the others. In addition, these students were all rapidly moving towards similarity of social class, as members of the teaching profession.

The verdict of teachers

Whatever the pupils might think, what is the opinion of the teachers? Moreton (1939) used an attitude scale with a large sample of secondary school teachers (not, of course, including secondary modern), and found 'a great preponderance in favour of co-education', with little difference according to sex, marital status, education, etc. Teachers with experience of co-education, however, had a higher opinion of it than had other teachers. Although his general results are confirmed by later research, some of the details are not, and one could not rely on his work independently because it was based on a mere 14 per cent return of forms. W. E. Davies (1950) used a large national sample of teachers in all types of secondary school and also found a favourable attitude to co-education, but, unlike Moreton, he concluded that men were more favourably inclined than women. This work is much more dependable, but as the return of questionnaires was, at best, only 63 per

* Results are statistically significant unless they are stated not to be so.

cent, there remain some elements of doubt. Readers who wish to explore the question further are also referred to the findings of the Swedish Commission of 1919 in favour of mixed schools, partly based on the opinion of teachers in such schools. A part translation of the findings appears in Clark (1937). A later minor inquiry confirmed these findings (Sweden 1947).

I began my own inquiry in 1946 and completed the major part of it by 1948 (Dale 1955). This latter part was deliberately confined to secondary grammar schools in Glamorgan, in order to secure a high percentage of completed questionnaires. To this end the forms were made as simple as possible, and 83 per cent of teachers responded. The reasons for the non-return of the remaining 17 per cent of forms were partly administrative—for example, one head-teacher was retiring the next day and another was ill. As head-teachers were asked to collect the forms (in sealed envelopes), the teachers themselves could not be held responsible for such administrative failures. Teachers were asked, simply and directly, 'Are you in favour of co-education in secondary schools?' Each individual had to weigh up the arguments, subconsciously using his own set of 'scale values', without the imposition of arbitrary scale values from outside. He was then able to vary the extent of his approval or disapproval by indicating a preference for full co-education, for co-educational schools with mostly single-sex classes, for dual schools (classified as single-sex in the analysis), for single-sex schools, or for 'undecided'. He could make further reservations in a 'comments' section.

The results are informative. An overwhelming majority of the staffs of co-educational schools (91 per cent) preferred their own system, but a majority of the staffs of single-sex schools voted against their own system and preferred co-education. This verdict might be criticized because many of the teachers had taught in only one type of school, so that they could not validly compare co-educational and single-sex schooling. A further analysis of the data, therefore, extracted the opinions of only those teachers, of whom there were 238, who had taught in both types of school. Eighty per cent of the men teaching in boys' schools were in favour of co-education, 62 per cent of the women in girls' schools, and 92 per cent of the teachers in mixed schools—the women more strongly than the men.

Though the preferences probably reflect in part the influences of the type of school in which the teacher is employed, some teachers will have chosen to teach in the kind of school which they prefer. If this argument is used about those teaching in co-educational schools, it must in fairness also be used about those in single-sex schools. Detailed analysis shows that another influence is the type of school in which a teacher is educated: those co-educated have a more favourable attitude towards that system than have those educated in single-sex schools.

General comments

Both pupils and teachers who have had experience of co-education tend to have an overwhelming preference for it, whether they have been in single-sex schools or not. The opposition has come very largely from those with no direct experience of it; in other words, it has been founded upon ignorance. It is possible that the belief in the value of single-sex education had its origins in the evolution of secondary education, was established by the Victorian attitude to the sexes, fortified by tradition, and entrenched behind established interests and stereotyped prejudice. The Victorian era has passed, tradition is relaxing its hold, and the prejudice is disappearing. Some of the established interests are understandably to be seen in the desire to preserve opportunities for the promotion of women to headships of schools, and, in fairness to the sex, these opportunities should be open to those women who want them and have the ability to use them.

The researches described have been mainly about day grammar schools, largely because there is a lamentable paucity of investigation of public boarding schools. A few of the public schools are included in the analysis of examination results and some of their students will be among the samples of intending teachers, but the under-representation is very marked. This is more of an advantage than a disadvantage as the single-sex and co-educational schools are then more fairly comparable, and the influence of boarding education does not affect the issue.

Within each type of school, co-educational or single-sex, there will be a wide range of academic attainment, of pupil happiness and of pupil-teacher relationships. Schools of both types may be good or bad. Moreover, the type of school which is best for one child may not be the best for another, though there seems to be a heavy preference in one direction. Another factor which should be watched is social class; so far its influence has not been detected, but this might be because the manual-working-class children considered have been finely selected and the schools have had a strong middle-class contingent.

Schools are set in society and in many ways are a reflection of that society. The success of a particular form of school organization will therefore depend at least in part upon its relation to the beliefs, attitudes and ideals of society. It will also depend upon the spirit in which the men and women in that organization serve the next generation. Co-education is no magic wand which would produce an Utopia in our school system, but as far as research has gone it appears to deserve a much higher prestige in this country than that accorded it by tradition.

Acknowledgments

Thanks are due to the Department of Education and Science for the provision of clerical assistance, to the colleges and schools who made the field work possible, to my colleagues Dr Philip Williams and Mr D. Sharp for kindly reading the manuscript and making useful suggestions, to my research assistant Mr G. Lyons for work on one of the questionnaires, and to my secretary Mrs R. Lewis for help with tabulation and statistical computation.

Stephen Wiseman

Educational Deprivation and Disadvantage

One of the things the newly qualified teacher is quickly brought up against, as he faces his first class of pupils, is the problem of individual differences. That such differences exist he has known since the time he was a schoolboy himself, and during his training he has, presumably, been given more precise information as to the range and extent of such variations. But now he is faced, day by day, with concrete evidence that some children learn quickly and easily, others more slowly and with difficulty, and some—apparently—not at all. He can react to this realization in one of two ways. He can view the situation as immutable and pre-ordained, a 'fact of life' to be accepted, with staff-room grumbles as the only palliative and expectations of a 'better lot next year' as the only hope. Or he can pin his hopes to the possibility of remedial treatment, in the belief that some, at least, of the slow learners can be brought on more quickly. His lack of experience, plus confidence in his own abilities as a teacher, may well lead him to believe that all that is necessary is more careful preparation of materials, more skill in presenting them, and as much individual attention as he can manage to give. The relative failure of this line of attack with some of his pupils may—we hope—lead him on to consider the *causes* of backwardness, since, presumably, remedial measures to be effective must bear some relation to diagnosis.

Our young teacher will find no shortage of books to help him in his search for understanding. A survey of them will reveal considerable differences in approach, and these differences will often be found to bear relation to the dates when the books were written. The authors of those produced in the thirties and forties will—generally speaking— consider backwardness to be a predominantly cognitive problem, related to level of intelligence or particular sensory defects, and will rely on diagnostic tests as preliminaries to carefully designed remedial teaching programmes. An honourable exception to this generalization is Sir Cyril Burt. His book *The Backward Child*, published in 1937, showed ineluctably that backwardness is nearly always a matter of multiple causation, that in addition to cognitive factors, personality, motivation and environment all play a part. The child guidance clinics have never been in doubt as to the importance of factors of personality in school progress: backwardness nearly always goes hand in hand with maladjustment. But, in this country at least, environmental factors have received very little attention. During the last few years increasing interest has been shown and some research has been done, but we are still in the very early stages of exploration in this field. The situation is rather better in the United States, where the civil rights movement has stirred educationists, psychologists and politicians to attack the problem of the slum schools in the cities of the north as well as in the segregated schools of the south. Research and curriculum development is being supported by federal funds, and many promising schemes of 'compensatory education' have been launched. Among the many relevant American publications, the following can be recommended: Bloom, Davis and Hess 1965, Deutsch 1960, Fusco 1966, Passow 1963. Nevertheless, even though our insights are far from complete, research in this country has already produced some results which are of significance for teachers; it is the purpose of this paper to describe these and their implications.

The role of intelligence

Before we do this, it is necessary to clear the ground and, in particular, to consider more closely a factor which is of central importance in the discussion of backwardness and environmental deprivation—the factor of intelligence. In many of the publications of the inter-war years, already referred to, in which backwardness was seen as predominantly a matter of cognitive deficiency, the diagnosis was simple. It depended upon a comparison of *mental age*, derived from an intelligence test, and *educational age*, derived from standardized attainment tests in English, arithmetic, etc. If the educational age lagged behind the mental age, the pupil was 'merely backward' (caused, perhaps, by absence from school) and the condition was remediable by individual coaching. If, on the other hand, mental age and educational age were the same, then the child was 'dull'; and, since he was working 'up to his potential', no special action on the teacher's part was necessary.

The rationale behind this procedure was apparently valid and unassailable. It derived from two assumptions: first, that intelligence is innate, and genetically determined; secondly, that existing tests are capable of measuring it. Later research has shown these assumptions not to be wrong, but to fall into the dangerous category of half-truths. First, there seems little doubt that intelligence, like height, is largely determined by genetic or inborn factors; but that—again like height—its development may be strongly affected by environmental conditions. Secondly, although many attempts have been made to construct culture-free or culture-fair tests of intelligence, all measures are forced to employ methods of communication between tester and testee (reading and writing; listening and speaking) which are learned, and therefore are the results of environmental processes.

One should beware of the temptation to swing the pendulum too far from the assumption of the 1930s. Some current writings in education and sociology suggest that the genetic element in intelligence is either so small as to be educationally insignificant, or is non-existent. For an up-to-date and authoritative statement by a geneticist, the reader should consult Huntley (1966) who, after a survey of research, concludes 'that certainly well over half the variability of this predominantly verbal kind of intelligence in the population is due to genetic differences between people. It is probably fair to suggest that for general operational intelligence genetic differences will be responsible for something nearer three-quarters, perhaps 70 per cent of the total variability' (p. 216). The partitioning of variability in this way, 70 per cent to nature, 30 per cent to nurture, is a sensible enough procedure for the geneticist, looking at the population as a whole. But the teacher, who is concerned with individual children, must be reminded that beneath such an overall average may lie considerable individual differences, and that for some of his pupils the effects of environment may be greater than the 30 per cent suggested by Huntley. Nevertheless, it must be borne in mind that genetic differences are far from insignificant: the notion that with highly skilled teachers and a perfect educational system, allied to the abolition of slums and the destruction of the class system, all children would be equally intelligent, and would progress at the same rate and reach the same level, is an egalitarian fantasy.

Having made the point about the importance of hereditary factors, however, let us look more closely at what it means. The correlation between the intelligence of parents and that of their children is around 0·5. This is far from perfect, and it permits very substantial differences to occur. It is therefore possible for a child of below-average parents to have a very high level of potential—and vice versa, of course. Whenever surveys of adult intelligence are made, a correlation is found between I.Q. and occupation. Men and women in professional jobs tend to be more intelligent than skilled workers, who in turn have, on average, higher I.Q.s than unskilled workers. Because of the parent-child correlation, the children of such occupational classes tend to follow—on average—the same trend. For this reason the percentage of children of professional parents with high I.Q.s is greater than the percentage of children of parents in the working class.

Since the parent-child relationship is only 0·5, however, and since the number of adults in the working class is so much greater than the number in professional jobs, the *total number* of bright children of skilled, semi-skilled and unskilled workers greatly exceeds the number who come from professional homes. But by no means all of these bright children of working-class origin succeed in gaining maximum profit from the educational system. Environmental forces—in which the school as well as the home is an active element—are responsible for a great deal of wasted talent.

What are the implications for the teacher of the present state of knowledge about intelligence and its measurement?

1. Intelligence is largely determined genetically. All children are *not* of equal educational potentiality.

2. Nevertheless, intelligence is a developmental concept, and the level of stimulation in the environment has a considerable effect on its development.

3. It follows that the device of comparing 'mental age' with 'educational age' is unsound, and can never provide justification for teachers' complacency.

4. The correlation between the intelligence of parents and the intelligence of their children is far from perfect. To base educational expectancy on occupational level is unjustified, and is bound to lead to non-recognition of talent and loss of potential.

5. Intelligence tests do not measure innate ability solely: their results are affected by environmental experiences. Nevertheless, they are less affected than are tests of educational attainment,

and so are important weapons in the diagnostic armoury. A high score is always significant; a low one *may* be.

Educational deprivation

This consideration of intelligence and its measurement is an essential preliminary to the discussion of the effect of environment on school progress and educational attainment, since intelligence is a central factor in the educational process. For the teacher, the I.Q. should be thought of as a measure of *scholastic aptitude*. It is, as we have suggested, an imperfect measure, and one which itself is affected by adverse environmental forces and this fact must be kept at the forefront of the teacher's mind.

Turning now to the effects of environment on the educational process, we may discern two ways in which adversity may operate. I propose to call these 'educational deprivation' and 'educational disadvantage'. By educational deprivation is meant the process by which certain groups of children within the population appear to have less *opportunity* for education than others. Over twenty years ago Burt (1943) surveyed the distribution of intelligence among elementary school pupils and concluded that 'in round numbers about 40 per cent, or two out of five, among the pupils from the elementary school, who are capable of a university education, never obtain it' (p. 87). Almost all these children were of working-class parents. In 1954 the then Ministry of Education produced a report on *Early Leaving* from the grammar school. This showed that of the pupils who gained high marks in the grammar school selection examination, 10 per cent of those with parents in professional jobs failed to get at least three G.C.E. 'O' level passes; but for the children of parents classified as 'unskilled workers', with an identical level at entry, the figure was 54 per cent. The well-known research of Floud, Halsey and Martin (1956) compared the situation in south-west Hertfordshire in the early fifties with what it had been sixty years earlier. The percentage of children of manual workers who gained grammar school places rose from 11 to 34 over this period—a not inconsiderable improvement. But in Middlesbrough, post war, they found 68 per cent of children of professional and managerial parents in grammar schools, compared with 14 per cent of children of skilled workers. These differences reflect fairly accurately the proportions to be expected on the results of group tests of verbal intelligence—but, as we have seen, the results of such tests are themselves subject to the effects of environment.

Perhaps the United States, of all the Western nations, provided the most dramatic evidence of educational deprivation in its segregated schools in the south in the immediate post-war years (see Passow 1963). And in the big cities of the north, the slum schools, with the added problems of colour, race and language, show an intensity of educational deprivation in the 1960s which surpasses anything we experience in this country. Cloward and Jones (1963) point out that 'because of the greater turn-over of teachers in slum schools, their relative inexperience, and the geographic mobility of low-income families, slum youth receive less actual instructional time than do school children in middle-class neighbourhoods' (p. 191). And Deutsch (1960) found that in some schools in deprived areas as much as 80 per cent of the school day was devoted to matters of discipline and organization; even with the best teachers the proportion never fell below 50 per cent.

Nearly all the research on educational deprivation uses social class or occupational level as the basis of analysis. There are obvious advantages in this: it is simple, quick and easy. But it is a very rough-and-ready measure: like nearly all such broad groupings the differences within classes are found to be greater than the differences between classes. Useful as it was in the early stages of research, it has now become almost a *de rigueur* approach for many educational sociologists, who seem unaware of its ability to conceal differences—differences that are important and even essential for a fuller understanding of the mechanisms underlying educational deprivation and disadvantage.

Educational disadvantage

Let us now turn to a consideration of the way in which environment affects educational attainment rather than educational opportunity. The first significant British work in this field will be found in Burt's (1937) *The Backward Child*. In that classic book is a map of London showing the incidence of educational backwardness, from which it is clear that the greatest intensity of backwardness is found in the poorest areas: Lambeth, Bermondsey, Shoreditch and Limehouse. Burt used the metropolitan boroughs as units of analysis, and found that the percentage of backward children in the boroughs had correlations of 0·9 or over with such social variables as the infantile mortality rate or the amount of overcrowding, and a correlation of 0·7 with juvenile delinquency.

Since 1951 we have been carrying out a series of researches in the Manchester area (Wiseman 1964, 1966, Department of Education and Science 1967a, Appendix), which have focused on the attainment of children in secondary schools and in primary schools, and relating this to environmental factors. In our 1951 and 1957 surveys of secondary school children, we used the city ward as the unit of analysis, and, like Burt in London, we were able to draw maps of the incidence of backwardness. Figure 1 shows the distribution of backwardness in reading in the city, and demonstrates the heavy incidence in the central slum areas, with a 'grey' area to the north and a 'white' area in the middle-class suburbs in the south. The correlation with socio-economic level is high. But when we compare other indices of social insufficiency, the picture is by no means so simple. Look at figure 2, which shows the incidence of infantile mortality. In Burt's time, this was mainly a product of poverty: he found a correlation of 0·8 between this and 'economic grade'. Our own data give a correlation of zero between infantile mortality and the juror index (at that time a quick and useful measure of socio-economic level). In the welfare state, deaths under one year are not produced by poverty and lack of material needs, but are rather associated with parental neglect; that is, it is a psychological rather than an economic factor. This underlines very clearly the fact that research findings at one point in time do not necessarily apply at a later point. The educational system exists in, and interacts with, the larger social system: changes in the latter may make significant changes in the way in which such interaction occurs.

One of the significant aspects of all the Manchester researches has been the investigation of the effect of environmental factors on bright children and on backward children as an extension of the effect on the average child. Few, if any, of the other investigators have done this. This is odd, for we have found important and significant differences here. The earliest of our surveys showed that backwardness and brightness are not just simple opposites in such a social context, that areas with little backwardness do not necessarily have a proportionately greater percentage of bright children—and vice versa. But this demonstration was linked with an even more important one, that of these two measures, brightness appears much *more* susceptible to the effects of environment, that bad homes and bad neighbourhoods are more

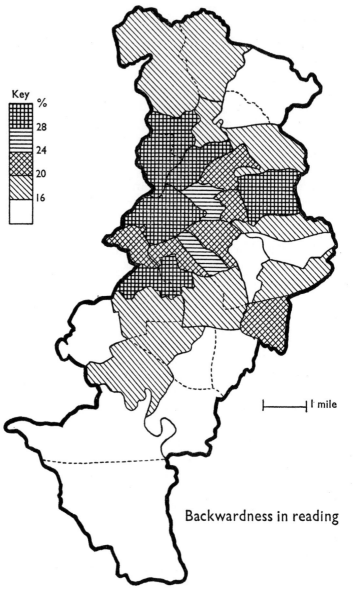

Key

%
28
24
20
16

Backwardness in reading

Figure 1   Distribution of backwardness (R.Q.<85) on reading
comprehension test

Reprinted from Wiseman, S., *Education and Environment*, Manchester University
Press, 1964, by permission of the author and publishers.

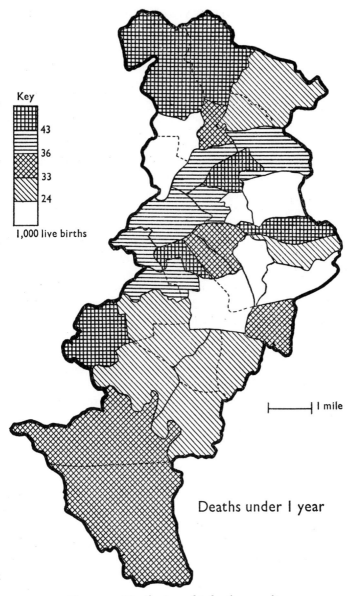

Key

43

36

33

24

1,000 live births

⊢——⊣ I mile

Deaths under I year

Figure 2   Distribution of infantile mortality

Reprinted from Wiseman, S., *Education and Environment*, Manchester University Press, 1964, by permission of the author and publishers.

effective in preventing the emergence of brightness than they are in producing backwardness. This supports Burt's (1943) finding of 'decidedly higher' correlations with environmental factors for brighter children; Fraser's (1959) significant relation between ability level and abnormal home background, with brighter children being the more affected; and Maxwell's (1953) finding from the 1947 Scottish Mental Survey that 'high intellectual ability is more widely distributed over different social environments than is low intellectual ability'.

The social variables that are strongly associated with educational attainment are certainly *economic*, since areas with a low J-index, and with a high proportion of children receiving free shoes and clothing, tend to be areas of poor attainment. But there are stronger associations with such variables as number of N.S.P.C.C. cases of cruelty and neglect, number of committals to care, and lack of immunization to whooping cough and diphtheria. These form a related bunch of variables that we have called 'maternal care', and affect all aspects of attainment but are particularly strongly associated with poor reading comprehension. Then there is a group of variables, associated with these, but emphasizing *dirt* rather than the more psychological aspects of maternal care: verminous conditions, scabies and cleansing notices. These are particularly associated with low percentages of high-scoring children.

These are some of the major results from the 1951 and 1957 surveys, and perhaps enough has been said to make it clear that they were explorations in an almost unknown field. We were trying to do two things: first, to try out techniques of exploration, and secondly, to find some significant signposts to guide us in further work.

In 1963 we began an investigation on the effect of environment on the educational attainment of *primary* school children, including school environment as well as home and neighbourhood environment. This gave us the opportunity of comparing results from our secondary school analysis, as well as enabling us to widen the scope of environmental factors (Department of Education and Science 1967a, Appendix).

We took a carefully chosen sample of 25 per cent of all Manchester primary schools, designed to be a representative sample in respect of school type, school size and geographical location. We studied the ten-year-old pupils in these schools—2,000 of them. Our research fell into two parts: first, the investigation of the forty-four schools and their environments—the level of educational attainment in each school, the percentage of bright and backward pupils on each of the measures of educational attainment, and the correlations of these measures with the various environmental variables. Secondly, we took a small sample of 200 children from half the schools studied, and did a more detailed investigation of these individual pupils. We had the benefit of interviews with parents conducted by the Social Survey team of the Central Office of Information for each of the pupils in the sub-sample.

The major limitation of our research—and this must be stressed very strongly—lay in the nature of our measures of educational attainment. Such measures must be common to all schools, and since we were working for the Plowden Committee, we had severe limitations on time. This made it impossible to consider the use of specially constructed tests; we had to make do with what was available. The only common measures available were the tests given to the children by the Manchester Authority—tests of arithmetic (problem and mechanical), of English (objective tests and an essay test), and of verbal intelligence. Such tests had been given to these ten-year-old children at ages 7 plus, 8 plus, 9 plus and 10 plus, so that we were able to look at age-trends. But these objective measures of performance in the tool subjects are far from a comprehensive measure of primary school attainment. As was said in the report to the Plowden Committee (Department of Education and Science 1967a, Appendix), 'Such measures are a necessary *part* of any criterion of primary school attainment, but they are far from giving a balanced picture. No account is taken of the many other activities which go on in the average primary school, the work in art and craft, in music, in science and geography and history, and in the many other pursuits which can often not be classified under the traditional "subject" labels, but which, nevertheless, are of very great significance educationally. Our choice of criterion measures must not be taken to indicate a belief that the three Rs are all that matter, nor should the limitations of our tests be forgotten in interpreting the results of our inquiry.'

There were twelve tests altogether (two at age 7, three at age 8, two at age 9, and five at age 10); each test gave us three 'scores' for each school (mean score, percentage bright and percentage backward), so we had thirty-six criterion variables. In addition to this we had fifty-two environmental variables, eighteen relating to the home and neighbourhood, thirty-four relating to the school itself—its building, its equipment, its teachers and its atmosphere. This gave us a total of eighty-eight variables and a matrix of nearly 4,000 correlations.

The average correlation of the eighteen 'home' variables with educational attainment was 0·295; the average of the thirty-four school variables was only 0·199. The environmental pressures of home and neighbourhood seem to be more powerful than those of the school itself. The highest correlations were for the percentage of verminous children, the cleanliness of the home, and the percentage of free meals, thus underlining the factors of maternal care and of poverty that we had found in our earlier secondary school studies. The highest school correlations were attendance (a highly predictable result) and streaming. Streamed schools had better records of attainment than unstreamed schools. Little weight should be attached to this result: the investigation of such a complex problem as streaming needs a much wider sample of schools than the forty-four we used—and of these, the majority of schools classified as 'unstreamed' were so because they had to be, being one-form entry schools. Nevertheless, we found no evidence that streaming has an adverse effect on pupils of *low* ability: streamed schools tended to have fewer backward children at all ages and in all tests.

Since we had test results for the 2,000 ten-year-old children at four different ages, it is of some interest to see what changes, if any, in correlations are shown over the years. Figure 3 shows average correlations for home and neighbourhood variables separately. There are a number of interesting points about these graphs. First, notice the higher correlations for home and neighbourhood effects—and the commanding position of the intelligence test here. Why is I.Q. more strongly associated with these variables than with the school environment? As I have suggested elsewhere (Wiseman 1966), 'the crucial difference between the school variable and the home and neighbourhood variables lies in the fact that the latter are affected by, and affect, the *parents* of the children, while school variables are those which affect children only. In other words, I am emphasizing the heavier *genetic* element in the results of the intelligence tests . . . Much of the quality of home and neighbourhood is related to the parents' intellectual level. Adverse environments tend both to be produced by the incompetent and the incapable and also to attract them. And since there is a correlation of 0·5 between the intelligence of parents and that of their children, this produces a significant correlation between children's I.Q. and the social variables' (pp. 71–2).

The upward slope of the lines in figure 3 is almost certainly an artifact, arising from the fact that the correlations are between *present* environmental measures and test results from earlier years. This will produce shrinkage in the correlations, and a shrinkage which is greater for the greater time-gap. Indeed, it seems highly probable that the true line of the graphs should be downwards, showing a decrease in

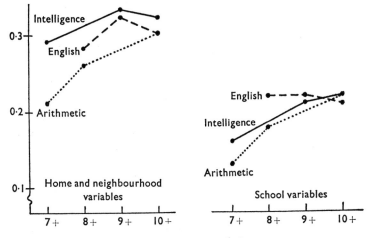

Figure 3   Mean correlations

Reprinted from Wiseman, S., 'Environmental and innate factors and educational attainment', in Meade, J. E. and Parkes, A. S. (eds.) *Genetic and Environmental Factors in Human Ability*, Oliver & Boyd, 1966, by permission of the author and publishers.

correlation between attainment and environment as the children get older. Two of our measures of environment were identical with those used in the 1957 secondary school survey: per cent of verminous children, and per cent receiving free shoes and clothing. The average correlations of the former with attainment were 0·483 at 10 plus, 0·383 at 14 plus; for the latter the figures are 0·237 and 0·173. The fall from 10 plus to 14 plus is apparent for all three types of test. Consider the implications of this. If one were to extrapolate the graphs back into the infant school, and thence to the pre-school years, we should then find the influence of environment becoming stronger and stronger, the younger the child. This receives powerful support from Bloom (1964). After making a very thorough survey of longitudinal studies of children's development, including physical characteristics as well as intelligence and educational attainment, he concludes, 'Intelligence is a developmental concept, just as is height, weight or strength. There is increased stability in intelligence measurements with time. However, we should be quick to point out that by about age 4, 50 per cent of the variation in intelligence at age 17 is accounted for. This would suggest the very rapid growth of intelligence in the early years and the possible great influence of environment on this development. We should expect the variations in environment to have relatively little effect on the I.Q. after age 8, but we should expect such variation to have marked effect on the I.Q. before that age, with the greatest effect likely to take place between the ages of about one to five' (p. 68). Bloom's study of the growth of educational attainment as distinct from intelligence is naturally complicated by the fact that its very nature restricts its study to the period of school attendance—apart, that is, from the growth of vocabulary. Nevertheless, his analysis suggests that 'learning patterns are partially established before children enter school'. Evidence on the growth of vocabulary shows that about one-third has been developed by this time. His estimate is similar for educational attainment in general. Thus he suggests that of the eventual attainment of eighteen-year-olds, one-third will have been developed by age 6 and three-quarters by age 13 (Bloom 1964, p. 110); he comments, 'although these figures may be debatable and further studies may modify them, we are of the opinion that the relative magnitude of these values will not change appreciably. We believe it is likely that more careful investigations will reveal even larger values for the pre-school period and the first three years of elementary school than is suggested by the studies we have been able to assemble to date . . . The home environment is very significant not only because of the large amount of educational growth which has already taken place before the child enters the first grade but also because of the influence of the home during the elementary school period.'

Allied to this American support of the thesis that environmental effects are greatest at the youngest ages, we have other evidence of the weakening of these influences at the upper end of the age-range. The Robbins Report (Ministry of Education 1963b) collected evidence on the relation between G.C.E. results and social class, and found that 'working-class children who do stay on to take "A" level examinations are on average as successful as their counterparts in other social groups'

(Appendix I, p. 46). The Committee provided data connecting 'A' level G.C.E. results with previous 11-plus results (see table 1), from which it is clear that differences of social class have ceased to be effective determinants of educational achievement at this level and by the age of about eighteen.

TABLE I

Percentage of school leavers aged 18 or over who have at least two G.C.E. 'A' levels

(From table 7, p. 45, Appendix I of the Robbins Report)

Father's occupation	11-plus grading		
	Upper third	Middle third	Lower third
Professional and managerial	79	63	43
Clerical	74	56	58
Skilled manual	77	59	51
Semi- and unskilled	81	58	53

Reprinted from *Higher Education*, Report of the Committee on Higher Education (The Robbins Report), H.M. Stationery Office, 1963, by permission of the Department of Education and Science and the publishers.

The pupil analysis

It will be remembered that, in addition to our investigation of the forty-four schools which contained our 2,000 primary school children, we also made a more intensive study of 200 individual children and their homes. Here it was necessary to perform three separate analyses, in order to investigate backwardness and brightness as well as total score on the tests. For the details of the three analyses the reader is referred to the full report (Department of Education and Science 1967a, Appendix); here we shall take an overall view.

There was a good deal of common ground in the three analyses. This is made evident by the fact that, if we take the 'top ten' environmental variables in each analysis (i.e. the ten which show the strongest association with attainment), *seven* of these appear in all three analyses: membership of library; parents' reading; number of books in house; child's reading; preferred age of leaving school; homework given; and parents' concern about the child's school progress. No clearer indication could be given of the importance of (a) the literacy of the home, and (b) the parents' attitude to education. Little connection is shown with social class (average correlation with father's occupation was 0·098). What matters is the attitude of parents towards books and towards school. These results emphasize the existence of many 'good' homes in the working class, and many 'bad' homes in the middle class. The differences between the three kinds of test are also interesting for the 'reading' variables. The child's reading understandably shows the highest correlations with the English tests; but if we average the correlations of the other three reading variables (membership of library, parents' reading, number of books) we get I.Q. 0·325, English 0·307 and arithmetic 0·283. It is not unreasonable to assume that the standard of literacy in the home and the interest the parents show in reading are—like their readiness to keep the child at school beyond the statutory leaving age—strongly correlated with the parents' level of intelligence. It is not surprising, therefore, to find a high correlation of these variables with the intelligence of the child. As in the schools analysis, variables which are parent-determined, or which are likely to be affected by parental action or attitude, tend to show higher correlations with the child's I.Q. than with the measures of attainment.

Notice again the relative lack of association with school variables. Only one appears in the 'top ten' lists—homework given. This is a measure of the parents' response to the interviewer's question, 'Have the teachers at school given the child any work to do at home?' This should not, in fact, be regarded as necessarily a *school* variable. A negative response may indicate the parents' ignorance and lack of interest—or, indeed, the child's refusal to conform.

When we consider differences between the three analyses, we find an interesting contrast between brightness and backwardness. The factors associated with backwardness tend to be those denoting maternal attitude to the *child*, while for brightness the parents' attitude to *education* seems the more important. The backward child is a pupil beset with problems. Support, affection and understanding at home help him to surmount these. The potentially bright child, on the other hand, needs not so much help in overcoming difficulties as encouragement to take full advantage of the opportunities offered. The parents' view of schooling and the value they put on education are the factors that are likely to affect the progress of the able child.

The effects of environmental deprivation

What conclusions can we draw from the results of the Manchester surveys? One of the difficulties we face here is one that is sometimes forgotten in interpreting researches which rely upon correlation co-efficients as a technique of analysis. A correlation is merely a measure of *association*; it does not necessarily imply *causality*. Two variables may, for example, show a high correlation, not because they themselves are directly related, but because each of them is related to a third, unmeasured, variable. As has been said elsewhere, 'a positive relation-ship between size of class and school attainment does not justify the corollary that increasing class size will improve scholastic ability. A similar association with the number of books in the home does not mean that if one made a present of a dozen books to a family, this would improve the child's school work. Winning the pools, and thus dramatically raising the family income, is unlikely to have any advan-tageous educational effects on the children, despite the correlation between income level and attainment. If the school nurse disinfests the hair of one or two children, this is irrelevant to their results on the next arithmetic test, in spite of the Manchester results on "cleanliness" ' (Department of Education and Science 1967a, p. 348). We must, there-fore, restrain our natural tendency to transform 'association' into 'direct causality'. Nevertheless, with this warning in mind, the points which seem to be established are as follows:

1. Factors in the home environment are overwhelmingly more important than those of the neighbourhood or the school.

2. Of these home influences, factors of maternal care and of parental attitude to education, to school and to books, are of far greater significance than social class and occupational level.

3. Environmental influences on educational attainment are greatest at the youngest ages, and get progressively less influential as the children get older. This does not deny the inevitable effect of 'cumulative deficit' if adequate remedial measures are not taken.

4. It seems more likely that the greatest damage occurs before the child ever reaches school, and this may well be the major reason why school factors appear so weak in their effects.

5. Adverse conditions of home and neighbourhood have their greatest impact on the more able children. This, perhaps, of all

our conclusions is the one that needs most stress—not only because of its intrinsic importance for national efficiency as well as individual self-fulfilment, but because it is at variance with the popular and generally accepted view of the effects of environmental deprivation. The man in the street and the teacher in the classroom both tend to think of slum neighbourhoods as those which produce dirty children, ragged children, weakly children, aggressive children, delinquent children—and backward children. And in this belief they are right; but they are wrong in thinking this is the whole of the story. The teacher must for ever be on the alert to respond to, and to cater adequately for, the slum child whose potentiality is well above that of many of his confrères from the neat and tidy homes of respectable suburbia. Such children are not rare occurrences: there are far more of them than we at present recognize. Consider the deprived child whose I.Q.—had he been born into a family with a richer and more educationally-advantageous background—would be in the region of 120 plus. His tested intelligence in the primary school is only 100. But he progresses at an average rate, he is not a slow learner, he does not fall behind. In view of his poor home background his teacher may view him as one of her 'successes'—and yet he is far from working at his true potential. The challenge to the teacher is a real one, and a difficult one. And unless we as teachers abandon the automatic equation 'slums=backwardness' and engage on a positive and deliberate search for buried talent, then most of these children will fumble their way through school, unidentified, unstimulated and unaware of their powers.

Remedial measures

Since the effects of environmental deprivation on educational attainment are so strong and so pervasive, what can we do to counteract them? Can the school compensate, at least in some degree, for the handicaps of home and neighbourhood? Many programmes of 'compensatory education' have been launched in the United States, and we in this country must watch them with close attention, and learn as quickly as possible which elements appear to be producing the most profit. This may seem a timid and rather negative approach to our own problems, but these American programmes must, we suggest, be viewed as being in the nature of operational research. We do not yet know enough about the mechanisms operating to produce educational disadvantage to be able to offer advice to the teacher in the classroom; we need more research. And this means not only research of the Manchester survey type, but also operational research of the American type. Let us hope that some of our larger urban authorities will mount some projects in compensatory education—but meanwhile let us learn from the initiative of our transatlantic cousins.

There are, however, at least two clear necessities for action here and now. Since the maximum impact of environment comes in the years before school, we must increase our nursery school provision in the large cities and conurbations. What is needed is the provision of proper nursery schools and classes, staffed by fully trained teachers, not mere nurseries to look after children while 'Mum' is at work. There already is evidence of the value of this. Goldberg (1963) quotes Lees' Philadelphia study, which finds that 'Philadelphia-born Negro pupils who had attended kindergarten scored higher at each grade level than those who had not attended . . . those born in the city had average I.Q.s of 92·1 in the first grade and 93·7 in the ninth grade. Only those who attended kindergarten reached a mean-I.Q. status of approximately 97—thus approaching the national norm' (p. 84). A pioneer of research in this field is Deutsch (1963, 1964), who believes that 'early intervention by well-structured programs will significantly reduce the attenuating influence of the socially marginal environment'. He emphasizes the central role of language (as does Bernstein 1960 in this country) but suggests that this arises—at least partly—from *perceptual* deficit: 'Perhaps the poverty of his experience has slowed his rate of maturation. Then by requiring, without the antecedent verbal preparation, a relatively high level of language skill, the school may contribute to an increase in the child's deficit in this area, relative to middle-class children . . . The remedy for such a situation would be emphasis on perceptual training in the early school, or, better, pre-school, years, combined with a more gradual introduction of language training and requirements' (Deutsch 1963, p. 176).

In addition to providing the enrichment of perceptual experience suggested by Deutsch, and the fuller oral language environment suggested by the work of Bernstein, the nursery school should also do much to change the child's attitude to school—and also that of his parents. As

Passow (1963) points out, 'Predilection towards school and academic achievements is determined fairly early in the child's development. Kahl (1953) has pointed out that early success in school raises the hopes of both child and parent for future achievements. 'Basic patterns of' school behaviour, affinity or distaste for educational achievement, are established in the early grades' (p. 182). In other words, nursery school experience would attempt to offset what Deutsch calls the 'formal, conceptual and attitudinal systems' of the child. The United States has already acted under the spur of research such as that mentioned above and instituted the 'Head start' programme. This is one that we should immediately copy in this country. We have long prided ourselves on a school starting age of five, compared with six or seven in other European countries—conveniently ignoring the fact that other countries, almost without exception, have kindergarten and nursery school provision far in excess of that available here. It is time we recognized this lack of educational opportunity which falls most heavily on the children least able to bear it. Generally speaking, it is the well-to-do middle-class children who get nursery school experience because their parents are able to pay for it in independent schools —but it is the slum children who need it.

The second line of immediate action is by changes in teacher training, both initial training and in-service training. All our college of education students need more guidance and more information on the problems and extent of educational deprivation and disadvantage. They must be made aware of the need for constant vigilance in the search for buried talent, and their responsibilities for the educational guidance of individual pupils must embrace knowledge of home background as well as the results of classroom tests. The walls of the Education lecture room might well bear a Victorian text, from a poet much revered by the Victorians, Gray:

> But Knowledge to their eyes her ample page
>> Rich with the spoils of time, did ne'er unroll;
> Chill Penury repress'd their noble rage,
>> And froze the genial current of the soul.

> Full many a gem of purest ray serene
>> The dark unfathom'd caves of ocean bear:
> Full many a flower is born to blush unseen,
>> And waste its sweetness on the desert air.

But there must also be an opportunity for those students who so wish to pursue a more specialized course concerned with cultural deprivation. This would not only delve more deeply into the researches in this field, but ought also to include practical work in collaboration with probation officers, youth leaders, children's officers and other workers in the welfare services. It may be true that teachers are middle class in outlook, but it is certainly true that very many are working class in origin. Many of our college of education students would welcome an option in their training which would help them to evaluate the positive as well as the negative aspects of working-class culture, and so equip them to do more constructive work with the deprived children in our schools, and with their parents.

In addition to such courses in our colleges, there ought to be more in-service courses, 'training courses for experienced teachers, so that they may be equipped to co-operate with the officers of the other social agencies within local authorities. Their task would be, not only to recognize cases of deprivation and to refer them to the appropriate experts, but also to bring home and school, parents and teachers, into closer relationship, to their mutual understanding and benefit. Such teachers are as necessary as remedial teachers, careers masters, or guidance counsellors, and would—like them—spend only part of their time within the classroom. The existence of a small corps of such "teachers-cum-social-workers" within an authority (and particularly within the large urban authorities) would be of the greatest benefit in increasing our knowledge of the complex interactions between environment and educational attainment, and in developing new strategies in our efforts to provide the conditions for the full flowering of every child's potentiality' (Department of Education and Science 1967a, vol. 2, p. 383).

D. F. Swift

Social Class and Educational Adaptation

The importance of social class

The concept of social class has become one of the vital weapons in the armoury of educational analysts. It would be unthinkable, nowadays, to avoid applying it in a book which reviews our present state of research in education. Whatever the educational problem, somewhere the analyst will have to deal with his material in terms of how social class factors influence it. But does this mean that research workers in education have found a sharp new instrument which greatly improves our understanding? In one way, it does; but in another, it does not. Certainly, during the last decade, ideas about social class have played an important part in our ability to *describe* what is going on in the educational system. On the other hand, the concept is neither new nor sharp. The intention behind this paper will be to emphasize the bluntness of the instrument without destroying confidence in the work it has already done.

First of all, then, what has it done? At the very simplest level it has shown that the impact of the system of formal education differs in different strata of societies. Because in social analysis all associations are assumed to be reciprocal, and because it is clearly true, we have to say that the different strata of society also have different kinds of effects upon the functioning of the educational system.

To put these ideas in a proper context, we must start with a model of society in our heads. It is important to realize that we will do this whether we intend to or not; that is, if we ignore a sociological perspective when we are thinking about education, we will be implicitly *assuming* things about how society functions. There will be a model implicitly contained in what we say. Occasionally this may not matter, but when we are dealing with such a social concern as education it is usually dangerous. It is sensible, therefore, to bring these implicit ideas out into the open, so as to ensure that they are as reasonable as we can make them.

Let us think of society as a system of interrelated parts. To simplify matters we will think of only its major parts—its institutions. These institutions are patterns of action and of values which have grown up in response to major needs of the whole society.

Thus, we have an institution of education consisting of patterns of action and of values which have produced a set of material artifacts—buildings and equipment. The major function of this sub-system is to transmit the beliefs, habits and skills of thought and action which exist or are believed to be needed in society. At the same time, we have certain regularized ways of arranging for the distribution of power in society, which we call the 'political sphere'. We have an institution known as 'the family' which attempts to provide for sexual needs, the procreation of children, and their initiation into society. How far we would wish to go in drawing up a list of such institutions would depend upon ourselves; but certainly the list would always contain these three basic institutions and the economy. The crucial point about all of them is that the patterns of behaviour which earn them their names are, to some extent, devised deliberately by the members of the society. We make rules and attempt to enforce them. We insist that one man should have one vote, one wife, some schooling and only his own money.

In addition to the formal structures, we can also see similar regularities which are not backed by a structure of formal rules, but which otherwise are similar in that they are reasonably distinct and fundamental patterns of action and values. Perhaps the two most important ones are religion and stratification. All these great institutions of society together form a structure which is rather like the skeleton of a ferro-concrete building. They are the backbone of society.

We now have the basis for a crude model of a functioning society. It comprises a number of people knowing, doing and valuing. What they know and do, and how they value what they know and do, is not just a disordered jumble of unconnected items. It forms inter-acting patterns which are relatively stable and hence predictable. The mutual influencing which goes on between these patterns we can call the 'social process'. We attempt to isolate an aspect of this social process when we ask questions like, 'Why do dockers' children do less well at school than the children of doctors?', or 'Why do we insist upon a school engaging in daily prayers?', or 'What are the consequences of teaching through note-taking?', or even 'Why does Johnny always play the fool in class?' This paper must deal with the way in which the system of stratification influences the system of education and vice versa. And this is why the instrument of class analysis cannot be called new. Such questions have been asked and sometimes even answered by many great educational thinkers. Plato himself devised a scheme whereby a system of stratification might be wedded to a system of education with what he hoped would be desirable consequences.

However, since the mid-fifties a kind of class analysis has been used simply to describe how the stratification and educational characteristics of individuals have tended to coincide. This has been important simply because it showed that factors from a system of stratification were clearly related to aspects of educational consequences which were neither intended nor thought to be desirable (Banks 1958, Floud *et al.* 1956, Little and Westergaard 1964, Ministry of Education 1954). For example, the Crowther Report (Ministry of Education 1959–60) found that two-thirds of the second highest ability group (out of six—hence reasonably 'able' children) left school at fifteen, and that 80 per cent of them came from manual worker homes. The best descriptive study on these lines was reported by a medical research worker (Douglas 1964), who showed that in a sample of all the children in England children of the upper middle class get three times as many selective (11-plus) places as children of the lower manual, twice as many as children of the upper manual and one and a half times as many as 'white-collar' children *when comparing children of equal verbal reasoning ability*.

This, then, is the major contribution to knowledge which has been made through the use of social class as an analytical tool. Chances of receiving and accepting education, however it is defined, are biased according to social class. Many questions of applied science can now be put which depend upon the values the observer holds about what the system of education *should* be doing. However, there is a pure science question which must be asked and which *has* been asked, but badly. What are the mechanisms by which this situation is brought about? Its sociological formulation looks for what happens in the social process to produce this pattern. Its social-psychological formulation is: 'How does a child from one kind of environment develop cognitive skills and motivations which differ from those of a child from another environment?' Because these are only two ways of looking at the same situation, the answers they arrive at will have to be consonant with each other. In both formulations we are concerned with the context of human learning as well as the psychological processes involved.

The message of the 'class-chances' research is that social class must have something to do with the process of learning in schools. What, then, is the social class factor that seems to interfere with the process of human interaction and mutual influencing which we describe as education? If we take our answer from the research itself, it is parents' occupation. Unfortunately, part of the Plowden research has taken this at its face value and has tried to isolate the influence of parents' occupation in school achievement when the effect of 'everything' else has been removed (Department of Education and Science 1967a, vol. 2, Appendix 4). This is exactly like testing the effects of chocolate upon the taste-buds by eating its wrapper. When we are discussing how a *particular environment affects an individual*, the term is a summary of a whole matrix of other factors rather than a thing in itself. We can fairly confidently predict a large number of future studies employing covariance and analogous techniques to 'partial out' the 'simultaneous' effect of 'social class' and other 'factors' which will find that parents' occupation did not have the most important 'effect' upon achievement. For example, Bruckman (1966) found, through such a research design, that intelligence was the dominant variable. The important underlying assumption of studies like these is that the conceptual status of each of the variables is equivalent. But this is not so. The concept 'occupational status' derives from social structural, rather than psycho-dynamic analysis. Such 'simultaneous effect' analyses, therefore, suffer from a weakness in articulation between theoretical framework and research design. This is different from the much more serious weakness implied in the logical jump from mathematical 'interaction' to social interaction. Both these problems, however, have to be lived with, and in the former case the difficulty is not insurmountable.

In order to elucidate the conceptual status of 'parents' occupation', two topics will be dealt with. The difference between social structural analysis and psycho-dynamics will be exemplified first. We can then go on to clarify what is meant by class analysis, and to try to show that it is not a sharp tool when we approach the question of how environment influences the individual.

Let us return for a moment to the system of stratification in our simple model of society in process. Stratification simply relates to a hierarchy of inequality. It is clear that there exists in our society (many sociologists would say in *all* societies) a series of hierarchies of inequalities. The three obvious hierarchies are those to do with income, prestige and power. (There are also others which relate to, say, height or strength, but these are best dealt with as attributes of individuals rather than of societies.) While it is true that we can distinguish *analytically* between these three hierarchies in any society, it is impossible to make a distinction between them in actual life. Power tends to go with income, which tends to go with prestige, and so on. A great deal of fairly fruitless effort has been expended in attempting to find the most important or perhaps even prime mover of the three elements. For our purposes there is no need to pursue that debate. The important point is that when a sociologist wishes to study the stratification system of a particular society, he has to specify how he will define it. How he does this will depend upon the kind of analysis he has in mind. Therefore, we must ask ourselves what relation we want stratification to bear to the education system.

Social structural analysis and psycho-dynamics

First, we must take a societal view of the process so as to minimize the danger of analytical myopia—which is an inability to see the wood because of the trees. We see the whole of society as a process in which patterns of behaviour and of valuing can be seen to be related to and to influence each other. This is social structural analysis. We think of the stratification system (of whatever kind) and the educational system as sub-systems of the wider social system. The ways in which they influence and adapt to each other are aspects of the integration of society. As an over-simplified example, we can see that the present class-chances picture of educational selection indicates the support which the education system gives the stratification system.

On the other hand—and this is the psycho-dynamic approach—we have to ask how experience in other sub-systems affects the adaptation *of an individual* to education. In doing this, we can expect to find that the problems which it sets him will be influenced by the problems it encounters in adapting to its own environment. Adaptation by an individual to a system is a problem of psycho-dynamics and a textbook of educational psychology would concentrate upon it. However, to the extent that such a discipline aims to improve the practice of education, it is a dangerous thing to do. Taking the education system and its adaptation to society as given involves concentrating upon the problems of adaptation it raises for individuals. But these very problems may be aspects of its own adaptation to the wider social structure, and as such may be better solved at that level. This is not necessarily so, but to assume that it was not so would deprive the analyst of the chance of ever finding out.

The distinction between the psycho-dynamics of adaptation to education and social structural analysis is not purely academic. It has important consequences for the interpretation of observed data, in that it is an important aspect of the definition of variables. It is also the cause of problems of interpretation which have arisen between psychologically and sociologically oriented researches. In this paper a conceptual framework will be put forward which is suitable to the perspectives of both disciplines.

Basically, the class–chances kind of head-counting has thrown us back upon explicit or implicit social-psychological theories about the adaptation of individuals to social situations. We have looked at data which shows that children of middle-class parents had six times as good a chance of selection at 11 plus as working-class children (Swift 1965b) and added some explanations for it which amount to a fairly unorganized amalgamation of single associations. The class–chances picture came about because potentially clever people have potentially clever children. They teach them to value education, and they teach them ways of behaving which will make them successful at school. Unfortunately, some of these ideas can be contradictory. Parents who force children to work hard will have more successful children than those who do not (Drews and Teahan 1957, Swift 1967b). On the other hand, children from democratic (i.e. 'nice') homes also appear to be more successful than those from non-democratic (Clausen and Williams 1963, Elder 1965, Fraser 1959, Griffiths 1959).

The point is that the number of potential single variables is limitless. For example, Orme (1965) found an association between climatic temperature changes during foetal development and subsequent ability. Clearly the associations a research worker finds will always be partly a function of what he chooses to treat as data. However, social class has been shown to matter so often that we must be on to something.

But what is it? Clearly, we must see social class as some kind of structuring of human experience which has consequences for the learning of social and cognitive behaviour.

The important questions from a psycho-dynamic point of view must be formulated in the following way. By what means does the structuring of social experience develop cognitive, cathectic and evaluative* skills and habits in children? Which aspects of this structuring foster the development of which kinds of skills and habits? Which skills and habits make adapting to the process of formal education easier?

The role of social class analysis in the formulation of questions such as these is fairly obvious. Social classes are social structures according to which experience is organized. Its value in research terms will lie in the extent to which it allows variables to be grouped. The aim of scientific research is to measure all possible stimulus variables efficiently, so as to either control or to randomize them. It only remains, then, to manipulate a single independent variable with a view to observing the consequences upon the dependent one. Ideally this is done by experiment or by statistical manipulation of data. Unfortunately, this state can never be reached in social research. It will always be possible to refine down our analysis of stimuli to the point at which we have discarded sociological or psychological descriptions of them and are concentrating upon physiological ones. These, in turn, could then be refined down into molecular structure analysis, and so on. No sociologist and few psychologists would be prepared to accept that the content of his own discipline can be reduced to that of sub-atomic physics.

Use of the concept social class, therefore, is a categorizing device which will have some value at a particular stage in the analysis of cognitive development, but which may be replaced as our ability to define the stimulus content of social class experience improves. On the other hand, from the point of view of sociological analysis, the concept will never become redundant, since it is related to an aspect of the societal structure. For our purposes, however, we need to think about what is contained in the social class structuring of experience for

* These are three terms used by sociologists to describe how an individual responds to his environment. They see the actor as having to make three kinds of response-channelling definitions. Cognition involves defining what is actually there, cathectic ideas indicate to him whether or not he derives pleasure from it, and evaluative ideas tell him whether he values it as good or bad.

the individual. To do this we must return to its definition. It is a set of interacting hierarchies of inequality. Principally we said that inequalities of income, power and prestige were the most important.

Social class analysis

What consequences for the developing child follow from differences in social experience? Perhaps the neatest of the early British studies on this question was carried out by Fraser (1959), who showed that a whole range of environmental factors related with scholastic achievement at age 11. All these could have been described as consequences of stratification (Swift 1966). By this we mean that differential access to income, prestige and power in society appears to induce styles of life which bear a clear relation to school achievement. The fact that the different social classes have different ways of living is too obvious to have to debate—it is one of the recurring themes in our literature. But these different styles of life are not simply settings within which people function. They are one way of describing *how* people function; that is, we can separate the members of different social strata according to the cognitive, cathectic and evaluative habits and skills they employ. Individually, the habits and skills will be a partial consequence of their social experience. And this will follow from their access to participation in the social process, which is based upon their position in the system of stratification.

Consequently, when we divide a population according to the occupation followed by the head of each family, we are not attempting to measure a single stimulus variable in the way that we might measure an electrical charge being applied to a rat in a maze. A much better analogy to the maze situation could be produced if we had a number of mazes comprising many different kinds of problems and hence different kinds of environments. One maze, perhaps, might be characterized as something which produces aggression, while another produces skill at manipulating certain kinds of objects, and so on. Whether it is the humidity, the sequence of electric shocks, the heat, the density of inhabitants in the maze, the breed of rat, atmospheric pressure during gestation or whatever, which 'really' produces the condition is not known. Of course, the response of an experimental psychologist would be to point out that this is not the way to conduct an experiment. Each of these factors should be treated as an independent variable, while all the others were controlled. In analysis of social class, this means that each social class is to be looked upon as a unique association of variables. Within its context any single variable is related to another in ways which are dependent upon their joint positions in the matrix. To put it in the very simplest way, factor X might be found to influence ability Y in situation A, but to have no influence in situation B. A factor which is important to educational achievement in the lowest social class may be irrelevant in the middle stratum. This destroys our hope that a factor X can be isolated which is simply a cause of Y (Farber 1965, Swift 1967b).

A vitally important methodological issue is raised here, because so much of our research is based upon an assumption that associations between factors and achievement will be linear and present in all other situations. Further point is added to this criticism by Child (1966), who showed that children of parents from the top and the bottom of the status continuum were significantly more introverted than children whose parents were in the middle of it.

The point underlying the theoretical perspective upon stratification is that *when we are concerned with describing the social environment of individuals and relating it to their development*, a social class must be looked upon as a summarizing variable and not an effective influencing factor. As one of the foremost exponents of social class analysis has written:

'. . . social class has proved to be so useful a concept because it refers to more than simply educational level, or occupation, or any of the large number of correlated variables. It is so useful because it captures the reality that the intricate interplay of all these variables creates different basic conditions of life at different levels of the social order. Members of different social classes, by virtue of enjoying (or suffering) different conditions of life, come to see the world differently—to develop different conceptions of social reality, different aspirations and hopes and fears, different conceptions of the desirable' (Kohn 1963, p. 471).

Even this is an over-simplification, because social classes do not exist as discrete entities around which it is possible to draw clear boundaries. They are analytical abstractions from reality. In real life, the boundaries shade into each other and are obscured by the presence of other social abstractions describing other factors. While it is analytically reasonable to think of the sub-culture of a social class, we can equally well distinguish a sub-culture founded upon regional factors or sheer historical accident (Roach and Gursslin 1967). It would be a great mistake to equate, for example, the working-class fisherman sub-culture of Hull with the working-class miner sub-culture of south Wales. Nevertheless, Kahan *et al.* (1966) have produced some recent proof that the simple split between white-collar and manual jobs is a subjectively real one in the British population.

Similarly, a single occupational or income category will not ne-cessarily produce a sub-culture in the accepted sense of the word. All bus conductors or all people earning £1,000-1,100 a year do not form a sub-culture. The problem, therefore, is to devise a criterion according to which the most meaningful collection of the relevant factors can be grouped. The two words 'meaningful' and 'relevant' are deliberately used here to emphasize the difficulties of the problem. The meaning-fulness will depend upon the associations among the factors on the one hand, and between the factors and important aspects of social structure on the other. Relevance relates to the extent to which a factor actually does influence school achievement.

A great deal of the necessary research has not yet been done; but there are many pointers to the way in which we will have to move if we are to try and specify the mechanisms by which adaptation comes about. Two areas of research which promise increased understanding will be dealt with in the remaining sections. They are the views which people hold of education and the influence which linguistic forms are believed to have upon the development of cognitive skills.

The perception of education and aspiration

It is probably true that all groups, except those to be found in the more alienated of slum cultures, would tend to agree at the verbal level that education is a good thing. On the other hand, there is no doubt that the degree of conviction behind the statement varies enormously. The evidence of research shows fairly conclusively that the more highly parents value education, the more they will support their child's educational endeavours and the more likely he is to succeed (Banfield *et al.* 1966, Douglas 1964, Wall *et al.* 1962). Furthermore, the more the child succeeds, the more likely he is to go on succeeding (Robinson 1964). But this is a very crude way of describing a very subtle set of processes. What do we mean when we say education is a good thing?

Clearly there are at least two kinds of criteria by which we can view its goodness: (a) education as an end in itself; and (b) education as a means to other ends. The stereotype in teaching folk-lore of an 'educogenic' environment contains an emphasis on the first aspect of judgment. On the other hand, most people actually have a view of education as a means to other ends. Education is for getting good jobs. In teaching children how to behave, it makes possible a quieter and more successful period of child-rearing for parents, and so on. We must also take into account differences, which are often based on class, in perception of what *success* actually is (Katz 1964, Lambert and Klineberg 1964). If we are to discover the mechanisms by which educational achievement is brought about, we will have to distinguish between the different conceptions of education and their relation to achievement motivation. Grossly we say that there are small sections of the middle classes where belief in education *as an end in itself* is more important to people than their knowledge that it is also a means to certain practical ends. Proportionately similar but numerically larger sections of the working class do not even conceive of it as a good thing, or are more likely to think of it as a bad thing, especially for girls.

We have seen that we must look for differences in ideas about what education is *for*; we can also expect to find differences in ideas about what it is. Obviously these two ways of 'seeing' education are related. Perhaps they are simply different aspects of the same generalized 'attitude towards education'. Nevertheless, we must be prepared for greatly differing pictures in the minds of parents about what actually goes on in education. Working-class students are often amused or annoyed by their parents' ideas of what happens to them at university. It is possible that if their parents really knew, many of them would be inclined to discourage their children from going at all.

A great deal of research has produced a large amount of evidence to show that middle-class children aspire to higher occupational and income levels than do those of the working class (Bruckman 1966, Jackson and Marsden 1961, Kahl 1953, Rosen 1956, Sewell *et al.* 1957, Stacey 1965, Swift 1967b, Turner, R. H., 1966). It is also probable that they try harder at *all* tasks, presumably because of the view of 'themselves in relation to task' which they are taught (Hyman 1953, Rosen and d'Andrade 1959). It has even been suggested (Davis 1948) that the child-rearing methods and stresses of middle-class life tend to produce a higher level of anxiety about all forms of achievement, but research has failed to confirm the hypothesis for Britain (Himmelweit 1955).

It is a truism, but an important one, to say that whether or not middle-class child-training produces generalized anxiety, it teaches the habits of responsibility (Clausen and Williams 1963, Cohen, E., 1965, Dale and Griffith 1966), restraint of physical aggression (Fraser 1959) and the extended time-span of attention to the world which is vitally necessary to educational adaptation (Campbell 1952, Elder 1965, Sugarman 1966). This is supported by an important rational process which inevitably follows from the 'instrumental' and individualistic life-orientations of middle-class parents (Bernstein 1965, Strauss 1962, Sugarman 1966). Their manifestations of love for the child are intelligently linked to the actual achievement of what are thought to be appropriate skills. From a different point of view this has been called emotional blackmail, but its success in achieving its short-term objective is undisputed.

In contrast, the child-training of the lower classes tends to emphasize unthinking acceptance of authority personified in the parents. Parents tend to rely upon physical punishment, which is often long delayed, inconsistent, vengeful and violent. Children tend to be unsupervised in play and allowed a great deal of unorganized freedom. This might be a much better way of convincing the children that their parents love them for themselves, since punishment, however violent, is irrationally and inconsistently related to behaviour; but it is not a particularly efficient way of encouraging the children to internalize the process of self-control. Authority, children learn, is partial, external and inexplicable. Such a set of ideas is likely to hinder rather than help the process of educational adaptation.

So far we have described some characteristics of social class sub-cultures and guessed how they might encourage or discourage the development of potentially adaptive cognitions, cathexes and evaluations in the child. To some extent this has fallen into the trap described earlier of assuming that single factors are linearly related to achievement throughout the stratification continuum. If we accept the criticism, we have to try to think in terms of matrices of factors rather than single ones. To some extent the folk-lore of teaching does this. There is a common stereotype of the educationally successful home, which is democratic, values learning as an end in itself, respects the authority of the teachers, supports school activities in a comprehending way, and so on. The problem with this stereotype is that it is unreal.

In order to emphasize that the characteristics of the 'good' family are seldom found in real life, Swift (1967b) suggested a second ideal type which might very well turn out to have much greater applicability. This family is found in the upper working class, but predominates in the lower white collar. Both parents are dissatisfied with the status they have achieved. They feel themselves to be able, but are convinced that promotion or social mobility does not depend upon ability. Connections and qualifications are better explanations. Commitment to education is very strong, but it is different from that found in the stereotypical 'good' home where education is seen to be *intellectually* liberating. In this situation it is seen to be *socially* liberating. Educational certificates are only a means to an end of social mobility.

Discipline of the children is traditional as a result of the need to project or 'introject' (Argyle 1964, Argyle and Robinson 1962) frustrated ambitions on to the child. At the same time, parents will have some understanding of the financial and social rewards which are open to the socially mobile. They will also have an adequate understanding of what is involved in successful school adaptation, even though, for reasons which they can usually explain, they were only initially successful themselves. Finally, and perhaps most importantly, they will not have the common working-class view of the middle and upper middle classes; that is, they will not look upon people of these strata as basically different from themselves. All these attitudes provide a climate which is likely to produce a high degree of achievement motivation.

Modes of speech and cognitive skills

There is much more to successful adaptation than the desire to adapt; it is not only a question, that is, of holding positive evaluations and cathexes of education. Adaptation is a consequence of a series of implicit and explicit accepting decisions made by other members of the organization over a period of time. These decisions are evaluations based on many facets of social behaviour. Amongst them exhibited cognitive skills are clearly of the first importance. To put it crudely, the existing members of the group (school) will tend to value thinking and valuing skills which are most like the ones they possess themselves. From the point of view of social class analysis we have to ask how the different social classes encourage the development of those thinking skills which have a bearing on successful school adaptation. Research at this level of complexity is non-existent in Britain. However, one of the best developed and most widely accepted theories concerning such processes has been suggested by Bernstein (1964, 1965), who posits the existence of two types of 'linguistic code', elaborated and restricted. The elaborated code makes precise use of words to communicate meaning, and a person who speaks in this way develops habits and skills in thinking which encourage him to view the environment as a structure to be manipulated. The restricted code, on the other hand, requires its user to employ gesture, intonation and posture to communicate adequately. As a result of this, a more emotional, less predictable approach to coping with the environment is encouraged. Cognitive and social skills so produced tend to be of the kind which are not valued in education. It is not too misleading a generalization to say that the lower reaches of the status continuum are more likely to employ only a restricted code.

The crucial factor from an educational point of view is Bernstein's argument that for a child sensitive to an elaborated code 'school experience is one of symbolic and social change'. He raises the suggestion that the linguistic code mediates between the environment and the individual's experience of it, so as to channel the development of his thought in specific directions. In arguing that the user of the elaborated code learns to take an instrumental view of the world around him, Bernstein is concerned with very much more than modes of communication. He is describing the development of intelligent behaviour in which the linguistic code plays a part of unknown importance. Unfortunately, Bernstein's work has received very little empirical validation. This has not been through lack of interest in a most persuasive theory, but because of the sheer complexity of the research which will be necessary. One such empirical test has been devised by Warren (1966), who reports 'a measure of support' for certain cognitive aspects of the theory. In addition, a great deal of social-psychological research is afoot, which promises an improvement in our present crudely conceived ideas about the development of cognitive style (Bruner et al. 1966, Triandis 1964).

Bernstein has argued that his theory does not *necessarily* evaluate the quality of symbolization which the restricted code is thought to produce: it 'carries its own aesthetic...will tend to develop a metaphoric range of considerable power, simplicity and directness, vitality and rhythm'. Nevertheless, it seems possible to argue that the conditions of life in some lower-class sub-cultures are intellectually *less* stimulating. They conduce to lower levels of intellectual efficiency and lower standards of judgment and reasoning. This can come about through inadequate conditions for physical functioning—poverty may still play a part. Again, there is no research backing for such a suggestion, but the possibility must be kept open.

Despite the shortage of research, Bernstein's theory, in conjunction with the findings of social anthropologists on the one hand, and psychometricians on the other, points the way towards future knowledge. It seems certain that our knowledge of social class sub-cultures will play an important part in this process.

Conclusion

This paper has attempted to develop a perspective, according to which the well-known head-counting association between social class and variations in school achievement may be used as a basis for investigation of the social and psychological processes which go to make up the system of education. The crucial distinction to be made is that between social class analysis as an aspect of societal functioning and the influence of cultural experience upon educational adaptiveness of the child.

Once we begin to concentrate upon the latter kind of question, we must place the social class background of the child in its proper context of other aspects of his culture. For example, the local community and its culture, his religion, his family structure, his peer-group and so on are all important aspects of the total cultural experience which 'produces' him before he goes to school and which influences his responses to the demands of school when he starts going to it. There is a large amount of British and American research which can provide data on the extent to which family background can be said to influence ideas about education and the need to achieve in it. But this is only the superficial aspect of the process of adaptation. We have also to consider how cultural experience provides the individual with the cognitive, cathectic and evaluative habits of thought which are important in the process of education. When we have done this, we will be in a better position to decide whether the explicit and implicit demands of the school system, as they are manifested in consequences upon children, are relevant to our aims for education.

J. Heywood

Technological Education

It is perhaps surprising that, with so much investment in technical and technological education, little research has been done on this institution or the organizations in it or, for that matter, into the effectiveness of the educational procedures used in those organizations. Few educationists at the universities have devoted themselves to extensive studies in this field. Inspection of the reports of research in progress between 1962 and 1964 shows, surprisingly, that many of the projects in technical education were being pursued by teachers either for their own sake or as part of study for a higher degree (Abel and Heywood 1965). So much interest has been shown in research by teachers that all the colleges of education training technical teachers have one member of staff appointed solely for research and its co-ordination in the district. Short courses in research methods for technical teachers have been organized with success.

Although there has been little research, *Technical Education Abstracts*, published at regular intervals by the N.F.E.R., illustrate the enormous volume of opinion published in more than 150 different journals. This is partly because Technical Education in England and Wales not only includes specialist technological studies, but undertakes teaching for qualifications as divergent as London University degrees on the one hand and the commercial examinations of the Royal Society of Arts on the other. It accounts for the diversity of kinds of research in the projects listed. The impossibility of connecting so many different threads in a short paper will, I hope, be understood and the restrictions consequent on this be readily acceptable. Because I have written elsewhere (Peters, A. J. 1968), about the researches relevant to technical and further education, I propose to limit most of this essay to issues raised by studies of the education of technologists (i.e. graduates or graduate equivalent).

Supply and demand

A) INVESTIGATIONS INTO THE SUPPLY, DEMAND AND USE OF QUALIFIED MAN-POWER

Much discussion in the press of recent years has been devoted to the controversial issue of the supply and demand for qualified man-power. A white paper (Ministry of Education 1961) in particular sparked off a great debate on whether or not there was a shortage of technologists. Generally speaking, however, the nation accepts the view that there is and will continue to be in the foreseeable future a shortage of qualified man-power. Little important research has been done on this problem, but relevant to the issue is a survey completed for the United States Government by Payne (1960), which describes developments up to that date. A report by Political and Economic Planning (1957) on the employment of graduates in industry was produced in 1957. Some of its findings are still pertinent. A more significant critical review of the situation in terms of the relations between technical education and social change was published by Cotgrove (1958). Various statistics are given in the reports of the Committee on Scientific Manpower; there is one independent report (Federation of British Industries 1961) of special interest.

The debate between 1961-3 has led to increasing interest in the methods of research into problems of man-power, and several important projects have been started at the London School of Economics (Roberts and Smith 1966). Several writers (Jewkes 1959, Pym 1967) have questioned the view that there is a shortage of qualified man-power. In the majority of seventy-three firms supporting Dip. Tech. schemes in an inquiry (Heywood 1968) made in 1962-3, there was no short supply. Some firms were discarding executives. More important, however, is the growing belief that technologists can and ought to be better used, although critics who take this line do not say how! Some studies (Turner, B. T., 1963) are being made in industry to see how engineers can be used more effectively. There is little doubt that poor utilization leads to discontent. It is surprising that very little is said of a survey into the conditions of employment of their own kind by two mechanical engineers Salek and Julius (1965), for the picture they paint is very similar to that of the poor image of technology held by sixth-formers (Hutchings 1963). Indeed, able sixth-formers seem to be justified in holding such attitudes.

In official circles there has been a growing awareness that too much effort was put into understanding the problem of qualified man-power at the expense of appreciating the relations between the various types of skilled and unskilled labour and, in particular, the relative roles of technician and technologist. They have also become increasingly worried by an increasing shortage of technicians (Department of Education and Science 1966c).

Another important trend has been the attempt to discuss shortages in terms of specific subjects (e.g. mechanical engineers, control enginers) (Department of Education and Science 1966c). These have brought to light divergencies of opinion between the committees forecasting national needs and employers in terms of the educational requirements of engineers and in particular of mechanical engineers. Employers of mechanical engineers seem to be particularly unwilling to depart from support of national certificate and day release courses to full-time sandwich or degree courses (Ministry of Education 1963c).

In the past the institutions have played an important role in providing an alternative route to professional membership (Prandy 1965). Their new regulations, which operate in favour of persons with full-time education possessing university degrees, may cause sufficient pressure to be brought on employers to give more support to such courses through an increasing employment of engineers qualified in this way. It remains to be seen whether in the future engineering graduates will be attracted to the professional institutions. In the past, Associate Member qualifications could be achieved by day release, and were equivalent to the possession of a degree. Many employers preferred the former. Much will depend on the emphasis placed by employers on the possession of the Chartered Engineers (C.Eng.) qualification (introduced by the Council of Engineering Institutions whose examinations will under Royal Charter replace those offered now by each institution). It is interesting to note in Heward's (1967) survey reported later that many of the 'drop-out' applied scientists did not continue their education. Is it not significant that the institutes catering for their needs do not have the status of the engineering societies? Within the last two years professional institutions have been established for electronic and electrical technicians, and the Junior Institution of Engineers is attempting to undertake the same role for mechanical technicians.

Interest has also been shown in the utilization of arts graduates in industry. Apart from the annual reports of the university appointments boards, which indicate the extent of this movement to industry, there has been one important investigation (Acton Society Trust 1962), which evaluates the experience of nearly 100 arts graduates employed in industry.

B) ATTITUDES TO TECHNOLOGY IN THE SCHOOLS

The adequate supply of technologists depends increasingly on the schools, not only because of increasing demands for university graduates, but also because of the changing pattern of the provision of education for adolescents in response to the demand for more full-time courses.

In the 1950s there was a considerable expansion in the provision of university places in science and technology. The first reports of the Universities Central Council on Admissions showed vacancies in technology departments and engineering departments. About the same time Hutchings (1963) gave evidence to the Robbins Committee which showed that sixth-formers with good 'A' levels preferred pure science to applied science and technology. Since then a great deal of attention has been paid to improving the image of engineering. The demand for a Royal Society of Technology has in part been met by the creation of the Council of Engineering Institutions with its Royal Charter award, C.Eng. G. Jones (1963) at the same time reported on sixth form stereotypes of several occupations to show the characteristics valued by sixth-formers. His results confirmed their poor image of engineering. Some researches in the United States yielded similar results (Beardslee and O'Dowd 1961). I myself (Heywood *et al.* 1966b) initiated inquiries among schoolmasters to ascertain their attitudes to technology, the colleges of advanced technology and sandwich courses. The colleges of advanced technology ran second best to the universities, but ahead of the technical colleges. School-teachers preferred the thick sandwich course to the thin, degree to Dip. Tech. Many sixth-formers who failed to get a university place at the end of the second year were encouraged to stay on at school instead of seeking places in the other sector.

One outcome of the concern with sixth form attitudes to technology has been the encouragement of engineering studies in schools highlighted in the report by G. T. Page (1965). Unfortunately, the debate about *to examine or not examine* this subject is overshadowed by the requirements of university entrance, and teachers in both schools and university departments fail to grasp the possibilities of influencing curriculum, teaching method and examining. For example, an important study which seems to have been overlooked in this debate is by MacFarlane Smith (1964). He suggests that spatial ability is a major underlying factor or type of ability, which is best defined as the capacity to perceive and hold in the mind the structure and proportions of a form or figure, grasped as a whole. It is in such activities as technical drawing and the Schools Council design projects that spatial ability might prosper. MacFarlane Smith argues that the English system of education has undervalued spatial ability, and this is one of the reasons why the schools and colleges have failed to produce the scientists, technologists and technicians required by industry. His findings show that 'spatially gifted pupils are relatively less gifted for the majority of the traditional grammar school subjects. In the past, many grammar school teachers may have inferred that such pupils are relatively less "intelligent" or "academically" gifted. That such inferences were made is borne out by the fact that many eminent engineers and scientists were reported to be dull or backward at school.'

Some writers both here and in the United States have suggested that the drift to the arts now creating vacancies in both arts and science departments (Department of Education and Science 1966a, Phillips, G., 1965) is in part due to the student's concern with people and a belief that science and engineering are *not* concerned primarily with human relationships. It has also been suggested that sixth-formers wish to delay their choice of career for as long as possible. Science and technology seem necessarily to imply commitment. I have suggested that it is this 'commitment' which is rejected rather than science or technology.

Nevertheless, these are opinions, and it is to be hoped that the committees set up to examine the problem will go beyond the collection of superficial statistics and look at these issues in some depth. The danger is that engineering science in the sixth form may be sponsored for motives which are less than educational, and so ignore those other possibilities of developing spatial ability through design and bridging the arts-science gap through a study of the macroscopic and microscopic human issues which have to be dealt with by technologists.

C) SUPPLY AS A FUNCTION OF WASTAGE

Unfortunate though it may be, the fact is that some students fail their academic courses and others leave for one reason or another. Wastage from technological courses offered by both universities and technical colleges tends to be high.

Three studies are of interest. The first, by Heward (1967), seeks to find out what happened to several hundred students after they had left the course. It is the subject of this section. The second, by Dickenson (1963), seeks to evaluate the relative performances of students with national certificate entry qualifications on the one hand and Advanced level G.C.E. on the other. The third, by Furneaux (1962), first shows how psychometric techniques can be applied to college records, and secondly relates certain course factors, in particular performance in examinations, to personality types.

Heward's study differs from Dickenson's, which was of academic records, in that its results were obtained from questionnaires answered by 224 withdrawals from the same college in which Dickenson did her work. Heward's study gives a substantially lower figure for the cause of withdrawal as academic failure than Dickenson, who had rated it at 99 per cent; but, as Heward points out, college records for the period of these surveys were less than adequate. Heward was concerned to test the hypothesis that students based on industry will adopt alternative routes to the goal of professional status, assuming that this goal does not change. When she made her inquiries, there were adequate alternative routes for engineering students of Dip.Tech. courses, but not for those in applied science subjects.

Mrs Heward found as follows:

'Only a minority (21 per cent) leave industry on withdrawing from the course. Few were asked to leave their sponsoring firm. College-based and applied science students left industry more frequently than engineers and builders. Of those who remained in industry a high proportion continued their education by studying the Higher National Certificate or Higher National Diploma (sixty-eight were gained by ex-students of engineering and metallurgy) and thirty-nine were making the attempt.' In the future professional qualification via the national certificate route will become more difficult, if not impossible. Will students in this position in the future adjust to a technician role? Will the courses of the future become more like the American, in which the initial years have a 'cooling-out' function so that weaker students are eased out into less exacting courses and often provided with new goals? In a selective system such as the English, where sixth-formers are highly motivated towards science or arts, the failure to achieve goals, whatever the reason, is much more serious, particularly if it occurs during the university course. Thus some readers may find Heward's findings about the fate of applied scientists more disquieting than the other outcomes of her investigation. She reports: 'Engineers and metallurgists continued their education more frequently than applied scientists who remained in industry. Fewer engineers than applied scientists did not continue their education at all. Engineers and metallurgists had better jobs and higher salaries than applied scientists who remained in industry; those with higher and more qualifications tended to have better jobs and salaries than those with poor or no qualification.'

There is need for many more follow-up studies of this kind.

D) PRE-ENTRY EXPERIENCE

Two kinds of pre-entry experience have been of interest to teachers. Comparisons have been made of the relative merits of entrants possessing either national certificates or Advanced level G.C.E., and also between students with and without industrial experience between leaving school and entering college. Indeed, many industrialists and teachers favour the student with such experience (Heywood 1965, Jackson, W. 1961).

The wastage rates reported by Dickenson (1963) for one college were: students with three or four 'A' levels 17 per cent; two 'A' levels 35 per cent; one 'A' level 41 per cent; O.N.C. 27 per cent of the intake. This places the O.N.C. student second in the order of merit. In her study it was shown that there was a closer relation between entry qualifications and success on the Dip.Tech. than exists between the school last attended and success on the Dip.Tech.

Other writers, including M. Jahoda (1964) and Chisholm and Walmsley (1964), have reported on the comparative success of O.N.C. students. Several principals of the ex-colleges of advanced technology have underlined the success of entrants via this route (Tait 1962). Such comparisons were made with students with relatively poor grades in 'A' level. But more important is the fact that many of the O.N.C.

students had been at grammar schools and possessed 'O' level G.C.E. certificates. With the raising of the school leaving age to sixteen and the increasing interest in sixth form education, it is not unreasonable to suppose that some, if not many, of those now entering O.N.C. courses will remain in the sixth form. The question which cannot be answered is whether or not these students will do better in the sixth form than the entrants with 'A' levels with whom they have been compared.

Ordinary National Certificate courses of that time differed considerably from traditional sixth form studies both in teaching method and syllabus. Closely related to the job done by the student, they might well have supplied a motivation and teaching structure that produced quite different responses to those which would be produced by the sixth form. The existence of this problem emphasizes the need to reconsider the recommendation of the Crowther Committee, which suggested that there should be an alternative road in the sixth form. The provision of technology projects in the sixth form is far from the answer. The existence of such routes in the sixth form would be insufficient of itself, unless universities are prepared to accept different intakes from different course structures and teaching methods. The sandwich course might be one such structure. Much depends on the teaching and examining methods adopted within the course.

The period between school and college may not only be used in industry to teach basic skills and develop interests, but can also be used for remedial treatment if it is accompanied by some form of education. Sir Willis Jackson (1961) has suggested that day release might be given for continuation of studies, particularly in mathematics. Twenty-two per cent of a sample of diplomates of technology required considerable help with mathematics during their first year (Heywood 1968). Such continuation studies could ease the transition from school to college.

The experience of higher technological education

Studies by Hornsby-Smith (1967), M. Jahoda (1964), Marris (1964), Matthews (Personal communication 1964) and Heywood (1966, 1967) have attempted to evaluate the effectiveness of the undergraduate experience. Hornsby-Smith followed through a complete course of thirty-seven students in a department offering thick and thin sandwich courses as well as traditional degree courses to try and establish relations between course structure, student attitudes, examination performance, and other factors contributing to success. This study is of particular interest, since it illustrates what can be accomplished by a practising teacher.

Jahoda was able to study the attitudes of a large number of students, staff and industrialists to the sandwich courses operated by Brunel University, then a college of advanced technology. Marris included a college of advanced technology (Northampton) in his study of student experience in six universities. Since both of these writers have published books, I have not referred in any detail to their work, since their observations cover the range of problems experienced by staff and students operating sandwich courses. Together with the investigations carried out by Matthews at Loughborough and by me, data (with many similarities) are available on the student experience of nine of the ten colleges of advanced technology in 1963, the year that the Robbins Committee recommended that these institutions become universities. I am using this data in writing a history of these colleges and the development of Dip.Tech. sandwich courses. It should be emphasized that these were not the only studies initiated in the colleges of advanced technology, which were institutions that sponsored a great deal of educational research. Much of this work has depended on the skills of the sociologist and social psychologist, and not so much of the psychologist. Practising teachers have made considerable contributions. Apart from Hornsby-Smith, whose work was related to one department, none of the studies mentioned are related to specific subjects. Student and staff respondents came from all disciplines. Nevertheless, attitudes to one subject in particular, liberal/general studies, have not only attracted the attention of these research workers, but of others as well.

Attitudes to liberal general studies

During the 1950s it was suggested that scientists and technologists were vocationally narrow. To quote L. Davies (1965), 'Perhaps our most persistent fear today is that in neglecting to provide a general education in a variety of forms of knowledge, we are delivering our future into the hands of immature specialists, whose skill may be sufficient to extinguish the human race, but whose wisdom cannot be looked upon to save and transfigure it.' C. P. Snow's two-culture thesis undoubtedly did much to enhance such views.

The chief effect of a circular by the Ministry of Education in 1957 (no. 323) was the inclusion of space in the timetable for additional studies to liberalize the curriculum of technologists. It suggested studies of human relations, English and the art of communication, law (the most popular subject at one college of advanced technology), foreign affairs, languages, political science and physical education. Departments of liberal or general studies were developed and, in some colleges, teachers of specialist subjects were encouraged to take an interest in the subject. Indeed, this is how I developed my interest in educational research.

Liberal studies were a compulsory part of Diploma in Technology courses. One of the reasons they were so controversial—supported by some staff and students, loathed by others—was because they intruded into an already heavily loaded timetable. One study of the attitudes of 363 diplomates of technology to liberal studies (Heywood 1967) showed they did not want liberal studies abolished, although suggestions were made for better teaching and a wider range and greater freedom of choice of subject. Only 23 per cent of the students in Jahoda's study wanted less liberal studies. Peers and Madgwick (1963) got a similar result. Bridger (1962) surveyed teachers' reactions to liberal studies. Most of them thought the subject should be examined, but like the students were divided in opinion about the best way of testing liberal studies. They were similarly divided about method.

L. Davies (1965), in whose book is to be found the most comprehensive survey of all the research into liberal studies, made a detailed study of student attitudes and abilities in the Welsh College of Advanced Technology. Among the many items of interest, he found that O.N.C. students were more favourably inclined to liberal studies than those with 'A' level. Engineers were also more favourably inclined than applied scientists. Davies is one of the few research workers to have administered tests of ability and personality to students taking compulsory liberal studies. He found a positive link between intelligence (non-verbal) and neuroticism; a similar positive relation existed between intelligence (verbal and non-verbal) and examination mark. A favourable attitude to liberal studies appeared to relate to success at the examination. Engineers were superior in achievement to applied scientists in liberal studies examinations.

The universities have not been unaware of the problem. Hutton and Gerstl (1963) recommended the inclusion of sociological and communication studies in the curriculum of engineers. Notwithstanding this recommendation, those universities offering such programmes seem not to have made them obligatory, although the permissive curriculum offered at Imperial College seems to have had some effect (Linstead *et al.* 1961), but, as Davies suggests, it is questionable whether the response would justify continuing the programme.

Other universities, notably Keele (Iliffe 1968) and the newest institutions, have also been aware of the arts students. Thus, with few exceptions arts students at Lancaster pursue a course in a science specially designed for their needs in the second year (Heywood and Montagu-Pollock 1966).

The pattern of liberal/general studies continues to change. Perhaps there will be a hardening towards the social sciences rather than the humanities.

It is likely that attitudes of staff and students will be similar in the future, unless teaching methods and curricula can be adjusted to tap the drives of students highly motivated to the study of their own subject. The mere acquisition of facts contributes little to needs and the development of personality. It may well be that, from a more rigorous awareness of the characteristics of their working environment provided by courses in social studies, education will affect occupation and improve not merely the status of technology but the reality of the job itself.

Curriculum studies

Three different methods have been used to examine various aspects of technological curricula. Furneaux (1962) uses the techniques of the psychologist in the analysis of success and failure in one department of Imperial College. He shows how psychometric techniques can be applied to data already available in a department of engineering. Thus, for example, there was little evidence of unusually high correlations between the marks obtained at the ends of years 1 and 2 in specially related subjects (e.g. thermodynamics in year 1 is analogous to applied heat in year 2). Further, 'every year-1 paper has a correlation with at least one year-2 paper with which it has no special link, which is as large as, or larger than, those relating it to its analogues'. With the exception of engineering drawing, it seemed that the examinations were measuring some kind of ability to pass exams. Such results raise many questions, which Furneaux considers in some detail. To quote: 'What is the appropriate criterion for a first-year pass? Suppose a candidate succeeds with every paper save mathematics, is it justifiable to require him to repeat this examination, in view of the evidence that his second-year performance in the same subject is predicted at least as well by applied electricity, in which he has passed, as by the paper in which he failed?' This emphasizes the lack of thought given, in planning degree courses, to the variety of skills to be sampled for examination. It also suggests that reorganization of curricula might reduce the well-known heavy loading of engineering syllabuses.

Furneaux also used personality/temperament measures on engineering students in the same department. Several fascinating relations were found between given groups of students (neurotic introverts, neurotic extroverts, stable introverts, stable extroverts). For example, on a measure of intellectual speed slower students in the stable extrovert group tended to obtain poor examination marks. The need for more studies of this kind in relation to curriculum structure is in my view self evident.

Post-evaluation studies seem to have been the most popular means of curriculum research. The most discussed of these is one on the education and careers of mechanical engineers by Hutton and Gerstl (1963), a collaboration between two professors, one an engineer, the other a sociologist. They compared the career patterns and educational needs of 1,000 mechanical engineers who had achieved professional membership of the Institution via graduate and non-graduate routes. Such studies can have an enormous impact on policy. For example, 89 per cent of this sample taken at a time of vigorous controversy over the suggested introduction of engineering into the school curriculum had no wish for engineering subjects at school. This serves to illustrate the dilemma of the educationists, who, in trying to cater, say, for the development of spatial ability or of thinking in problem-solving situations, want to introduce some form of design based on value analysis and simple quality control. The engineering public is attuned to the results of attitude surveys but not to depth studies, say, of the type made by MacFarlane Smith in *Spatial Ability*. Whereas few engineers have heard of this work, many have heard of Hutchings' (1963) survey of sixth form attitudes to engineering.

Surveys do provide considerable information about the value and use of the subjects studied at college. They create moods for change and help to remove irrelevancies from the curriculum.

The fact that differently structured methods of teaching and examining might lead to different links between the subjects or help reduce wastage cannot really be studied in such investigations. So there is the need for different kinds of study. The curriculum model deduced by Hutton and Gerstl has some considerable significance, for there is a demand for 31 per cent of course time to be divided between English, technical report writing, humanities, industrial administration, economics and social science.

In terms of an ideal university course of study, these engineers wanted 23 per cent of the time to be devoted to mathematics, physics and chemistry, 27 per cent to basic engineering science, 13 per cent to design engineering, and 6 per cent to a speciality engineering. The need for courses in design is fully supported by the recommendations of the Feilden Committee (Ministry of Education 1963a).

Hutton and Gerstl asked them to give their views of the general objectives of engineering education. Ranked in order of importance, they suggested, first, to teach the fundamentals of the main engineering subjects; secondly, to teach students the techniques of scientific method, and thirdly, to stimulate them to think about their subject, etc. Many commentators now speak of a philosophy of engineering. There is no mention of this in the ideal curriculum described above. In a recent pilot study Moon (1967) has collected data which suggests that engineers do not believe their education contributed to their philosophy of engineering! In view of the possibility that sixth-formers may be tending to show more interest in people and values than hitherto, the inclusion of fundamental considerations of ethics in an engineering course might well improve the image of the technologist and technological education.

Metallurgists were also subjected to similar inquiries. Hopkins (1967) sent a questionnaire to all Associates and Licentiates of the Institution of Metallurgists in January 1964; 1,689 persons returned them. The major deficiencies that respondents found in their training were the inclusion of too great a proportion of subjects dealing with extraction metallurgy and the omission of formal instruction in report writing. The importance of studies in industrial management and engineering subjects was also revealed.

Finally, mention should be made of a case study into the education of professional engineers for design and manufacture (Heywood *et al.* 1966a), which was undertaken by a group of industrial engineers, teachers and professional educationists. This report is of interest if only for its listing of the controversies encompassing engineering education.

Mathematics

Three investigations have tried to establish the mathematical requirements of industry. Langton (1962) considered the teaching of theoretical subjects to students of high polymer technology. He attempted to discover what theoretical subjects to teach students of polymer technology. His reason for doing this was 'the unsatisfactory nature of the mathematical portion of the course'. He found in the course of his inquiries that it was impossible to avoid comment on other theoretical topics included in the curriculum. Forty-four firms were visited. During each visit he learned sufficient about the firm's activities to be able to describe in some detail their activities and scientific and mathematical needs. Having got this data, he balanced it with information collected from the literature and a theory of teaching, which would be acceptable to teachers and educationists. His belief in the role of the teacher as an integrator of many diverse requirements is of fundamental importance. In the last chapter of his book he remarks, 'What is really being advocated here is the fundamental idea that learning should be considered as a unity, and not as something that can be broken up into compartments. The mathematics taught to students of technology must, therefore, be taught as a subject interwoven into the other branches of his course and not as an unrelated subject as it is so often regarded. If this integration of mathematics is attempted, then it will be found that technology students have a much greater potential capacity for the subject than is immediately apparent.' The possibility of such integration comes through in some of the details of industrial projects. From the teacher's point of view, this report full of life-size examples must be welcome; the research worker, however, is often faced with the job of disentangling facts from opinion. Some of the facts undoubtedly surprised Dr Langton. For example, only one firm refused to help. The surveys reflect the changing needs of industry; most of the firms stated that a student with a good theoretical knowledge would be preferable to one with a more detailed knowledge of manufacturing technique and the properties of materials.

Langton found that the mathematics requirements of the industry were much greater than was thought. One of the reasons for this was the attitude of mind associated with the acquisition of mathematics. Possibly it is beliefs about the development of an 'attitude of mind' that accounts for the demand for more mathematics in other technologies, such as mechanical engineering, when many senior mechanical engineers are opposed to excessive study of mathematics. Langton also found that some subjects, such as engineering drawing, chemical analysis and others which would seem important to the industry, are not required to the extent one would imagine at first sight. The enthusiasm shown by industrialists for his inquiry also highlighted the dichotomy between industry and the educational establishments. There was need for much greater co-operation.

Clarke (1967) has reported on a survey of about 9 per cent of the Associates of the Institution of Metallurgists. These metallurgists thought that all students should take courses in basic mathematics, statistics and computation. There should be the option for selected students to read further mathematics. The teaching should be by mathematicians and, whenever possible, it should be illustrated by practical applications.

Scott and three colleagues in the Department of Mathematics at Salford University (Scott *et al.* 1966) used both questionnaire and interview techniques to study the applications of mathematics in the electrical engineering industry in order to comment on syllabuses and the teaching of mathematics to both engineers and mathematicians. Prior to the inquiry, British and American syllabuses were compared, and each member of the team spent six months in industry. From these studies questionnaires were sent to 5,000 electrical engineers (3,159 replied). As a follow up to the study senior engineers and academics were interviewed.

Among the many interesting facts brought to light was that six out of seven research workers felt that their work was impeded by a lack of mathematics. Teachers felt the same. Following this up with questions about the action taken to remedy this defect, Scott *et al.* found that 'reading literature is more popular with non-graduates than with graduates, who prefer to go to a mathematician . . . There is no doubt that the fear of an unsympathetic reception deters some engineers from consulting mathematicians.'

But so much for the facts too numerous to report in these paragraphs. It is the general implications for teaching which are of interest. They do not, for example, conclude that the best teacher of mathematics to engineers is likely to be an engineer, and although they recognize that mathematics is taught badly by maths departments, they suggest that it should be taught by a mathematician with specialist interest in industrial problems.

They also comment on the effects of external examinations, and suggest that students should be allowed to bring textbooks to the examination, as this would encourage a different outlook. In my own opinion, the form of question could be more significant in structuring outlook. Questions designed to help students to formulate engineering problems in mathematical terms would structure one mode of thought, while others designed to solve mathematical problems would create another. To overcome the fact that 70 per cent of the engineers in the pilot study found the formulation of engineering problems in mathematical terms the most difficult, these research workers suggest a case study approach in teaching.

On the issue of whether to teach more or less mathematics they suggest the provision of two Honours courses—special and general, with a single Ordinary course. The special course would be primarily for the research worker; it would devote more time to the relevant branches of mathematics and physics than the general course, which while still maintaining a high academic standard, would be more broadly based.

Important to the study of mathematics is motivation. These research workers found that two out of three engineers said that an engineering application provided an incentive to mathematical study, while three out of four found that an engineering application was an aid to mathematical understanding. They write, 'Mathematicians who are teaching engineers are urged to take note of this latter result, as it runs counter to their own attitudes as mathematicians.' We might add that it runs counter to the views of scientists in other fields. The theorem to be demonstrated or the principle to be illustrated leads to a certain technique of teaching associated with an analytical strategy of tackling problems demanding single solutions. The idea of starting with a real engineering problem as a means of illustrating basic principles is seen either as too difficult or as specialization. As one conceptual study has shown, it can lead to the breaking down of subject divisions. The importance of investigating teaching methods as well as conducting surveys of the kind described cannot be over-emphasized. There is a need to come to a better understanding of the relation between technique, principles, knowledge and the extent to which their combination in the learning situation can be transferred to the understanding of new techniques in the industrial situation.

Both inquiries by Langton and Scott reveal the belief that technologists should study mathematics, since it is an intellectual discipline which develops a grasp of concepts which may be transferred to other fields. We might ask whether, in fact, transfer of the rigour of traditional mathematics teaching to engineering problems in industry is an important factor inhibiting the engineer in his synthesis of open-ended situations. Teaching methods are thus of great importance, and the case study approach recommended by the research workers to help engineers formulate the problem in mathematical terms coupled with the idea of teaching out of practical problems are, in my view, of more significance to the mathematical education of engineers than changes in syllabus.

Of interest is the view of the research workers that engineers should have a broad mathematical training with one topic studied in depth. It may not be as easy as this, for if it should turn out, as one recent research suggests, that while some students are motivated best through broad studies to study in depth, others come to the broad path by way of depth. A unique educational experiment might be conducted in a department prepared to offer one course based on breadth and another on depth.

Conclusion

Most research into problems of technological education has been outside the classroom. The studies within departments and colleges have not been geared to detailed analysis of assessment, teaching methods and course structure. The need for such analysis cannot be over-emphasized.

Much of the research has been done either by practising teachers or visitors to the field. This accounts for the diversity of topics studied and the technique used. There is need for continuity and development of research. One might hope that in the not too distant future a university might find a home for a centre devoted to the problems of technological education.

Brian Cane

Teachers, Teaching and Teacher Education

The salary bill for teachers in maintained schools was £450 million in 1963-4—nearly half the total l.e.a. and Ministry educational expenditure. This considerable annual investment in some 300,000 teachers on the staff of maintained schools is backed by astonishingly little information about teacher education and by few research projects which might be of assistance to those concerned with educating teachers. Reviewing research on teacher education, E. A. Allen (1963) commented: 'We need . . . to know about what happens in professional training itself, and on this there is not so much research.' The situation has not changed greatly during the last few years, although, on the credit side, the start of several regional research projects can be noted as well as the completion of several limited but nevertheless useful surveys.

Ideally the development of programmes of teacher education should take account of the research on teachers and teaching which has been reported. Much of this work has been concerned with establishing the characteristics of the 'good teacher' and the hallmark of 'successful teaching'. To this end, teaching ability and personality factors have been analysed; the attitudes expressed by teachers have been studied and related to their particular teaching functions and programmes; the intellectual attainments and background of student teachers have been correlated with their performance in school practice and 'education' examinations; and attempts have been made to determine which tests prove the best predictors of success in teaching. A large part of the recent reviews of research on teaching and teaching ability has been concerned with research of this kind.

An alternative approach focuses attention upon teaching situations rather than the teachers themselves. Teaching roles adopted in different circumstances are identified; group relationships within the classroom and the relationships between the children and the teacher are analysed and recorded; the teacher's day and individual lessons are observed and recorded; the organization and direction of children's learning is carefully considered, including the introduction of new aids to learning.

Since the research into the characteristics of 'good teachers' and 'successful teaching' is still at an infant stage of growth, it is hardly surprising that teacher trainers have given little consideration to such research when developing their college or department courses. This does not mean that staff have ignored the need for radical changes and bold experiments, and indeed many changes and experiments have been initiated and undertaken in colleges throughout Britain during recent years. Nevertheless, there appears to be a continuing need in teacher education for systematic curriculum development and research, so organized as to link the best efforts of individual colleges; to evaluate these efforts in relation to the present and future tasks of the teaching profession; and to feed back research results into new patterns for college and department courses.

But such developments in the initial training of teachers would not be sufficient. Teacher education is now seen to be a process which must continue throughout the teacher's career. The pace of educational change before the Second World War was comparatively slow compared with that since the war. There has been a quiet revolution in British state education during the last two decades, which has presented many new problems to teachers and administrators: the school leaving age has been raised to fifteen, and will shortly be raised to sixteen; more and more children are staying at school until the age of eighteen, and then proceeding to some form of higher or further education; the provision for university and professional education has been greatly expanded; new methods and curricula in mathematics, modern languages, sciences and other subjects have been introduced at all levels of schooling; the extent to which backwardness arises from environmental factors such as home or school conditions has been increasingly recognized; techniques of diagnosis and guidance have steadily gained acceptance; new forms of school organization such as the several varieties of comprehensive school and the intermediate school, previously ignored or rejected, have suddenly found favour and support. In this exciting period of change, teachers face many professional challenges which they are often ill equipped to meet—either by experience or by training. On every side, the need for expanded programmes of in-service training has been recognized, but the needs and the provision have yet to be charted and related. Virtually no research has been undertaken in this vital area of teacher education.

In view of the rapid changes taking place in teaching and in teacher education, and the tentative nature of the findings which have emerged from the limited research so far undertaken, it might seem pointless to consider the *effectiveness* of present and past programmes of teacher education. Yet there has been much indirect pressure from teachers and administrators that this consideration should go ahead. This pressure has been applied by those who feel that there is much that is fundamental, constant and well defined in the teacher's job, and that colleges and departments have not been as effective as they might have been in preparing students for the practical realities of classroom routine. There is a small but growing interest in research which attempts to investigate this possibility objectively by conducting longitudinal studies.

These, then, are some of the chief areas of research and investigation relevant to British teaching and teacher education today. In what follows, an attempt is made to survey the current position of British research in these several areas. Inevitably these surveys are selective, but every effort has been made to include most of the British researches that are relevant.

Selection, personality and attitudes

There has been considerable research on the selection of students for teacher training. This partly reflects concern for the effectiveness of training, and partly the interest of teacher trainers and others in diagnosing the qualities expected from good student teachers.

In recent years, British investigators have given particular attention to the value of the interview and of personality tests in selection. Burroughs (1958) found that the interview was as good a predictor of teaching success as most other measures, and that ratings for observable features of the applicant and his intellectual maturity and powers of self-expression gave the best prediction of teaching marks. Ratings for personality traits were less important. M. Allen (1962) made an interesting comparison of group selection procedure with an individual selection procedure, correlating the rating from each procedure with final teaching marks. The latter were best predicted by the group selection procedure, i.e. groups of ten applicants taking part in leader-less and controlled discussions on educational topics and mock staff meetings.

In a recent report of an investigation into the selection of student teachers and the effects of training, Halliwell (1965) reviewed a large number of works on aspects of teaching and the qualities of teachers, and reported the lack of any convincing agreement between the various measures of teaching efficiency. He found the College Interview Rating to be one of the most important predictors of success in the training course; the predictive value of other measures, such as attitude and personality tests, varied according to the category of student under consideration. Perhaps it is not surprising that interview ratings correlate well with teaching marks within colleges; a detailed analysis and comparison of the assessment of students at the pre-training interview and on school practice might reveal common ground between these assessments in individual colleges. It is likely that a fair proportion of this common area would be assessment of personality and attitudes.

Warburton, Butcher and Forrest (1963) reported a study of 100 teachers in training in the University of Manchester Department of Education. They found that whilst the degree class was the best single predictor of the mark in education theory and the final Certificate award, the best single predictor of the teaching mark was Cattell's 16 P.F. questionnaire. They commented: 'It would, therefore, appear best in selecting potential teachers to concentrate on attainment and general culture rather than ability, on stability rather than on extraversion or introversion, on academic rather than aesthetic interests, and on participation in social activities rather than on social or domestic background.' An Irish research by Tarpey (1965) reported that correlations between several test scores and teaching marks were varied and contradictory, but that there were some significant correlations between Cattell's 16 P.F. questionnaire and the teaching mark. She suggested that the teaching mark itself might account for a good deal of the variation and contradiction in the correlations, and could not be regarded as a reliable statistical measure. There was great diversity of opinion in the colleges as to what constituted a good teacher, and the teaching mark was necessarily a subjective measure: it was prophetic as well as prognostic. Clearly more research is needed on the reliability and validity of college assessment of teaching practice. Brimer and his team at Bristol are giving some consideration to the nature of these assessments.

Many of the personality and attitude tests employed in such research have been American in origin. Some workers have questioned the administration of such tests to British teachers or students. Referring to the Minnesota Inventory, K. M. Evans (1966) comments: 'All who have used it in this country agree that the American norms are not applicable here and it is also probable that some rewording of items would be desirable.' A recent comparative study of student teachers in the United States and the United Kingdom (University of Toledo 1965) indicates some points to bear in mind. A British advisory group reviewed the content of the Minnesota Inventory and the Ryans Teacher Characteristic Measures, and recommended changes which were adopted. The modified instruments were used in the study. Results for five groups out of six ('elementary' students in three college years and 'secondary' students in three college years) showed no significant difference between British and American students in the case of the Minnesota Inventory. There was a significant difference in mean score for the sixth group (first-year 'elementary' students) in favour of the American students. The results for the modified Ryans Measures showed few consistent differences: however, the Ryans B measure (Learning-centred v. Child-centred) gave the surprising result that the American students obtained significantly greater mean scores than their British counterparts in all six student categories. The American students were more 'learning-centred'. It remains to be shown whether differences of this kind are real differences or differences arising from the content and construction of the test or from weaknesses in the sampling design.

Herbert and Turnbull (1963) studied 499 Scottish diploma students on a three-year course, and related several personality tests and the Minnesota Inventory to the criteria of teaching marks. They divided the students into two contrasting groups: those awarded an A or B teaching grade on a five-point scale, and those awarded a D or E grade. The Minnesota Inventory discriminated most consistently between these two groups, and the students increased their scores on the Inventory during the three-year course. The sense of humour test (Social Intelligence Test 1930) also discriminated between the two groups in the third year of the course. Herbert and Turnbull regarded the Minnesota Inventory as a successful predictor of college teaching and educational assessments.

However, it seems that the Minnesota Inventory cannot be employed as a satisfactory instrument for use in the selection of students without modification. Herbert and Turnbull recommended restandardization of the Inventory and rewording of the items. K. M. Evans (1966) has pointed out that even though differences in mean scores of more and less successful students may be significant, 'there is generally considerable overlapping of scores in the two groups and consequent difficulty of discrimination among individual members'. She analyses and criticizes the form of the Minnesota Inventory, and recommends that it should be improved and standardized in Britain.

A number of current N.F.E.R. research projects concerned with the investigation of school organization or teaching methods have included in the research design measures of the attitudes of teachers. An account of one such measure, used in the N.F.E.R. 'Streaming' project, has been reported by Tuppen (1966). Six Guttman scales concerned with 'permissiveness', and attitudes towards physical punishment, 11-plus selection, noise in the classroom, streaming, children in A streams, were devised and used. The teachers taking part in this project were also asked to indicate how often they used various types of lesson, for example, 'formal sums'. The responses were used to derive two scores: a 'traditional lessons' score, and a 'progressive lessons' score; these are described in an interim report, by Barker-Lunn (1967). The application of such measures has been fruitful in gaining further insight into the influence of a school on the child's education: the form of school organization may not be as critical as the attitudes of teachers and their teaching methods.

Eleven of the thirty-five points on a scale of 'Teacher's contribution assessments', used in the N.F.E.R. Kent reading research project, include teachers' beliefs about the acquisition of reading skills and pupil-teacher relationships. The remaining twenty-four points of the scale were concerned with professional competence and knowledge. J. M. Morris (1966) has reported the use of this assessment scale with sixty-three teachers of 200 selected children from ten different schools. She showed that 'poor readers' invariably suffered 'poor teachers', and that there were significant associations of 'good assessments' with longer training, experience outside junior schools (e.g. secondary), and longer total experience of teaching.

Teachers' attitudes became a major focus in the N.F.E.R. London Infant School Study, 'Teaching beginners to read', and were given special study by Goodacre (1968). The responses of 275 teachers to a Home Background (General) Scale which indicated attitudes towards good/poor homes, and towards children from these homes, were obtained, and 148 teachers agreed to respond to a further questionnaire which included attitudes towards people's behaviour, children's behaviour, and statements of opinion about homes and parents. Goodacre examined the effect of teachers' expectations and attitudes towards pupils' home background upon their estimates of pupils' attributes, personality characteristics and reading readiness, progress and attainment. She reported that the teachers' general expectations seemed to operate most strongly in schools in the highest and lowest social areas; teachers' professional values made them selective in their perceptions of their pupils, rather than their own social background. There were different findings for different school social areas; the importance of the head-teacher's personality and attitudes were also investigated.

Studies of teachers in the school or classroom

The shortage of teachers and general interest in new patterns of teaching has led to much discussion of the teacher's job. The Department of Education and Science has conducted an inquiry in 300 secondary schools, which included investigation of the qualifications and deployment of teachers in relation to the courses which make up a curriculum. The inquiry is referred to in a recent publication of the Schools Council (1965), but it has not yet been published.

The Scottish Council for Research in Education is conducting a job analysis of teaching in some Scottish primary schools, and the N.F.E.R. is making an exploratory study of the techniques available for classroom observation and job analysis of the teacher's day. There has been only one major scientific experiment in classroom observation reported, and that is the work conducted in ten Manchester secondary schools under the direction of Professor R. W. Revans of the Department of Industrial Administration at the University of Manchester. Poole (1964) has described the filming and tape-recording of five mathematics lessons in each of the schools, and the subsequent analysis of the observations of the children's activities. The thesis investigated in this experiment was 'whether it was possible to collect data about classroom activity of sufficient quantity and quality to enable us eventually to identify the assumptions on which teaching effectiveness may be said to be based'. It was concluded that this was certainly possible. A final list of seven activities was agreed: listening or looking, referring, writing, answering, not attending, settling down or leaving, obscured (not evident from film record). Each lesson contained 'so much varied information as to warrant the application of computational and statistical techniques'. These techniques enabled an analysis of the children's activities which suggested that there were substantial differences between the structure of the lessons with an agreed subject content in different schools, and that the opportunities for feedback differed significantly. On average, the teacher presented three units of spoken or written information for every one obtained from the class as a whole. The verbal and written 'outputs' from the classes were found to contain evidence of a great deal of misconception and misunderstanding on the part of the pupils, and the efficiency of the 'inputs' from the teachers was therefore questioned. T. A. Birkin, a Senior Research Associate at the University of Birmingham, is investigating some major dimensions of classroom groups and their relations to the verbal behaviour within these groups. He is using interaction process measures and relating these to personality and motivational characteristics of teachers and pupils.

There have been several recent studies of the teacher's role and the perception that different educationists have of this role, for instance, those of L. Cohen (1965) and Burnham (1965). Recent sociological studies include those of Floud (1962) and B. R. Wilson (1962). Wilson has argued that the teacher's role must become more general and diffuse, although the roles of many professional persons have become more specialized and restricted. Musgrove and Taylor (1965) administered questionnaires on the teacher's role to 470 teachers and 237 parents; their purpose was to estimate the extent to which teachers in different types of schools saw their roles in a narrow sense, to investigate the teacher's perception of parents' views of teachers, and to establish the parents' actual viewpoint. Musgrove and Taylor found that teachers in all the types of school saw their role in rather restricted terms, chiefly moral and intellectual, and were comparatively indifferent to the social aims of education. Parents were generally in agreement, but the teachers thought that parents were indifferent to moral training but very concerned with social advance.

The N.F.E.R. 'Constructive education' project is currently considering the way in which role analysis can be used as part of the approach to estimating school 'climate' and 'organization'. Instruments are being developed for assessing roles played by heads, deputy heads, teachers and pupils. The communications structure of a school is being studied. An officer in this project has recently discussed the need to reassess the role of the head (Westwood 1966).

There have been a number of British studies of group relationships in the classroom. K. M. Evans (1959b, 1962) has summarized the research position and outlined problems requiring consideration. Emmett (1964) has made an experimental study of the personal interaction in the classroom of teacher and pupils with special reference to the self-concept of teachers. Twelve student teachers under training took part, lessons being tape-recorded or observed in detail. The aim was to explore the different approaches to a class, and to relate these to teaching success.

The curriculum for teacher education

Curriculum development involves a recognition of syllabus content and its parts in relation to one another, as well as possible changes in teaching methods and the disposition of staff. Curriculum research, as contrasted with curriculum development, seeks to evaluate the teaching programme in syllabus, methods and procedure—by measurements of the success of the students taking part: the criteria employed are related to the stated objectives of the curriculum. Curriculum research succeeds, but cannot precede, curriculum development.

In teacher training there has been a breeze of healthy, continuous development blowing since the war, but in recent years the wind has been intensified almost to gale force by a number of pressures from outside the colleges and by the enterprise and initiative of staff themselves. In these conditions, there is a clear need for objective surveys of the many experiments taking place, followed by objective evaluation of these experiments. There have been a number of rather incomplete surveys of teacher training curricula and methods in the last six years, but little evaluative research has been attempted or, indeed, has been feasible.

THE EDUCATION COURSE

A survey of the study of education in teacher training (A.T.C.D.E. 1962) reported on the practices found in the colleges in May 1960 and made suggestions, but warned that these practices and suggestions were exploratory, and that 'no evaluation of them was yet possible'. The survey sought information from colleges about practical issues, such as the size of working groups and methods of examination. On the question of the size and classification of 'working groups', for example, replies were received from one-third of the total number of colleges, and a considerable variation in practice was evident. The information obtained from this survey is now out of date in the sense that it was obtained right at the start of the two-year course. There is an urgent need for another and more comprehensive survey of procedures.

Much of the A.T.C.D.E. document was concerned with discussing the natures of the education course in familiar terms. The report declared that whilst the immediate purpose of the course in education was to prepare the student for the profession of teaching, 'its deeper purpose' was to contribute to the general education of the students. The aim of the education course was seen to be the understanding of human beings. Moreover, colleges of education were thought to be the 'only institutions of higher education in this country in which all the lecturers' had to accept 'the personal development of every student as their primary concern'. The implication is that all college staff are concerned with the general and professional education of students, as well as with their personal development. The practical problem for colleges in pursuing these aims has been to find solutions to questions of balance as between different parts of the education course, between the contributions of staffs of education and other college departments, and between education and other courses.

These problems of balance underline the question, 'What is the study of education?' There has been much discussion of this question since the A.T.C.D.E. report of 1962. Bramwell (1962) considered that 'education was a discipline which could provide a point of view to select and give coherence to content, whilst at the same time providing a discipline of thinking'. The viewpoint was 'the introduction of children to their world'. W. Taylor (1964) has questioned the habit of regarding education as an autonomous discipline. He felt that so regarded, the education course might become 'a rather aimless wandering among educational topics, in which hortatory injunction and a concern with group process takes the place of systematic analysis'; such a study was unlikely to provide an adequate basis for the work of a student who wished to investigate an educational problem, since elementary areas of other, relevant disciplines would not have been mastered. A. R. and A. Kelly

(1965) have reviewed the various approaches to a study of education, and concluded that 'one has to abandon the view that the course can be covered satisfactorily by the running together of assorted subjects, each handled by a specialist in that field'. Such specialists should assist and supplement specialists in education and method. Given this premise, they regard the central premise as one of organization of time. S. Morris (1965) has seen the clash between supporters of interrelation of the branches of educational theory and the supporters of differentiation of these branches, as a contributory cause to the lack of development of the philosophy of education course in teacher training. The purpose, organization, and the content of the education course, and the interrelation of the disciplines underlying the study of education, were discussed at an important conference in March 1964. In the introductory address, Gill summarized the problem (Department of Education and Science 1965b):

'We are faced with the old problem of how to bring specialist knowledge and individual interests and enthusiasms to bear on specific topics in such a way as to give students some insight into the topic under discussion. With the desire to give a rigorous theoretical basis to what a student sees and does in schools, there is the desire to help him to relate subject content, methods and materials to children, at the same time giving him values and a sense of purpose and direction. With the advent of education as a degree subject . . . departments will be faced with the question of whether they can continue to be all things to all men; whether, to achieve recognition as an academic discipline, unification of the studies should be attempted or whether, to avoid too superficial a treatment of, say, psychology or sociology, some degree of specialization will be called for.'

The policy of the Government and national needs have made it extremely difficult for college staff to find the time to sit back and consider these questions. Yet until these issues have been more thoroughly considered and some kind of consensus achieved, evaluative research of curriculum and procedures will have much less impact than might otherwise be possible. Detailed investigations into questions such as the educational effects of different staffing policies, and the merits of continuous assessment of course work, make little sense in the shadow of uncertainty about curriculum objectives. Nevertheless, it might be feasible to conduct 'case studies' of individual college programmes which had well-defined objectives and procedures, and such studies, taken together, might be of great value to teacher trainers generally.

Detailed surveys of certain aspects of the education syllabus have been made, and exploratory discussions have ensued. Three of these aspects—educational psychology, the sociology of education, and the philosophy of education—will be reviewed here by way of illustration, without intending to minimize the importance of other aspects.

1. *Educational psychology*

'Educational psychology' has been given form and definition over the last few decades; there has been less uncertainty as to the definition of this aspect of educational studies than there has been perhaps in the case of, say, the sociology or the philosophy of education. Both the sociologists and philosophers have been making good their positions, to the future advantage of student teachers. A survey of 'the position of psychology in training colleges at the end of the two-year course' was made in January 1960 by the B.P.S. and A.T.C.D.E. (1962). The average time spent on teaching psychology in seventy colleges was 40 per cent of the time spent on education as a whole, and this time allocation was reckoned to be 10 to 15 per cent of the whole college course. The qualifications of those teaching the subject were less than satisfactory, but in colleges which had a specialist teacher there was a strong tendency for psychology to be taught separately rather than as part of an integrated course. The report listed the teaching methods used by colleges, and commented on the standard of the students. It was thought that there was a good case for teaching psychology at more than one level. Now that the three-year course has been operated for six student intakes, it would seem appropriate to investigate the question of student ability with a national sample. Amongst the recommendations of the report were two which concerned the need for greater variety of psychology textbooks in college libraries, and the plea that the methods of setting, marking and combining scores should embody sound psychometric principles. It would be worth repeating the 1960 survey if only to check on improvements in these two areas.

Some of the practical problems involved in teaching psychology to student teachers have been discussed by Collier (1960), Hollins (1963) and Thyne (1963). With reference to future investigation, Hollins looks forward to 'a deeper, more searching study of psychology in the training colleges', and Thyne suggests a further task, namely, 'to discover the major problems actually faced by lecturers in psychology, and the ways in which they have been tackled. For example, what criteria are cited in selecting psychological material for a course? And why? Is there an optimum order of presentation? How do we solve the problem of breadth versus depth?'

Himmelweit (1961b) and Wiseman (Department of Education and Science 1965b) have both given detailed discussions of the possible content of a psychology course. Wiseman advocates research and development work on college examinations in psychology, and Himmelweit considers the manner in which the study of sociology and psychology complement each other in training courses.

2. *The sociology of education*

The place of the sociology of education in a training course was given extensive consideration at the Fourth Interprofessional Conference at Keele. Halsey (1961b) commented that courses in colleges 'consist typically of lectures on general sociology of education properly so called'. His contribution to the conference provided some detailed practical suggestions for a college syllabus, following upon a rigorous definition of the subject. Suggestions have been made by Bernstein (Department of Education and Science 1965b), Floud and Halsey (1958), Musgrave (1965), Otley (1966), W. Taylor (1961), and others. Mac-Guire (1963) based a report on the position of sociological teaching in colleges, on replies to a questionnaire returned by seventy-three colleges and sixteen departments in the academic year 1961–2. Most of these training centres did not run specific courses in sociology. Less than half of these included sociology, and sociological topics in college programmes largely depended on the extent to which university departments of education had courses in the sociology of education available at the post-graduate level.

3. *The philosophy of education*

The debate on the nature of the philosophy of education suitable for inclusion in training courses has had some notable contributors, to whom trainers owe a considerable debt: for instance, L. A. Reid (1962) for his notion of the educative teacher; Hirst (1963) for his concept of 'education theory' functioning as the determinant of educational practice, with the theoretical problems clarified by the 'comprehensive contribution of distinctly philosophical methods of investigation'; and

R. S. Peters (Department of Education and Science 1965b) for his detailed suggestions for an initial training course. Squire (1965) has reported a survey of the teaching of philosophy in training institutions carried out during 1963–4. The survey provides some evidence for the earlier claim of Harrison (1962) that 'what generally purports to be "philosophy of education" is nothing more or less than *reflections* on education'. Not more than six out of 208 training institutions, surveyed by Squire in England and Wales, offered courses which included in their titles the words 'philosophy of education'. Squire found that the degree of emphasis on philosophy in 'principles of education' courses varied enormously. Only a minority of colleges presented a dynamic approach which treated educational philosophy as an activity rather than a body of knowledge.

Particular teaching methods and courses

J. McLeish, a Research Fellow at the Cambridge Institute of Education, is comparing the effects of 'participatory' and 'oracular' methods of college teaching. The primary objective of the research is to discover the effects of teaching methods on students' attitudes, especially their attitudes to knowledge and to teaching as a profession. All students entering ten colleges in the Cambridge Institute are involved. A 'survey of opinions' questionnaire is being administered at different stages of the students' courses. A second part of the project consists of experimental studies of the communication process and the ways in which it differs in different teaching methods.

At the University of Keele, a comparative study is being made of two education courses at the university.

Professional training

Surprisingly few researches have been reported relating to training procedures, although perhaps this is one area in which specific reforms can be most easily investigated and evaluated. A systematic attempt to record the opinions of students and teachers was made by R. H. Williams (1963). He reported replies to a questionnaire on details of professional training from fifty-three colleges and thirteen institutes of education. The answers of 1,736 students to another questionnaire giving their opinions on their training were compared with those of 222 recently qualified teachers, and twenty-four teachers who had had ten or more years of experience. The students were preoccupied with their ability to teach in the classroom, and emphasized teaching practice, whilst teachers laid stress on instruction in teaching method. Other differences of emphasis were related to the age-ranges of children the students intended to teach.

Primary method courses have received some attention. Waddington (1952) has considered the effect of contact with children in play centres or junior clubs in relation to the training of teachers. Ingram of Rolle College, Exmouth, is conducting research on a similar topic. J. M. Morris (1966) reporting the N.F.E.R. reading research in Kent junior schools, has considered the relevance of college professional training to the problem of teaching reading in schools.

There is considerable current discussion and investigation of teaching practice methods, although as yet the strictures of the survey of the study of education (A.T.C.D.E. 1962), have not received a satisfactory reply: 'No serious attempt has been made to investigate the effects of the length or placing of the school practices in the student's course upon her development as a teacher.

'No reasonably based answer can be given even to the question whether a student who has done twelve weeks' school practice is likely to develop into a better teacher than one who has done six; there is no evidence on which to decide whether school practice with young children should follow a different distribution of time from practice with children of secondary age.'

Some of these questions, and others, are receiving attention in an important study of the function of teaching practice in courses of teacher training being undertaken at present at the Bristol Institute of Education by a research team led by M. J. Brimer. Their research will include a follow-through study of first-, second- and third-year student samples to determine role conformity of tutors, functional relations between means and objectives, and directional changes towards attainment of objectives.

Discussing the crises in school practice, Price (1964) suggested new measures which involved closed-circuit television, college-linked practice schools, and team teaching in the schools. Coltham (1966) described an interesting attempt to introduce a combination of two of these methods. Caspari and Egglestone (1965) have reported an experiment to test the relevance of a modified casework method of teaching practice supervision, set up at the School of Education, Leicester, in the session 1964–5. The method attempted to overcome the limitations of traditional practice supervision arising from the actual presence of a tutor in a classroom. The experiment was evaluated in a qualitative manner.

The Department of Education and Science is financing a two-year research project into relations between liberal and professional studies in the field of teacher training. This project is part of a programme of studies in the field of tertiary education being undertaken at the Centre for the Study of Educational Policies, University of London Institute of Education, under the direction of Professor W. R. Niblett. The following kinds of questions are being asked: 'How far is the concentration upon the production of expert professionals? What understanding of "general education" is implicit in the training they are given during their period at a university or college?'

In-service training

The recent attention given to curriculum reform and development in Britain, as instanced by the work of the Nuffield Foundation, the Schools Council, and the Scottish Council, has spotlighted the need for more in-service training. Yet there has been surprisingly little investigation of this aspect of teacher education. There have been one or two reports of in-servicing programmes: the Joint Mathematics Council has considered the in-service training of mathematics teachers (1965), and an interesting account of in-service training in Oxfordshire has been given by Moorhouse (1965). But, generally, there has been a noticeable absence of any large surveys of the provision and need for in-service training, or of any evaluation research. The Royal Institute of Chemistry established a research fund in 1965, which will be partly devoted to evaluating the effectiveness of some of the Institute's in-service courses and seminars for school teachers. The N.F.E.R. has undertaken a pilot survey of aspects of in-service training in a local area, and there are plans to proceed to a national survey in 1968.

Effectiveness of teacher training

A major British research project in this field is under the direction of Professor S. Wiseman at the School of Education, Manchester. The team is conducting a longitudinal study of training college students to assess the effectiveness of selection, training and examining in the light of subsequent teaching performance. A number of separate follow-up and follow-back studies of student teachers are involved.

The first of these was reported recently by Wiseman and Start (1965). Of the teachers who consented to take part 248 had complete data, which included their performance at the final examination at the training college, the headmaster's report on the teacher five years after qualifying, and details of the teachers' careers. One finding was that there seemed to be little agreement between college assessment and the headmaster's reference after five years. Wiseman and Start suggest that the colleges and the headmasters may be using different criteria: this suggestion seems worth further investigation, if only because an explanation may help both tutor and headmaster as they make their contributions to teacher training.

This report of one of the smaller Manchester projects found little association between professional training courses and factors such as promotion, head-teacher's assessment or satisfaction in the profession. However, the research projects which follow are being conducted on a larger scale and with other samples; they are likely to provide a greater understanding of the effectiveness of training.

Evans (Cardiff) is studying the effect of the graduate training year on the values and attitudes of her students, using control groups of theological students and mature teachers. Work of this kind, though necessarily limited in scope, can be extremely helpful in the task of objectively assessing the effectiveness of training courses.

Conclusion

There has been some progress in Britain in applying the disciplines of psychology and sociology to the study of teaching and teachers. The tools of psychometrics and sociometrics have been used in recent investigations on the selection of teachers, and the study of the factors which determine 'good teaching'. Several major studies have stressed the importance of the teachers' attitudes in determining the outcome of education. A start has been made on the job analysis of teaching, studies of teachers' roles, and group relationships in the classroom; but these are all areas in which increased support for research is required.

The curriculum and methods of teacher education have received limited attention; some useful surveys of course objectives and content have been made, but little in the way of curriculum evaluation has been attempted. Progress in this direction will remain slow, since apart from the absence of extensive research on teaching noted above, there are many immediate practical issues which preoccupy the staff of colleges and departments and minimize the opportunities for research.

During recent years the staffs of colleges and departments of education have been performing miraculous feats in solving problems of rapid expansion concurrent with the raising of standards, and at the same time many experiments in curriculum and organization have been attempted. Yet the pressure of development has prevented an adequate interchange of ideas and information, or the systematic evaluation of procedures.

Many fundamental questions which are in the minds of active staff, and which might be thought by outsiders to require their attention, have often been 'left on the table' because of commitment to college or institute policy, or continued discussion at a level higher than that of ordinary staff. Now that the three-year course has been established, and the B.Ed. degree introduced, it may be realistic to expect a developing concern for more research into teacher education. The fact that the professional association for the staff of colleges of education, the A.T.C.D.E., has established a Research Committee suggests that there will be increasing participation of college staff in such research, provided that funds for research are made available to colleges.

It can be argued that there are many aspects of teacher education about which quick guidance is required rather than long-term complex studies, important though these may be. For this reason, thorough national surveys of training methods and procedures, and short-term regional evaluation of specific alternatives in the training curriculum or methods, may be considered the immediate requirement. Nevertheless, if duplication is to be avoided, it would be wise to seek some degree of national concensus, and certainly there will be a clear need for close co-operation between colleges and between institutes in any research which is undertaken.

H. J. Butcher

University Education

Students have long served as useful guinea-pigs for the experiments of academic psychologists, to such an extent that psychological theory has sometimes been criticized as explaining the behaviour of under-graduates rather than human behaviour in general. But in such in-quiries the subjects have not usually been studied *as students*; their main role has been to provide fodder for experiments, and the fact of their being students has been a nuisance rather than an advantage, making the experimental results less widely generalizable than they would be from a random or stratified sample of the whole population.

With few exceptions studies within British universities of their own functioning, of student performance, of the characteristics and motivation of staff, of teaching methods, of the examination system, and so on have until very recently been timid, rare and on a small scale. An obvious and important turning-point was the publication of the report of the Robbins Committee on higher education in Britain, which was in itself a massive piece of sociological research, and which settled for some time to come disputes and controversies about, for instance, the so-called pool of ability in the country and the desirability of expansion in higher education.

The Robbins Report, when seen in perspective after the lapse of a decade or two, will very possibly appear quite as important for having changed attitudes to research in higher education as for having brought about great expansion and for having recommended major admini-strative changes. Some of its major recommendations have not been adopted by the Government—for example, the appointment of a senior Minister responsible for higher education, and the loosening of the control of local education authorities over colleges of education. It is arguable, too, that expansion would soon have been achieved even without publication of the report, though perhaps rather more grudgingly and slowly. But it seems certain that the report gave an enormous boost to the idea of planning, and more especially to the idea that extensive research is required if planning is to be anything but another name for guesswork. None of this was novel in principle to anyone with training in the social sciences, but it was a revolutionary innovation for survey methods and statistical analysis to be used seriously, competently and on a nation-wide scale in the study of higher education. The information provided in the several volumes of appendices has still hardly been fully digested, and contains a mine of data suitable as starting-points for further investigations.

One respect in which the recommendations of the Robbins Report have not been fully adopted is worth mentioning because it is relevant to the scope and coverage of this paper. 'Higher education'—meaning whole-time education in degree-giving or equivalent institutions—has in the past been distinguished from 'further education', arbitrarily understood to mean education received (by someone who has left school) in a college or other institution controlled by the local authorities. The recommendations of the Robbins Committee were aimed at reducing differences between these two spheres and at producing a continuum, rather than a dichotomy. The distinction, as applied in practice, refers to the autonomy or dependence of the institution; but it sounds as if it implies differences in the nature or quality of the courses provided. Now that institutions of 'further education' provide numerous degree courses, and now that the avowed hope of the Department of Education and Science is that such degrees, awarded by the Council for National Academic Awards, should be of equal status and repute to those bestowed by the universities, the arbitrary distinction between 'higher' and 'further' education should be treated as obsolete. 'Tertiary education' will serve as a less tendentious description of both.

Official policy at present (June 1967) is for the main 'further education' institutions doing advanced work to be re-grouped into a smaller number (some twenty-eight or thirty) of 'polytechnics'. This 'binary system', under which there is apparently to remain rather a deep gulf between, on the one hand, the autonomous sector of tertiary education (the universities, including those that were until recently colleges of advanced technology) and, on the other, the public, grant-aided section, has been severely criticized by Lord Robbins (Robbins 1966, Robbins and Ford 1965) writing as a private individual. Recent issues of *Universities Quarterly* have contained evidence of general, almost unanimous, support for these criticisms from staff in both kinds of institution (Atkinson 1965, Ford 1965, Venables 1965). A recent discussion of these issues can also be found in the proceedings of the Home Universities Conference (1966).

The fragmentation of tertiary education has produced a consequent fragmentation of research, which is partly reflected in the organization of this book. Technical and technological education and the training of teachers are treated in separate papers, and this is by no means an artificially imposed treatment. In general, the study of technical students undergoing 'further education', that of teachers in training, and that of university students have been carried out by different investigators with different interests. The Robbins Report was a pioneering survey in producing extensive factual evidence about all these kinds of institution and their students, and in considering together their several needs and abilities so as to form a general plan for the whole pattern of tertiary education.

Despite Robbins, and despite moves towards closer co-operation between the various kinds of institution (Ford 1966), few other research teams, even if they have had the inclination, have had the facilities or the man-power to carry out 'cross-cultural' investigations involving more than one kind of educational institution. One very hopeful development, however, has been the formation of the flourishing and rapidly expanding Society for Research into Higher Education, with regional branches in major areas of the country. This organization has greatly speeded up the post-Robbins tendency for institutions of higher education to study their own functions, processes and people, and is commendably broad in its terms of reference. One of the most useful of its activities is the provision of an abstracting service, covering almost all the relevant publications in Britain and a fair selection from the United States. Similarly, a register of research in progress has been formed and circulated to members (including corporate members, such as universities or departments).

In this preamble an attempt has been made to sketch some of the background, and to suggest the general atmosphere in which research into higher education has recently been and is being carried on. Obviously this survey must needs be somewhat sketchy and even inconsequent, if only to reflect the present state of research. Even when 'further education' and the training of teachers are excluded (as treated in other papers) and also some aspects of university education, such as the examination system, a large number of aspects remain, many of which have as yet given rise only to scattered and piecemeal researches. To provide some semblance of unity, the rest of this paper will be concerned mainly with student selection, performance and 'wastage' of both undergraduates and graduates, and to a lesser degree with university teaching methods. An analysis by Oxtoby (1967) shows that about half of all current research in higher education comes under these heads, or (if one excludes topics treated in other papers and also historical and philosophical research) rather more than two-thirds.

Methods of student selection

Four main kinds of information used in student selection may be distinguished, of which the first three have been widely used, but the fourth quite infrequently, having met with considerable suspicion and opposition. These are (a) examination results, pre-eminently those of the General Certificate of Education at Advanced level, and of the Scottish Higher Grade examination; (b) reports from headmasters and headmistresses; (c) information obtained from the interviewing of candidates by university staff; (d) scores on standardized psychological tests.

The report of the Robbins Committee (sects. 228–33) recommended one 'old-fashioned' and one 'new-fashioned' development, corresponding to (b) and (d) above. These recommendations were that reports from schools should be fuller, more systematic, and presented in a form to be determined jointly by representatives of schools and universities; and that research should be carried out in this country into the efficacy of tests similar to those widely used in the United States, such as the so-called scholastic aptitude tests of the College Entrance Examinations Board.

Drever (1963) and Kelsall (1963) have surveyed the literature on the effectiveness of the main means of selection. Drever's paper contains a useful bibliography of more than a hundred earlier references, including almost all the British ones.

a) THE PREDICTIVE VALUE OF EXAMINATIONS SUCH AS 'A' LEVEL G.C.E.

Although university selection has in the past relied so heavily on examination results, this reliance has to a large degree been a matter of faith and tradition. The assumptions underlying such reliance have, until very recently, rarely been made explicit, but a recent symposium in *Universities Quarterly* (June 1967) is evidence of a welcome rethinking. Although the technical defects in most examination procedures have been well known to specialists since the alarming results reported by Hartog and Rhodes (1935), they have not been fully recognized by most university staff. Equally, the various G.C.E. examinations boards have until recently been somewhat inactive in research, particularly in respect of comparing standards between boards. This situation has been changing rapidly in the last few years, with the appointment of research workers and with increased communication and exchange of information between boards. Recent research in this area is described in the paper by Pilliner.

In one of the earlier studies relating academic performance at school with that at university, E. M. Williams (1950), compared results in Higher School Certificate with results in first-year university examinations. The students concerned were those entering the Faculties of Arts, Science and Medicine at Sheffield University over a five-year period who had taken the Northern Universities Joint Matriculation Board Higher School Certificate. Thirty-one of sixty-eight correlations were not statistically significant; but this is not surprising, since the subjects were often unrelated. Some correlations, indeed, were negative, such as between subsidiary English in Higher School Certificate and both chemistry and physics in university intermediate examinations. What is more of interest is that several correlations were decidedly high, particularly between the same or similar subjects as examined at school and university. A value of + 0·79 was found between performances in Latin at the two levels, and one of + 0·77 in the case of biology. In general, results at university were more predictable in science than in arts subjects. This finding was in agreement with those of the Scottish Council for Research in Education (1936).

In another study from Sheffield, Austwick (1960) studied the relation between performance in G.C.E. ('A' and 'S' level) and subsequent performance in the Faculty of Arts. The number of students was fairly small, and the results consequently not analysed in great detail; but there was clearly a moderate degree of correspondence between the two sets of performances. The extent of correlation, however, was not so high that a clear dividing line could be set at any particular G.C.E. mark that would serve for selecting students. Austwick's research produced lower coefficients of correlation that had been found by Williams, but their order of size was approximately similar. An incidental interesting finding was that, over the three years studied, the standard of university entrants rose steadily in terms of G.C.E. marks previously obtained. Austwick interpreted this as representing a genuine rise in standards.

The results of Gould and McComisky (1958), who compared performance in S.C.E. with that in the University of Edinburgh Faculty of Arts, again confirmed the general impression that there is a significant but moderate degree of overall relation between leaving certificate and university performance right through to final Honours examinations.

An extensive investigation was carried out by Petch (1961, 1963), following up those candidates in the Northern Universities Joint Matriculation Board G.C.E. examination of 1956 who went on to universities. Most of the results are presented in tables of frequencies and percentages, but a more elaborate statistical analysis of these data was made by Barnett and Lewis (1963). They found, after dividing the universities into eleven groups (six groups consisting each of a large provincial university, one group being Oxford and Cambridge combined, and so on), that there was no significant difference between university groups in the proportion of Firsts obtained nor in the proportion of students failing Finals, but that there were substantial differences in proportions of Seconds, Thirds and Pass and Ordinary degrees obtained. This analysis, and most of the others to be described, was based on some 1,300 students. Other findings, all statistically significant, were that boys did better than girls, obtaining more Firsts and less Thirds, that students from maintained grammar schools and independent schools did equally well, but those from direct grant schools less well, and that those who were younger when they took 'A' level G.C.E. did better in Finals. Rather surprisingly, there was only a faint tendency, not significant, for state scholars to do better than other students.

The most original part of Barnett and Lewis' work was the use of a sophisticated multivariate technique known as canonical analysis to investigate the predictive values, individual and joint, of the various G.C.E. marks at 'O', 'A' and 'S' level and of the other descriptive variables such as age and type of school. One reason for using this technique, rather than the more familiar multiple regression, was that, instead of assuming that the various degree results (including Pass or General, Ordinary, Fail but successful at second attempt, and so on) formed an ordered scale, the technique in effect treated these as discrete categories initially and tested whether they could be meaningfully ordered. It was found that they could, and that the provisional ordering adopted was confirmed. Barnett and Lewis also found that 'O' level grade in English language had no appreciable value as a predictor of degree performance, that average G.C.E. grade, whether in 'O', 'A' or 'S' level was a positive predictor in all groups without exception, but that the 'A' level average was the most important. Useful prediction could be achieved without including 'O' or 'S' level results, and without giving special weight to main subjects. In all these findings it was clear that prediction was impaired by ignoring differences between universities, and that if these were taken into account, different predictive formulas would be required for success at particular universities, or at least types of university. Finally it was shown that the formulas obtained from this detailed statistical analysis gave much better prediction of university success than an empirical grading developed by the Joint Matriculation Board.

Another thorough and detailed research into the predictive value of examinations taken at school was that of Pilliner (1960). This deserves quite a full description, particularly as it was not published (except as a duplicated memo). The students studied were those entering the Faculty of Arts, Edinburgh University, in 1953 and 1954 whose record at ordinary and higher grade examinations in the Scottish Leaving Certificate could be traced. The criteria were various university examinations from first Ordinary to final Honours. The size of the samples was, for 1953 and 1954 respectively, 136 Ordinary and ninety-three Honours degree students, and 148 Ordinary and seventy Honours.

Pilliner investigated the correlation between overall performance in the Leaving Certificate and overall success at university. Clearly, to assess 'overall' performance in this way, rather arbitrary assumptions have to be made about how to combine and weight the elements. For the criterion of university success, passing or failing the degree examination within a particular length of time was adopted. How best to combine the parts of the Leaving Certificate is more of a problem; Pilliner formed four different weighted aggregates, as follows. All included performance at both Ordinary and Higher Grade, and all counted one Higher as worth two Ordinary. Of the first three aggregates, one (A) assessed mainly 'quantity', giving main weight to number of passes in the Leaving Certificate; the second (B) assessed mainly 'quality', giving greater weight to high marks in a few subjects than to middling marks in many; the third (C) attempted to balance these two factors. All these three were concerned only with *passes* in the Leaving Certificate; the fourth aggregate took into account also marks obtained in subjects attempted but failed.

The results of this analysis showed rather clearly the limitations of the Leaving Certificate as an 'overall' predictor of university success. The correlations between the first three aggregates and degree performance are shown in table 1.

TABLE I

Correlations of overall success in Scottish Leaving Certificate with overall university success (1953 and 1954 entries to Edinburgh University Faculty of Arts)

			Ord. M.A. in 3 years	Hons M.A. in 4 years	Hons M.A. in 5 years
	Entry				
		No.	108	83	83
1953		A	0·48	0·16	0·02
	Aggregates	B	0·41	0·26	0·11
		C	0·53	0·23	0·07
		No.	149	70	70
1954		A	0·14	0·33	0·40
	Aggregates	B	0·20	0·43	0·30
		C	0·17	0·38	0·29

These figures are interesting and rather surprising. Two facts stand out immediately. It appears to make relatively little difference which of the three aggregates is employed, whether 'quantity' or 'quality' or a mixture of the two. Secondly, there is a disturbing inconsistency from one year to another. Among the 1953 entrants, Ordinary degree result is more predictable, but in the next year-group the reverse is true.

Pilliner's research included also the prediction of success in particular courses at university from the corresponding subjects in the Leaving Certificate and from various aggregates. As expected, he found a higher degree of correlation in the case of particular subjects than with 'overall' measures. For Latin and French, for instance, the correlations were in the range $+ 0.4$ to $+ 0.7$, but were markedly lower for mathematics.

Much less research appears to have been done into the prediction of success in technological subjects (but see the paper by Heywood). It is worth mentioning a recent study by Bagg (1968), in which he has investigated the correlation of G.C.E. 'A' level grades with performance at a university course in chemical engineering. The most surprising finding in Bagg's paper is the low relation between 'A' level maths and degree results.

The conclusions to be drawn from these studies are that a positive and significant correlation has almost always been found, but that G.C.E. or Scottish Leaving Certificate examination results could not be considered adequate as a means of selection unless they were supported by other evidence. Moreover, the results of these surveys have been subject, as Pilliner points out, to three separate kinds of error, (a) sampling error, (b) predictive error, and (c) errors due to unreliability both of the predictive and the criterion measures.

Similarly, Kelsall (1963) has summarized some of the reasons for caution in interpretation, including the restriction of range of ability in any student sample, the unreliability of marking examinations, and the fact that examinations such as the Leaving Certificate are not primarily designed as predictive instruments.

The general pattern of these results and the consequent reservations one must make about them are paralleled in other countries. If one makes some allowance for local differences in examination systems and university courses, it appears from, for instance, the review of Parkyn (1959) that similar findings have been typical in Australia, New Zealand, South Africa and the United States.

Considerable space has been given to the first of the four main sources of information used in student selection, i.e. the results of G.C.E. 'A' level and similar examinations, both because in practice it is the most influential and also because there is most favourable evidence for its predictive validity. The remaining three kinds of data must be treated much more succinctly.

B) TEACHERS' ESTIMATES

University selectors have commonly made use of reports from headmasters. There is little doubt that in principle these could be very relevant and effective, but equally little doubt that they may in practice be almost useless, or indeed worse than useless if they counter-act and decrease reliance on more reliably predictive measures.

Some thirty years ago, the Scottish Council for Research in Educa-tion inquiry found that teachers' ratings of success in the Leaving Certificate examination were virtually as effective in predicting univer-sity success as the Certificate results themselves, and sometimes even more effective. Kelsall (1963), however, points out that this high prognostic value was probably peculiar to pre-war Scotland and would not apply universally to teachers' estimates of 'A' level G.C.E. per-formance. Further research in this area would be useful. It would certainly be unwise to extrapolate these results to the reports from headmasters seen by university selectors.

'He shows promise as a left-handed spin bowler, and is a great comfort to his widowed mother' is, according to Drever (1963), not untypical of such reports. Moreover, Himmelweit (1963) has shown that the overall assessment provided by headmasters varies with the ratio of applicants to places, so that the average picture of candidates is more glowing when places are in shorter supply. She concludes that both headmasters' letters (and 'O' level G.C.E. information) 'are totally inadequate data on which to decide whether to look at an applicant or reject him. It is only slightly better than deciding on a random basis.'

This is not to say, however, that they could not be much more useful in the future. Fifteen years ago Warburton (1952) made a number of suggestions about how this might be achieved, including, for instance, a greater standardization of the form in which information is requested, the clear specification of particular areas of information (to reduce 'halo effect'), the ranking of candidates within a school, and so on. Another important possibility of improvement is in greater 'feedback' to the schools of progress at university; the headmasters' insight into their own bases of assessment would thereby be greatly facilitated. There is no reason in principle, if some of these improve-ments become standard practice, why headmasters' estimates should not add to the predictive value of 'A' level results in much the same way as estimates were shown to add to the predictive value of test data at age 11.

c) INTERVIEWING OF CANDIDATES FOR UNIVERSITY PLACES

If headmasters' reports as typically required and received are of uncertain prognostic value, the prognostic value of the ordinary interview is probably even more dubious. Albrow (1967) reminds us of the number of man-hours employed by busy lecturers and of the fact that in many faculties the whole procedure has taken on the nature of a ritual. Oxford and Cambridge colleges have usually placed great faith in the value of interviewing. Rose and Ziman (1964), in spite of stigmatizing the college admission procedures as in general 'clumsy and cranky', believe that 'a quarter of an hour of pumping and probing, pushing and prodding, needling and knifing, although done with such gentlemanly skill it might seem to be mere cocktail party chit-chat, can yield a rich harvest of information'. Well, perhaps this is so, but it remains an article of faith, not an established fact. What experimental evidence we have about the value of even the most skilfully conducted interviews is at best ambivalent. Ulrich and Trumbo (1965), surveying an extensive literature (mainly American) on selection interviews, conclude that their main use is in assessing competence in social relations and level of motivation. Ability and attainment are more effectively appraised by other means, but the interviews can be as good as any other technique for ascertaining whether the candidate is likely to work hard and adjust to the social conditions of work. It is perhaps an implicit realization of this fact that makes so many university lecturers remain convinced supporters of the selection interview. Even at Oxford and Cambridge, however, the realization is increasing that justice must not only be done but be seen to be done, and that the interview is particularly open to criticism in this respect, being essentially subjective and private. Brock (1965), writing as an Oxford Senior Tutor, argues in favour of a revision of the Oxford admission system so as to make it fairer (or at least more attractive) to candidates from the maintained secondary schools within the state system, which at present provide less than half of the entrants.

d) STANDARDIZED PSYCHOLOGICAL TESTS

Himmelweit (1950, 1963, Himmelweit and Summerfield 1951a, b) has been one of the most consistent advocates of tests of ability as instruments of student selection. Having calculated multiple correlations between selected psychological tests and Finals results in law and sociology, she drew attention to the interesting result that the most crucial predictor is the limiting ability, 'without which the student might come a cropper in that particular course', and not necessarily the one most typically employed in studying the subject. This finding has obvious relevance to 'wastage rates', and requires further study.

Not all psychologists have been so convinced of the usefulness of tests of ability at university level. Correlations in many other studies have been low to the point of insignificance. But it seems likely that the use of such tests has often been abandoned before their potentialities have been fully explored. It also seems likely that tests of creativity or divergent thinking and of personality factors may ultimately prove useful in selecting and placing students, but at present their practical value has not been adequately demonstrated. Possibly they will be more valuable in guidance than in selection. Hudson (1966) has claimed that arts specialists are predominantly 'divergent' and science specialists predominantly 'convergent' thinkers. M. B. Cameron (1967) has found some support for this thesis in a study of Scottish students. Tests of divergent thinking may prove particularly useful in identifying students with talent for such subjects as architecture (cf. the work of Mackinnon in the United States). Research on these lines is in progress in the University of Manchester, and a preliminary report has been published by Freeman (1967).

There are indications of systematic relations between personality factors, particularly introversion, and success in academic courses (Furneaux 1962), but it is hardly likely that these findings will affect selection procedures in the near future. The correlations are not very large, and usually depend on results obtained from questionnaires, which are too easily fakable to be suitable for purposes of selection; but there is certainly a need for more research in this direction. One comprehensive study still in progress is that of Dr Vernon Hamilton at the University of Reading, who is using, among other measures, a personality inventory developed by Grygier.

At present, however, the most active tendency is to develop scholastic aptitude tests, rather than tests of intelligence or personality for selection purposes (Oliver 1962). A large experimental project, sponsored by the Committee of Vice-chancellors and Principals, is at present well advanced, with the work of test construction, adaptation and try-out being shared between units at the Universities of London and Manchester. The unit at London is responsible for preparation of the mathematical part of the battery, and that at Manchester, under Professor R. A. C. Oliver, for the verbal part. Extensive trials of the new instrument and administration to more than 30,000 sixth-formers are in progress at the time of writing.

A rather similar project has been carried on for some years in Scotland jointly by the Scottish Council for Research in Education and the Department of Psychology at the University of Edinburgh. All pupils who took Scottish Certificate of Education Higher Grade examinations for the first time in 1962 were also tested in that year with a scholastic aptitude test. Those entering universities and other institutes of tertiary education are being followed up, their performances recorded throughout their subsequent academic career, and the relative predictive values of the Scottish Certificate of Education, the scholastic aptitude test, teachers' estimates and headmasters' and headmistresses' assessments compared. Most of the students concerned have now graduated. M. C. Killcross of the Applied Psychology Unit, Department of Psychology, University of Edinburgh, is in charge of the project, 'Assessment for higher education', and first results are due to be published fairly soon.

Very recently a research report has appeared (Pilkington and Harrison 1967) which is one of the few so far published to compare the value of tests and G.C.E. results in a single survey and also to assess their joint predictive value. It is particularly interesting in that the two tests of ability used were 'high-level' ones, and therefore presumably more appropriate to student selection than most such. Nevertheless, it was found that the 'A' level results were rather more predictive than the intelligence test results against degree marks as criterion. When multiple correlations were calculated, the addition of intelligence tests to 'A' level marks as predictors increased the correlation very little.

'Wastage' of undergraduate students

Mountford (1957) studied the university career of three years' entry to Liverpool University. His account is still valuable, particularly with reference to 'wastage', and factors affecting it. His findings about students who took more than the usual time to complete their courses are also useful. These were commonest in the Schools of Dentistry, Veterinary Science, Architecture and the Faculty of Medicine, in that order. Mountford points out that these are professional schools in which the student has to adjust to a new or virtually new subject, with little help from what he has learned at school. They are also long courses, and ones for which the selection procedures based on school achievement and school records have little predictive validity.

High proportions of delays were found amongst overseas students and amongst students who were privately financed. Rather lower proportions of women were delayed. This last finding perhaps reflects the higher degree of selection among women.

Of the whole three-year enrolment, just over 13 per cent abandoned their courses entirely. Causes external to the university itself that were particularly relevant appeared to be unsuitable working conditions at home, frictions within the family, undue demands on the student for household chores, family financial worries, and strain and waste of time in travelling too great a distance every day between home and university. In some cases there is a general lack of physical tone; in others there are emotional disturbances; and in the case of overseas students there are many problems arising from life in a strange environment. Some students are found to be taking a course simply because of pressure from their parents; others appear to have misjudged their aptitude for the subject they have chosen. Excess of zeal in the activities of student societies or in outside organizations proves to be the undoing of some, while a streak of sheer laziness brings disaster to others. In most instances, however, it is not really possible to put one's finger on a single cause and say, 'This lies at the bottom of the trouble'; most failures are due to a combination of factors.

Mountford believed that the best ways in which the university could try to ensure that student 'wastage' was kept fairly low were (a) to improve methods of selection; (b) to take pains to strengthen the tutorial system and to ensure staff-student contact; (c) to make sure (though illness was only a small factor in failure) that the Health Service was fully used; (d) to check that timetables were not overloaded; and (e) to improve teaching techniques.

Craig and Duff (1961) investigated failure rates in the Faculty of Science, University of Edinburgh, of students entering in the period 1954–9. The average rate of 'wastage', after deaths, illnesses and transfers, had been excluded, ranged between 16 and 19 per cent. Men were again found to have a higher failure rate than women; and those who had changed their subject, transferring to pure science from other courses, were also worse risks than the average. Another interesting finding in this research dealt with the relative performance of entrants who had taken the Scottish Leaving Certificate (i.e. in Scottish schools) and those whose qualification was a number of G.C.E. 'A' levels, (i.e. mainly students from English schools). Overall performance showed little difference, but Leaving Certificate students who failed nearly all failed in their first year, whereas the G.C.E. students who failed nearly all failed in subsequent years. This, no doubt, reflects the fact that many of the G.C.E. entrants will have had an extra year in the sixth form, will have specialized to a greater extent, and will have found the transition to university work rather easier.

J. D. Nisbet and Welsh (1966) describe a study of student performance in the Faculties of Arts and Sciences at Aberdeen University that was particularly concerned with failure and drop-out. After attempting to predict students' performance from Scottish Certificate in Education Higher Grade results and from head-teachers' reports, they concluded that the degree of prediction was too low and too variable from year to year (as in Pilliner's research already described) to be put to practical use. It would appear that a substantial part of the variation in students' performance at university is basically unpredictable from evidence available at time of entry to university. They decided that a more promising line of inquiry was to try to develop a kind of 'early-warning' system during the crucial first year. The criterion for considering first-year students to be at risk was fixed, after some trial and error, as their falling in the bottom third of the class in two or more subjects in the December examinations. Although no remedial action was taken beyond notifying the names of these students to their main supervisors, the rate of failure, which had been rising sharply and had reached 23 per cent, declined through 17 to 14 per cent in the next two years. These figures apply to science students; the 'early-warning' system was not attempted with arts students. The authors do not claim that the change in trend was directly due to the introduction of the system, but the evidence is at least suggestive.

There has been little study of what happens to students who have to abandon their courses; the main information available is provided by Kendall (1964a, b). His starting-point was the work by Mountford at Liverpool, already discussed in this section, and also that of Malleson (1958) at University College, London. Following up the students in these two groups who had failed to graduate, he was able to obtain an overall response rate to his questionnaire of about 50 per cent. This figure appears to have been based not only on the 'drop-outs' but on the entire sample including a control group of successful students (who provided a higher response rate). Thus it is not quite clear from the article how far below 50 per cent was the response rate among the people with whom the research was mainly concerned. One may suspect, too, that the more 'successful' failed students may have been more willing to respond.

If these reservations are borne in mind, some of Kendall's results are suggestive, particularly the relatively high number of 'failed' students who managed nevertheless ultimately 'to gain a university degree diploma or certificate, or some other qualification of relatively high standing, generally awarded by a professional body such as the R.I.B.A. or the Institution of Mechanical Engineers. Many of these qualifications are regarded by the Ministry of Education as equivalent to degrees in the calculation of teachers' salaries (Kendall 1964a, p. 401). These he described as the 'recouped' group, and they formed over 50 per cent of the men from University College, London, who answered the questionnaire, and about 35 per cent of the Liverpool men. In the former group the 'recouping' generally meant obtaining a degree; but the Liverpool 'recoupers' generally obtained some other kind of qualification, as described in the passage just quoted. The corresponding figures for women were lower. Kendall's second paper compares 'recoups' and 'non-recoups' with the control group in terms of occupation and income. Here the findings were generally in line with expectation. On the whole, the control group were earning more than the 'recoups', and the 'recoups' rather more than the 'non-recoups'. For the women it appeared, Kendall points out, that marriage was an alternative to qualifying for a large proportion of those who had failed. Only one in five of the 'non-recoups' had remained single compared with about one in three in the other two groups (see also the paper by Heywood).

Graduate students

Until recently, virtually no research had been carried out in Britain into the selection, academic performance or wastage rate of graduate students, and even in the United States reliable findings are still scarce. Rudd, at the University of Essex, has recently carried out an extensive investigation; but no published account is available as this book goes to press, although one is shortly due.

The only large-scale research yet reported (except for the information assembled by the Robbins Committee) is that of Glennerster (1966), dealing with graduate students in the London School of Economics; this will consequently be discussed in some detail.

Glennerster's book describes only retrospective statistical findings unearthed from college records, whereas a longitudinal ongoing study of graduate students would have many obvious advantages, such as the possibility of questioning and interviewing the people concerned. None the less, Glennerster succeeded in revealing a great deal of useful information that has important practical consequences for the future policy of universities.

Before this, published empirical research into the success and failure of graduate students in Britain appeared to amount to only two fragmentary accounts, (a) a report of Oxford students embarking on courses in 1953 (contained in the report of the Franks Commission), and (b) a small survey of London graduates carried out by the Association of University Teachers and described by Hatch in *New Society* (17 June 1965). Glennerster's book is therefore a useful one, particularly perhaps in showing how little was known, and how readily the required data were available in existing records. When classified and tabulated, these provide indications for future policy about, for instance, admissions policy and about the degree of supervision needed by graduate students.

That such information was urgently needed is suggested by the sharp increase, absolutely and proportionately, in the number of graduate students at the London School of Economics. Taking full-time students only, the respective numbers in 1950/51, 1960/61 and 1963/64 were 383, 732 and 933. The ratio of graduate to undergraduate students had also been rising sharply (from 20 to 39 per cent in the nine years from 1954/55 to 1963/64), with the result that the London School of Economics is well on the way to becoming primarily a graduate college. (Moreover, the figures quoted do not include graduate students in education.) A parallel but much more gradual increase in the proportion of graduate students in British universities as a whole has taken place (from 11 to 15 per cent in the same period).

On admissions, Glennerster starts from the assumption that the intake of students to a college is chiefly affected by three factors: the number and kind of applications received, the college's admissions policy, and the current policy of the Government about student grants. These three factors may interact, and admissions policy, for instance, may affect applications, or vice versa.

In the case of the London School of Economics, it was found that over the period 1952–64 applications for graduate places increased by 123 per cent, and that this increase was about the same among home and overseas students. Selection policy and grants policy appear to have worked in opposite directions during that period. The college selection procedure became more formalized and more rigorously selective; yet the ratio of entrants to applicants increased, since a far higher proportion of those accepted were able to obtain adequate financial assistance. Other facts discovered were that the proportion of women graduate students had remained practically constant, that far more overseas students came from developed than from under-developed countries, and that overseas students were accepted less readily (in terms of the number of applicants) but had a lower drop-out ratio. The effect of more readily obtainable grants was seen not only in the ratio of entrants to acceptances, but also in the considerably increased ratio of full-time to part-time graduate students.

The question of 'drop-outs' or wastage is complex and treated with proper caution. Here the research suffers particularly from being retrospective and statistical, and from not being concerned with reasons for discontinuance of study. The analysis was also made more difficult because only partial information was available about students switching from, for example, a Ph.D. course to a Master's degree course. As a consequence, apparent wastage on the Master's course was inflated, since an unknown number of those dropping out had originally intended to obtain a Ph.D. degree. Furthermore, results were not yet complete; some of the students in the group studied might still eventually obtain a degree. The most general conclusions about 'wastage', subject to all these reservations, were that it was substantially higher than among undergraduates both at the London School of Economics and nationally; that there had been some tendency for the rate to increase in the period studied, and that it was considerably lower among science than among arts graduate students. It appears from this study of the London School of Economics and from the scattered evidence available in the few other British and American researches, that, in very round figures, 50 to 60 per cent of students enrolled for higher degrees obtain them sooner or later. This is probably a higher rate of wastage than has been fully realized or taken into account in most university planning. Further research into the determining factors would be welcome.

The amount of formal and informal teaching and supervision received by graduate students was investigated, and some of the results were rather surprising. Full-time graduate students at the London School of Economics (as reported in November 1964) received a little over three hours a week of teaching, compared with eight and a half hours received by undergraduates. A larger proportion of the graduates' time was spent in tutorials than at lectures, compared with the undergraduates, but this amounted to only half an hour per week on average (including both individual tutorials and small classes). There were naturally differences between the amounts of teaching received by Ph.D. and Master's degree students, and by each at different stages of their courses. Thus full-time students for a Master's degree received twice as much teaching as the average full-time graduate student, about six hours a week compared with three. Ph.D. students received correspondingly less; teaching received by full-time Ph.D. students averages throughout their course just over one hour a week. In both kinds of higher degree the amount of teaching was greater in the earlier years of the course.

Teaching time has so far been considered from the point of view of the student. How does it appear to the university teacher? The University Grants Committee has laid down, for calculations of staff-student ratios, that one graduate student should be treated as equivalent to two undergraduates in demands on staff time (one to three in science faculties). Glennerster produces detailed tables and estimations to show that, as regards the London School of Economics, these assumptions have little foundation in actual practice. It was found that the average full-time graduate student received only just over half as much teaching time as did an undergraduate. A part-time graduate student consumed only one-third as much staff time as a full-time one, and therefore only about one-sixth as much as an undergraduate. Nor was it found that the teaching and supervision of graduate students took more staff time per student in terms of preparation. Apparently the only sense in which graduate students are more demanding of staff time is that their tuition is largely concentrated among senior staff. In addition, what was found to apply to staff in general, namely that supervision of graduates was less time-consuming than of undergraduates, did not apply to professional staff.

University teaching methods

Powell (1964) summarized research on teaching methods in a succinct and critical review. His general theme was the essential amateurishness of most British university teachers, since the profession is the only major one for which there is no recognized course of training. Very few university teachers are familiar with the suggestive findings of social psychologists, particularly about small groups; many of these are directly relevant to the organization of tutorial groups.

Other research results with which, according to Powell, the university teacher ought to be familiar concern the best size for classes and a comparison of lectures with teaching in small tutorial groups. Small classes are not necessarily more effective than large. For the intake and recording of information, large ones can be perfectly effective. Small classes and tutorial groups are superior in effectiveness only with fairly able students, and with those who are prepared to take an active part. Staff and students alike tend to underestimate the complexity of small-group discussions, and the research evidence suggests that it is easier to become an effective lecturer than an effective tutor. In particular, experiment has shown that tutors tend to underestimate the extent to which they are monopolizing discussion; yet if a tutorial group becomes in effect a small lecture class, it is likely to have the worst of both worlds. According to other experiments quoted, the best size for a tutorial or discussion group is from about seven to nine. Leaderless group discussions—i.e. discussions between groups of students without a member of staff—have sometimes produced excellent results, but such discussions cannot be expected to develop as spontaneous 'happenings'; they require careful preparation, briefing and subsequent analysis.

Students' ratings of how well members of staff lecture appear to be reliable, and the judgments of undergraduate and graduate students agree closely. Senior and more experienced lecturing staff are not in general rated more highly. 'The fact that . . . there was not improvement with rise in rank will surprise nobody but professors.'

Three papers in the same (June 1966) issue of *Universities Quarterly* described enterprising attempts to study and improve methods of university teaching. Those by Collier and S. Nisbet dealt with experimental methods of handling small groups, that by Kerr is more concerned with how to help inexperienced lecturers.

Collier adapted a 'syndicate' method of organizing classes, as used in a course for business executives at the Harvard Business School, to the teaching of a six-week course in educational sociology. Groups of five or six students were given assignments and were required to furnish joint reports, both oral and written, and sometimes to sit as a forum to answer questions. Lectures were used to summarize, and, if necessary, to extend or correct the conclusions of the student groups. Collier found that this method (used on a visit to Temple University, U.S A.) improved student 'involvement' and lecturer-student relations without impairing academic standards.

Nisbet tried out a not dissimilar technique in a seminar for advanced students of education at Glasgow University. Again the emphasis was on helping the student to think for himself, to prepare a case, and to defend it in the face of criticism from fellow students; but in Nisbet's seminar the individual student rather than the 'syndicate' bore responsibility. The novel feature in this seminar was that the students taking part were asked to produce 'six statements worth making' on the topic under discussion—worth making, that is, in the sense of being clear, succinct and important, of being controversial enough to stimulate discussion and argument and as representing in each case 'the personal belief, based on study, experience and reflection of its author'. Nisbet suggests a number of advantages in this procedure, which is admittedly suitable only for rather mature students, in particular, that the tutor is enabled more easily to sustain his desired role of *primus inter pares*.

Kerr described briefly a series of meetings arranged at Leicester University in order to put into effect some of the recommendations of the report of the Hale Committee on university teaching methods. The meetings included lectures about the work of Senate and of Faculty Boards, about the mental health of students, about teaching arts subjects, science subjects and social science subjects; also demonstrations by means of closed-circuit television of personal tutorials, seminars and group tutorials, followed by discussion between the tutors concerned and the members of staff attending the course. Other demonstrations were provided of various teaching aids, such as projectors, duplicating machines, programmed texts and a language laboratory. Staff attending the course agreed almost unanimously that it could be profitably repeated, perhaps every two years.

McLeish (1966) reported a study of students' attitudes to lectures, tutorials and seminars, and of their preferences for one or other of these kinds of teaching. He found that preferences were systematically related to more general measures of personality and attitude. Among these students, who were not undergraduates, but mainly mature teachers taking the advanced Diploma in Education at the Cambridge Institute, there was a very marked preference for tutorials and seminars as against lectures. This preference was stronger on average among women than among men, and also stronger among the more able students. Those favouring tutorials and seminars without reservation tended to be more radical in political opinions and also in opinions about educational issues as assessed by Manchester scales of educational attitudes (Butcher 1965, Oliver and Butcher 1962). McLeish's results appear to be in accord with those of some American research concerned with 'the authoritarian personality', such as those of Haythorn *et al.* (1956).

Two extensive surveys, in which the field work has been completed, but of which the results are still unpublished at the time of writing, have been carried out by Koc of the University of Lancaster, and by Healey, Hartley and Freeman at the University of Manchester. Koc's research (see Koc 1966 for an interim report) involved visiting seven universities and, in addition to collecting other kinds of data, attending some 200 tutorials and seminars, almost all of which were tape-recorded. The study was limited to undergraduate work in arts and social sciences; but apart from this restriction, it was planned to have a very broad coverage in terms of subjects taught. Russian and North American studies were represented, for instance, in a few sessions, although a higher proportion was given to the more popular subjects, such as history, sociology and English. The study by Healey and his colleagues in university teaching methods, also unpublished as yet, was limited to Manchester University, and depended mainly on a detailed question-naire to be completed by staff. This was given to lecturers in all faculties, except those of Medicine and Dentistry, and was answered by more than 450, who formed a sample representative by departments and academic grades.

Just as this book is about to go to press, a valuable and detailed review of research into teaching methods in higher education has been published by Beard (1967), which provides a far more adequate cover-age than has been possible in this brief section. It is confined mainly to British research, and has a bibliography of 105 items. On many topics there is still a dearth of research, including many of the most important and central. For instance, 'There does not appear to be any British experimental work on techniques of giving lectures' (p. 16); similarly, 'only two experiments described in British journals are specifically concerned with class size' (p. 7). But Beard also points out that inquiries into teaching in higher education are rapidly gaining momentum, and that of the researches she surveyed, only five dated from before 1950, fifteen between 1950 and 1959, the remaining eighty-five having appeared since 1960.

Finally, it must be mentioned that much of the most interesting work in this field is concerned with programmed learning, which was discussed from a general viewpoint in the paper by Kay. The list of current researches on university teaching methods provided by Oxtoby (1967) includes a number of projects concerned specifically with programmed instruction.

Bibliography

ABEL, R. A. and HEYWOOD, J. (eds.) (1965) *Technical Education and Training.* Occasional publication no. 8. London: N. F. E. R.

ABRAMS, M. (1963) 'Cambridge recruits to university teaching.' *Universities Quarterly*, **17**, 260–70.

Acton Society Trust (1962) *The Arts Graduate in Industry.* London: Acton Society Trust.

AGER, M. and WELTMAN, J. (1967) 'The present structure of university examinations.' *Universities Quarterly*, **21**, 272–85.

AINSWORTH, M. D. (1962) 'The effects of maternal deprivation: a review of findings in the context of research strategy.' In *Deprivation of Maternal Care: A Reassessment of its Effects.* Geneva: W. H. O. Public Health Paper.

ALBROW, M. C. (1967) 'Ritual and reason in the selection of students.' *Universities Quarterly*, **21**, 141–51.

ALLEN, E. A. (1959) 'Attitudes to school and teachers in a secondary modern school.' M.A. thesis, University of London.

ALLEN, E. A. (1963) 'Professional training of teachers: a review of research.' *Educ. Research*, **5**, no. 3, 200.

ALLEN, L. E. (1965) 'Toward autotelic learning of mathematical logic by the WEF'N PROOF games.' In MORRISETT, L. N. and VINSONHALER, J. (eds.) *Mathematical Learning.* Monograph of the Society for Research in Child Development 30, no. 1 (serial no. 99), 29–41.

ALLEN, M. (1962) 'A comparison between group and individual selection procedures in a training college.' M.Ed. thesis, University of Manchester.

ALLINSMITH, W. (1960) 'The learning of moral standards.' In MILLER, D. R. and SWANSON, G. E. (eds.) *Inner Conflict and Defence.* New York: Holt, Rinehart and Winston.

AMARIA, R. P. (1967) 'Learning in pairs.' Proceedings of the A. P. L.-N. C. P. L. Programmed Learning Conference, April 1967. London: Association for Programmed Learning.

AMARIA, R. P., BIRAN, L. A. and LEITH, G. O. M. (1966) *Learning in Pairs.* Research notes on programmed learning no. 10. National Centre for Programmed Learning, University of Birmingham.

American Psychologist (1967) 'Privacy and behaviour research.' **22**, no. 5, 345–9.

ANDRY, R. G. (1960) *Delinquency and Parental Pathology*. London: Methuen.

ANTHONY, E. J. (1956) 'Jean Piaget and child psychiatry.' *Brit. J. Med. Psychol.*, **29**, 20–34.

ANTHONY, E. J. (1957) 'Symposium on the contribution of current theories to an understanding of child development 4. The system makers: Piaget and Freud.' *Brit. J. Med. Psychol.*, **30**, 255–69.

ARGYLE, M. (1964) 'Introjection: a form of social learning.' *Brit. J. Psychol.*, **55**, 391–402.

ARGYLE, M. and ROBINSON, J. (1962) 'Two origins of achievement motivation.' *Brit. J. Soc. Clin. Psychol.*, **1**, 107–20.

ARMSTRONG, H. G. (1965) 'Special educational treatment in the ordinary schools.' *Brit. J. Educ. Psychol.*, **35**, 242–4.

ARONFREED, J. (1961) 'The nature, variety and social patterning of moral responses to transgression.' *J. Abn. Soc. Psychol.*, **63**, 223–41.

ASHBY, E. (1963) 'Investment in man' (Presidential address to the British Association). *The Advancement of Science*, **20**, no. 85, 1–8.

ASTINGTON, E. (1960) 'Personality assessments and academic performance in a boys' grammar school.' *Brit. J. Med. Psychol.*, **30**, 225–36.

A. T. C. D. E. (1962) 'The study of education in colleges of education for teaching.' A. T. C. D. E. Education Section.

ATKINSON, G. S. (1965) 'Mr Crosland's binary inclinations.' *Universities Quarterly*, **20**, 109–10 (letter to the editor).

AUSTWICK, K. (1960) 'G.C.E. to B.A.' *Universities Quarterly*, **15**, 64–71.

BAGG, D. G. (1968) 'The correlation of G.C.E. 'A' level grades with university examinations in chemical engineering.' *Brit. J. Educ. Psychol.*, **38**.

BANDURA, A. and WALTERS, R. H. (1963) *Social Learning and Personality Development*. New York: Holt, Rinehart and Winston.

BANFIELD, J., BOWYER, C. and WILKIE, E. (1966) 'Parents and education.' *Educ. Research*, **9**, 63–6.

BANKS, O. (1958) 'Social mobility and the English system of education.' *International Review of Education*, **4**, 196–202.

BANNATYNE, A. D. (1964) 'Research needs in dyslexia.' *Word Blind Committee Bulletin*, **1**, no. 4, 5–7.

BANNATYNE, A. D. (1966) 'The colour phonics system.' In MONEY, J. (ed.) *The Disabled Reader*. Baltimore: Johns Hopkins Press.

BANNISTER, H. and RAVDEN, M. (1944) 'The problem child and his environment.' *Brit. J. Psychol.*, **24**, 82–7.

BARKER-LUNN, J. (1967) 'The effects of streaming and non-streaming in junior schools: second interim report.' *New Research in Education*, **1**, 46–75.

BARNES, E. (1902) 'The growth of social judgments.' *Studies in Education*, **2**, 203–17.

BARNETT, V. D. and LEWIS, T. (1963) 'Study of the relation between G.C.E. and degree results.' *J. Royal Stat. Soc.*, series A, **126**, 187–226.

BEARD, R. M. (1962) 'The order of concept development studied in two fields 1. Number concepts in the infant school.' *Educ. Review*, **15**, 105–17.

BEARD, R. M. (1967) *Research into Teaching Methods in Higher Education* (mainly in British universities). London: Society for Research into Higher Education.

BEARD, R. M., LEVY, P. M. and MADDOX, H. (1964) 'Academic performance at university.' *Educ. Review*, **16**, 163–74.

BEARDSLEE, D. and O'DOWD, D. (1961) 'The college student image of the scientist.' *Science*, **133**, 997.

BEILIN, H. (1965) 'Learning and operational convergence in logical thought development.' *J. Exp. Child Psychol.*, **2**, 317–39.

BEILIN, H., KAGAN, J. and RABINOWITZ, R. (1966) 'Effects of verbal and perceptual training on water level representation.' *Child Development*, **37**, 317–29.

BELFIELD, D. J. (1963) 'The social adjustment of most-accepted and least-accepted children in junior schools.' M.Ed. thesis, University of Manchester.

BENE, E. (1958) 'Suppression of hetero-sexual interest and of aggression by middle-class and working-class grammar school boys.' *Brit. J. Educ. Psychol.*, **28**, 226–31.

BERNBAUM, G. (1967) 'Educational expansion and the teacher's role.' *Universities Quarterly*, **21**, 152–66.

BERNSTEIN, B. (1960) 'Language and social class.' *Brit. J. Psychol.*, **51**, 271–6.

BERNSTEIN, B. (1964) 'Elaborated and restricted codes: their social origins and some consequences.' In *American Anthropologist*, special publication: GUMPERTZ, J. J. and HUMES, D. (eds.) 'The ethnography of communication.' **66**, 55–69.

BERNSTEIN, B. (1965) 'A socio-linguistic approach to social learning.' In *Penguin Survey of the Social Sciences*, pp. 144–66. Harmondsworth, Middlesex: Penguin Books.

BIGGS, J. B. (1959) 'The teaching of mathematics 2. Attitudes to arithmetic-number anxiety.' *Educ. Research*, **1**, 6–21.

BIGGS, J. B. (1962) 'The relation of neuroticism and extraversion to intelligence and educational attainment.' *Brit. J. Educ. Psychol.*, **32**, 188–95.

BIGGS, J. B. (1967) *Mathematics and the Conditions of Learning*. London: N. F. E. R.

BIRCH, H. G. and LEFFORD, A. (1963) *Intersensory Development in Children*. Monograph of the Society for Research in Child Development 28, no. 5 (serial no. 89).

BLOOM, B. S. (ed.) (1956) *Taxonomy of Educational Objectives*. London: Longmans.

BLOOM, B. S. (1964) *Stability and Change in Human Characteristics*. New York: Wiley.

BLOOM, B. S., DAVIS, A. and HESS, R. (1965) *Compensatory Education for Cultural Development*. New York: Holt, Rinehart and Winston.

Board of Education (1926) *The Education of the Adolescent*. Report of the Consultative Committee (The Hadow Report). London: H.M. Stationery Office.

Board of Education (1938a) *The Organization and Curriculum of Sixth Forms in Secondary Schools*. Educational pamphlet no. 114. London: H.M. Stationery Office.

Board of Education (1938b) *Secondary Education with Special Reference to Grammar Schools and Technical High Schools*. Report of the Consultative Committee on Secondary Education (The Spens Report). London: H.M. Stationery Office.

BOEHM, L. (1962) 'The development of conscience: a comparison between students in Catholic parochial and in public schools.' *Child Development*, **33**, 591–602.

BOOTE, D. W. (1967) 'An experimental study of concept attainment with reference to concrete and formal modes of thinking.' M.Ed. thesis, University of Manchester.

BOWLBY, J. (1946) *Forty-four Juvenile Thieves*. London: Ballière, Tindall and Cox.

BOWLBY, J. (1957) 'Symposium on the contribution of current theories to an understanding of child development 1. An ethological approach to research in child development.' *Brit. J. Med. Psychol.*, **30**, 230–40.

BOWLBY, J., AINSWORTH, M., BOSTON, M. and ROSENBLUTH, D. (1956) 'The effects of mother-child separation: a follow-up study.' *Brit. J. Med. Psychol.*, **29**, 211–43.

BOWYER, L. R., MARSHALL, A. and WEDDELL, K. (1963) 'The relative personality adjustment of severely deaf and partially deaf children.' *Brit. J. Educ. Psychol.*, **33**, 85–7.

B. P. S. and A. T. C. D. E. (1962) *Teaching Educational Psychology in Training Colleges*.

BRADBURN, E. (1964) 'The teacher's role in the moral development of children in primary schools.' Ph.D. thesis, University of Liverpool.

BRADLEY, D. R. (1966) 'An investigation of a theory of reading.' Dissertation for Dip. Applied Linguistics, University of Edinburgh.

BRAMWELL, R. D. (1962) 'Education as a discipline.' *Education for Teaching*, **59**, 23.

BRANDON, S. (1960) 'An epidemiological study of maladjustment in childhood.' M.D. thesis, University of Durham.

BRAY, D. H. (1962) 'A study of children's writing on an admired person.' *Educ. Review*, **15**, 44–53.

BREARLEY, M. and HITCHFIELD, E. (1966) *A Teacher's Guide to Reading Piaget.* London: Routledge & Kegan Paul.

BRENNAN, W. K. (1962) 'The relation of social adaptation, emotional adjustment and moral judgment to intelligence in primary school children.' M.Ed. thesis, University of Manchester (Abstract in *Brit. J. Educ. Psychol.,* **32,** 200–4).

BRIDGER, P. R. (1962) 'Liberal education and the teenage world.' *J. Assoc. for Liberal Education,* **1,** no. 2, 4–6.

BROCK, M. G. (1965) 'Admissions: an Oxford view.' *Universities Quarterly,* **19,** 259–66.

BROCKINGTON, F. and STEIN, Z. (1963) 'Admission, achievement and social class.' *Universities Quarterly,* **18,** 52–73.

BRONOWSKI, J. (1960) *The Common Sense of Science.* Harmondsworth, Middlesex: Penguin Books.

BRUCE, D. J. (1964) 'The analysis of word sounds by young children.' *Brit. J. Educ. Psychol.,* **34,** pt 2, 158–69.

BRUCKMAN, I. R. (1966) 'The relationship between achievement motivation and sex, age, social class, school stream and intelligence.' *Brit. J. Soc. Clin. Psychol.,* **5,** 211–20.

BRUNER, J. S., (1959) 'Inhelder and Piaget's *The Growth of Logical Thinking:* a psychologist's viewpoint.' *Brit. J. Psychol.,* **50,** 363–70.

BRUNER, J. S. (1966) 'On the conservation of liquid.' In BRUNER, J. S., OLVER, R. R. and GREENFIELD, P. M. (eds.) *Studies in Cognitive Growth.* New York: Wiley.

BRUNER, J. S., GOODNOW, J. J. and AUSTIN, G. A. (1956) *A Study of Thinking.* New York: Wiley.

BRUNER, J. S., OLVER, R. R. and GREENFIELD, P. M. (1966) *Studies in Cognitive Growth.* New York: Wiley.

BULL, G. M. (1956) 'An examination of the final examination in medicine.' *Lancet,* **2,** 268–72.

BURNHAM, P. S. (1965) 'The role of the deputy head in a secondary school.' M.Ed. thesis, University of Liverpool.

BURROUGHS, G. E. R. (1958) 'A study of the interview in the selection of students for teacher training.' *Brit. J. Educ. Psychol.,* **28,** 37–46.

BURSTALL, C. (1967) 'The French project: an interim report.' *New Research in Education,* **1,** 76–81.

BURT, C. (1937) *The Backward Child.* London: University of London Press Ltd.

BURT, C. (1943) 'Ability and income.' *Brit. J. Educ. Psychol.,* **13,** 83–98.

BURT, C. and HOWARD, M. (1952) 'The nature and causes of maladjustment among children of school age.' *Brit. J. Statist. Psychol.,* **5,** pt 1, 39–60.

BUTCHER, H. J. (1965) 'The attitudes of student teachers to education.' *Brit. J. Soc. Clin. Psychol.,* **4,** 17–24.

BUTCHER, H. J., AINSWORTH, M. and NESBITT, J. E. (1963) 'Personality factors and school achievement.' *Brit. J. Educ. Psychol.*, **33**, 276–85.

CALLARD, M. P. and GOODFELLOW, C. L. (1962) 'Neuroticism and extraversion in schoolboys as measured by the J. M. P. I.' *Brit. J. Educ. Psychol.*, **32**, 241–50.

CAMERON, A. E. (1923) 'A comparative study of the mathematical abilities of boys and girls in secondary schools.' M.A. thesis, University of London.

CAMERON, M. B. (1967) 'An investigation of cognitive differences in first-year arts and science students.' M.Ed. thesis, University of Aberdeen.

CAMPBELL, W. J. (1952) 'The influence of home environment on the educational progress of selective secondary school children.' *Brit. J. Educ. Psychol.*, **22**, 89–100.

CANE, B. S. (1966) 'A review of recent research on reading and related topics with a selected bibliography.' Appendix E in MORRIS, J. M. (ed.) *Standards and Progress in Reading*. London: N. F. E. R.

CANNON, C. (1964) 'Social studies in secondary schools.' *Educ. Review*, **17**, 18–30.

CARNEY, P. (1963) 'A study of the relations between home background, attainment and social adjustment among children in a junior school.' M.Ed. thesis, University of Manchester.

CASE, D. and COLLINSON, J. M. (1962) 'The development of formal thinking in verbal comprehension.' *Brit. J. Educ. Psychol.*, **32**, 103–11.

CASHDAN, A., PUMFREY, P. and LUNZER, E. A. (1967) 'A survey of children receiving remedial education in reading.' Paper read to Annual Conference of the British Psychological Society.

CASPARI, I. E. and EGGLESTONE, J. (1965) 'A new approach to supervision of teaching practice.' *Education for Teaching*, **98**, 42.

CAST, B. M. D. (1939) 'The efficiency of different methods of marking English composition.' *Brit. J. Educ. Psychol.*, **9**, 257–69.

CHAZAN, M. (1959) 'Maladjusted children in grammar schools.' *Brit. J. Educ. Psychol.*, **29**, 198–206.

CHAZAN, M. (1962) 'School phobia.' *Brit. J. Educ. Psychol.*, **32**, 209–17.

CHAZAN, M. (1963) 'Maladjustment, attainment and sociometric status.' *University College of Swansea Faculty of Education Journal*, 4–7.

CHAZAN, M. (1964) 'The incidence and nature of maladjustment among children in schools for the E. S. N.' *Brit. J. Educ. Psychol.*, **34**, 292–304.

CHAZAN, M. (1965) 'Factors associated with maladjustment in E. S. N. children.' *Brit. J. Educ. Psychol.*, **35**, 277–85.

CHILD, D. (1964) 'The relationship between introversion-extraversion, neuroticism and performance in school examinations.' *Brit. J. Educ. Psychol.*, **34**, 187–96.

CHILD, D. (1965) 'The sixth form myth.' *Education*, **126**, no. 3280, 1144 ff.

CHILD, D. (1966) 'Personality and social status.' *Brit. J. Soc. Clin. Psychol.*, **5**, 196–9.

CHISHOLM, A. W. and WALMSLEY, B. J. (1964) Cyclostyled report to N. F. E. R. Conference, April 1964.

CHURCHILL, E. M. (1958) 'The number concepts of the young child.' *Researches and Studies*, **17**, 34–49 and **18**, 28–46.

CLARK, G. (1937) 'Co-education: an analysis of the work and principles of the mixed school.' M.A. thesis, University of Liverpool.

CLARKE, R. J. (1967) 'Mathematics and metallurgists.' *Lancaster Studies in Higher Education*, **2**, B1–15.

CLAUSEN, J. A. and WILLIAMS, J. (1963) 'Sociological correlates of child behaviour.' In STEVENSON, H. W., KAGAN, J. and SPIKER, C. (eds.) *Yearbook of National Society for Studies in Education*, **62**, 62–107.

CLOWARD, R. A. and JONES, J. A. (1963) 'Social class: educational attitude and participation.' In PASSOW, A. H. (ed.) *Education in Depressed Areas*, pp. 190–216. New York: Teachers College Press.

CLYNE, M. (1966) *Absent: School Refusal as an Expression of Disturbed Family Relationships*. London: Tavistock.

COCKBURN, J. M. (1960) 'Psychological aspects of cerebral palsy.' Ph.D. thesis, University of St Andrews.

COCKBURN, J. M. (1961) 'Psychological and educational aspects.' In HENDERSON, J. L. (ed.) *Cerebral Palsy in Childhood and Adolescence*. Edinburgh: Livingstone.

COHEN, A. K. (1955) *Delinquent Boys*. Glencoe, Illinois: Free Press.

COHEN, E. (1965) 'Parental factors in educational mobility.' *Sociology of Education*, **38**, 404–25.

COHEN, L. (1965) 'An exploratory study of the teacher's role as perceived by head-teachers, tutors and students in a training college.' M.Ed. thesis, University of Liverpool.

COLLIER, K. G. (1960) 'The teaching of educational psychology in training colleges.' *Brit. J. Educ. Psychol.*, **30**, pt 2, 103.

COLLIER, K. G. (1966) 'An experiment in university teaching.' *Universities Quarterly*, **20**, 336–48.

COLTHAM, J. B. (1960) 'Junior school children's understanding of some terms commonly used in the teaching of history.' Ph.D. thesis, University of Manchester.

COLTHAM, J. B. (1966) 'An experiment in school practice.' *Education for Teaching*, **69**, 71.

COOPER, M. G. (1966a) 'School refusal.' *Educ. Research*, **8**, 115–27.

COOPER, M. G. (1966b) 'School refusal: an inquiry into the part played by school and home.' *Educ. Research*, **8**, 223–9.

COTGROVE, S. (1958) *Technical Education and Social Change*. London: Allen & Unwin.

COTGROVE, S. and FRIEND, D. (1965) 'Social studies at school.' *New Society*, **153**, 15–16.

COX, R. (1966) *Examinations and Higher Education: Survey of the Literature*. London: Society for Research into Higher Education.

COX, R. (1967) 'Examinations and higher education.' *Universities Quarterly*, **21**, 292–340.

CRAIG, G. Y. and DUFF, P. MCL. (1961) 'Academic success among pure science students.' *University of Edinburgh Gazette*, May.

CRAWFORD, A. (1961) 'Reading and ability survey of representative samples of Liverpool school children.' Paper to Annual Conference of the British Psychological Society (Abstract in *B.P.S. Bulletin*, May 1961).

CRITCHLEY, C. (1963) 'An investigation into the moral judgments of two age-groups of delinquents and non-delinquents.' B.A. dissertation, University of Durham.

CRITCHLEY, M. (1964) *Developmental Dyslexia*. London: Heinemann.

CRONBACH, L. J. (1951) 'Coefficient alpha and the internal structure of tests.' *Psychometrika*, **16**, 297–334.

CRONBACH, L. J. (1963) 'Evaluation for course improvement.' *Teachers' College Record*, **64**, no. 8.

CUMMINGS, A. and GOLDSTEIN, L. S. (1962) *The Effect of Overt and Covert Responding on New Kinds of Learning Task*. Technical report 620919, Centre for Programmed Instruction, Teachers College, Columbia, New York.

CURETON, E. E. (1951) 'Validity.' In LINDQUIST, E. F. (ed.) *Mental Measurement*. Washington D.C.: American Council on Education.

CURR, W. and HALLWORTH, H. J. (1965) 'An empirical study of the concept of retardation.' *Educ. Review*, **18**, 5–15.

CURRIE, K. (1962) 'A study of the English comprehensive school, with particular reference to the educational, social and cultural effects of the single-sex and co-educational types of school.' Ph.D. thesis, University of London.

DAKIN, J. (1967) 'Reading.' In FRASER, H. (ed.) *Applied Linguistics in the English Classroom*. London: Longmans.

DALE, R. R. (1955) 'Co-education: the verdict of experience.' *Brit. J. Educ. Psychol.*, **25**, 3.

DALE, R. R. (1962a) 'Co-education 1. A critical analysis of research on the effects of co-education on academic attainment in grammar schools.' *Educ. Research*, **4**, no. 3, 207–17.

DALE, R. R. (1962b) 'Co-education 2. An analysis of research on comparative attainment in mathematics in single-sex and co-educational maintained grammar schools.' *Educ. Research*, **5**, no. 1, 10–15.

DALE, R. R. (1964) 'Co-education 3. Research on comparative attainment in English in single-sex and co-educational grammar schools.' *Educ. Research,* **6**, no. 3, 170–8.

DALE, R. R. (1965a) 'Teachers of mathematics in N. Ireland grammar schools.' *The Northern Teacher,* **8**, 3.

DALE, R. R. (1965b) 'Co-education: the verdict of experience 2. A qualitative approach.' *Brit. J. Educ. Psychol.,* **35**, pt 2.

DALE, R. R. (1966a) 'A comparison of the academic qualifications of teachers of mathematics in single-sex and co-educational grammar schools respectively, in three contrasted areas.' *Educ. Review,* **18**, 2.

DALE, R. R. (1966b) 'The happiness of pupils in co-educational and single-sex grammar schools.' *Brit. J. Educ. Psychol.,* **36**, pt 1, 41–7.

DALE, R. R. (1966c) 'School days are happy days.' *Where,* **28**.

DALE, R. R. (1966d) 'Pupil-teacher relationships in co-educational and single-sex grammar schools.' *Brit. J. Educ. Psychol.,* **36**, pt 3, 267–71.

DALE, R. R. (1968) *Mixed or Single-sex Schools.* London: Routledge & Kegan Paul.

DALE, R. R. and GRIFFITH, S. (1965) *Down Stream.* London: Routledge & Kegan Paul.

DALE, R. R. and GRIFFITH, S. (1966) 'Selected findings from a five-year study of academic deteriorators in a grammar school.' *Educ. Research,* **8**, 146–54.

DALE, R. R. and JONES, I. (1957) 'The interest shown by boys and girls in the principal aspects of history in grammar schools.' *Educ. Review,* **10**, no. 1.

DALE, R. R. and JONES, J. A. (1964) 'An investigation into the comparative response of boys and girls to scripture in certain co-educational grammar schools.' *Brit. J. Educ. Psychol.,* **34**, pt 2.

DANIELS, J. C. (1967) 'Waiting for Plowden.' *Reading,* **1**, pt 1.

DANIELS, J. C. and DIACK, H. (1956) *Progress in Reading.* University of Nottingham Institute of Education.

DANIELS, J. C. and DIACK, H. (1960) *Progress in Reading in the Infant School.* University of Nottingham Institute of Education.

DAVIDSON, M. A., MCINNES, R. G. and PARNELL, R. W. (1957) 'The distribution of personality traits in seven-year-old children: a combined psychological, psychiatric and somatotype study.' *Brit. J. Educ. Psychol.,* **27**, 48–61.

DAVIDSON, S. (1961) 'School phobia as a manifestation of family disturbance: its structure and treatment.' *J. Child Psychol. Psychiat.,* **1**, pt 2, 130–6.

DAVIES, L. (1965) *Liberal Studies and Higher Technology.* Cardiff: University of Wales Press.

DAVIES, W. E. (1950) 'A study of the attitudes of secondary school teachers towards co-education, differentiation of curriculum and sex teaching.' Ph.D. thesis, University of London.

DAVIS, A. (1948) *Social Class Influences upon Learning.* Cambridge, Mass.: Harvard University Press.

DAVYDOV, V. (1965) 'Learning barriers.' *New Education*, **1**, no. 3, 12–15.

DEARBORN, W. F. and ROTHNEY, J. W. M. (1941) *Predicting the Child's Development*. Harvard Growth Study. Cambridge, Mass.: Sci.-Art Publications.

DE MONCHAUX, C. (1957) 'Symposium on the contribution of current theories to an understanding of child development 3. The contributions of psycho-analysis to the understanding of child development.' *Brit. J. Med. Psychol.*, **30**, 250–4.

Department of Education and Science (1964, 1965c, 1966d) *Statistics of Education*. London: H. M. Stationery Office.

Department of Education and Science (1965a) *The Organization of Secondary Education*. Circular 10/65. London: H. M. Stationery Office.

Department of Education and Science (1965b) Report of a conference on the Course in Education in the Education of Teachers, Hull University, 16–21 March 1964. London: distributed by the Department of Education and Science and H. M. Stationery Office.

Department of Education and Science (1966a) *Inquiry into the Flow of Candidates in Science and Technology into Higher Education*. Interim report, Cmnd 2893. London: H. M. Stationery Office.

Department of Education and Science (1966b) *Progress in Reading, 1948–64*. Pamphlet no. 50. London: H. M. Stationery Office.

Department of Education and Science (1966c) *Report on the 1965 Triennial Manpower Survey of Engineers, Technologists, Scientists and Technical Supporting Staff*. Cmnd 3103. London: H. M. Stationery Office.

Department of Education and Science (1967a) *Children and their Primary Schools* (The Plowden Report). 2 vols. London: H. M. Stationery Office.

Department of Education and Science (1967b) *Comprehensive Schools Research*. Report on education no. 36. London: H. M. Stationery Office.

DEUTSCH, M. (1960) *Minority Group and Class Status as Related to Social and Personality Factors in Scholastic Achievement*. Monograph no. 2. Ithaca, New York: Society for Applied Anthropology.

DEUTSCH, M. (1963) 'The disadvantaged child and the learning process.' In PASSOW, A. H. (ed.) *Education in Depressed Areas*, pp. 163–80. New York: Teachers College Press.

DEUTSCH, M. (1964) 'Early social environment: its influence on school adaptation.' In SCHREIBER, D. (ed.) *The School Drop-out*, pp. 89–100. Washington D.C.: National Education Association.

DIACK, H. (1960) *Reading and the Psychology of Perception*. Nottingham: Peter Skinner.

DICKENSON, H. (1963) 'Students in a C.A.T.: qualifications and success.' *Universities Quarterly*, **18**, 407–15.

DIENES, Z. P. (1963) *An Experimental Study of Mathematics Learning*. London: Hutchinson.

DIENES, Z. P. (1965) *Modern Mathematics for Young Children*. Harlow, Essex: Educational Supply Association.

DIXON, S. (1962) 'Some aspects of school life and progress in a comprehensive school in relation to pupils' social background.' M.A. thesis, University of London Institute of Education.

DOCKRELL, W. B. (1966) 'Secondary education, social class and the development of abilities.' *Brit. J. Educ. Psychol.*, **36**, 7–14.

DODD, B. T. (1964) 'Goodbye, Nellie.' *New Education*, **1**, no. 2.

DODWELL, P. C. (1962) 'Relations between the understanding of the logic of classes and of cardinal number in children.' *Canad. J. Psychol.*, **16**, 152–60.

DODWELL, P. C. (1963) 'Children's understanding of spatial concepts.' *Canad. J. Psychol.*, **17**, 141–61.

DONALDSON, M. (1963) *A Study of Children's Thinking*. London: Tavistock.

DOUGLAS, J. W. B. (1964) *The Home and the School: a Study of Ability and Attainment in the Primary School*. London: MacGibbon & Kee.

DOUGLAS, J. W. B. and BLOMFIELD, J. M. (1958) *Children under Five*. London: Allen & Unwin.

DOUGLAS, J. W. B. and ROSS, J. M. (1964) 'The later educational progress and emotional adjustment of children who went to nursery schools or classes.' *Educ. Research*, **8**, 73–80.

DOUGLAS, J. W. B. and ROSS, J. M. (1966) 'Single-sex or co-ed? The academic consequences.' *Where*, **25**, 5–8.

DOUGLAS, J. W. B., ROSS, J. M., HAMMOND, W. A. and MULLIGAN, D. G. (1966) 'Delinquency and social class.' *Brit. J. Criminol.*, **5**, 294–302.

DOUVAN, E. and ADELSON, J. (1958) 'The psycho-dynamics of social mobility in adolescent boys.' *J. Abn. Soc. Psychol.*, **56**, 31–44. Reprinted in CHARTERS, W. W. and GAGE, N. L. (eds.) (1963) *Readings in the Social Psychology of Education*. Boston, Mass.: Allyn and Bacon.

DOWNING, J. (1961) 'How your children are being taught to read with the Initial Teaching Alphabet.' Edinburgh: Chambers.

DOWNING, J. (1964a) (ed.) *The First International Reading Symposium, Oxford, 1964*. London: Cassell.

DOWNING, J. (1964b) *The Initial Teaching Alphabet*. London: Cassell; New York: Macmillan.

DOWNING, J. (1967a) *Evaluating the Initial Teaching Alphabet*. London: Cassell.

DOWNING, J. (1967b) *The i.t.a. Symposium: Research Report on the British Experiment with i.t.a.* London: N. F. E. R.

DOWNING, J. (1967c) 'Pro-active interference in transfer from i.t.a. to traditional orthography.' Paper to the Annual Conference of the British Psychological Society, Belfast, 1967 (Abstract in *B. P. S. Bulletin*, **20**, no. 67, 18a–19a).

DOWNING, J. and JONES, B. (1966) 'Some problems of evaluating i.t.a.: a second experiment.' *Educ. Research*, **8**, no. 2, 100–14.

DREVER, J. (1963) 'Prediction, placement and choice in university selection.' Annex A, appendix 2(B), Report of the Robbins Committee.

DREWS, E. M. and TEAHAN, J. E. (1957) 'Parental attitudes and academic achievement.' *J. Clin. Psychol.*, **13**, 328–32. Reprinted in CHARTERS, W. W. and GAGE, N. L. (eds.) (1963) *Readings in the Social Psychology of Education*. Boston, Mass.: Allyn and Bacon.

DRILLIEN, C. M. (1964) *The Growth and Development of the Prematurely Born Infant*. Edinburgh: Livingstone.

DUNSDON, M. I. (1952) *The Educability of Cerebral Palsied Children*. London: Newnes.

Educational Testing Service *et al.* (1963) *Multiple-choice Questions: A Close Look*. Princeton, N.J.: Educational Testing Service.

EDWARDS, J. B. (1965a) 'Some moral attitudes of boys in a secondary modern school, pt 1.' *Educ. Review*, **17**, 114–27.

EDWARDS, J. B. (1965b) 'Some moral attitudes of boys in a secondary modern school, pt 2.' *Educ. Review*, **17**, 234–44.

EGGLESTONE, S. J. (1965) 'Staying-on in non-selective secondary schools.' M.A. (Ed.) thesis, University of London.

EIGEN, L. D. and MARGULIES, S. (1963) 'Response characteristics as a function of information level.' *J. Programmed Instruction*, **2**, 45–54.

EKMAN, G. (1962) 'Measurement of moral judgment: a comparison of scaling methods.' *Perceptual and Motor Skills*, **15**, 3–9.

ELDER, G. H. (1965) 'Life opportunity and personality: some consequences of stratified secondary education in Britain.' *Sociology of Education*, **38**, 173–202.

ELVIN, H. L. (1966) 'Research in the planning of higher education.' *Paedagogica Europaea*, **2**, 233–49.

EMMETT, R. G. (1964) 'An experimental study of personal interaction in the classroom with special reference to the self-concept of teachers.' Ph.D. thesis, University of London.

EVANS, D. (1956) 'An experimental study of a group of seriously-maladjusted E.S.N. children.' M.A. (Ed.) thesis, University of Birmingham.

EVANS, K. M. (1959a) 'Research on teaching ability.' *Educ. Research*, **1**, no. 3, 22.

EVANS, K. M. (1959b) 'The teacher-pupil relationship.' *Educ. Research*, **2**, no. 1, 3–8.

EVANS, K. M. (1961) 'An annotated bibliography of British research on teaching and teaching ability.' *Educ. Research*, **4**, no. 1, 67.

EVANS, K. M. (1962) *Sociometry and Education*. London: Routledge & Kegan Paul.

EVANS, K. M. (1966) 'The Minnesota Teacher Attitude Inventory.' *Educ. Research*, **8**, 134–41.

EWING, A. (1958) *Educational Guidance and the Deaf Child*. London: University of London Press Ltd.

EYSENCK, H. J. (1960a) 'The contribution of learning theory.' *Brit. J. Educ. Psychol.*, **30**, 11–21.

EYSENCK, H. J. (1960b) *The Structure of Human Personality*. London: Methuen.

EYSENCK, H. J. (ed.) (1960c) *Handbook of Abnormal Psychology*. London: Pitman.

EYSENCK, H. J. (1964) *Crime and Personality*. London: Routledge & Kegan Paul.

EYSENCK, H. J. and RACHMAN, S. J. (1965) 'The application of learning theory to child psychiatry.' In HOWELLS, J. G. (ed.) *Perspectives in Child Psychiatry*. Edinburgh: Oliver & Boyd.

FARBER, B. (1965) 'Social class and intelligence.' *Social Forces*, **44**, 215–25.

Federation of British Industries (1961) *Industrial Research in Manufacturing Industry: 1959–60*. London: Federation of British Industries.

FINLAYSON, D. S. (1951) 'The reliability of marking essays.' *Brit. J. Educ. Psychol.*, **21**, 126–34.

FISHER, B. (1966) 'The social and emotional adjustment of children with impaired hearing attending ordinary classes.' *Brit. J. Educ. Psychol.*, **36**, 319–21.

FISHER, G. H. (1965) 'Developmental features of behaviour and perception.' *Brit. J. Educ. Psychol.*, **35**, 69–78.

FLAVELL, J. H. (1963) *The Developmental Psychology of Jean Piaget*. Princeton, N.J.: Van Nostrand.

FLOUD, J. (1962) 'Teaching in the affluent society.' *Brit. J. Sociol.*, **13**, 299–308.

FLOUD, J. and HALSEY, A. H. (1957) 'Intelligence tests, social class and selection for secondary schools.' *Brit. J. Sociol.*, **8**, 33–9.

FLOUD, J. and HALSEY, A. H. (1958) 'The sociology of education.' *Current Sociology*, **7**, no. 3, 165.

FLOUD, J. and HALSEY, A. H. (1961) 'Homes and schools: social determinants of educability.' *Educ. Research*, **3**, 83–8.

FLOUD, J., HASLEY, A. H. and MARTIN, F. (1956) *Social Class and Educational Opportunity*, London: Heinemann.

FLOYER, E. B. (1955) *A Psychological Study of a City's Cerebral Palsied Children*. London: British Council for the Welfare of Spastics.

FORD, B. (1965) 'Mr Crosland's binary inclinations.' *Universities Quarterly*, **19**, 225–6 and 266 (editorial).

FORD, B. (1966) 'From Manchester to Brighton: conversations on higher education.' *Universities Quarterly*, **20**, 209–25.

FORREST, G. M. (1961) 'An experimental study of concept attainment in children.' M.Ed. thesis, University of Manchester.

FORRESTER, J. F. F. (1946) 'A study of the attitudes of adolescents towards their own intellectual, social and spiritual development.' Ph.D. thesis, University of London.

FRANKLIN, W. (ed.) (1962) Word Blindness or Specific Developmental Dyslexia. London: Pitman.

FRASER, E. (1959) Home Environment and the School. S.C.R.E. publication no. 43. London: University of London Press Ltd.

FREEMAN, J. (1967) 'Convergent and divergent thinking among students of architecture.' Unpublished report.

FREEMAN, J., MCCOMISKY, J. G. and BUTTLE, D. (1968) 'Research into convergent and divergent thinking.' International J. Electrical Engineering Education (to appear).

FRYE, C. H. (1963) Group versus Individual Pacing in Programmed Instruction. Oregon State System of Higher Education, title 7, project no. 847.

FURNEAUX, W. D. (1961) The Chosen Few. London: Oxford University Press.

FURNEAUX, W. D. (1962) 'The psychologist and the university.' Universities Quarterly, 17, 33–47.

FUSCO, G. C. (1966) 'Reaching the parents.' In STROM, R. D. (ed.) The Inner-city Classroom: Teacher Behaviour, pp. 145–62. Columbus, Ohio: Charles E. Merrill.

GABRIEL, J. (1957) An Analysis of the Emotional Problems of the Teacher in the Classroom. Melbourne: F. W. Cheshire.

GEORGIADES, N. J. (1967) 'The Initial Teaching Alphabet in remedial reading groups: an experiment.' Unpublished report to Department of Education and Science.

GESELL, A. (1940) The First Five Years of Life. New York: Harper.

GESELL, A. (1946) The Child from Five to Ten. New York: Harper.

GESELL, A., ILG, F. L. and AMES, L. B. (1956) Youth: the Years from Ten to Sixteen. New York: Harper.

GIFFEN, E. (1962) 'Reflections on the Institution's role in engineering education.' Proceedings of the Institution of Mechanical Engineering, 176, 947.

GLENNERSTER, H. (1966) Graduate School: A Study of Graduate Work at the London School of Economics. Edinburgh: Oliver & Boyd.

GOLDBECK, R. A. and CAMPBELL, V. N. (1962) 'The effects of response mode and response difficulty on programmed learning.' J. Educ. Psychol., 53, 110–18.

GOLDBERG, M. L. (1963) 'Factors affecting educational attainment in depressed urban areas.' In PASSOW, A. H. (ed.) Education in Depressed Areas, pp. 68–100. New York: Teachers College Press.

GOLDMAN, R. J. (1964) Religious Thinking from Childhood to Adolescence. London: Routledge & Kegan Paul.

GOLDMAN, R. J. (1965) 'The application of Piaget's schema of operational thinking to religious story data by means of the Guttman scalogram.' *Brit. J. Educ. Psychol.*, **35**, 158–70.

GOODACRE, E. J. (1961) 'Teachers and the socio-economic factor.' *Educ. Research*, **4**, 56–61.

GOODACRE, E. J. (1968) *Teaching Beginners to Read.* The second report of the N. F. E. R. London Infant School Study. London: N. F. E. R.

GOODNOW, J. J. and BETHON, G. (1966) 'Piaget's tasks: the effects of schooling and intelligence.' *Child Development*, **37**, 573–82.

GORDON, E. W. and WILKERSON, D. A. (1966) *Compensatory Education for the Disadvantaged.* New York: College Entrance Examination Board.

GOTT, B. (1928) In HOWARD, B. J. *The Mixed School.* London: University of London Press Ltd.

GOULD, E. M. and MCCOMISKY, J. G. (1958) 'Attainment level in leaving certificate and academic performance at university.' *Brit. J. Educ. Psychol.*, **28**, 129–34.

GRANT, E. C. (1965) 'The contribution of ethology to child psychiatry.' In HOWELLS, J. G. (ed.) *Modern Perspectives in Child Psychiatry.* Edinburgh: Oliver & Boyd.

GRÉCO, P. (1959) 'L'apprentissage dans une situation à structure opératoire concrète: les inversions de l'ordre linéaire par des rotations de 180°.' In GRÉCO, P. and PIAGET, J. (eds.) *Apprentissage et Connaissance.* Etudes d'épistémologie génétique 7, pp. 68–182. Paris: Presses Universitaires de France.

GRÉCO, P. (1962) 'Quantité et qualité.' In GRÉCO, P. and MORF, A. (eds.) *Structures Numériques Elémentaires.* Etudes d'épistémologie génétique 13, pp. 1–70. Paris: Presses Universitaires de France.

GREENFIELD, P. M. (1966) 'On culture and conservation.' In BRUNER, J. S., OLVER, R. R. and GREENFIELD, P. M. (eds.) *Studies in Cognitive Growth.* New York: Wiley.

GREGORY, R. E. (1965) 'Unsettledness, maladjustment and reading failure: a village study.' *Brit. J. Educ. Psychol.*, **35**, 63–8.

GRIFFITHS, S. (1959) 'An examination of the causes of deterioration in academic performance among pupils in a grammar school.' *Brit. J. Educ. Psychol.*, **29**, 167–9.

GROSS, L. and GRUSSLIN, O. R. (1963) 'Middle- and lower-class beliefs and values: a heuristic model.' In GOULDNER, A. and H. P. (eds.) *Modern Sociology*, pp. 168–77. New York: Harcourt, Brace and World.

Gulbenkian Educational Discussion (1962) 'Research into higher education.' *Universities Quarterly*, **17**, 111–76.

Gulbenkian Educational Discussion (1963) 'Attention to graduates.' *Universities Quarterly*, **18**, 229–300.

GUYLER, K. R. (1966) 'The effects of variations in task contents and materials on conservation and transitivity.' M.Ed. thesis, University of Manchester.

HALL, S. (1904) *Adolescence*. 2 vols. New York: Appleton.
HALLIWELL, K. (1965) 'An investigation into the selection of students admitted to a teachers' training college; the effect of training on students selected by different methods; a comparison of teachers receiving two and three years training.' Ph.D. thesis, University of Sheffield.
HALLWORK, H. (1964) 'Anxiety in school examinations.' *Educ. Review*, **16**, 3.
HALLWORTH, H. J. (1961) 'Anxiety in secondary modern and grammar school children.' *Brit. J. Educ. Psychol.*, **31**, 281–92.
HALLWORTH, H. J. (1964) 'Personality ratings of adolescents: a study in a comprehensive school.' *Brit. J. Educ. Psychol.*, **34**, 171–7.
HALLWORTH, H. J. and WAITE, G. (1966) 'A comparative study of value judgments of adolescents.' *Brit. J. Educ. Psychol.*, **36**, 202–9.
HALSEY, A. H. (ed.) (1961a) *Ability and Educational Opportunity*. Paris: Organization for Economic Co-operation and Development.
HALSEY, A. H. (1961b) 'Sources for teaching the sociology of education.' In HALMOS, P. (ed.) *Sociol. Review*, Monograph no. 4, p. 115.
HALSEY, A. H. (1964) 'Second thoughts on Robbins: the academic hierarchy —appendix 3.' *Universities Quarterly*, **18**, 129–35.
HARLOW, H. F. (1949) 'The formation of learning-sets.' *Psychol. Review*, **56**, 51–65.
HARRISON, J. L. (1962) 'Towards a philosophy of education.' *Education for Teaching*, **59**, 13.
HARROWER, M. H. (1934) 'Social status and moral development.' *Brit. J. Educ. Psychol.*, **4**, 75–95.
HARTLEY, J. (1963) 'Some guides for evaluating programmes.' London: Association for Programmed Learning.
HARTLEY, J. (1966) 'Some guides for evaluating programmes.' In CAVANAGH, P. and JONES, C. (eds.) *Programmes in Print*. London: Association of Programmed Learning.
HARTLEY, J. (1967) 'Some factors affecting student performance in programmed learning.' Paper to 3rd International Congress on Problems of Programmed Learning and Teaching Machines, Prague, May 1967.
HARTLEY, J. and COOK, A. (1967) 'Programmed learning in pairs: the results of miniature experiments.' Proceedings of the A.P.L.-N.C.P.L. Programmed Learning Conference, April 1967. London: Association of Programmed Learning.
HARTOG, P. and RHODES, E. C. (1935) *An Examination of Examinations*. London: Macmillan.
HARTSHORNE, H. and MAY, M. A. (1930, 1931) 'The training of teachers for the work of character.' *J. Educ. Sociol.*, **18**, no. 14–17, 426.

HASHIM, A. (1948) 'A study of the attitude of secondary school pupils towards certain school subjects.' M.A. thesis, University of London.

HAVIGHURST, R. J. and TABA, H. (1949) *Adolescent Character and Personality.* New York: Wiley.

HAYTHORN, W., COUCH, A., HAEFNER, D., LANGHAM, P. and LANNOR, F. C. (1956) 'The behaviour of authoritarian and egalitarian personalities in groups.' *Human Relations,* **9,** 57–74.

HERBERT, N. and TURNBULL, G. H. (1963) 'Personality factors and effective progress in teaching.' *Educ. Review,* **16,** 24–31.

HERRIOTT, R. E. (1963) 'Some social determinants of educational aspiration.' *Harvard Educ. Review,* **33,** 157–77.

HERRIOTT, R. E. and ST JOHN HOYT, N. (1966) *Social Class and the Urban School.* New York: Wiley.

HERSOV, L. A. (1960a) 'Persistent non-attendance at school.' *J. Child Psychol. Psychiat.,* **1,** pt 2, 130–6.

HERSOV, L. A. (1960b) 'Refusal to go to school.' *J. Child Psychol. Psychiat.,* **1,** pt 2, 137–45.

HEWARD, C. H. (1967) 'A study of withdrawals from one college of advanced technology.' Sent for publication to *Proceedings of the Institution of Mechanical Engineering.*

HEWITT, L. E. and JENKINS, R. L. (1946) *Fundamental Patterns of Maladjustment: the Dynamics of their Origin.* Illinois: Green.

HEYWOOD, J. (1965) 'The interim year.' *J. Careers Research and Advisory Centre,* **1,** no. 4.

HEYWOOD, J. (1966) 'Attitudes to compulsory liberal studies in sandwich courses for the education of technologists.' Unpublished manuscript.

HEYWOOD, J. (1967) 'The effectiveness of undergraduate (Dip. Tech.) industrial training.' *International J. Electrical Engineering Education,* **5,** 281.

HEYWOOD, J. (1968) *Innovation in Technological Education* (in press).

HEYWOOD, J. and MONTAGU-POLLOCK, H. (1966) '*An Explanatory Study in the Teaching and Examining of a Section of a Principles of Physics Course for Arts Students.*' Bulletin no. 1 of Department of Higher Education, University of Lancaster.

HEYWOOD, J. *et al.* (1966a) 'The education of professional mechanical engineers for design and manufacture (a model curriculum).' *Lancaster Studies in Higher Education,* **1,** 1–151.

HEYWOOD, J., POLLITT, J. and MASH, V. (1966b) 'The schools and technology.' *Lancaster Studies in Higher Education,* **1,** 153–305.

HIBBERT, F. S. (1961) 'Dyslexia.' In Proceedings of the Society of British Neurological Surgeons: 62nd Meeting. *J. Neurol. Neurosurg. Psychiat.,* **24,** 92.

HILL, W. S. (1959) 'An investigation of the organization of comprehensive schools and its relation to their avowed purpose.' M.Ed. thesis, University of Leeds.

HILLIARD, F. H. (1959) 'The influence of religious education upon the development of children's moral ideas.' *Brit. J. Educ. Psychol.*, **29**, 50–9.

HILLIARD, F. H. (1965) 'Children's religious thinking.' *Learning for Living*, **5**, no. 2, 13–15.

HIMMELWEIT, H. T. (1950) 'Student selection—an experimental investigation, pt 1.' *Brit. J. Sociol.*, **1**, 328–46.

HIMMELWEIT, H. T. (1955) 'The psychological aspects of social differentiation.' *International Social Science Bulletin*, **7**, 29–35.

HIMMELWEIT, H. T. (1961a) 'The role of intelligence in modifying social class differences in outlook.' *Acta Psychologica*, **19**, 273–81.

HIMMELWEIT, H. T. (1961b) 'The teaching of social psychology to students of education and social work.' In HALMOS, P. (ed.) *Sociol. Review*, Monograph no. 4, p. 77.

HIMMELWEIT, H. T. (1963) 'Student selection: implications derived from two student selection inquiries.' In HALMOS, P. (ed.) *Sociol. Review*, Monograph no. 7, pp. 79–98.

HIMMELWEIT, H. T. (1967) 'Towards a rationalization of examination procedures.' *Universities Quarterly*, **21**, 3.

HIMMELWEIT, H. T. and SUMMERFIELD, A. (1951a) 'Student selection—an experimental investigation, pt 2.' *Brit. J. Sociol.*, **2**, 59–75.

HIMMELWEIT, H. T. and SUMMERFIELD, A. (1951b) 'Student selection—an experimental investigation, pt 3.' *Brit. J. Sociol.*, **2**, 340–53.

HIMMELWEIT, H. T., OPPENHEIM, A. N. and VINCE, P. (1958) *Television and the Child.* London: Oxford University Press.

HIND, A. G. (1964) 'The comprehensive school with special reference to the house system.' Dip. Ed. thesis, University of Nottingham Institute of Education.

HINDLEY, C. B. (1957) 'Symposium on the contribution of current theories to an understanding of child development 2. Contributions of associative learning theory to an understanding of child development.' *Brit. J. Med. Psychol.*, **30**, 241–50.

HIRST, P. H. (1963) 'Philosophy and educational theory.' *Brit. J. Educ. Studies*, **12**, no. 1, 51.

H. M. Inspectorate of England and Wales, Northern Division (1967) 'Sixth form survey.' *Trends in Education*, **7**, 46–9.

HOLLING, K. (1964) 'The feedback classroom.' *Programmed Learning*, **1**, 17–20.

HOLLINS, T. H. B. (1955) 'Teachers' attitudes to children's behaviour.' M.Ed. thesis, University of Manchester.

HOLLINS, T. H. B. (1963) 'Teaching educational psychology in training colleges.' *Brit. J. Educ. Psychol.*, **33**, pt 2, 187.

HOLLOWAY, P. J. (1966) 'The effect of lecture time on learning.' *Brit. J. Educ. Psychol.*, **36**, 255–8.

HOLLY, D. N. (1963) 'Social and academic selection in a London comprehensive school.' M.A. thesis, University of London Institute of Education.

HOLLY, D. N. (1965) 'Profiting from a comprehensive school—class, sex and ability: investigation in a London comprehensive school.' *Brit. J. Sociol.*, **16**, no. 2, 150.

Home Universities Conference (1966) *The Universities in the Future Pattern of Higher Education.* Report of proceedings. London: Association of Commonwealth Universities.

HOOD, H. B. (1962) 'An experimental study of Piaget's theory of the development of number in children.' *Brit. J. Psychol.*, **53**, 273–86.

HOPKINS, A. D. (1967) 'The training of professional metallurgists.' *Lancaster Studies in Higher Education*, **2**, A1–89.

HORNSBY-SMITH, M. P. (1967) 'The study of three parallel degree level courses in a department of metallurgy.' *Lancaster Studies in Higher Education*, **2**, C1–66.

HUBBARD, J. P. and CLEMANS, M. V. (1961) *Multiple-choice Examinations in Medicine.* London: Kimpton.

HUDSON, L. (1966) *Contrary Imaginations.* London: Methuen.

HUNT, J. MCV. (1961) *Intelligence and Experience.* New York: Ronald.

HUNTLEY, R. M. C. (1966) 'Heritability of intelligence.' In MEADE, J. E. and PARKES, A. S. (eds.) *Genetic and Environmental Factors in Human Ability*, pp. 201–18. Edinburgh: Oliver & Boyd.

HUSÉN, T. (ed.) (1967) *International Study of Achievement in Mathematics: a Comparison of Twelve Countries.* International Project for the Evaluation of Education Achievement (I.E.A.). 2 vols. New York: Wiley; Stockholm: Almqvist and Wiksell.

HUTCHINGS, D. G. (1963) *Technology and the Sixth Form Boy.* University of Oxford Institute of Education.

HUTTON, S. P. and GERSTL, J. E. (1963) 'Engineering education and careers.' *Proceedings of the Institution of Mechanical Engineering*, **178** (3F), 1–16.

HYDE, D. M. (1959) 'An investigation of Piaget's theories of the development of the concept of number.' Ph.D. thesis, University of London.

HYMAN, H. H. (1953) 'The value systems of different classes.' In BENDIX, R. and LIPSET, S. (eds.) *Class, Status and Power*, pp. 426–42. Glencoe, Illinois: Free Press.

ILIFFE, A. H. (1968) 'Foundation year in the University of Keele.' *Sociol. Review*.

Incorporated Association of Assistant Masters in Secondary Schools (1962) *General Education in Grammar Schools.* Cambridge: Cambridge University Press.

INGRAM, T. T. S. (1960) 'Paediatric aspects of specific developmental dysphasia, dyslexia and dysgraphia.' *Cerebral Palsy Bulletin*, **2**, 254–77.

INGRAM, T. T. S. (1964) 'The dyslexic child.' *The Practitioner*, April.

INGRAM, T. T. S. and REID, J. F. (1956) 'Developmental aphasia observed in a department of child psychiatry.' *Archives of Disease in Childhood*, **31**, 161–72.

INHELDER, B. (1956) 'Criteria of the stages of mental development.' In TANNER, J. M. and INHELDER, B. (eds.) *Discussions on Child Development*, vol. I, pp. 75–107. London: Tavistock.

INHELDER, B. and PIAGET, J. (1958) *The Growth of Logical Thinking from Childhood to Adolescence*. London: Routledge & Kegan Paul.

INHELDER, B. and PIAGET, J. (1964) *The Early Growth of Logic in the Child (Classification and Seriation)*. London: Routledge & Kegan Paul.

INHELDER, B., BOVET, M., SINCLAIR, H. and SMOCK, C. D. (1966) 'On cognitive development.' *Amer. Psychologist*, **21**, 160–4.

JACKSON, B. and MARSDEN, D. (1961) *Education and the Working Class*. London: Routledge & Kegan Paul.

JACKSON, S. (1965) 'The growth of logical thinking in normal and subnormal children.' *Brit. J. Educ. Psychol.*, **35**, 255–8.

JACKSON, W. (1961) *The 1961 Viscount Nuffield Paper* (to the Institution of Production Engineers), pp. 21–6.

JAHODA, G. (1963a) 'The development of children's ideas about country and nationality.' *Brit. J. Educ. Psychol.*, **33**, 47–60 and 143–53.

JAHODA, G. (1963b) 'Children's concepts of time and history.' *Educ. Review*, **15**, 87–104.

JAHODA, M. (1964) *The Education of Technologists*. London: Tavistock.

JAHODA, M. et al. (1967) 'Examining in universities.' *Universities Quarterly*, **21**, 3.

JEWKES, J. (1959) 'How much science?' *Advancement of Science*, **62**, 67.

JOHNSON, J. C. (1962) *Educating Hearing-impaired Children in Ordinary Schools*. Manchester: Manchester University Press.

Joint Mathematics Council (1965) *Report on the In-service Training of Mathematics*.

JONES, G. (1963) 'Why is there a shortage of engineers?' *Engineering*, September, 340.

JONES, H. E. (1943) *Development in Adolescence*. California Adolescent Growth Study. New York: Progressive Education Association.

JONES, J. K. (1965) 'Colour as an aid to visual perception in early reading.' *Brit. J. Educ. Psychol.*, **35**, pt I, 21–7.

JONES, V. (1936) *Character and Citizenship Training in the Public School*. Cambridge: Cambridge University Press.

KAHAN, M., BUTLER, D. and STOKES, D. (1966) 'On the analytical division of social class.' *Brit. J. Sociol.*, **17**, 122–32.

KAHL, J. A. (1953) 'Educational and occupational aspirations of "common man" boys.' *Harvard Educ. Review*, **23**, 186–203.

KAHN, J. H. (1958) 'School refusal.' *Medical Officer*, **100**, 337–40.

KAHN, J. H. and NURSTEN, J. (1964) *Unwillingly to School*. London: Pergamon.

KATZ, F. M. (1964) 'The meaning of success: some differences in value systems of social classes.' *J. Soc. Psychol.*, **62**, 141–8.

KAY, H. (1964) 'General introduction to teaching machine procedures.' In AUSTWICK, K. (ed.) *Teaching Machines and Programming*. London: Pergamon.

KAY, H. and WARR, P. B. (1962) 'Teaching by machine.' *The Chartered Mechanical Engineer*, **9**, 472–5.

KAY, H., DODD, B. T. and SIME, M. E. (1968) *Teaching Machines*. Harmondsworth, Middlesex: Penguin Books.

KELLY, A. R. and A. (1965) 'Education as a degree subject.' *Education for Teaching*, **67**, 13.

KELLY, M. B. (1967) 'An inquiry into the ability of E. S. N. children to handle money in practical situations in relation to their mathematical understanding.' M.Ed. thesis, University of Manchester.

KELSALL, R. K. (1963) 'University student selection in relation to subsequent academic performance: a critical appraisal of the British evidence.' In HALMOS, P. (ed.) *Sociol. Review*, Monograph no. 7, pp. 99–115.

KENDALL, M. (1964a) 'Those who failed 1. The further education of former students.' *Universities Quarterly*, **18**, 398–406.

KENDALL, M. (1964b) 'Those who failed 2. Occupation and income.' *Universities Quarterly*, **19**, 69–77.

KERR, J. F. (1966) 'Teaching in universities.' *Universities Quarterly*, **20**, 356–8.

KING, E. (1965) 'Tertiary education, U.K.' *The World Yearbook of Education*, 215–33.

KING, W. H. (1949) 'A critical analysis of the results of a school certificate examination.' Ph.D. thesis, University of London Institute of Education.

KING, W. H. (1966) 'Experimental evidence on comparative attainment in mathematics in single-sex and co-educational secondary schools.' *Educ. Research*, **8**, no. 2, 74–80.

KINSBOURNE, H. and WARRINGTON, E. K. (1966a) 'Developmental factors in reading and writing backwardness.' In MONEY, J. (ed.) *The Disabled Reader*. Baltimore: Johns Hopkins Press.

KINSBOURNE, H. and WARRINGTON, E. K. (1966b) 'Disorders of spelling.' In MONEY, J. (ed.) *The Disabled Reader*. Baltimore: Johns Hopkins Press.

KOC, W. T. (1966) 'Sociology of learning, teaching and communication within the system of higher education.' Unpublished manuscript.

KOHLBERG, L. (1963) 'The development of children's orientations toward a moral order 1. Sequence in the development of moral thought.' *Vita Humana*, **6**, 11–33.

KOHN, M. L. (1963) 'Social class and parent-child relationships: an interpretation.' *Amer. J. Sociol.*, **69**, 471–80.

KOHNSTAMM, G. A. (1967) *Teaching Children to Solve a Piagetian Problem of Class-inclusion.* The Hague: Mouton.

KOSHE, G. (1957) 'A comparative study of the attainments and intelligence of children in certain comprehensive, grammar and modern schools.' M.A. thesis, University of London.

KRESS, G. C. and GROPPER, G. L. (1964) *The Influence of External Pacing on Learning from Programmed Instruction.* Report no. 2. Studies in Televised Instruction: Individualizing Group Instruction. Pittsburgh: American Institute for Research.

KRETSCHMER, E. (1921) *Körperbau und Charakter.* Berlin: Springer.

LAMBERT, P., MILLER, D. M. and WILEY, D. E. (1962) 'Experimental folk-lore and experimentation: the study of programmed learning in the Wanwatosa public schools.' *J. Educ. Research*, **55**, 485–94.

LAMBERT, W. E. and KLINEBERG, O. (1964) 'Cultural comparisons of boys' occupational status aspirations.' *Brit. J. Soc. Clin. Psychol.*, **3**, pt 1, 56–65.

LAND, F. W. (1961) *The Language of Mathematics.* London: Murray.

LANGTON, N. R. (1962) *The Teaching of Theoretical Subjects to Students of High Polymer Technology.* Report to the Nuffield Foundation.

LATHAM, W. and GEORGIADES, N. J. (1967) *Reading*, **1**, 2 (letter to the editor).

LAVIN, D. E. (1965) *The Prediction of Academic Performance.* New York: Russell Sage Foundation.

LAWRENCE, P. (1964) *Advanced Level 1963 and After.* Occasional publication 20. Manchester: Joint Matriculation Board.

LEE, M. (1965) 'Children's reactions to moral transgression.' M.Ed. thesis, University of Durham.

LEEDHAM, J. and UNWIN, D. (1965) *Programmed Learning in Schools.* London: Longmans.

LEITH, G. O. M. (1966) *Abstracts of Research.* National Centre for Programmed Learning, University of Birmingham.

LEITH, G. O. M. and BUCKLE, E. F. (1965) *Mode of Response and Non-specific Background Knowledge.* Interim technical report. National Centre for Programmed Learning, University of Birmingham.

LERNER, E. (1937) 'Perspectives in moral reasoning.' *Amer. J. Sociol.*, **63**, 249–69.

LEVITT, E. E. (1957) 'The results of psychotherapy with children: an evaluation.' *J. Consult. Psychol.*, **21**, 189–96.

LEVY, P. M. (1962) 'Ability and attainment: a new psychometric formulation of the concept of educational retardation.' *Brit. J. Statist. Psychol.*, **15**, 137–47.

LEWIS, B. N. and PASK, G. (1965) 'The theory and practice of adaptive teaching systems.' In GLASER, R. (ed.) *Teaching Machines and Programmed Learning*, vol. 2. Washington D.C.: National Education Association.

LEWIS, D. G. (1961) 'The relations between grammar school subjects.' *Educ. Review*, **14**, 134.

LEWIS, D. G. and GREEN, P. M. (1965) 'The effects of auditory rhythmic distraction upon the task performance of educationally subnormal children.' *Educ. Review*, **18**, 54–9.

LEWIS, H. (1954) *Deprived Children*. London: Oxford University Press.

LINSTEAD, P., BARNARD, G. A. and MCCREATH, M. (1961) '1,800 students of science and technology.' *Universities Quarterly*, **16**, 36.

LITTLE, A. and WESTERGAARD, J. (1964) 'The trend of class differentials in educational opportunity in England and Wales.' *Brit. J. Sociol.*, **15**, 301–16.

LOCKE, C. D. (1960) 'A record of student performance at Keele.' *Universities Quarterly*, **15**, 46–53.

LODWICK, A. R. (1958) 'An investigation of the question whether the inferences that children draw in learning history correspond to the stages of mental development that Piaget postulates.' Dip.Ed. dissertation, University of Birmingham.

LORENZ, K. Z. (1950) 'The comparative method in studying innate behaviour patterns.' In *Physiological Mechanisms in Animal Behaviour*, Symposia of the Society for Experimental Biology no. 4. Cambridge: Cambridge University Press.

LOTTES, J. J., PALMER, G. and OAKES, H. (1963) 'An experimental comparison of differential rules of pacing programmed mathematics.' In CARPENTER, C. R. and GREENHILL, L. P. (eds.) *Comparative Research on Methods and Media for Presenting Programmed Courses in Mathematics and English*. University Park, Pa.: Pennsylvania State University.

LOUGHRAN, R. (1967) 'A pattern of development in moral judgments made by adolescents derived from Piaget's schema of its development in childhood.' *Educ. Review*, **19**, 79–98.

LOVELL, K. (1959) 'A follow-up study of some aspects of the work of Piaget and Inhelder on the child's conception of space.' *Brit. J. Educ. Psychol.*, **29**, 104–17.

LOVELL, K. (1961) 'A follow-up of Inhelder and Piaget's *The Growth of Logical Thinking*.' *Brit. J. Psychol.*, **52**, 143–53.

LOVELL, K. (1963) 'Informal *v.* formal education and reading achievement in the junior school.' *Educ. Review*, **6**, 71–6.

LOVELL, K. (1965) *The Growth of Basic Mathematical and Scientific Concepts in Children* (4th edition). London: University of London Press Ltd.

LOVELL, K. and BRADBURY, B. (1967) 'The learning of English morphology in educationally subnormal special school children.' *Amer. J. Mental Deficiency*, **71**, 609–15.

LOVELL, K. and BUTTERWORTH, I. B. (1966) 'Abilities underlying the understanding of proportionality.' *Mathematics Teaching*, **37**, 5–9.

LOVELL, K. and DIXON, E. M. (1967) 'The growth of the control of grammar in imitation, comprehension and production in normal and E. S. N. special school children.' *J. Child Psychol. Psychiat*, **8**, 31–9.

LOVELL, K. and OGILVIE, E. (1960) 'A study of the conservation of substance in the junior school child.' *Brit. J. Educ. Psychol.*, **30**, 109–18.

LOVELL, K. and OGILVIE, E. (1961a) 'A study of the conservation of weight in the junior school child.' *Brit. J. Educ. Psychol.*, **31**, 138–44.

LOVELL, K. and OGILVIE, E. (1961b) 'The growth of the concept of volume in junior school children.' *J. Child Psychol. Psychiat.*, **2**, 118–26.

LOVELL, K. and SLATER, A. (1960) 'The growth of the concept of time: a comparative study.' *J. Child Psychol. Psychiat.*, **1**, 179–90.

LOVELL, K. and WOOLSEY, M. E. (1964) 'Reading disability, non-verbal reasoning and social class.' *Educ. Research*, **6**, 226–9.

LOVELL, K., BYRNE, C. and RICHARDSON, M. (1963) 'A further study of the long-term effects of remedial education.' *Brit. J. Educ. Psychol.*, **33**, 3–9.

LOVELL, K., GRAY, E. and OLIVER, D. E. (1964) 'A further study of some cognitive and other disabilities in backward readers of average non-verbal reasoning scores.' *Brit. J. Educ. Psychol.*, **34**, 275–9.

LOVELL, K., HEALEY, D. and ROWLAND, A. D. (1962) 'Growth of some geometrical concepts.' *Child Development*, **33**, 751–67.

LOVELL, K., JOHNSON, E. and PLATTS, D. (1962) 'A summary of the reading ages of children who have been given remedial teaching.' *Brit. J. Educ. Psychol.*, **32**, 66–71.

LOVELL, K., KELLETT, V. L. and MOORHOUSE, E. (1962) 'The growth of the concept of speed: a comparative study.' *J. Child Psychol. Psychiat.*, **3**, 101–10.

LOVELL, K., MITCHELL, B. and EVERETT, I. R. (1962) 'An experimental study of the growth of some logical structures.' *Brit. J. Psychol.*, **53**, 175–88.

LOVELL, K., SHAPTON, D. L. and WARREN, N. S. (1964) 'A study of some cognitive and other disabilities in backward readers of average intelligence as assessed by a non-verbal test.' *Brit. J. Educ. Psychol.*, **34**, 58–64.

LOVELL, K., WHITE, C. and WHITELEY, R. (1965) 'Studying backward readers.' *Special Education*, **54**, 9–13.

LUNN, J. B. (1967) 'The effects of streaming and other forms of grouping in junior schools.' *New Research in Education*, **1**, 4–75.

LUNZER, E. A. (1960a) 'Aggressive and withdrawing children in the normal school 1. Patterns of behaviour.' *Brit. J. Educ. Psychol.*, **30**, 1–10.

LUNZER, E. A. (1960b) 'Aggressive and withdrawing children in the normal school 2. Disparity in attainment.' *Brit. J. Educ. Psychol.*, **30**, 119–23.

LUNZER, E. A. (1960c) *Recent Studies in Britain based on the Work of Jean Piaget*. Occasional publication no. 4. London: N. F. E. R.

LUNZER, E. A. (1960d) 'Some points of Piagetian theory in the light of experimental criticism.' *J. Child Psychol. Psychiat.*, **1**, 191–202.

LUNZER, E. A. (1965a) 'Les co-ordinations et les conservations dans le domaine de la géométrie.' In VINH BANG and LUNZER, E. A. *Conservations Spatiales.* Etudes d'épistémologie génétique 19, pp. 59–148. Paris: Presses Universitaires de France.

LUNZER, E. A. (1965b) 'Problems of formal reasoning in test situations.' In MUSSEN, P. H. (ed.) *European Research in Cognitive Development.* Monograph of Society for Research in Child Development 30, no. 2 (serial no. 100), pp. 19–46.

LUNZER, E. A. (1968a) (ed.) *Development in Learning* 1. *The Regulation of Behaviour.* London: Staples.

LUNZER, E. A. (1968b) 'Formal reasoning.' In LUNZER, E. A. and MORRIS, J. F. (eds.) *Development in Learning* 2. *Development in Human Learning.* London: Staples.

LUNZER, E. A. and PUMFREY, P. D. (1966) 'Understanding proportionality.' *Mathematics Teaching*, **34**, 7–13.

LYNN, R. (1957) 'Temperamental characteristics related to disparity of attainment in reading and arithmetic.' *Brit. J. Educ. Psychol.*, **27**, 62–7.

LYTTON, H. (1967) 'Follow-up of an experiment in selection for remedial education.' *Brit. J. Educ. Psychol.*, **37**, 1–9.

MACAULAY, E. and WATKINS, S. M. (1926) 'An investigation into the development of the moral conceptions of children.' *Forum of Education*, **4**.

MCCLELLAND, W. (1942) *Selection for Secondary Education.* S. C. R. E. publication no. 19. London: University of London Press Ltd.

MACFARLANE, J. W., ALLEN, L. and HONZIK, P. (1954) *A Developmental Study of the Behaviour Problems of Normal Children between 12 months and 14 years.* Berkeley Guidance Study. Berkeley: University of California Press.

MACFARLANE SMITH, I. (1964) *Spatial Ability: its Educational and Social Significance.* London: University of London Press Ltd.

MACGUIRE, J. M. (1963) 'Sociology for teachers.' *Education for Teaching*, **61**, 14.

MCLAUGHLIN, G. H. (1963) 'Psycho-logic: a possible alternative to Piaget's formulation.' *Brit. J. Educ. Psychol.*, **33**, 61–7.

MCLEISH, J. (1966) 'Lecture, tutorial, seminar: the students' view.' Paper to Annual Meeting of Society for Research into Higher Education.

MCPHERSON, D. (1950) 'An investigation into a system of moral instruction.' Ed.B. thesis, University of Glasgow (Abstract in *Brit. J. Educ. Psychol.*, **20**, 139.)

MACPHERSON, J. S. (1958) *Eleven-year-olds Grow Up.* S. C. R. E. publication no. 42. London: University of London Press Ltd.

MACRAE, D., jr (1954) 'A test of Piaget's theories of moral development.' *J. Abn. Soc. Psychol.*, **49**, 14–18.

MAGOWAN, S. A. (1966) 'A study of immanent justice in the moral development of the child.' Ed.B. thesis, University of St Andrews.

MALLESON, N. (1957) 'Treatment of pre-examination strain.' *Brit. Med. J.*, **2**, 551.

MALLESON, N. (1958) 'Student performance at University College, London, 1948–51.' *Universities Quarterly*, **12**, 288–319.

MALLESON, N. (1960) 'University students, 1953 4. Different sorts of students.' *Universities Quarterly*, **15**, 54–63.

MANNIX, J. B. (1959) 'The number concepts of a group of E. S. N. children.' M.Ed. thesis, University of Manchester.

MARRIS, P. (1964) *The Experience of Higher Education*. London: Routledge & Kegan Paul.

MASON, A. (1966) 'La dyslexie spécifique d'évolution et ses rapports avec le retard dans l'acquisition du langage.' *Revue de Neuropsychiatrie Infantile*, **14**, 7–8.

MATTHEW, G. C. (1963) 'The post-school social adaptation of educationally subnormal boys.' *Brit. J. Educ. Psychol.*, **33**, 329–31.

MAXWELL, J. (1953) *Social Implications of the 1947 Scottish Mental Survey*. S. C. R. E. publication no. 35. London: University of London Press Ltd.

MAYS, W. (1953) 'An elementary introduction to Piaget's logic.' In PIAGET, J. *Logic and Psychology*. Manchester: Manchester University Press.

MAYS, W. (1965) 'Logic for juniors.' *Teaching Arithmetic*, **3**, no. 3, 3–10.

MAYS, W. (1966) 'A philosophical critique of intelligence tests.' *Educ. Theory*, **16**, 318–32.

MEEK, L. H. (1940) *The Personal-social Development of Boys and Girls*. New York: Progressive Education Association.

MEREDITH, P. (1966) 'Principles and methods of analytical programming for the treatment of dyslexia.' *Programmed Learning*, **3**, no. 2, 115–16.

MILLER, T. G. W. (1958) 'A critical and empirical study of the emergence, development and significance of the comprehensive secondary school in England with special reference to certain educational and social effects.' Ph.D. thesis, University of Birmingham. (Published as a monograph *Values in the Comprehensive School: an Experimental Study*. Edinburgh: Oliver & Boyd, 1961).

Ministry of Education (1947) Circular no. 144. London: H. M. Stationery Office.

Ministry of Education (1950) *Report of the Departmental Committee on Children and the Cinema* (The Wheare Report). Cmnd 7945. London: H. M. Stationery Office.

Ministry of Education (1951) *The Road to the Sixth Form*. Pamphlet no. 19. London: H. M. Stationery Office.

Ministry of Education (1954) *Early Leaving*. Report of the Central Advisory Council for Education (England). London: H. M. Stationery Office.

Ministry of Education (1959–60) *15 to 18*. Report of the Central Advisory Council for Education (The Crowther Report). 2 vols. London: H. M. Stationery Office.

Ministry of Education (1961) *The Long-term Demand for Scientific Manpower*. Cmnd 1490. London: H. M. Stationery Office.

Ministry of Education (1963a) *Engineering Design*. Report of a D. S. I. R. Committee (The Feilden Committee). London: H. M. Stationery Office.

Ministry of Education (1963b) *Higher Education*. Report of the Committee on Higher Education (The Robbins Report). London: H. M. Stationery Office.

Ministry of Education (1963c) *Scientific and Technological Manpower in Great Britain 1962*. Cmnd 2146. London: H. M. Stationery Office.

Ministry of Education (1963d) *Statistics of Education*. London: H. M. Stationery Office.

MITCHELL, S. and SHEPHERD, M. (1966) 'A comparative study of children's behaviour at home and at school.' *Brit. J. Educ. Psychol.*, **36**, 248–54.

MODEL, A. and SHEPHEARD, E. (1958) 'The child who refuses to go to school.' *Medical Officer*, **100**, 39–41.

MONTGOMERY, R. J. (1965) *Examinations*. London: Longmans.

MOON, J. (1967) *The Influence of Ethical Behaviour on the Role of the Professional Mechanical Engineer*. London: Register of Research into Higher Education.

MOORE, D. L. (1967) 'Group teaching by programmed instruction.' *Programmed Learning and Educ. Technology*, **4**, 37–46.

MOORE, T. W. (1959) 'Studying the growth of personality: a discussion on the uses of psychological data obtained in a longitudinal study of child development.' *Vita Humana*, **2**, 65–87.

MOORE, T. W. (1966) 'Difficulties of the ordinary child in adjusting to primary school.' *J. Child Psychol. Psychiat.*, **7**, 17–38.

MOORE, T. W., HINDLEY, C. B. and FALKNER, F. (1954) 'A longitudinal research in child development and some of its problems.' *Brit. Med. J.*, **2**, 1132–7.

MOORHOUSE, E. (1965) 'In-service training in Oxfordshire.' *Froebel Journal*, **3**, 25–8.

MORETON, F. E. (1939) 'Co-education: a statistical inquiry into the attitude of teachers towards co-education and a comparative study of the emotional development of children trained in co-educational and other institutions.' Ph.D. thesis, University of London (Abstract in *Brit. J. Educ. Psychol.*, **16**, no. 2, 82–95).

MORETON, F. E. (1944) 'Attitudes to religion among adolescents and adults.' *Brit. J. Educ. Psychol.*, **14**, 69–79.

MORGAN, G. A. V. (1959) 'Children who refuse to go to school.' *Medical Officer*, **102**, 221–4.

MORRIS, J. F. (1958) 'The development of adolescent value judgments.' *Brit. J. Educ. Psychol.*, **28**, 1–14.

MORRIS, J. M. (1959) *Reading in the Primary School.* London: Newnes.

MORRIS, J. M. (1964) 'How far can reading backwardness be attributed to school conditions?' In DOWNING, J. (ed.) *The First International Reading Symposium, Oxford 1964.* London: Cassell.

MORRIS, J. M. (1966) *Standards and Progress in Reading.* Research reports, 2nd series, no. 1. London: N. F. E. R.

MORRIS, N. (1961) 'An historian's view of examinations.' In WISEMAN, S. (ed.) *Examinations and English Education.* Manchester: Manchester University Press.

MORRIS, S. (1965) 'Aims and content of courses in philosophy of education.' *Educ. Review*, **17**, no. 3, 184.

MOUNTFORD, J. (1957) *How They Fared: a Survey of a Three-year Student Entry.* Liverpool: Liverpool University Press.

MULLIGAN, G., DOUGLAS, J. W. B., HAMMOND, W. A. and TIZARD, J. (1963) 'Delinquency and symptoms of maladjustment: the findings of a longitudinal study.' *Proceedings of the Royal Society of Medicine*, **56**, pt 12, 1083–6.

MUSGRAVE, P. W. (1965) 'Sociology in the training of teachers.' *Aspects of Education*, **3**, 41.

MUSGROVE, F. (1966) 'Social needs and satisfactions of some young people   2. At school.' *Brit. J. Educ. Psychol.*, **36**, 137–49.

MUSGROVE, F. and TAYLOR, P. H. (1965) 'Teachers' and parents' conception of the teacher's role.' *Brit. J. Educ. Psychol.*, **35**, pt 2, 171–8.

NESBITT, J. E. (1962) 'The development of character integration in children aged from 9–14 years.' Ph.D. thesis, University of Manchester.

New Society (1964) 'School social studies.' *New Society*, **4**, no. 101.

NEWSON, J. and E. (1965) *Patterns of Infant Care in an Urban Community.* Harmondsworth, Middlesex: Penguin Books.

NEWSON, J. and E. (1967) 'Some social differences in the process of child-rearing.' In *Penguin Survey of the Social Sciences.* Harmondsworth, Middlesex: Penguin Books.

NISBET, J. D. and ENTWISTLE, N. J. (1966) *The Age of Transfer to Secondary Education.* S. C. R. E. publication no. 53. London: University of London Press Ltd.

NISBET, J. D. and WELSH, J. (1966) 'Predicting student performance.' *Universities Quarterly*, **20**, 468–80.

NISBET, S. (1966) 'A method for advanced seminars.' *Universities Quarterly*, **20**, 349–55.

Northern Universities Joint Matriculation Board (1964) 61st Annual Report. Manchester: Joint Matriculation Board.

Northern Universities Joint Matriculation Board (1966) 63rd Annual Report. Manchester: Joint Matriculation Board.

O'CONNOR, N. and FRANKS, C. (1960) 'Childhood upbringing and other environmental factors.' In EYSENCK, H. J. (ed.) *Handbook of Abnormal Psychology*. London: Pitman.

OLIVER, R. A. C. (1961) 'Education and selection.' In WISEMAN, S. (ed.) *Examinations and English Education*. Manchester: Manchester University Press.

OLIVER, R. A. C. (1962) 'The selection of university students: a "scholastic aptitude test".' *Universities Quarterly*, **16**, 264–73.

OLIVER, R. A. C. (1966) 'University entrance requirements: whence and whither?' *Universities Quarterly*, **20**, 307–16.

OLIVER, R. A. C. and BUTCHER, H. J. (1962) 'Teachers' attitudes to education: the structure of educational attitudes.' *Brit. J. Soc. Clin. Psychol.*, **1**, 56–69.

OPPENHEIM, A. N., JAHODA, M. and JAMES, R. L. (1967) 'Assumptions underlying the use of university examinations.' *Universities Quarterly*, **21**, 3.

ORME, J. E. (1965) 'Ability and season of birth.' *Brit. J. Psychol.*, **56**, 471–5.

OTLEY, C. B. (1966) 'Sociology in the college of education.' *Education for Teaching*, **69**, 56.

Oxford University Department of Education (1960) *Arts and Science Sides in the Sixth Form*. Report to the Gulbenkian Foundation.

Oxford University Department of Education (1963) *Technology and the Sixth Form Boy: a Study of Recruitment to Higher Scientific and Technological Education in England and Wales*. Report to C. R. E. I. Washington D.C.

OXTOBY, R. (1967) *A Review of Current Research into Higher Education*. London: Society for Research into Higher Education. Duplicated.

PACE, C. R. (1963) *C.U.E.S.: College and University Environment Scales*. Technical manual. Princeton, N.J.: Educational Testing Service.

PAGE, E. I. (1959) 'Haptic perception.' *Educ. Review*, **11**, 115–24.

PAGE, G. T. (1965) *Engineering among the Schools*. Oxford: Institution of Mechanical Engineers.

PAPE, G. V. (1961) 'Mixing in the comprehensive school.' *Forum of Education*, **3**, 71–4.

PARKYN, G. W. (1959) *Success and Failure at the University*. 2 vols. Wellington: New Zealand Council for Educational Research.

PARNELL, R. W. (1958) *Behaviour and Physique*. London: Arnold.

PASCUAL LEONE, J. and BOVET, M. C. (1966) 'L'apprentissage de la quantification de l'inclusion et la théorie opératoire.' *Acta Psychologica*, **25**, 339–56.

PASK, G. (1960) 'Adaptive teaching with adaptive machines.' In LUMSDAINE, A. A. and GLASER, R. (eds.) *Teaching Machines and Programmed Learning*. Washington D.C.: National Education Association.

PASSOW, A. H. (ed.) (1963) *Education in Depressed Areas*. New York: Teachers College Press.

PAYNE, G. L. (1960) *Britain's Scientific and Technological Manpower*. Stanford, San Francisco: Stanford University Press.

PEAKER, G. F. (1953) 'A sampling design used by the Ministry of Education.' *J. Royal Statist. Soc.* series A, no. 116, 140–65.

PEARSON, V. (1963) 'An investigation into the nature of moral judgment in six-year-old children.' B.A. dissertation, University of Durham.

PEEL, E. A. (1959) 'Experimental examination of some of Piaget's schemata.' *Brit. J. Educ. Psychol.*, **29**, 89–103.

PEEL, E. A. (1960) *The Pupil's Thinking*. London: Oldbourne.

PEEL, E. A. (1966) 'A study of differences in the judgments of adolescent pupils.' *Brit. J. Educ. Psychol.*, **36**, 77–86.

PEEL, E. A. (1968a) 'Explainer thinking.' In LUNZER, E. A. and MORRIS, J. F. (eds.) *Development in Learning 2. Development in Human Learning*. London: Staples.

PEEL, E. A. (1968b) 'A method for investigating children's understanding of certain logical connectives.' (Abstract in *B.P.S. Bulletin, 81*, 26.)

PEERS, R. and MADGWICK, P. J. (1963) 'Problems and attitudes in higher technological education.' *Vocational Aspect*, **15**, 69.

PELUFFO, N. (1964) 'La nozione di conservazione del volume e le operazioni di combinazione come indice di sviluppo del pensiero operatorio in soggetti appartenenti ad ambienti fisici e socioculturi diversi.' *Rivista di Psicologia Sociale* (Turin), **11**, 99–132.

PETCH, J. A. (1961) *G.C.E. and Degree* (pt 1). Manchester: Joint Matriculation Board.

PETCH, J. A. (1963) *G.C.E. and Degree* (pt 2). Manchester: Joint Matriculation Board.

PETERS, A. J. (ed.) (1968) *The Expansion of Further Education in England and Wales*. London: MacGibbon & Kee.

PETERS, M. (1967a) 'The influence of reading methods on spelling.' *Brit. J. Educ. Psychol.*, **37**, pt 1, 47–53.

PETERS, M. (1967b) 'Learning to spell.' *New Education, 3*, 11–13.

PETERS, R. S. (1960) 'Freud's theory of moral development in relation to that of Piaget.' *Brit. J. Educ. Psychol.*, **30**, 250–8.

PETERSON, A. G. (1960) 'The myth of "subject-mindedness".' *Universities Quarterly, 14*, 223–32.

PETRIE, I. R. J. (1962) 'Residential treatment of maladjusted children: a study of some factors related to progress in adjustment.' *Brit. J. Educ. Psychol.*, **32**, 29–37.

PHEASANT, T. H. (1961) 'The influence of the school on the choice of science careers.' *Brit. J. Educ. Psychol.*, **31**, 38–42.

PHEMISTER, A. (1960) 'An investigation into children's understanding of number on school entry and of the effectiveness of infant classroom teaching based on Piaget's theory.' Dissertation, University of Manchester.

PHILLIPS, C. J. (1966) 'Reading abilities among senior E. S. N. pupils: prediction of gain.' Paper to Annual Conference of the British Psychological Society.

PHILLIPS, G. (1965) 'Science and arts subjects at G. C. E. level.' *Times Educ. Supp.*, 19 November.

PIAGET, J. (1928) *Judgment and Reasoning in the Child*. London: Kegan Paul.

PIAGET, J. (1932) *The Moral Judgment of the Child*. London: Routledge & Kegan Paul.

PIAGET, J. (1946a) *Le Développement de la Notion de Temps chez l'Enfant*. Paris: Presses Universitaires de France.

PIAGET, J. (1946b) *Les Notions de Mouvement et de Vitesse chez l'Enfant*. Paris: Presses Universitaires de France.

PIAGET, J. (1953) *The Origin of Intelligence in the Child*. London: Routledge & Kegan Paul.

PIAGET, J. (1955) *The Child's Construction of Reality*. London: Routledge & Kegan Paul.

PIAGET, J. (1957) 'Logique et équilibre dans les comportements du sujet.' In APOSTEL, L., MANDELBROT, B. and PIAGET, J. (eds.) *Logique et Équilibre*. Etudes d'épistémologie génétique 2, pp. 27–117. Paris: Presses Universitaires de France.

PIAGET, J. and INHELDER B. (1956) *The Child's Conception of Space*. London: Routledge & Kegan Paul.

PIAGET, J. and INHELDER, B. (1962) *Le Développement des Quantités Physiques chez l'Enfant* (2ème édition augmentée). Neuchâtel: Delachaux et Niestlé.

PIAGET, J. and SZEMINSKA, A. (1952) *The Child's Conception of Number*. London: Routledge & Kegan Paul.

PIAGET, J., INHELDER, B. and SZEMINSKA, A. (1960) *The Child's Conception of Geometry*. London: Routledge & Kegan Paul.

PIDGEON, D. A. (ed.) (1967) *Achievement in Mathematics: a National Study in Secondary Schools*. London: N. F. E. R.

PILKINGTON, G. W. and HARRISON, G. J. (1967) 'The relative value of two high-level intelligence tests, Advanced level, and first-year university examination marks for predicting degree classification.' *Brit. J. Educ. Psychol.*, **37**, 382–8.

PILLINER, A. E. G. (1960) 'Prediction of success in the Arts Faculty of the University of Edinburgh by marks attained at the Scottish Leaving Certificate examination.' Unpublished report.

PILLINER, A. E. G. (1961) 'The measurement of educational achievement in Israel.' Report to Unesco.

PILLINER, A. E. G. (1965) 'Review of the marking of scripts in Advanced level history.' *Brit. J. Educ. Psychol.*, **35**, 110–11.

PILLINER, A. E. G. (1968) 'A comparison of two methods of marking English essays.' *Bulletin of the Planning Centre for the Teaching of English*. Israel.

PITMAN, I. J. (1961) 'Learning to read: an experiment.' *J. Royal Society of Arts*, **109**, 149–80.

Political and Economic Planning (1957) *Graduates in Industry*. London: Allen & Unwin.

POOLE, J. (1964) 'A scientific experiment in classroom observation.' M.Sc. thesis, University of Manchester.

POWELL, J. P. (1964) 'Experimentation and teaching in higher education.' *Educ. Research*, **6**, 171–91.

RANDY, K. (1965) *Professional Employees*. London: Faber.

PRICE, G. (1964) 'The crisis in school practice.' *Education for Teaching*, **65**, 36.

PRICE-WILLIAMS, D. R. (1961) 'A study concerning concepts of conservation of quantities among primitive children.' *Acta Psychologica*, **18**, 297–305.

PRICE-WILLIAMS, D. R. (1962) 'Abstract and concrete modes of classification in a primitive society.' *Brit. J. Educ. Psychol.*, **32**, 50–61.

PRINGLE, M. L. K. (1965) *Deprivation and Education*. London: Longmans.

PRINGLE, M. L. K. and BOSSIO, V. (1958) 'A study of deprived children 1. Intellectual, emotional and social development.' *Vita Humana*, **1**, 65–92.

PRINGLE, M. L. K. and BUTLER, N. R. (1966) 'Studying 16,000 children.' *Special Education*, **55**, 9–12.

PRINGLE, M. L. K. and EDWARDS, J. B. (1964) 'Some moral concepts and judgments of junior school children.' *Brit. J. Soc. Clin. Psychol.*, **3**, 196–215.

PRINGLE, M. L. K., BUTLER, N. R. and DAVIE, R. (1967) *11,000 Seven-year-olds* (1958 Cohort). Study in Child Development. London: Longmans.

PUMFREY, P. D. (1965) 'The growth of the schema of proportionality.' M.Ed. thesis, University of Manchester.

PYM, D. (1967) 'The misuse of professional manpower.' *Chartered Mechanical Engineer*, **14**, no. 5, 221.

RABINOWITCH, R. D. (1962) 'Dyslexia: psychiatric considerations.' In MONEY, J. and SCHIFFMAN, G. (eds.) *Reading Disability*. Baltimore: Johns Hopkins Press.

REED, G. and SCHONFIELD, D. (1958) 'Disparity of attainment in reading and arithmetic.' *Brit. J. Educ. Psychol.*, **38**, 271–6.

REID, B. H. (1966) 'A study of some aspects of the religious behaviour of a group of Protestant and Catholic adolescents.' M.A. thesis, University of Glasgow.

REID, J. F. (1958) 'A study of thirteen beginners in reading.' *Acta Psychologica*, **14**, no. 4, 295–313.

REID, J. F. (1966) 'Learning to think about reading.' *Educ. Research*, **9**, no. 1, 56–62.

REID, J. F. (1967) In *The i.t.a. Symposium*. An evaluation. London: N. F. E. R.

REID, L. A. (1962) *Philosophy and Education*. London: Heinemann.

RICHARDS, J. P. G. and WILSON, A. J. C. (1961) ' "A" level and pass degree in physics.' *Universities Quarterly*, **15**, 389–92.

RICHMOND, K. (1963) *Culture and General Education*. London: Methuen.

ROACH, J. L. and GURSSLIN, O. R. (1967) 'An evaluation of the concept "culture of poverty".' *Social Forces*, **45**, 383–92.

ROBBINS, Lord (1966) *The University in the Modern World*. London: Macmillan.

ROBBINS, Lord and FORD, B. (1965) 'Report on Robbins.' *Universities Quarterly*, **20**, 5–15.

ROBERTS, B. C. and SMITH, J. H. (eds.) (1966) *Manpower Policy and Employment Trends*. London School of Economics, University of London.

ROBERTS, G. (1967) 'Towards a linguistic approach to reading.' *Reading*, **1**, no. 1.

ROBINSON, W. P. (1964) 'The achievement motive, academic success and intelligence test scores.' *Brit. J. Soc. Clin. Psychol.*, **4**, 98–103.

ROE, M. C. (1963–4) 'Attitudes towards specialization among senior grammar school pupils.' *Educ. Review*, **16**, 227.

ROE, M. (1965) *Survey into Progress of Maladjusted Pupils*. Inner London Education Authority.

ROGERS, K. W. (1967) 'Concepts of time in secondary school children of above average I.Q.' *Brit. J. Educ. Psychol.*, **37**, 99–109.

ROSE, J. and ZIMAN, J. (1964) *Camford Revisited*. London: Gollancz.

ROSEN, B. C. (1956) 'The achievement syndrome: a psycho-cultural dimension of social stratification.' *Amer. Sociol. Review*, **21**, 203–11.

ROSEN, B. C. and D'ANDRADE, R. (1959) 'The psycho-social origins of achievement motivation.' *Sociometry*, **22**, 185–218.

RUSHTON, J. (1966) 'The relationship between personality characteristics and scholastic success in eleven-year-old children.' *Brit. J. Educ. Psychol.*, **36**, 178–84.

RUSHTON, C. S. and STOCKWIN, A. E. (1963) 'Change in Terman-Merrill I.Q.s of educationally subnormal boys.' *Brit. J. Educ. Psychol.*, **33**, 132–42.

RUTTER, M. and GRAHAM, P. (1966) 'Psychiatric disorder in ten- and eleven-year-old children.' *Proceedings of the Royal Society of Medicine*, **59**, no. 4, 382–7.

RYLE, A., POND, D. A. and HAMILTON, M. (1965) 'The prevalence and patterns of psychological disturbance in children of primary age.' *J. Child Psychol. Psychiat.*, **6**, 101–13.

SALEK, A. M. and JULIUS, W. P. (1965) 'Problems of the young graduate.' *Chartered Mechanical Engineer*, **12**, no. 5, 271.

SAMPSON, O. C. (1966a) 'Maladjustment in an urban nine-year-old population.' Paper to British Psychological Society (Education section), September 1966.

SAMPSON, O. C. (1966b) 'Reading and adjustment: a review of the literature. *Educ. Research*, **8**, no. 3, 184–90.

SAPIR, E. (1921) *Language*. New York: Harcourt Brace.

SAVAGE, R. D. (1966) 'Personality factors and academic attainment in junior school children.' *Brit. J. Educ. Psychol.*, **36**, 91–2.

SAWYER, W. W. (1955) *Prelude to Mathematics*. Harmondsworth, Middlesex: Penguin Books.

SCEATS, J. (1967) *i.t.a. and the Teaching of Literacy*. London: Bodley Head.

SCHAFFER, H. R. (1958) 'Objective observations of personality development in early infancy.' *Brit. J. Med. Psychol.*, **31**, 174–83.

SCHOFIELD, M. (1965) *The Sexual Behaviour of Young People*. London: Longmans.

SCHONELL, F. J. (1949) *Diagnostic and Attainment Testing*. Edinburgh: Oliver & Boyd.

SCHONELL, F. J., ROE, E. and MEDDLETON, I. G. (1962) *Promise and Performance*. London: University of London Press Ltd.

Schools Council (1965) *Raising the School Leaving Age*. Working paper no. 2, pp. 26–7. London: H. M. Stationery Office.

Schools Council (1966) *Sixth Form: Curriculum and Examinations*. Working paper no. 5. London: H. M. Stationery Office.

SCOTT, M. R., BROOKS, A., LEE, A. W. and RAMSAY, H. B. (1966) *The Use o Mathematics in the Electrical Industry*. London: Pitman.

Scottish Council for Research in Education (1933) *The Intelligence of Scottish Children: a National Survey of an Age Group*. S. C. R. E. publication no. 5. London: University of London Press Ltd.

Scottish Council for Research in Education (1936) *The Prognostic Value of University Entrance Examinations in Scotland*. S. C. R. E. publication no. 9. London: University of London Press Ltd.

Scottish Council for Research in Education (1949) *The Trend of Scottish Intelligence*. S. C. R. E. publication no. 30. London: University of London Press Ltd.

Scottish Council for Research in Education (1953) *Social Implications of the 1947 Scottish Mental Survey*. S. C. R. E. publication no. 35. London: University of London Press Ltd.

Scottish Council for Research in Education (1958) *Educational and Other Aspects of the 1947 Scottish Mental Survey*. S. C. R. E. publication no. 41. London: University of London Press Ltd.

Scottish Council for Research in Education (1963) *The Scottish Scholastic Survey, 1953*. S. C. R. E. publication no. 48. London: University of London Press Ltd.

Scottish Council for Research in Education (1967) *The Scottish Standardisation of the Wechsler Intelligence Scale for Children*. S. C. R. E. publication no. 55. London: University of London Press Ltd.

Scottish Council for Research in Education (1968) *Rising Standards in Scottish Primary Schools, 1953–63.* S. C. R. E. publication no. 56. London: University of London Press Ltd.

SEALEY, L. G. W. (1967) 'An outline of curricular changes in Great Britain.' In WILLIAMS, J. D. (ed.) *Mathematics Reform in the Primary School.* Hamburg: Unesco Institute of Education.

Secondary Schools Examination Council (1943) *Curriculum and Examinations in Secondary Schools.* London: H. M. Stationery Office.

Secondary Schools Examination Council (1960) *Examinations in Secondary Schools: the G.C.E. and Sixth Form Studies.* Third report. London: H. M. Stationery Office.

SEWELL, W. H., HALLER, A. O. and STRAUS, M. A. (1957) 'Social status and educational and occupational aspiration.' *Amer. Sociol. Review*, **22**, 67–73.

SHANKWEILER, D. (1964) 'A study of developmental dyslexia.' *Neuropsychologia*, **I**, 267–86.

SHELDON, W. H. and STEVENS, S. S. (1942) *The Varieties of Temperament.* New York: Harper.

SHELDON, W. H. and TUCKER, W. B. (1940) *Varieties of Human Physique.* New York: Harper.

SHEPHERD, M., OPPENHEIM, A. N. and MITCHELL, S. (1966) 'Childhood behaviour disorders and the child guidance clinic: an epidemiological study.' *J. Child Psychol. Psychiat.*, **7**, 39–52.

SHIELDS, J. (1962) *Monozygotic Twins Brought Up Apart and Brought Up Together.* London: Oxford University Press.

SIGEL, I. E., ROEPER, A. and HOOPER, F. H. (1966) 'A training procedure for acquisition of Piaget's conservation of quantity.' *Brit. J. Educ. Psychol.*, **36**, 301–11.

SILVERMAN, R. E. and ALTER, M. (1961) *Response Mode, Pacing and Motivational Effects in Teaching Machines.* Port Washington, N. Y.: U.S. Naval Training Device Centre.

SIME, M. E. (1964) 'The elements of a teaching system.' In AUSTWICK, K. (ed.) *Teaching Machines and Programming.* London: Pergamon.

SINHA, U. (1963) 'Educational abilities and streaming in comprehensive schools.' Ph.D. thesis, University of London.

SKEMP, R. R. (1962) 'The teaching of mathematical concepts.' *Mathematics Teaching*, **20**, 13–15.

SKEMP, R. R. (1963a) 'Schematic learning and rote learning.' *Mathematics Teaching*, **21**, 9–11.

SKEMP, R. R. (1963b) 'Sensori-motor intelligence and reflective intelligence.' *Mathematics Teaching*, **22**, 17–19.

SKINNER, B. F. (1938) *The Behaviour of Organisms.* New York: Appleton-Century-Crofts.

SMEDSLUND, J. (1959) 'Apprentissage des notions de la conservation et de la transitivité du poids.' In PIAGET, J. (ed.) *La Logique des Apprentissages.* Etudes d'épistémologie génétique 9, pp. 85-124. Paris: Presses Universitaires de France.

SMEDSLUND, J. (1961a) 'The acquisition of conservation of substance and weight in children 2. External reinforcement of conservation of weight and of the operations of addition and substraction.' *Scand. J. Psychol.*, 2, 71-84.

SMEDSLUND, J. (1961b) 'The acquisition of conservation of substance and weight in children 5. Practice in conflict situations without external reinforcement.' *Scand. J. Psychol.*, 2, 156-60.

SMEDSLUND, J. (1961c) 'The acquisition of conservation of substance and weight in children 6. Practice on continuous *v.* discontinuous material in problem situations without external reinforcement.' *Scand. J. Psychol.*, 2, 203-10.

SMEDSLUND, J. (1963) 'Patterns of experience and the acquisition of conservation of length.' *Scand. J. Psychol.*, 4, 257-64.

SMEDSLUND, J. (1964) *Concrete Reasoning: a Study of Intellectual Development.* Monograph of the Society for Research in Child Development 29, no. 2 (serial no. 92).

SMEDSLUND, J. (1966) 'Micro-analysis of concrete reasoning.' *Scand. J. Psychol.*, 7, 145-67.

SOCHET, M. A. (1964) 'Social class awareness of lower-class children as revealed in their concepts of adult preferences, ideals and self-images.' *International Review of Education*, 10, 341-6.

SONSTROEM, A. McK. (1966) 'On the conservation of solids.' In BRUNER, J. S., OLVER, R. R. and GREENFIELD, P. M. (eds.) *Studies in Cognitive Growth.* New York: Wiley.

SPEARMAN, C. (1936) 'Note on the reliability and validity of examinations.' In *Essays on Examinations.* London: Macmillan.

SPENCE, J., WALTON, W. S., MILLER, F. J. W. and COURT, S. D. M. (1954) *1,000 Families in Newcastle-upon-Tyne.* London: Oxford University Press.

SQUIRE, W. H. (1965) 'Philosophy of education and the training of teachers: some notes on present practice.' *Educ. Review*, 17, no. 3, 181.

STACEY, B. G. (1965) 'Some psychological aspects of inter-generation occupational mobility.' *Brit. J. Soc. Clin. Psychol.*, 4, 275-86.

STAINES, J. W. (1958) 'The self-picture as a factor in the classroom.' *Brit. J. Educ. Psychol.*, 28, 97-111.

STALNAKER, J. M. (1951) 'The essay type of examination.' In LINDQUIST, E. F. (ed.) *Educational Measurement.* Washington D.C.: American Council on Education.

STEIN, Z. A. and STORES, G. (1965) 'I.Q. changes in educationally subnormal children at special school.' *Brit. J. Educ. Psychol.*, 35, 379-81.

STEPHEN, E. (1965) 'Cerebral palsy and mental defect.' In CLARKE, A. M. and A. D. B. (eds.) *Mental Deficiency: the Changing Outlook* (2nd edition). London: Methuen.

STEPHENSON, G. M. (1966) *The Development of Conscience.* London: Routledge & Kegan Paul.

STERN, G. G. (1968) *People in Context.* Syracuse, U.S.A.: Syracuse University Press.

STEVENS, F. (1960) *The Living Tradition.* London: Hutchinson.

STOLUROW, L. M. and WALKER, C. C. (1962) 'A comparison of overt and covert response modes in programmed learning.' *J. Educ. Research*, **55**, 421–9.

STOTT, D. H. (1957) 'Physical and mental handicap following a disturbed pregnancy.' *Lancet*, **I**, 1006–12.

STOTT, D. H. (1959) 'Evidence for pre-natal impairment of temperament in mentally retarded children.' *Vita Humana*, **2**, 125–48.

STOTT, D. H. (1963) *The Social Adjustment of Children: Manual to the Bristol Social Adjustment Guides* (2nd edition). London: University of London Press Ltd.

STOTT, D. H. (1964) *Thirty-three Troublesome Children.* London: National Children's Home.

STOTT, D. H. (1966) *Studies of Troublesome Children.* London: Tavistock.

STRAUSS, M. A. (1962) 'Deferred gratification, social class, and the achievement syndrome.' *Amer. Sociol. Review*, **27**, 326–35.

SUGARMAN, B. N. (1966) 'Social class and values as related to achievement and conduct in school.' *Sociol. Review*, **14**, 287–301.

SUPPES, P. (1965) 'On the behavioral foundations of mathematical concepts.' In MORRISETT, L. N. and VINSONHALER, J. (eds.) *Mathematical Learning.* Monograph of the Society for Research in Child Development 30, no. 1, (serial no. 99), 60–94.

SUTHERLAND, M. (1961) 'Co-education and school attainment.' *Brit. J. Educ. Psychol.*, **31**, 2.

Sweden (1923) Report of the Commission of 1919. Stockholm.

Sweden (1947) 'Flickskolan', 1940, Ars Skolutrednings Betankanded Och Utredningar (tr. by Oke Olden). Stockholm: Statens Offentliga Utredningar.

SWIFT, D. F. (1965a) 'Educational psychology, sociology and the environment: a controversy at cross-purposes.' *Brit. J. Sociol.*, **16**, 334–50.

SWIFT, D. F. (1965b) 'Meritocratic and social class selection at age 11.' *Educ. Research*, **8**, 65–73.

SWIFT, D. F. (1966) 'Social class and achievement motivation.' *Educ. Research*, **8**, 83–95.

SWIFT, D. F. (1967a) 'Family environment and 11-plus success: some basic predictors.' *Brit. J. Educ. Psychol.*, **37**, 10–21.

SWIFT, D. F. (1967b) 'Social class mobility ideology and 11-plus success.' *Brit. J. Sociol.*, **18**, no. 2, 165–86.

TAIT, J. S. (1962) 'Colleges of advanced technology: fact, fiction and future.'
    B. A. C. I. E. Report of Annual Conference.

TANNER, J. M. (1961) *Education and Physical Growth*. London: University of
    London Press Ltd.

TANSLEY, A. E. (1951) 'The use of mental and scholastic test data and case his-
    tory information as indications for the treatment of E. S. N. children.' M.Ed.
    thesis, University of Leeds.

TANSLEY, A. E. and GULLIFORD, R. (1960) *The Education of Slow-learning
    Children*. London: Routledge & Kegan Paul.

TARPEY, M. S. (1965) 'Personality factors in teacher trainee selection.' *Brit. J.
    Educ. Psychol.*, **35**, 140–9.

TAYLOR, H. J. (1964) 'Operation passmark: an account of the method used in the
    matriculation examination of 1963.' University of Gauhati.

TAYLOR, W. (1961) 'The sociology of education in the training college.'
    Education for Teaching, **54**, 45.

TAYLOR, W. (1964) 'The organization of educational studies.' *Education for
    Teaching*, **65**, 28.

TERMAN, L. M. (1925, 1926, 1930, 1947) *Genetic Studies of Genius*. 4 vols.
    Stanford, San Francisco: Stanford University Press.

THOMPSON, D. (1966) 'Streaming in the secondary school.' *Educ. Review*, **18**,
    no. 3, 196–204.

THOMSON, G. H. (1921) 'The Northumberland Mental Tests.' *Brit. J. Educ.
    Psychol.*, **12**, 201ff.

THYNE, J. (1963) 'Teaching educational psychology in training colleges.' *Brit. J.
    Educ. Psychol.*, **33**, pt 2, 190.

The Times (1967) 'Teaching by machine.' 30 March.

TINBERGEN, N. (1951) *The Study of Instinct*. London: Oxford University Press.

TRASLER, G. B. (1962) *The Explanation of Criminality*. London: Routledge &
    Kegan Paul.

TRASLER, G. B. (1963) 'Theoretical problems in the explanation of delinquent
    behaviour.' *Educ. Research*, **6**, 42–9.

TRASLER, G. B. (1966) 'The process of socialization.' *The Listener*, **75**, 341–3.

TRIANDIS, H. C. (1964) 'The influence of culture on cognitive processes.' In
    BERKOWITZ, L. (ed.) *Advances in Experimental Social Psychology*. New York:
    Academic Press.

TUPPEN, C. J. S. (1966) 'The measurement of teachers' attitudes.' *Educ. Research*,
    8, no. 2, 142.

TURNER, B. T. (1963) 'The effective use of engineers in the changing industrial
    environment.' *Proceedings of the Institution of Mechanical Engineering*, **178** (3F).

TURNER, G. H. N. (1966) 'A re-examination of certain of Piaget's inquiries on
    children's moral judgments in the light of his later theory.' M.Ed. thesis,
    University of Manchester.

TURNER, R. H. (1966) 'Acceptance of irregular mobility in Britain and the United States.' *Sociometry*, **29**, 334–52.

TYERMAN, M. J. (1958) 'A research into truancy.' *Brit. J. Educ. Psychol.*, **28**, 217–25.

TYERMAN, M. J. (1968) *Truancy*. London: University of London Press Ltd.

TYSON, G. (1928) 'Some apparent effects of co-education suggested by a statistical investigation of examination results.' M.Ed. thesis, University of Manchester.

ULRICH, L. and TRUMBO, D. (1965) 'The selection interview since 1949.' *Psychol. Bulletin*, **63**, 110–16.

Unesco Institute for Education (1962) *Educational Achievements of Thirteen-year-olds in Twelve Countries*. Hamburg: Unesco.

Universities Central Council on Admissions (1966) 3rd report 1964–5. London: Universities Central Council on Admissions.

University of London, Goldsmith's College Curriculum Laboratory (1965) *The Raising of the School Leaving Age: Second Pilot Course for Experienced Teachers*, p. 2. New Cross, London.

University of Toledo (1965) *The Characteristics of Teacher Education Students in the British Isles and the United States*. Research Foundation of the University of Toledo, Ohio, U.S.A.

VALENTINE, J. (1967) 'G.C.E.—a comedy and tragedy of errors.' *New Education*, **3**, 2.

VAN DER EYKEN, W. (ed.) (1965) 'Educational research and the teacher.' Report of a one-day conference at the University of London Institute of Education. London : N. F. E. R.

VENABLES, P. (1965) 'Dualism in higher education.' *Universities Quarterly*, **20**, 16–29.

VERNON, M. D. (1957) *Backwardness in Reading*. Cambridge: Cambridge University Press.

VERNON, M. D. (1960) 'The investigation of reading problems today.' *Brit. J. Educ. Psychol.*, **30**, 146.

VERNON, M. D. (1962) 'Specific dyslexia.' *Brit. J. Educ. Psychol.*, **32**, 143–50.

VERNON, P. E. (ed.) (1957) *Secondary School Selection*. London: Methuen.

VERNON, P. E. (1961) *Intelligence and Attainment Tests*. London: University of London Press Ltd.

VERNON, P. E. (1965) 'Environmental handicaps and intellectual development.' *Brit. J. Educ. Psychol.*, **35**, 9–20 and 117–26.

VERNON, P. E. (1966) 'Educational and intellectual development among Canadian Indians and Eskimos.' *Educ. Review*, **18**, 79–91 and 186–95.

WADDINGTON, M. (1952) 'An investigation of the effects of contact with children in play centre or junior club in relation to the training of teachers.' M.A. thesis, University of London.

WALKER, M. (1965) 'Perceptual, coding, visuo-motor and spatial difficulties and the neurological correlates: a progress note.' *Develop. Med. Child Neurol.*, **7**, 543–8.

WALL, W. D. (1948) *The Adolescent Child*. London: Methuen.

WALL, W. D. (1959) *Educational Research and the Needs of the Schools*. National Association of Inspectors of Schools and Educational Organizers. London: N. F. E. R.

WALL, W. D. and SIMSON, W. A. (1950) 'The emotional responses of adolescent groups to certain films, pt 1.' *Brit. J. Educ. Psychol.*, **20**, 153–63.

WALL, W. D. and SIMSON, W. A. (1951) 'The responses of adolescent groups to certain films, pt 2.' *Brit. J. Educ. Psychol.*, **21**, 81–8.

WALL, W. D., SCHONELL, F. J. and OLSON, W. C. (1962) *Failure in School*. Hamburg: Unesco Institute for Education. Reviewed by CHAZAN, M. (1963) in *Brit. J. Educ. Psychol.*, **33**, pt 3, 338.

WALLACE, J. G. (1965) *Concept Growth and the Education of the Child*. London: N. F. E. R.

WALLACH, L. and SPROTT, R. L. (1964) 'Inducing number conservation in children.' *Child Development*, **35**, 1057–71.

WALLACH, M. A. (1963) 'Research on children's thinking.' In *Child Psychology 62nd Year Book. National Society for Student Education*, pt 1, pp. 236–76.

WALLACH, M. A. and KOGAN, N. (1965) *Modes of Thinking in Young Children*. New York: Holt, Rinehart and Winston.

WALLIS, D., DUNCAN, K. D. and KNIGHT, M. A. G. (1966) *Programmed Instruction in the British Armed Forces*. London: H. M. Stationery Office.

WALTON, H. M. (c.1934) Unpublished typescript. Middlesex Education Committee.

WARBURTON, F. W. (1952) *The Selection of University Students*. Manchester: Manchester University Press.

WARBURTON, F. W. (1962) 'The measurement of personality, pt 3.' *Educ. Research*, **4**, 193–206.

WARBURTON, F. W., BUTCHER, H. J. and FORREST, G. M. (1963) 'Predicting student performance in a university department of education.' *Brit. J. Educ. Psychol.*, **23**, 68.

WARREN, N. (1966) 'Social class and construct systems: examination of the cognitive structure of two social class groups.' *Brit. J. Soc. Clin. Psychol.*, **5**, 254–63.

WESTWOOD, L. J. (1966) 'Re-assessing the role of the head.' *Education for Teaching*, **71**, 65.

WHYTE, W. F. (1937) *Street Corner Society*. Chicago: University of Chicago Press.

WIDLAKE, P. (1964) 'The effects of mode of response on learning.' *Educ. Review*, **16**, 120–9.

WILKINSON, N. W. (1952) 'An inquiry into the reliability and validity of essay marks.' M.Ed. thesis, University of Edinburgh.

WILLIAMS, A. A. (1958) 'Number readiness.' *Educ. Review*, **11**, 31–46.

WILLIAMS, D. J. (1965) 'A five-year follow-up study of fifteen children assessed as possibly dyslexic in 1960.' Dissertation for Dip. in Education of Backward Children, University College of Swansea.

WILLIAMS, E. M. (1950) 'Higher School Certificate as a predictor of success at university.' *Brit. J. Educ. Psychol.*, **20**, 83–98.

WILLIAMS, J. D. (1965) 'Some problems involved in the experimental comparison of teaching methods.' *Educ. Research*, **8**, no. 1.

WILLIAMS, J. D. (1967) *Tentative Proposals for Investigating the Dienes Modern Mathematics Learning Situations*. Internal Mathematics Research Bulletin no. 1. London: N. F. E. R.

WILLIAMS, J. P. (1963) 'Comparison of several response modes in a review program.' *J. Educ. Psychol.*, **54**, 253–60.

WILLIAMS, N. (1966) 'The moral development of children: notes towards a research project.' Unpublished paper.

WILLIAMS, P. (1964) 'Date of birth, backwardness and educational organization.' *Brit. J. Educ. Psychol.*, **34**, 247–55.

WILLIAMS, R. H. (1963) 'Professional studies in teacher training.' *Education for Teaching*, **61**, 29.

WILLINGTON, G. W. (1967) 'The development of the mathematical understanding of primary school children.' M.Ed. thesis, University of Manchester.

WILSON, B. R. (1962) 'The teacher's role: a sociological analysis.' *Brit. J. Sociol.*, **13**, 15–32.

WILSON, J. (1968) *Approach to Moral Education*. Harmondsworth, Middlesex: Penguin Books.

WISEMAN, S. (1949) 'The marking of English composition in grammar school selection.' *Brit. J. Educ. Psychol.*, **19**, 200–9.

WISEMAN, S. (1959) 'Trends in educational psychology.' *Brit. J. Educ. Psychol.*, **29**, 128–35.

WISEMAN, S. (1961) 'The efficiency of examinations.' In WISEMAN, S. (ed.) *Examinations and English Education*. Manchester: Manchester University Press.

WISEMAN, S. (1964) *Education and Environment*. Manchester: Manchester University Press.

WISEMAN, S. (1965) 'Learning versus teaching.' In NIBLETT, W. R. (ed.) *How and Why do we Learn?* pp. 15–41. London: Faber.

WISEMAN, S. (1966) 'Environmental and innate factors and educational attainment.' In MEADE, J. E. and PARKES, A. S. (eds.) *Genetic and Environmental Factors in Human Ability*, pp. 64–80. Edinburgh: Oliver & Boyd.

WISEMAN, S. and START, K. (1965) 'A follow-up of teachers five years after completing their training.' *Brit. J. Educ. Psychol.*, **35**, pt 3, 342.

WOHLWILL, J. F. (1959) 'Un essai d'apprentissage dans le domaine de la conservation du nombre.' In PIAGET, J. (ed.) *La Logique des Apprentissages*. Etudes d'épistémologie génétique 9, pp. 125–35. Paris: Presses Universitaires de France.

WOHLWILL, J. F. and LOWE, R. C. (1962) 'Experimental analysis of the development of the conservation of number.' *Child Development*, **33**, 153–67.

WOOD, R. (1967) *Item Bank Project*. Research information. London: N. F. E. R.

WOODWARD, M. (1961) 'Concepts of number of the mentally subnormal studied by Piaget's method.' *J. Child Psychol. Psychiat.*, **2**, 249–59.

WOODWARD, M. (1962) 'Concepts of space in the mentally subnormal studied by Piaget's method.' *Brit. J. Soc. Clin. Psychol.*, **1**, 25–37.

WOODWARD, M. (1965) 'Piaget's theory.' In HOWELLS, J. G. (ed.) *Modern Perspectives in Child Psychiatry*. Edinburgh: Oliver & Boyd.

WRIGHT, D. and COX, E. (1967) 'A study of the relationship between moral judgment and religious belief in a sample of English adolescents.' *J. Soc. Psychol.*, **72**, 135–44.

WRIGHT, P. (1966) 'An investigation of the importance of the question and answer technique in programmed instruction.' Ph.D. thesis, University of London.

ZAHRAN, H. A. S. (1965) 'A study of the personality differences between blind and sighted children.' *Brit. J. Educ. Psychol.*, **35**, 329–38.

ZANGWILL, O. L. (1960) *Cerebral Dominance and its Relation to Psychological Function*. Edinburgh: Oliver & Boyd.

ZANGWILL, O. L. (1962) 'Dyslexia in relation to cerebral dominance.' In MONEY, J. and SCHIFFMAN, G. (eds.) *Reading Disability*. Baltimore: Johns Hopkins Press.

Index